Wireless Networking in the Developing World

Second Edition

A practical guide to planning and building low-cost telecommunications infrastructure

Wireless Networking in the Developing World

For more information about this project, visit us online at *http://wndw.net/*

First edition, January 2006
Second edition, December 2007

Many designations used by manufacturers and vendors to distinguish their products are claimed as trademarks. Where those designations appear in this book, and the authors were aware of a trademark claim, the designations have been printed in all caps or initial caps. All other trademarks are property of their respective owners.

The authors and publisher have taken due care in preparation of this book, but make no expressed or implied warranty of any kind and assume no responsibility for errors or omissions. No liability is assumed for incidental or consequential damages in connection with or arising out of the use of the information contained herein.

Contents

Where to Begin 1

Purpose of this book...2
Fitting wireless into your existing network................................3
Wireless networking protocols..3
Question & Answer...5

A Practical Introduction to Radio Physics 9

What is a wave?..9
Polarization...13
The electromagnetic spectrum..13
Bandwidth...15
Frequencies and channels..15
Behavior of radio waves..15
Line of sight..22
Power..24
Physics in the real world..26

Network Design 27

Designing the physical network..51
802.11 wireless networks...54
Mesh networking with OLSR..56
Estimating capacity..65
Traffic optimization...79
Internet link optimization...89
More information...93

Antennas & Transmission Lines 95

Cables...95
Waveguides...97
Connectors and adapters...100
Antennas & radiation patterns..102
Reflector theory...114
Amplifiers...115
Practical antenna designs...116

Networking Hardware
135

Wired wireless...135
Choosing wireless components...137
Commercial vs. DIY solutions..139
Building an access point from a PC..143

Security & Monitoring
157

Physical security..158
Threats to the network..160
Authentication..162
Privacy..167
Network Monitoring...174
What is normal?..203

Solar Power
211

Solar energy...211
Photovoltaic system components..212
The solar panel...217
The battery...222
The power charge regulator..229
Converters..231
Equipment or load..232
How to size your photovoltaic system.....................................238
Cost of a solar installation...246

Building an Outdoor Node
249

Waterproof enclosures...249
Providing power...250
Mounting considerations..251
Safety..257
Aligning antennas on a long distance link................................258
Surge and lightning protection...263

Troubleshooting
267

Building your team...267
Proper troubleshooting technique..270
Common network problems...271

Economic Sustainability   281

Create a Mission Statement..282
Evaluate the Demand for Potential Offerings..283
Establish Appropriate Incentives...284
Research the Regulatory Environment for Wireless....................................286
Analyze the Competition..286
Determine Initial and Recurring Costs and Pricing....................................287
Secure the Financing...291
Evaluate the Strengths and Weaknesses of the Internal Situation...............293
Putting it All Together..294
Conclusion...297

Case Studies   299

General advice...299
Case study: Crossing the divide with a simple bridge in Timbuktu...............302
Case study: Finding solid ground in Gao..305
Case Study: Fantsuam Foundation's Community Wireless Network...............308
Case study: The quest for affordable Internet in rural Mali.........................319
Case study: Commercial deployments in East Africa...................................325
Case study: Dharamsala Community Wireless Mesh Network.......................332
Case study: Networking Mérida State...334
Case study: Chilesincables.org...345
Case study: Long Distance 802.11..355

Appendix A: Resources   371

Appendix B: Channel Allocations   379

Appendix C: Path Loss   381

Appendix D: Cable Sizes   382

Appendix E: Solar Dimensioning   383

About This Book

This book is part of a set of related materials about the same topic: Wireless Networking in the Developing World. The WNDW project includes:

- Printed books, available on demand

- Several translations, including French, Spanish, Portuguese, Italian, Arabic, and others

- A DRM-free PDF and HTML version of the book

- An archived mailing list for discussion of the concepts and techniques described in the book

- Additional case studies, training course material, and related information

For all of this material and more, see our website at *http://wndw.net/*

The book and PDF file are published under a Creative Commons **Attribution-ShareAlike 3.0** license. This allows anyone to make copies, and even sell them for a profit, as long as proper attribution is given to the authors and any derivative works are made available under the same terms. Any copies or derivative works **must** include a prominent link to our website, *http://wndw.net/*. See *http://creativecommons.org/licenses/by-sa/3.0/* for more information about these terms. Printed copies may be ordered from Lulu.com, a print-on-demand service. Consult the website (*http://wndw.net/*) for details on ordering a printed copy. The PDF will be updated periodically, and ordering from the print-on-demand service ensures that you will always receive the latest revision.

The website will include additional case studies, currently available equipment, and more external website references. Volunteers and ideas are welcome. Please join the mailing list and send ideas.

The training course material was written for courses given by the Association for Progressive Communications and the Abdus Salam International Center for Theoretical Physics. See *http://www.apc.org/wireless/* and *http://wireless.ictp.trieste.it/* for more details on those courses and their material. Additional information was provided by the International Network for the Availability of Scientific Publications, *http://www.inasp.info/*. Some of this material has been incorporated directly into this book. Additional material was adapted from *How To Accelerate Your Internet*, *http://bwmo.net/*.

Credits

This book was started as the BookSprint project at the 2005 session of WSFII, in London, England (*http://www.wsfii.org/*). A core team of seven people built the initial outline over the course of the event, presented the results at the conference, and wrote the book over the course of a few months. Throughout the project, the core group has actively solicited contributions and feedback from the wireless networking community. Add your own feedback and updates to the WNDW wiki at *http://wiki.wndw.net/*.

- **Rob Flickenger** was the lead author and editor of this book. Rob has written and edited several books about wireless networking and Linux, including *Wireless Hacks* (O'Reilly Media) and *How To Accelerate Your Internet* (*http://bwmo.net/*). He is proud to be a hacker, amateur mad scientist, and proponent of free networks everywhere.

- **Corinna "Elektra" Aichele**. Elektra's main interests include autonomous power systems and wireless communication (antennas, wireless long shots, mesh networking). She made a small linux distro based on slackware geared to wireless mesh networking. This information is of course redundant if one reads the book... *http://www.scii.nl/~elektra*

- **Sebastian Büttrich** (*http://wire.less.dk/*) is a generalist in technology with a background in scientific programming and physics. Originally from Berlin, Germany, he worked with IconMedialab in Copenhagen from 1997 until 2002. He holds a Ph.D. in quantum physics from the Technical University of Berlin. His physics background includes fields like RF and microwave spectroscopy, photovoltaic systems, and advanced maths.

He is also a performing and recording musician.

- **Laura M. Drewett** is a Co-Founder of Adapted Consulting Inc., a social enterprise that specializes in adapting technology and business solutions for the developing world. Since Laura first lived in Mali in the 1990s and wrote her thesis on girls' education programs, she has strived to find sustainable solutions for development. An expert in sustainability for ICT projects in developing world environments, she has designed and managed projects for a diversity of clients in Africa, the Middle East and Eastern Europe. Laura holds a Bachelors of Arts with Distinction in Foreign Affairs and French from the University of Virginia and a Master's Certificate in Project Management from the George Washington University School of Business.

- **Alberto Escudero-Pascual** and **Louise Berthilson** are the founders of IT +46, a Swedish consultancy company with focus on information technology in developing regions. IT +46 is internationally known for promoting and implementing wireless Internet infrastructure in rural areas of Africa and Latinoamerica. Since 2004, the company has trained over 350 people in 14 countries and released over 600 pages of documentation under Creative Commons License. More information can be found at *http://www.it46.se/*

- **Carlo Fonda** is a member of the Radio Communications Unit at the Abdus Salam International Center for Theoretical Physics in Trieste, Italy.

- **Jim Forster** has spent his career in software development, mostly working on operating systems and networking in product companies. He has experience with several failed startup companies in Silicon Valley, and one successful one, Cisco Systems. After a lot of product development work there, his more recent activities involve projects and policies for improving Internet access in developing countries. He can be reached at *jrforster@mac.com*.

- **Ian Howard.** After flying around the world for seven years as a paratrooper in the Canadian military, Ian Howard decided to trade his gun for a computer.

  After finishing a degree in environmental sciences at the University of Waterloo he wrote in a proposal, "Wireless technology has the opportunity to bridge the digital divide. Poor nations, who do not have the infrastructure for interconnectivity as we do, will now be able to create a wireless infrastructure." As a reward, Geekcorps sent him to Mali as the Geekcorps Mali Program Manager, where he led a team equipping radio stations with wireless interconnections and designed content sharing systems.

  He is now a consultant on various Geekcorps programs.

- **Kyle Johnston,** *http://www.schoolnet.na/*

- **Tomas Krag** spends his days working with *wire.less.dk*, a registered non-profit, based in Copenhagen, which he founded with his friend and colleague Sebastian Büttrich in early 2002. wire.less.dk specialises in community wireless networking solutions, and has a special focus on low-cost wireless networks for the developing world.

  Tomas is also an associate of the Tactical Technology Collective *http://www.tacticaltech.org/*, an Amsterdam-based non-profit "to strengthen social technology movements and networks in developing and transition countries, as well as promote civil society's effective, conscious and creative use of new technologies." Currently most of his energy goes into the Wireless Roadshow (*http://www.thewirelessroadshow.org/*), a project that supports civil society partners in the developing world in planning, building and sustaining connectivity solutions based on license-exempt spectrum, open technology and open knowledge.

- **Gina Kupfermann** is graduate engineer in energy management and holds a degree in engineering and business. Besides her profession as financial controller she has worked for various self-organised community projects and non-profit organisations. Since 2005 she is member of the executive board of the development association for free networks, the legal entity of freifunk.net.

- **Adam Messer**.   Originally trained as an insect scientist, Adam Messer metamorphosed into a telecommunications professional after a chance conversation in 1995 led him to start one of Africa's first ISPs.   Pioneering wireless data services in Tanzania, Messer worked for 11 years in eastern and southern Africa in voice and data communications for startups and multinational cellular carriers. He now resides in Amman, Jordan.

- **Juergen Neumann** (*http://www.ergomedia.de/*) started working with information technology in 1984 and since then has been looking for ways to deploy ICT in useful ways for organizations and society. As a consultant for ICT strategy and implementation, he has worked for major German and international companies and many non-profit projects.   In 2002 he co-founded *www.freifunk.net*, a campaign for spreading knowledge and social networking about free and open networks. Freifunk is globally regarded as one of the most successful community-projects in this field.

- **Ermanno Pietrosemoli** has been involved in planning and building computer networks for the last twenty years. As president of the Latin American Networking School, Escuela Latinoamericana de Redes "EsLaRed", *www.eslared.org.ve*, he has been teaching wireless data communications in several countries while keeping his base at Mérida, Venezuela.

- **Frédéric Renet** is a co-founder of Technical Solutions at Adapted Consulting, Inc. Frédéric has been involved in ICT for more than 10 years and has worked with computers since his childhood. He began his ICT career in the early 1990s with a bulletin board system (BBS) on an analog modem and has since continued to create systems that enhance communication. Most recently, Frédéric spent more than a year at IESC/Geekcorps Mali as a consultant. In this capacity, he designed many innovative solutions for FM radio broadcasting, school computer labs and lighting systems for rural communities.

- **Marco Zennaro**, aka marcusgennaroz, is an electronic engineer working at the ICTP in Trieste, Italy. He has been using BBSes and ham radios since he was a teenager, and he is happy to have merged the two together working in the field of wireless networking. He still carries his Apple Newton.

Support

- **Lisa Chan** (*http://www.cowinanorange.com/*) was the lead copy editor.

- **Casey Halverson** (*http://seattlewireless.net/~casey/*) provided technical review and suggestions.

- **Jessie Heaven Lotz** (http://jessieheavenlotz.com/) provided several updated illustrations for this edition.

- **Richard Lotz** (*http://greenbits.net/~rlotz/*) provided technical review and suggestions. He works on SeattleWireless projects and would like to take his node (and his house) off the grid.

- **Catherine Sharp** (*http://odessablue.com/*) provided copy edit support.

- **Lara Sobel** designed the cover for WNDW 2nd Edition. She is an artist currently living in Seattle, WA.

- **Matt Westervelt** (*http://seattlewireless.net/~mattw/*) provided technical review and copy edit support. Matt is the founder of SeattleWireless (*http://seattlewireless.net/*) and is an evangelist for FreeNetworks worldwide.

About the solar power guide

The source material for the Solar Power chapter was translated and developed by Alberto Escudero-Pascual. In 1998, the organization Engineering without Borders (Spanish Federation) published the first version of a handbook titled "Manual de Energía Solar Fotovoltaica y Cooperación al Desarrollo". The handbook was written and published by members of the NGO and experts of the Institute of Energy Solar of the Polytechnical University of Madrid. By curiosities of life, none of the members of the editorial team kept the document in electronic format and more editions were never made. They have passed almost ten years from that very first edition and this document is an effort to rescue and to extend the handbook.

As part of this rescue operation Alberto would like to thank the coordinators of the first original edition and his mentors in his years at University: Miguel Ángel Eguido Aguilera, Mercedes Montero Bartolomé y Julio Amador. This new work is licensed under Creative Commons **Attribution-ShareAlike 3.0**. We hope that this material becomes a new departure point for new editions including new contributions by the community.

This second and extended edition of the solar power guide has received valuable input from Frédéric Renet and Louise Berthilson.

Special thanks

The core team would like to thank the organizers of WSFII for providing the space, support, and occasional bandwidth that served as the incubator for this project. We would especially like to thank community networkers everywhere, who devote so much of their time and energy towards fulfilling the promise of the global Internet. Without you, community networks could not exist.

The publication of this work has been supported by Canada's International Development Research Centre, *http://www.idrc.ca/*. Additional support was provided by *NetworktheWorld.org*.

The Abdus Salam
International Centre
for Theoretical Physics

1

Where to Begin

This book was created by a team of individuals who each, in their own field, are actively participating in the ever-expanding Internet by pushing its reach farther than ever before. The massive popularity of wireless networking has caused equipment costs to continually plummet, while equipment capabilities continue to sharply increase. We believe that by taking advantage of this state of affairs, people can finally begin to have a stake in building their own communications infrastructure. We hope to not only convince you that this is possible, but also show how we have done it, and to give you the information and tools you need to start a network project in your local community.

Wireless infrastructure can be built for very little cost compared to traditional wired alternatives. But building wireless networks is only partly about saving money. By providing people in your local community with cheaper and easier access to information, they will directly benefit from what the Internet has to offer. The time and effort saved by having access to the global network of information translates into wealth on a local scale, as more work can be done in less time and with less effort.

Likewise, the network becomes all the more valuable as more people are connected to it. Communities connected to the Internet at high speed have a voice in a global marketplace, where transactions happen around the world at the speed of light. People all over the world are finding that Internet access gives them a voice to discuss their problems, politics, and whatever else is important to their lives, in a way that the telephone and television simply cannot compete with. What has until recently sounded like science fiction is now becoming a reality, and that reality is being built on wireless networks.

But even without access to the Internet, wireless community networks have tremendous value. They allow people to collaborate on projects across wide distances. Voice communications, email, and other data can be exchanged for very little cost. By getting local people involved in the construction of the network, knowledge and trust are spread throughout the community, and people begin to understand the importance of having a share in their communications infrastructure. Ultimately, they realize that communication networks are built to allow people to connect with each other.

In this book we will focus on wireless data networking technologies in the 802.11 family. While such a network can carry data, voice, and video (as well as traditional web and Internet traffic), the networks described in this book are data networks. We specifically do not cover GSM, CDMA, or other wireless voice technologies, since the cost of deploying these technologies is well beyond the reach of most community projects.

Purpose of this book

The overall goal of this book is to help you build affordable communication technology in your local community by making best use of whatever resources are available. Using inexpensive off-the-shelf equipment, you can build high speed data networks that connect remote areas together, provide broadband network access in areas that even dialup does not exist, and ultimately connect you and your neighbors to the global Internet. By using local sources for materials and fabricating parts yourself, you can build reliable network links with very little budget. And by working with your local community, you can build a telecommunications infrastructure that benefits everyone who participates in it.

This book is not a guide to configuring a radio card in your laptop or choosing consumer grade gear for your home network. The emphasis is on building infrastructure links intended to be used as the backbone for wide area wireless networks. With that goal in mind, information is presented from many points of view, including technical, social, and financial factors. The extensive collection of case studies present various groups' attempts at building these networks, the resources that were committed to them, and the ultimate results of these attempts.

Since the first spark gap experiments at the turn of the last century, wireless has been a rapidly evolving area of communications technology. While we provide specific examples of how to build working high speed data links, the techniques described in this book are not intended to replace existing wired infrastructure (such as telephone systems or fiber optic backbone). Rather, these techniques are intended to augment existing systems, and provide connectivity in areas where running fiber or other physical cable would be impractical.

We hope you find this book useful for solving your communication challenges.

Fitting wireless into your existing network

If you are a network administrator, you may wonder how wireless might fit into your existing network infrastructure. Wireless can serve in many capacities, from a simple extension (like a several kilometer Ethernet cable) to a distribution point (like a large hub). Here just a few examples of how your network can benefit from wireless technology.

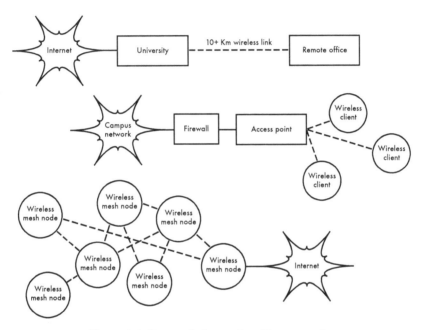

Figure 1.1: Some wireless networking examples.

Wireless networking protocols

The primary technology used for building low-cost wireless networks is currently the 802.11 family of protocols, also known in many circles as **Wi-Fi**. The 802.11 family of radio protocols (802.11a, 802.11b, and 802.11g) have enjoyed an incredible popularity in the United States and Europe. By implementing a common set of protocols, manufacturers world wide have built highly interoperable equipment. This decision has proven to be a significant boon to the industry and the consumer. Consumers are able to use equipment that implements 802.11 without fear of "vendor lock-in". As a result, consumers are able to purchase low-cost equipment at a volume which has benefitted manufacturers. If manufacturers had chosen to implement their own proprietary protocols, it is unlikely that wireless networking would be as inexpensive and ubiquitous as it is today.

While new protocols such as 802.16 (also known as WiMax) will likely solve some difficult problems currently observed with 802.11, they have a long way to go to match the popularity and price point of 802.11 equipment. As equipment that supports WiMax is just becoming available at the time of this writing, we will focus primarily on the 802.11 family.

There are many protocols in the 802.11 family, and not all are directly related to the radio protocol itself.   The three wireless standards currently imple-mented in most readily available gear are:

• **802.11b**. Ratified by the IEEE on September 16, 1999, 802.11b is proba-bly the most popular wireless networking protocol in use today. Millions of devices supporting it have shipped since 1999. It uses a modulation called *Direct Sequence Spread Spectrum* (**DSSS**) in a portion of the ISM band from 2.400 to 2.495 GHz. It has a maximum rate of 11 Mbps, with actual usable data speeds up to about 5 Mbps.

• **802.11g**. As it wasn't finalized until June 2003, 802.11g is a relative late-comer to the wireless marketplace. Despite the late start, 802.11g is now the de facto standard wireless networking protocol as it now ships as a standard feature on virtually all laptops and most handheld devices. 802.11g uses the same ISM range as 802.11b, but uses a modulation scheme called *Orthogonal Frequency Division Multiplexing* (**OFDM**). It has a maximum data rate of 54 Mbps (with usable throughput of about 22 Mbps), and can fall back to 11 Mbps DSSS or slower for backwards compatibility with the hugely popular 802.11b.

• **802.11a**. Also ratified by the IEEE on September 16, 1999, 802.11a uses OFDM. It has a maximum data rate of 54 Mbps, with actual throughput of up to 27 Mbps.   802.11a operates in the ISM band between 5.745 and 5.805 GHz, and in a portion of the UNII band between 5.150 and 5.320 GHz. This makes it incompatible with 802.11b or 802.11g, and the higher frequency means shorter range compared to 802.11b/g at the same power. While this portion of the spectrum is relatively unused compared to 2.4 GHz, it is unfortunately only legal for use in a few parts of the world. Check with your local authorities before using 802.11a equipment, particu-larly in outdoor applications. 802.11a equipment is still quite inexpensive, but is not nearly as popular as 802.11b/g.

In addition to the above standards, there are a number of vendor-specific exten-sions to equipment, touting higher speeds, stronger encryption, and increased range. Unfortunately these extensions will not operate between equipment from different manufacturers, and purchasing them will effectively lock you into that vendor for every part of your network. New equipment and standards (such as

802.11y, 802.11n, 802.16, MIMO and WiMAX) promise significant increases in speed and reliability, but this equipment is just starting to ship at the time of this writing, and availability and vendor interoperability is still uncertain.

Due to the ubiquity of equipment and unlicensed nature of the 2.4 GHz ISM band, this book will concentrate on building networks using 802.11b and 802.11g.

Question & Answer

If you are new to wireless networking, you likely have a number of questions about what the technology can do and what it will cost. Here are some commonly asked questions, with answers and suggestions on the listed page.

Power

- How can I supply power to my radio equipment, if there is no grid power available? **Page 211**

- Do I need to run a power cable all the way up the tower? **Page 250**

- How can I use solar panel to power my wireless node while keeping it online overnight? **Page 217**

- How long will my access point run on a battery? **Page 238**

- Can I use a wind generator to power my equipment at night? **Page 212**

Management

- How much bandwidth will I need to purchase for my users? **Page 65**

- How can I monitor and manage remote access points from my office? **Page 174**

- What do I do when the network breaks? **Page 174, 267**

- What are the most common problems encountered on wireless networks, and how do I fix them? **Page 267**

Distance

- How good is the range of my access point? **Page 67**

- Is there any formula I can use to know how far I can go with a given access point? **Page 67**

- How can I know if a remote place can be connected to Internet using a wireless link? **Page 67**

- Is there any software that can help me estimate the feasibility of a long distance wireless link? **Page 74**

- The manufacturer says my access point has a range of 300 meters. Is that true? **Page 67**

- How can I provide wireless connectivity to many remote clients, spread all around the city? **Page 53**

- Is it true that I can reach a much greater distance adding a tin can or aluminum foil to my AP's antenna? **Page 116**

- Can I use wireless to connect to a remote site and share a single central Internet connection? **Page 51**

- My wireless link looks like it will be too long to work well. Can I use a repeater in the middle to make it better? **Page 77**

- Should I use an amplifier instead? **Page 115**

Installation

- How can I install my indoor AP on the top of a mast on my roof? **Page 249**

- Is it really useful to add a lightning protector and proper grounding to my antenna mast, or can I go without them? **Page 263**

- Can I build an antenna mast by myself? How high can I go? **Page 251**

- Why does my antenna work much better when I mount it "sideways"? **Page 13**

- Which channel should I use? **Page 15**

- Will radio waves travel through buildings and trees? What about people? **Page 16**

- Will radio waves travel through a hill that is in the way? **Page 17**

- How do I build a mesh network? **Page 56**

- What kind of antenna is the best one for my network? **Page 102**

- Can I build an access point using a recycled PC? **Page 143**

- How can I install Linux on my AP? Why should I do so? **Page 152**

Money

- How can I know if a wireless link is achievable with a limited amount of money? **Page 281**

- Which is the best AP with the lowest price? **Page 137**

- How can I track and bill customers for using my wireless network? **Page 165, 190**

Partners and Customers

- If I am supplying connectivity, do I still need service from an ISP? Why? **Page 27**

- How many customers do I need to cover my costs? **Page 287**

- How many customers will my wireless network support? **Page 65**

- How do I make my wireless network go faster? **Page 79**

- Is my Internet connection as fast as it can be? **Page 90**

Security

- How can I protect my wireless network from unauthorized access? **Page 157**

- Is it true that a wireless network is always insecure and open to attacks by hackers? **Page 160**

- Is it true that the use of open source software makes my network less secure? **Page 167**

- How can I see what is happening on my network? **Page 174**

Information and Licensing

- What other books should I read to improve my wireless networking skills? Page 355

- Where can I find more information online? **Page 349,** *http://wndw.net/*

- Can I use parts of this book for my own teaching? Can I print and sell copies of this book? **Yes.** See **About This Book** for more details.

2

A Practical Introduction to Radio Physics

Wireless communications make use of electromagnetic waves to send signals across long distances. From a user's perspective, wireless connections are not particularly different from any other network connection: your web browser, email, and other applications all work as you would expect. But radio waves have some unexpected properties compared to Ethernet cable. For example, it's very easy to see the path that an Ethernet cable takes: locate the plug sticking out of your computer, follow the cable to the other end, and you've found it! You can also be confident that running many Ethernet cables alongside each other won't cause problems, since the cables effectively keep their signals contained within the wire itself.

But how do you know where the waves emanating from your wireless card are going? What happens when these waves bounce off of objects in the room or other buildings in an outdoor link? How can several wireless cards be used in the same area without interfering with each other?

In order to build stable high-speed wireless links, it is important to understand how radio waves behave in the real world.

What is a wave?

We are all familiar with vibrations or oscillations in various forms: a pendulum, a tree swaying in the wind, the string of a guitar - these are all examples of oscillations.

What they have in common is that something, some medium or object, is swinging in a periodic manner, with a certain number of cycles per unit of time. This kind of wave is sometimes called a ***mechanical wave***, since it is defined by the motion of an object or its propagating medium.

When such oscillations travel (that is, when the swinging does not stay bound to one place) then we speak of waves propagating in space. For example, a singer singing creates periodic oscillations in his or her vocal cords. These oscillations periodically compress and decompress the air, and this periodic change of air pressure then leaves the singers mouth and travels, at the speed of sound. A stone plunging into a lake causes a disturbance, which then travels across the lake as a ***wave***.

A wave has a certain ***speed***, ***frequency***, and ***wavelength***. These are connected by a simple relation:

```
Speed = Frequency * Wavelength
```

The wavelength (sometimes referred to as ***lambda***, **λ**) is the distance measured from a point on one wave to the equivalent part of the next, for example from the top of one peak to the next. The frequency is the number of whole waves that pass a fixed point in a period of time. Speed is measured in meters/second, frequency is measured in cycles per second (or Hertz, abbreviated ***Hz***), and wavelength is measured in meters.

For example, if a wave on water travels at one meter per second, and it oscillates five times per second, then each wave will be twenty centimeters long:

```
1 meter/second = 5 cycles/second * W
W = 1 / 5 meters
W = 0.2 meters = 20 cm
```

Waves also have a property called ***amplitude***. This is the distance from the center of the wave to the extreme of one of its peaks, and can be thought of as the "height" of a water wave. The relationship between frequency, wavelength, and amplitude are shown in **Figure 2.1**.

Waves in water are easy to visualize. Simply drop a stone into the lake and you can see the waves as they move across the water over time. In the case of electromagnetic waves, the part that might be hardest to understand is: "What is it that is oscillating?"

In order to understand that, you need to understand electromagnetic forces.

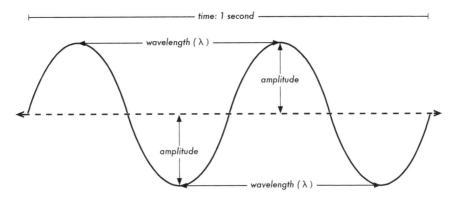

Figure 2.1: Wavelength, amplitude, and frequency. For this wave, the frequency is 2 cycles per second, or 2 Hz.

Electromagnetic forces

Electromagnetic forces are the forces between electrical charges and currents. Our most direct access to those is when our hand touches a door handle after walking on synthetic carpet, or brushing up against an electrical fence. A more powerful example of electromagnetic forces is the lightning we see during thunderstorms. The ***electrical force*** is the force between electrical charges. The ***magnetic force*** is the force between electrical currents.

Electrons are particles that carry a negative electrical charge. There are other particles too, but electrons are responsible for most of what we need to know about how radio behaves.

Let us look at what is happening in a piece of straight wire, in which we push the electrons from one and to the other and back, periodically. At one moment, the top of the wire is negatively charged - all the negative electrons are gathered there. This creates an electric field from plus to minus along the wire. The next moment, the electrons have all been driven to the other side, and the electric field points the other way. As this happens again and again, the electric field vectors (arrows from plus to minus) are leaving the wire, so to speak, and are radiated out into the space around the wire.

What we have just described is known as a dipole (because of the two poles, plus and minus), or more commonly a ***dipole antenna***. This is the simplest form of omnidirectional antenna. The motion of the electric field is commonly referred to as an ***electromagnetic wave***.

Let us come back to the relation:

```
Speed = Frequency * Wavelength
```

In the case of electromagnetic waves, the speed is **c**, the speed of light.

```
c = 300,000 km/s = 300,000,000 m/s = 3*10⁸ m/s
c = f * λ
```

Electromagnetic waves differ from mechanical waves in that they require no medium in which to propagate. Electromagnetic waves will even propagate through the vacuum of space.

Powers of ten

In physics, math, and engineering, we often express numbers by powers of ten. We will meet these terms again, e.g. in Giga-Hertz (GHz), Centi-meters (cm), Micro-seconds (µs), and so on.

Powers of Ten			
Nano-	10^{-9}	1/1000000000	n
Micro-	10^{-6}	1/1000000	μ
Milli-	10^{-3}	1/1000	m
Centi-	10^{-2}	1/100	c
Kilo-	10^{3}	1 000	k
Mega-	10^{6}	1 000 000	M
Giga-	10^{9}	1 000 000 000	G

Knowing the speed of light, we can calculate the wavelength for a given frequency. Let us take the example of the frequency of 802.11b wireless networking, which is

```
f = 2.4 GHz
  = 2,400,000,000 cycles / second

wavelength lambda (λ) = c / f
                      = 3*10⁸ / 2.4*10⁹
                      = 1.25*10⁻¹ m
                      = 12.5 cm
```

Frequency and wavelength determine most of an electromagnetic wave's behavior, from antennas that we build to objects that are in the way of the networks we intend to run. They are responsible for many of the differences between different standards we might be choosing. Therefore, an understanding of the basic ideas of frequency and wavelength helps a lot in practical wireless work.

Polarization

Another important quality of electromagnetic waves is **polarization**. Polarization describes the direction of the electrical field vector.

If you imagine a vertically aligned dipole antenna (the straight piece of wire), electrons only move up and down, not sideways (because there is no room to move) and thus electrical fields only ever point up or down, vertically. The field leaving the wire and traveling as a wave has a strict linear (and in this case, vertical) polarization. If we put the antenna flat on the ground, we would find horizontal linear polarization.

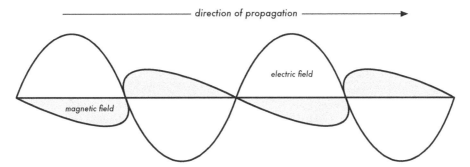

Figure 2.2: Electric field and complementary magnetic field components of an electromagnetic wave. Polarization describes the orientation of the electric field.

Linear polarization is just one special case, and is never quite so perfect: in general, we will always have some component of the field pointing other directions too. The most general case is elliptic polarization, with the extremes of linear (only one direction) and circular polarizations (both directions at equal strength).

As one can imagine, polarization becomes important when aligning antennas. If you ignore polarization, you might have very little signal even though you have the strongest antennas. We call this **polarization mismatch**.

The electromagnetic spectrum

Electromagnetic waves span a wide range of frequencies (and, accordingly, wavelengths). This range of frequencies and wavelengths is called the **electromagnetic spectrum**. The part of the spectrum most familiar to humans is probably light, the visible portion of the electromagnetic spectrum. Light lies roughly between the frequencies of $7.5*10^{14}$ Hz and $3.8*10^{14}$ Hz, corresponding to wavelengths from circa 400 nm (violet/blue) to 800 nm (red).

We are also regularly exposed to other regions of the electromagnetic spectrum, including **Alternating Current** (**AC**) or grid electricity at 50/60 Hz, Ultraviolet (on the higher frequencies side of visible light), Infrared (on the lower frequencies side of visible light), X-Rays / Roentgen radiation, and many others. **Radio** is the term used for the portion of the electromagnetic spectrum in which waves can be generated by applying alternating current to an antenna. This is true for the range from 3 Hz to 300 GHz, but in the more narrow sense of the term, the upper frequency limit would be 1 GHz.

When talking about radio, many people think of FM radio, which uses a frequency around 100 MHz. In between radio and infrared we find the region of microwaves - with frequencies from about 1 GHz to 300 GHz, and wavelengths from 30 cm to 1 mm.

The most popular use of microwaves might be the microwave oven, which in fact works in exactly the same region as the wireless standards we are dealing with. These regions lie within the bands that are being kept open for general unlicensed use. This region is called the **ISM band**, which stands for Industrial, Scientific, and Medical. Most other parts of the electromagnetic spectrum are tightly controlled by licensing legislation, with license values being a huge economic factor. This goes especially for those parts of the spectrum that are suitable for broadcast (TV, radio) as well as voice and data communication. In most countries, the ISM bands have been reserved for unlicensed use.

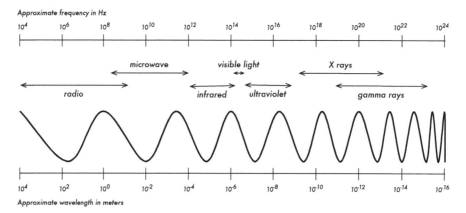

Figure 2.3: The electromagnetic spectrum.

The frequencies most interesting to us are 2.400 - 2.495 GHz, which is used by the 802.11b and 802.11g radio standards (corresponding to wavelengths of about 12.5 cm). Other commonly available equipment uses the 802.11a standard, which operates at 5.150 - 5.850 GHz (corresponding to wavelengths of about 5 to 6 cm).

Bandwidth

A term you will meet often in radio physics is **bandwidth**. Bandwidth is simply a measure of frequency range. If a range of 2.40 GHz to 2.48 GHz is used by a device, then the bandwidth would be 0.08 GHz (or more commonly stated as 80MHz).

It is easy to see that the bandwidth we define here is closely related to the amount of data you can transmit within it - the more room in frequency space, the more data you can fit in at a given moment. The term bandwidth is often used for something we should rather call a data rate, as in "my Internet connection has 1 Mbps of bandwidth", meaning it can transmit data at 1 megabit per second.

Frequencies and channels

Let us look a bit closer at how the 2.4GHz band is used in 802.11b. The spectrum is divided into evenly sized pieces distributed over the band as individual **channels**. Note that channels are 22MHz wide, but are only separated by 5MHz. This means that adjacent channels overlap, and can interfere with each other. This is represented visually in **Figure 2.4**.

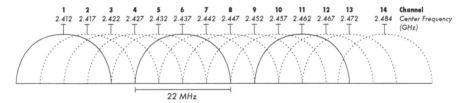

Figure 2.4: Channels and center frequencies for 802.11b. Note that channels 1, 6, and 11 do not overlap.

For a complete list of channels and their center frequencies for 802.11b/g and 802.11a, see **Appendix B**.

Behavior of radio waves

There are a few simple rules of thumb that can prove extremely useful when making first plans for a wireless network:

• The longer the wavelength, the further it goes

• The longer the wavelength, the better it travels through and around things

• The shorter the wavelength, the more data it can transport

All of these rules, simplified as they may be, are rather easy to understand by example.

Longer waves travel further

Assuming equal power levels, waves with longer wavelengths tend to travel further than waves with shorter wavelengths. This effect is often seen in FM radio, when comparing the range of an FM transmitter at 88MHz to the range at 108MHz. Lower frequency transmitters tend to reach much greater distances than high frequency transmitters at the same power.

Longer waves pass around obstacles

A wave on water which is 5 meters long will not be stopped by a 5 mm piece of wood sticking out of the water. If instead the piece of wood were 50 meters big (e.g. a ship), it would be well in the way of the wave. The distance a wave can travel depends on the relationship between the wavelength of the wave and the size of obstacles in its path of propagation.

It is harder to visualize waves moving "through" solid objects, but this is the case with electromagnetic waves. Longer wavelength (and therefore lower frequency) waves tend to penetrate objects better than shorter wavelength (and therefore higher frequency) waves. For example, FM radio (88-108MHz) can travel through buildings and other obstacles easily, while shorter waves (such as GSM phones operating at 900MHz or 1800MHz) have a harder time penetrating buildings. This effect is partly due to the difference in power levels used for FM radio and GSM, but is also partly due to the shorter wavelength of GSM signals.

Shorter waves can carry more data

The faster the wave swings or beats, the more information it can carry - every beat or cycle could for example be used to transport a digital bit, a '0' or a '1', a 'yes' or a 'no'.

There is another principle that can be applied to all kinds of waves, and which is extremely useful for understanding radio wave propagation. This principle is known as the **Huygens Principle**, named after Christiaan Huygens, Dutch mathematician, physicist and astronomer 1629 - 1695.

Imagine you are taking a little stick and dipping it vertically into a still lake's surface, causing the water to swing and dance. Waves will leave the center of the stick - the place where you dip in - in circles. Now, wherever water particles are swinging and dancing, they will cause their neighbor particles to do the same: from every point of disturbance, a new circular wave will start. This is, in simple form, the Huygens principle. In the words of *wikipedia.org*:

> *"The Huygens' principle is a method of analysis applied to problems of wave propagation in the far field limit. It recognizes that each point of an advancing wave front is in fact the center of a fresh disturbance and the source of a new train of waves; and that the advancing wave as a whole may be regarded as the sum of all the secondary waves arising from points in the medium already traversed. This view of wave propagation helps better understand a variety of wave phenomena, such as diffraction."*

This principle holds true for radio waves as well as waves on water, for sound as well as light - only for light the wavelength is far too short for human beings to actually see the effects directly.

This principle will help us to understand diffraction as well as Fresnel zones, the need for line of sight as well as the fact that sometimes we seem to be able to go around corners, with no line of sight.

Let us now look into what happens to electromagnetic waves as they travel.

Absorption

When electromagnetic waves go through 'something' (some material), they generally get weakened or dampened. How much they lose in power will depend on their frequency and of course the material. Clear window glass is obviously transparent for light, while the glass used in sunglasses filter out quite a share of the light intensity and also the ultraviolet radiation.

Often, an absorption coefficient is used to describe a material's impact on radiation. For microwaves, the two main absorbent materials are:

- **Metal**. Electrons can move freely in metals, and are readily able to swing and thus absorb the energy of a passing wave.

- **Water**. Microwaves cause water molecules to jostle around, thus taking away some of the wave's energy[1].

For the purpose of practical wireless networking, we may well consider metal and water perfect absorbers: we will not be able to go through them (al-

---

1. A commonly held myth is that water "resonates" at 2.4 GHz, which is why that frequency is used in microwave ovens. Actually, water doesn't appear to have any particular "resonant" frequency. Water spins and jostles around near radio, and will heat when in the presence of high power radio waves at just about any frequency. 2.4 GHz is an unlicensed ISM frequency, and so was a good political choice for use in microwave ovens.

though thin layers of water will let some power pass). They are to microwave what a brick wall is to light. When talking about water, we have to remember that it comes in different forms: rain, fog and mist, low clouds and so forth all will be in the way of radio links. They have a strong influence, and in many circumstances a change in weather can bring a radio link down.

There are other materials that have a more complex effect on radio absorption. For **trees** and **wood**, the amount of absorption depends on how much water they contain. Old dead dry wood is more or less transparent, wet fresh wood will absorb a lot.

Plastics and similar materials generally do not absorb a lot of radio energy- but this varies depending on the frequency and type of material. Before you build a component from plastic (e.g. weather protection for a radio device and its antennas), it is always a good idea to measure and verify that the material does not absorb radio energy around 2.4 GHz. One simple method of measuring the absorption of plastic at 2.4 GHz is to put a sample in a microwave oven for a couple of minutes. If the plastic heats up, then it absorbs radio energy and should not be used for weatherproofing.

Lastly, let us talk about ourselves: humans (as well as other animals) are largely made out of water. As far as radio networking is concerned, we may well be described as big bags of water, with the same strong absorption. Orienting an office access point in such a way that its signal must pass through many people is a key mistake when building office networks. The same goes for hotspots, cafe installations, libraries, and outdoor installations.

Reflection

Just like visible light, radio waves are reflected when they come in contact with materials that are suited for that: for radio waves, the main sources of reflection are metal and water surfaces. The rules for reflection are quite simple: the angle at which a wave hits a surface is the same angle at which it gets deflected. Note that in the eyes of a radio wave, a dense grid of bars acts just the same as a solid surface, as long as the distance between bars is small compared to the wavelength. At 2.4 GHz, a one cm metal grid will act much the same as a metal plate.

Although the rules of reflection are quite simple, things can become very complicated when you imagine an office interior with many many small metal objects of various complicated shapes. The same goes for urban situations: look around you in city environment and try to spot all of the metal objects. This explains why *multipath effects* (i.e. signal reaching their target along different paths, and therefore at different times) play such an important role in wireless networking. Water surfaces, with waves and ripples changing all the time, effectively make for a very complicated reflection object which is more or less impossible to calculate and predict precisely.

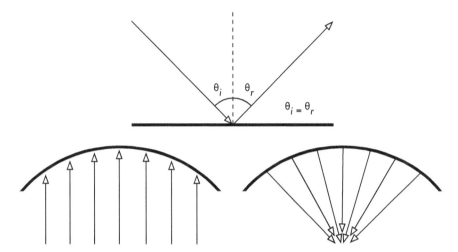

Figure 2.5: Reflection of radio waves. The angle of incidence is always equal to the angle of reflection. A parabolic uses this effect to concentrate radio waves spread out over its surface in a common direction.

We should also add that polarization has an impact: waves of different polarization in general will be reflected differently.

We use reflection to our advantage in antenna building: e.g. we put huge parabolas behind our radio transmitter/receiver to collect and bundle the radio signal into a fine point.

Diffraction

Diffraction is the apparent bending of waves when hitting an object. It is the effect of "waves going around corners".

Imagine a wave on water traveling in a straight wave front, just like a wave that we see rolling onto an ocean beach. Now we put a solid barrier, say a wooden solid fence, in its way to block it. We cut a narrow slit opening into that wall, like a small door. From this opening, a circular wave will start, and it will of course reach points that are not in a direct line behind this opening, but also on either side of it. If you look at this wavefront - and it might just as well be an electromagnetic wave - as a beam (a straight line), it would be hard to explain how it can reach points that should be hidden by a barrier. When modeled as a wavefront, the phenomenon makes sense.

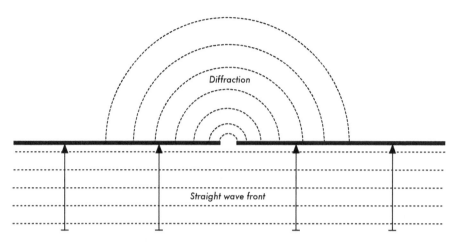

Figure 2.6: Diffraction through a narrow slit.

The Huygens Principle provides one model for understanding this behavior. Imagine that at any given instant, every point on a wavefront can be considered the starting point for a spherical "wavelet". This idea was later extended by Fresnel, and whether it adequately describes the phenomenon is still a matter of debate. But for our purposes, the Huygens model describes the effect quite well.

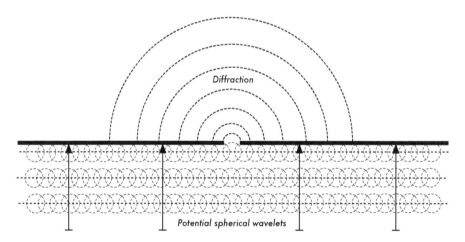

Figure 2.7: The Huygens Principle.

Through means of the effect of diffraction, waves will "bend" around corners or through an opening in a barrier. The wavelengths of visible light are far too small for humans to observe this effect directly. Microwaves, with a wavelength of several centimeters, will show the effects of diffraction when waves hit walls, mountain peaks, and other obstacles. It seems as if the obstruction causes the wave to change its direction and go around corners.

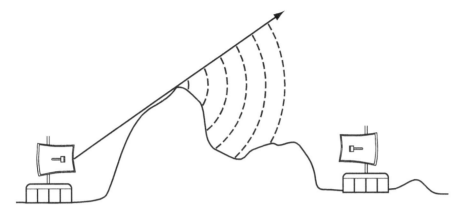

Figure 2.8: Diffraction over a mountain top.

Note that diffraction comes at the cost of power: the energy of the diffracted wave is significantly less than that of the wavefront that caused it.   But in some very specific applications, you can take advantage of the diffraction effect to circumvent obstacles.

Interference

When working with waves, one plus one does not necessarily equal two. It can also result in zero.

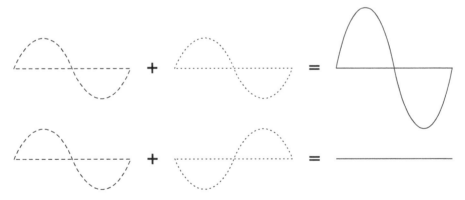

Figure 2.9: Constructive and destructive interference.

This is easy to understand when you draw two sine waves and add up the amplitudes. When peak hits peak, you will have maximum results (1 + 1 = 2). This is called **constructive interference**. When peak hits valley, you will have complete annihilation ((1 + (-)1 = 0) - **destructive interference**.

You can actually try this with waves on water and two little sticks to create circular waves - you will see that where two waves cross, there will be areas of higher wave peaks and others that remain almost flat and calm.

In order for whole trains of waves to add up or cancel each other out perfectly, they would have to have the exact same wavelength and a fixed phase relation, this means fixed positions from the peaks of the one wave to the other's.

In wireless technology, the word Interference is typically used in a wider sense, for disturbance through other RF sources, e.g. neighboring channels. So, when wireless networkers talk about interference they typically talk about all kinds of disturbance by other networks, and other sources of microwave. Interference is one of the main sources of difficulty in building wireless links, especially in urban environments or closed spaces (such as a conference space) where many networks may compete for use of the spectrum.

Whenever waves of equal amplitude and opposite phase cross paths, the wave is annihilated and no signal can be received. The much more common case is that waves will combine to form a completely garbled waveform that cannot be effectively used for communication. The modulation techniques and use of multiple channels help to deal with the problem of interference, but does not completely eliminate it.

Line of sight

The term **line of sight**, often abbreviated as **LOS**, is quite easy to understand when talking about visible light: if we can see a point B from point A where we are, we have line of sight. Simply draw a line from A to B, and if nothing is in the way, we have line of sight.

Things get a bit more complicated when we are dealing with microwaves. Remember that most propagation characteristics of electromagnetic waves scale with their wavelength. This is also the case for the widening of waves as they travel. Light has a wavelength of about 0.5 micrometers, microwaves as used in wireless networking have a wavelength of a few centimeters. Consequently, their beams are a lot wider - they need more space, so to speak.

Note that visible light beams widen just the same, and if you let them travel long enough, you can see the results despite of their short wavelength. When pointing a well focussed laser at the moon, its beam will widen to well over 100 meters in radius by the time it reaches the surface. You can see this effect for yourself using an inexpensive laser pointer and a pair of binoculars on a clear night. Rather than pointing at the moon, point at a distant mountain or unoccupied structure (such as a water tower). The radius of your beam will increase as the distance increases.

The line of sight that we need in order to have an optimal wireless connection from A to B is more than just a thin line - its shape is more like that of a cigar, an ellipse. Its width can be described by the concept of Fresnel zones.

Understanding the Fresnel zone

The exact theory of Fresnel (pronounced "Fray-nell") zones is quite complicated. However, the concept is quite easy to understand: we know from the Huygens principle that at each point of a wavefront new circular waves start, We know that microwave beams widen as they leave the antenna. We know that waves of one frequency can interfere with each other. Fresnel zone theory simply looks at a line from A to B, and then at the space around that line that contributes to what is arriving at point B. Some waves travel directly from A to B, while others travel on paths off axis. Consequently, their path is longer, introducing a phase shift between the direct and indirect beam. Whenever the phase shift is one full wavelength, you get constructive interference: the signals add up optimally. Taking this approach and calculating accordingly, you find there are ring zones around the direct line A to B which contribute to the signal arriving at point B.

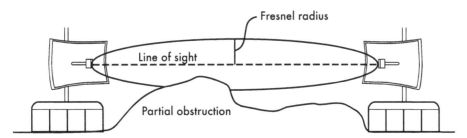

Figure 2.10: The Fresnel zone is partially blocked on this link, although the visual line of sight appears clear.

Note that there are many possible Fresnel zones, but we are chiefly concerned with zone 1. If this area were partially blocked by an obstruction, e.g. a tree or a building, the signal arriving at the far end would be diminished. When building wireless links, we therefore need to be sure that these zones be kept free of obstructions. Of course, nothing is ever perfect, so usually in wireless networking we check that about 60 percent of the radius of the first Fresnel zone should be kept free.

Here is one formula for calculating the first Fresnel zone:

```
r = 17.31 * sqrt((d1*d2)/(f*d))
```

...where **r** is the radius of the zone in meters, **d1** and **d2** are distances from the obstacle to the link end points in meters, **d** is the total link distance in meters, and **f** is the frequency in MHz. Note that this gives you the radius of the zone, not the height above ground. To calculate the height above ground, you need to subtract the result from a line drawn directly between the tops of the two towers.

For example, let's calculate the size of the first Fresnel zone in the middle of a 2km link, transmitting at 2.437 GHz (802.11b channel 6):

```
r = 17.31 sqrt((1000 * 1000) / (2437 * 2000))
r = 17.31 sqrt(1000000 / 4874000)
r = 7.84 meters
```

Assuming both of our towers were ten meters tall, the first Fresnel zone would pass just 2.16 meters above ground level in the middle of the link. But how tall could a structure at that point be to clear 60% of the first zone?

```
r = 0.6 * 17.31 sqrt((1000 * 1000) / (2437 * 2000))
r = 0.6 * 17.31 sqrt(600000 / 4874000)
r = 4.70 meters
```

Subtracting the result from 10 meters, we can see that a structure 5.3 meters tall at the center of the link would block up to 40% of the first Fresnel zone. This is normally acceptable, but to improve the situation we would need to position our antennas higher up, or change the direction of the link to avoid the obstacle.

Power

Any electromagnetic wave carries energy - we can feel that when we enjoy (or suffer from) the warmth of the sun. The amount of energy received in a certain amount of time is called **power**. The power **P** is of key importance for making wireless links work: you need a certain minimum power in order for a receiver to make sense of the signal.

We will come back to details of transmission power, losses, gains and radio sensitivity in **Chapter 3**. Here we will briefly discuss how the power P is defined and measured.

The electric field is measured in V/m (potential difference per meter), the power contained within it is proportional to the square of the electric field

$$P \sim E^2$$

Practically, we measure the power by means of some form of receiver, e.g. an antenna and a voltmeter, power meter, oscilloscope, or even a radio card and laptop. Looking at the signal's power directly means looking at the square of the signal in Volts.

Calculating with dB

By far the most important technique when calculating power is calculating with **decibels** (**dB**). There is no new physics hidden in this - it is just a convenient method which makes calculations a lot simpler.

The decibel is a dimensionless unit[2], that is, it defines a relationship between two measurements of power. It is defined by:

```
dB = 10 * Log (P1 / P0)
```

where **P1** and **P0** can be whatever two values you want to compare. Typically, in our case, this will be some amount of power.

Why are decibels so handy to use? Many phenomena in nature happen to behave in a way we call exponential. For example, the human ear senses a sound to be twice as loud as another one if it has ten times the physical signal.

Another example, quite close to our field of interest, is absorption. Suppose a wall is in the path of our wireless link, and each meter of wall takes away half of the available signal. The result would be:

```
0 meters    =      1 (full signal)
1 meter     =      1/2
2 meters    =      1/4
3 meters    =      1/8
4 meters    =      1/16
n meters    =      1/2ⁿ  = 2⁻ⁿ
```

This is exponential behavior.

But once we have used the trick of applying the logarithm (log), things become a lot easier: instead of taking a value to the n-th power, we just multiply by n. Instead of multiplying values, we just add.

Here are some commonly used values that are important to remember:

```
 +3 dB = double power
 -3 dB = half the power
+10 dB = order of magnitude (10 times power)
-10 dB = one tenth power
```

_____

2. Another example of a dimensionless unit is the percent (%) which can also be used in all kinds of quantities or numbers. While measurements like feet and grams are fixed, dimensionless units represent a relationship.

In addition to dimensionless dB, there are a number of relative definitions that are based on a certain base value P0. The most relevant ones for us are:

```
dBm    relative to P0 = 1 mW
dBi    relative to an ideal isotropic antenna
```

An *isotropic antenna* is a hypothetical antenna that evenly distributes power in all directions. It is approximated by a dipole, but a perfect isotropic antenna cannot be built in reality. The isotropic model is useful for describing the relative power gain of a real world antenna.

Another common (although less convenient) convention for expressing power is in *milliwatts*. Here are equivalent power levels expressed in milliwatts and dBm:

```
  1 mW        = 0  dBm
  2 mW        = 3  dBm
100 mW        = 20 dBm
  1 W         = 30 dBm
```

Physics in the real world

Don't worry if the concepts in this chapter seem challenging. Understanding how radio waves propagate and interact with the environment is a complex field of study in itself. Most people find it difficult to understand phenomenon that they can't even see with their own eyes. By now you should understand that radio waves don't travel in a straight, predictable path. To make reliable communication networks, you will need to be able to calculate how much power is needed to cross a given distance, and predict how the waves will travel along the way.

There is much more to learn about radio physics than we have room for here. For more information about this evolving field, see the resources list in **Appendix A**.

3

Network Design

Before purchasing equipment or deciding on a hardware platform, you should have a clear idea of the nature of your communications problem. Most likely, you are reading this book because you need to connect computer networks together in order to share resources and ultimately reach the larger global Internet. The network design you choose to implement should fit the communications problem you are trying to solve. Do you need to connect a remote site to an Internet connection in the center of your campus? Will your network likely grow to include several remote sites? Will most of your network components be installed in fixed locations, or will your network expand to include hundreds of roaming laptops and other devices?

In this chapter, we will begin with a review of the networking concepts that define TCP/IP, the primary family of networking protocols currently used on the Internet. We will then see examples of how other people have built wireless networks to solve their communication problems, including diagrams of the essential network structure. Finally, we will present several common methods for getting your information to flow efficiently through your network and on to the rest of the world.

Networking 101

TCP/IP refers to the suite of protocols that allow conversations to happen on the global Internet. By understanding TCP/IP, you can build networks that will scale to virtually any size, and will ultimately become part of the global Internet.

If you are already comfortable with the essentials of TCP/IP networking (including addressing, routing, switches, firewalls, and routers), you may want to skip ahead to **Designing the Physical Network** on **Page 51**. We will now review the basics of Internet networking.

Introduction

Venice, Italy is a fantastic city to get lost in. The roads are mere foot paths that cross water in hundreds of places, and never go in a simple straight line. Postal carriers in Venice are some of the most highly trained in the world, specializing in delivery to only one or two of the six *sestieri* (districts) of Venice. This is necessary due to the intricate layout of that ancient city. Many people find that knowing the location of the water and the sun is far more useful than trying to find a street name on a map.

Figure 3.1: Another kind of network mask.

Imagine a tourist who happens to find papier-mâché mask as a souvenir, and wants to have it shipped from the studio in S. Polo, Venezia to an office in Seattle, USA. This may sound like an ordinary (or even trivial) task, but let's look at what actually happens.

The artist first packs the mask into a shipping box and addresses it to the office in Seattle, USA. They then hand this off to a postal employee, who attaches some official forms and sends it to a central package processing hub for international destinations. After several days, the package clears Italian customs and finds its way onto a transatlantic flight, arriving at a central import processing location in the U.S. Once it clears through U.S. customs, the package is sent to the regional distribution point for the northwest U.S., then on to the Seattle postal processing center. The package eventually makes its way onto a delivery van which has a route that brings it to the proper address, on the proper street, in the proper neighborhood. A clerk at the office accepts the package and puts it in the proper incoming mail box. Once it arrives, the package is retrieved and the mask itself is finally received.

The clerk at the office in Seattle neither knows nor cares about how to get to the *sestiere* of S. Polo, Venezia. His job is simply to accept packages as they arrive, and deliver them to the proper person. Similarly, the postal carrier in Venice has no need to worry about how to get to the correct neighborhood in Seattle. His job is to pick up packages from his local neighborhood and forward them to the next closest hub in the delivery chain.

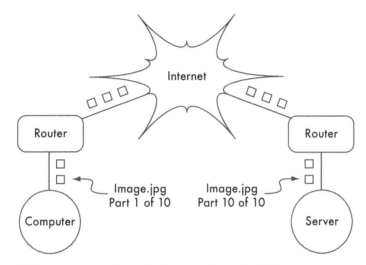

Figure 3.2: Internet networking. Packets are forwarded between routers until they reach their ultimate destination.

This is very similar to how Internet routing works. A message is split up into many individual **packets**, and are labeled with their source and destination. The computer then sends these packets to a **router**, which decides where to send them next. The router needs only to keep track of a handful of routes (for example, how to get to the local network, the best route to a few other local networks, and one route to a gateway to the rest of the Internet). This list of possible routes is called the **routing table**. As packets arrive at the router, the destination address is examined and compared against its internal routing table. If the router has no explicit route to the destination in question, it sends the packet to the closest match it can find, which is often its own Internet gateway (via the **default route**). And the next router does the same, and so forth, until the packet eventually arrives at its destination.

Packages can only make their way through the international postal system because we have established a standardized addressing scheme for packages. For example, the destination address must be written legibly on the front of the package, and include all critical information (such as the recipient's name, street address, city, country, and postal code). Without this information, packages are either returned to the sender or are lost in the system.

Packets can only flow through the global Internet because we have agreed on a common addressing scheme and protocol for forwarding packets. These standard communication protocols make it possible to exchange information on a global scale.

Cooperative communications

Communication is only possible when the participants speak a common language. But once the communication becomes more complex than a simple conversation between two people, protocol becomes just as important as language. All of the people in an auditorium may speak English, but without a set of rules in place to establish who has the right to use the microphone, the communication of an individual's ideas to the entire room is nearly impossible. Now imagine an auditorium as big as the world, full of all of the computers that exist. Without a common set of communication protocols to regulate when and how each computer can speak, the Internet would be a chaotic mess where every machine tries to speak at once.

People have developed a number of communications frameworks to address this problem. The most well-known of these is the ***OSI model***.

The OSI model

The international standard for Open Systems Interconnection (OSI) is defined by the document ISO/IEC 7498-1, as outlined by the International Standards Organization and the International Electrotechnical Commission. The full standard is available as publication "ISO/IEC 7498-1:1994," available from *http://standards.iso.org/ittf/PubliclyAvailableStandards/*.

The OSI model divides network traffic into a number of ***layers***. Each layer is independent of the layers around it, and each builds on the services provided by the layer below while providing new services to the layer above. The abstraction between layers makes it easy to design elaborate and highly reliable ***protocol stacks***, such as the ubiquitous ***TCP/IP*** stack. A protocol stack is an actual implementation of a layered communications framework. The OSI model doesn't define the protocols to be used in a particular network, but simply delegates each communications "job" to a single layer within a well-defined hierarchy.

While the ISO/IEC 7498-1 specification details how layers should interact with each other, it leaves the actual implementation details up to the manufacturer. Each layer can be implemented in hardware (more common for lower layers) or software. As long as the interface between layers adheres to the standard, implementers are free to use whatever means are available to build their protocol stack. This means that any given layer from manufacturer A can operate with the same layer from manufacturer B (assuming the relevant specifications are implemented and interpreted correctly).

Here is a brief outline of the seven-layer OSI networking model:

Layer	Name	Description
7	Application	The **Application Layer** is the layer that most network users are exposed to, and is the level at which human communication happens. HTTP, FTP, and SMTP are all application layer protocols. The human sits above this layer, interacting with the application.
6	Presentation	The **Presentation Layer** deals with data representation, before it reaches the application. This would include MIME encoding, data compression, formatting checks, byte ordering, etc.
5	Session	The **Session Layer** manages the logical communications session between applications. NetBIOS and RPC are two examples of a layer five protocol.
4	Transport	The **Transport Layer** provides a method of reaching a particular service on a given network node. Examples of protocols that operate at this layer are TCP and UDP. Some protocols at the transport layer (such as TCP) ensure that all of the data has arrived at the destination, and is reassembled and delivered to the next layer in the proper order. UDP is a "connectionless" protocol commonly used for video and audio streaming.
3	Network	IP (the Internet Protocol) is the most common **Network Layer** protocol. This is the layer where routing occurs. Packets can leave the link local network and be retransmitted on other networks. Routers perform this function on a network by having at least two network interfaces, one on each of the networks to be interconnected. Nodes on the Internet are reached by their globally unique IP address. Another critical Network Layer protocol is ICMP, which is a special protocol which provides various management messages needed for correct operation of IP. This layer is also sometimes referred to as the **Internet Layer**.

Layer	Name	Description
2	Data Link	Whenever two or more nodes share the same physical medium (for example, several computers plugged into a hub, or a room full of wireless devices all using the same radio channel) they use the **Data Link Layer** to communicate. Common examples of data link protocols are Ethernet, Token Ring, ATM, and the wireless networking protocols (802.11a/b/g). Communication on this layer is said to be link-local, since all nodes connected at this layer communicate with each other directly. This layer is sometimes known as the **Media Access Control** (**MAC**) layer. On networks modeled after Ethernet, nodes are referred to by their **MAC address.** This is a unique 48 bit number assigned to every networking device when it is manufactured.
1	Physical	The **Physical Layer** is the lowest layer in the OSI model, and refers to the actual physical medium over which communications take place. This can be a copper CAT5 cable, a fiber optic bundle, radio waves, or just about any other medium capable of transmitting signals. Cut wires, broken fiber, and RF interference are all physical layer problems.

The layers in this model are numbered one through seven, with seven at the top. This is meant to reinforce the idea that each layer builds upon, and depends upon, the layers below. Imagine the OSI model as a building, with the foundation at layer one, the next layers as successive floors, and the roof at layer seven. If you remove any single layer, the building will not stand. Similarly, if the fourth floor is on fire, then nobody can pass through it in either direction.

The first three layers (Physical, Data Link, and Network) all happen "on the network." That is, activity at these layers is determined by the configuration of cables, switches, routers, and similar devices. A network switch can only distribute packets by using MAC addresses, so it need only implement layers one and two. A simple router can route packets using only their IP addresses, so it need implement only layers one through three. A web server or a laptop computer runs applications, so it must implement all seven layers. Some advanced routers may implement layer four and above, to allow them to make decisions based on the higher-level information content in a packet, such as the name of a website, or the attachments of an email.

The OSI model is internationally recognized, and is widely regarded as the complete and definitive network model. It provides a framework for manufacturers and network protocol implementers that can be used to build networking devices that interoperate in just about any part of the world.

From the perspective of a network engineer or troubleshooter, the OSI model can seem needlessly complex. In particular, people who build and troubleshoot TCP/IP networks rarely need to deal with problems at the Session or Presentation layers. For the majority of Internet network implementations, the OSI model can be simplified into a smaller collection of five layers.

The TCP/IP model

Unlike the OSI model, the TCP/IP model is not an international standard and its definitions vary. Nevertheless, it is often used as a pragmatic model for understanding and troubleshooting Internet networks. The vast majority of the Internet uses TCP/IP, and so we can make some assumptions about networks that make them easier to understand. The TCP/IP model of networking describes the following five layers:

Layer	Name
5	Application
4	Transport
3	Internet
2	Data Link
1	Physical

In terms of the OSI model, layers five through seven are rolled into the topmost layer (the Application layer). The first four layers in both models are identical. Many network engineers think of everything above layer four as "just data" that varies from application to application. Since the first three layers are interoperable between virtually all manufacturers' equipment, and layer four works between all hosts using TCP/IP, and everything above layer four tends to apply to specific applications, this simplified model works well when building and troubleshooting TCP/IP networks. We will use the TCP/IP model when discussing networks in this book.

The TCP/IP model can be compared to a person delivering a letter to a downtown office building. The person first needs to interact with the road itself (the Physical layer), pay attention to other traffic on the road (the Data Link layer), turn at the proper place to connect to other roads and arrive at the correct address (the Internet layer), go to the proper floor and room number (the Transport layer), and finally give it to a receptionist who can take the letter from there (the Application layer). Once they have delivered the message to the receptionist, the delivery person is free to go on their way.

The five layers can be easily remembered by using the mnemonic "**P**lease **D**on't **L**ook **I**n **T**he **A**ttic," which of course stands for "**P**hysical / **D**ata **L**ink / **I**nternet / **T**ransport / **A**pplication."

The Internet protocols

TCP/IP is the protocol stack most commonly used on the global Internet. The acronym stands for *Transmission Control Protocol* (*TCP*) and *Internet Protocol* (*IP*), but actually refers to a whole family of related communications protocols. TCP/IP is also called the *Internet protocol suite*, and it operates at layers three and four of the TCP/IP model.

In this discussion, we will focus on version four of the IP protocol (IPv4) as this is now the most widely deployed protocol on the Internet.

IP Addressing

In an IPv4 network, the address is a 32-bit number, normally written as four 8-bit numbers expressed in decimal form and separated by periods. Examples of IP addresses are 10.0.17.1, 192.168.1.1, or 172.16.5.23.

If you enumerated every possible IP address, they would range from 0.0.0.0 to 255.255.255.255. This yields a total of more than four billion possible IP addresses (255 x 255 x 255 x 255 = 4,228,250,625); although many of these are reserved for special purposes and should not be assigned to hosts. Each of the usable IP addresses is a unique identifier that distinguishes one network node from another.

Interconnected networks must agree on an IP addressing plan. IP addresses must be unique and generally cannot be used in different places on the Internet at the same time; otherwise, routers would not know how best to route packets to them.

IP addresses are allocated by a central numbering authority that provides a consistent and coherent numbering method. This ensures that duplicate addresses are not used by different networks. The authority assigns large blocks of consecutive addresses to smaller authorities, who in turn assign smaller consecutive blocks within these ranges to other authorities, or to their customers. These groups of addresses are called sub-networks, or *subnets* for short. Large subnets can be further subdivided into smaller subnets. A group of related addresses is referred to as an *address space*.

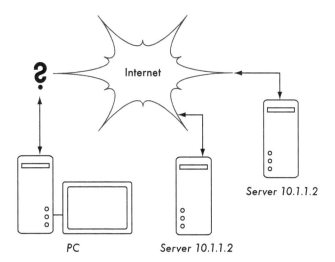

Figure 3.3: Without unique IP addresses, unambiguous global routing is impossible. If the PC requests a web page from 10.1.1.2, which server will it reach?

Subnets

By applying a **subnet mask** (also called a **network mask**, or simply **netmask**) to an IP address, you can logically define both a host and the network to which it belongs. Traditionally, subnet masks are expressed using dotted decimal form, much like an IP address. For example, 255.255.255.0 is one common netmask. You will find this notation used when configuring network interfaces, creating routes, etc. However, subnet masks are more succinctly expressed using **CIDR notation**, which simply enumerates the number of bits in the mask after a forward slash (/). Thus, 255.255.255.0 can be simplified as /24. CIDR is short for **Classless Inter-Domain Routing**, and is defined in RFC1518[1].

A subnet mask determines the size of a given network. Using a /24 netmask, 8 bits are reserved for hosts (32 bits total - 24 bits of netmask = 8 bits for hosts). This yields up to 256 possible host addresses ($2^8 = 256$). By convention, the first value is taken as the **network address** (.0 or 00000000), and the last value is taken as the **broadcast address** (.255 or 11111111). This leaves 254 addresses available for hosts on this network.

Subnet masks work by applying AND logic to the 32 bit IP number. In binary notation, the "1" bits in the mask indicate the network address portion, and "0" bits indicate the host address portion. A logical AND is performed by comparing two bits. The result is "1" if both of the bits being compared are

---

1. RFC is short for Request For Comments. RFCs are a numbered series of documents published by the Internet Society that document ideas and concepts related to Internet technologies. Not all RFCs are actual standards. RFCs can be viewed online at http://rfc.net/

also "1". Otherwise the result is "0". Here are all of the possible outcomes of a binary AND comparison between two bits.

Bit 1	Bit 2	Result
0	0	0
0	1	0
1	0	0
1	1	1

To understand how a netmask is applied to an IP address, first convert everything to binary. The netmask 255.255.255.0 in binary contains twenty-four "1" bits:

```
255       255       255        0
11111111.11111111.11111111.00000000
```

When this netmask is combined with the IP address 10.10.10.10, we can apply a logical AND to each of the bits to determine the network address.

```
  10.10.10.10: 00001010.00001010.00001010.00001010
255.255.255.0: 11111111.11111111.11111111.00000000
               -----------------------------------
   10.10.10.0: 00001010.00001010.00001010.00000000
```

This results in the network 10.10.10.0/24. This network consists of the hosts 10.10.10.1 through 10.10.10.254, with 10.10.10.0 as the network address and 10.10.10.255 as the broadcast address.

Subnet masks are not limited to entire octets. One can also specify subnet masks like 255.254.0.0 (or /15 CIDR). This is a large block, containing 131,072 addresses, from 10.0.0.0 to 10.1.255.255. It could be further subdivided, for example into 512 subnets of 256 addresses each. The first one would be 10.0.0.0-10.0.0.255, then 10.0.1.0-10.0.1.255, and so on up to 10.1.255.0-10.1.255.255. Alternatively, it could be subdivided into 2 blocks of 65,536 addresses, or 8192 blocks of 16 addresses, or in many other ways. It could even be subdivided into a mixture of different block sizes, as long as none of them overlap, and each is a valid subnet whose size is a power of two.

While many netmasks are possible, common netmasks include:

CIDR	Decimal	# of Hosts
/30	255.255.255.252	4
/29	255.255.255.248	8
/28	255.255.255.240	16
/27	255.255.255.224	32
/26	255.255.255.192	64
/25	255.255.255.128	128
/24	255.255.255.0	256
/16	255.255.0.0	65 536
/8	255.0.0.0	16 777 216

With each reduction in the CIDR value the IP space is doubled. Remember that two IP addresses within each network are always reserved for the network and broadcast addresses.

There are three common netmasks that have special names. A /8 network (with a netmask of 255.0.0.0) defines a **Class A** network. A /16 (255.255.0.0) is a **Class B**, and a /24 (255.255.255.0) is called a **Class C**. These names were around long before CIDR notation, but are still often used for historical reasons.

Global IP Addresses

Have you ever wondered who controls the allocation of IP space? **Globally routable IP addresses** are assigned and distributed by **Regional Internet Registrars** (**RIR**s) to ISPs. The ISP then allocates smaller IP blocks to their clients as required. Virtually all Internet users obtain their IP addresses from an ISP.

The 4 billion available IP addresses are administered by the **Internet Assigned Numbers Authority** (**IANA**, *http://www.iana.org/*). IANA has divided this space into large subnets, usually /8 subnets with 16 million addresses each. These subnets are delegated to one of the five regional Internet registries (RIRs), which are given authority over large geographic areas.

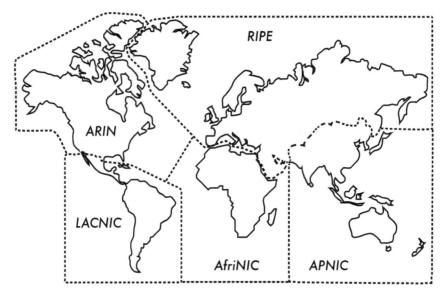

Figure 3.4: Authority for Internet IP address assignments is delegated to the five Regional Internet Registrars.

The five RIRs are:

- African Network Information Centre (AfriNIC, *http://www.afrinic.net/*)
- Asia Pacific Network Information Centre (APNIC, *http://www.apnic.net/*)
- American Registry for Internet Numbers (ARIN, *http://www.arin.net/*)
- Regional Latin-American and Caribbean IP Address Registry (LACNIC, *http://www.lacnic.net/*)
- Réseaux IP Européens (RIPE NCC, *http://www.ripe.net/*)

Your ISP will assign globally routable IP address space to you from the pool allocated to it by your RIR. The registry system assures that IP addresses are not reused in any part of the network anywhere in the world.

Once IP address assignments have been agreed upon, it is possible to pass packets between networks and participate in the global Internet. The process of moving packets between networks is called ***routing***.

Static IP Addresses

A static IP address is an address assignment that never changes. Static IP addresses are important because servers using these addresses may have DNS mappings pointed towards them, and typically serve information to other machines (such as email services, web servers, etc.).

Blocks of static IP addresses may be assigned by your ISP, either by request or automatically depending on your means of connection to the Internet.

Dynamic IP Addresses

Dynamic IP addresses are assigned by an ISP for non-permanent nodes connecting to the Internet, such as a home computer which is on a dial-up connection.

Dynamic IP addresses can be assigned automatically using the ***Dynamic Host Configuration Protocol*** (***DHCP***), or the ***Point-to-Point Protocol*** (***PPP***), depending on the type of Internet connection. A node using DHCP first requests an IP address assignment from the network, and automatically configures its network interface. IP addresses can be assigned randomly from a pool by your ISP, or might be assigned according to a policy. IP addresses assigned by DHCP are valid for a specified time (called the ***lease time***). The node must renew the DHCP lease before the lease time expires. Upon renewal, the node may receive the same IP address or a different one from the pool of available addresses.

Dynamic addresses are popular with Internet service providers, because it enables them to use fewer IP addresses than their total number of customers. They only need an address for each customer who is **active at any one time**. Globally routable IP addresses cost money, and some authorities that specialize in the assignment of addresses (such as RIPE, the European RIR) are very strict on IP address usage for ISP's. Assigning addresses dynamically allows ISPs to save money, and they will often charge extra to provide a static IP address to their customers.

Private IP addresses

Most private networks do not require the allocation of globally routable, public IP addresses for every computer in the organization. In particular, computers which are not public servers do not need to be addressable from the public Internet. Organizations typically use IP addresses from the ***private address space*** for machines on the internal network.

There are currently three blocks of private address space reserved by IANA: 10.0.0.0/8, 172.16.0.0/12, and 192.168.0.0/16. These are defined in RFC1918. These addresses are not intended to be routed on the Internet, and are typically unique only within an organization or group of organizations which choose to follow the same numbering scheme.

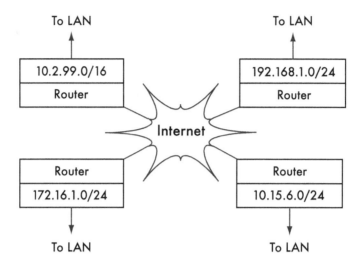

Figure 3.5: RFC1918 private addresses may be used within an organization, and are not routed on the global Internet.

If you ever intend to link together private networks that use RFC1918 address space, be sure to use unique addresses throughout all of the networks. For example, you might break the 10.0.0.0/8 address space into multiple Class B networks (10.1.0.0/16, 10.2.0.0/16, etc.). One block could be assigned to each network according to its physical location (the campus main branch, field office one, field office two, dormitories, and so forth). The network administrators at each location can then break the network down further into multiple Class C networks (10.1.1.0/24, 10.1.2.0/24, etc.) or into blocks of any other logical size. In the future, should the networks ever be linked (either by a physical connection, wireless link, or VPN), then all of the machines will be reachable from any point in the network without having to renumber network devices.

Some Internet providers may allocate private addresses like these instead of public addresses to their customers, although this has serious disadvantages. Since these addresses cannot be routed over the Internet, computers which use them are not really "part" of the Internet, and are not directly reachable from it. In order to allow them to communicate with the Internet, their private addresses must be translated to public addresses. This translation process is known as **Network Address Translation** (**NAT**), and is normally performed at the gateway between the private network and the Internet. We will look at NAT in more detail on **Page 43**.

Routing

Imagine a network with three hosts: A, B, and C. They use the corresponding IP addresses 192.168.1.1, 192.168.1.2 and 192.168.1.3. These hosts are part of a /24 network (their network mask is 255.255.255.0).

For two hosts to communicate on a local network, they must determine each others' MAC addresses. It is possible to manually configure each host with a mapping table from IP address to MAC address, but normally the **Address Resolution Protocol** (**ARP**) is used to determine this automatically.

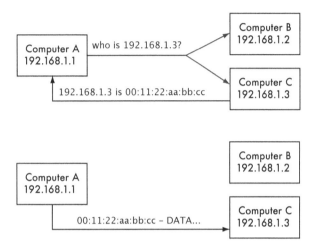

Figure 3.6: Computer A needs to send data to 192.168.1.3. But it must first ask the whole network for the MAC address that responds to 192.168.1.3.

When using ARP, host A broadcasts to all hosts the question, "Who has the MAC address for the IP 192.168.1.3?" When host C sees an ARP request for its own IP address, it replies with its MAC address.

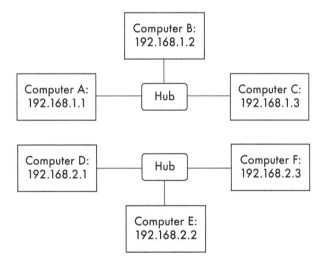

Figure 3.7: Two separate IP networks.

Consider now another network with 3 hosts, D, E, and F, with the corresponding IP addresses 192.168.2.1, 192.168.2.2, and 192.168.2.3. This is another /24 network, but it is not in the same range as the network above. All three hosts can reach each other directly (first using ARP to resolve the IP address into a MAC address, and then sending packets to that MAC address).

Now we will add host G. This host has two network cards, with one plugged into each network. The first network card uses the IP address 192.168.1.4, and the other uses 192.168.2.4. Host G is now link-local to both networks, and can route packets between them.

But what if hosts A, B, and C want to reach hosts D, E, and F? They will need to add a route to the other network via host G. For example, hosts A-C would add a route via 192.168.1.4. In Linux, this can be accomplished with the following command:

```
# ip route add 192.168.2.0/24 via 192.168.1.4
```

...and hosts D-F would add the following:

```
# ip route add 192.168.1.0/24 via 192.168.2.4
```

The result is shown in **Figure 3.8**. Notice that the route is added via the IP address on host G that is link-local to the respective network. Host A could not add a route via 192.168.2.4, even though it is the same physical machine as 192.168.1.4 (host G), since that IP is not link-local.

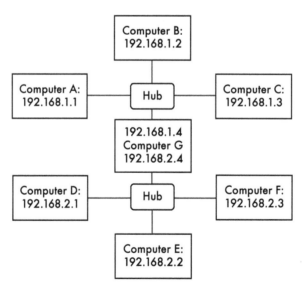

Figure 3.8: Host G acts as a router between the two networks.

A route tells the OS that the desired network doesn't lie on the immediate link-local network, and it must **forward** the traffic through the specified router. If host A wants to send a packet to host F, it would first send it to host G. Host G would then look up host F in its routing table, and see that it has a direct connection to host F's network. Finally, host G would resolve the hardware (MAC) address of host F and forward the packet to it.

This is a very simple routing example, where the destination is only a single *hop* away from the source. As networks get more complex, many hops may need to be traversed to reach the ultimate destination. Since it isn't practical for every machine on the Internet to know the route to every other, we make use of a routing entry known as the **default route** (also known as the **default gateway**). When a router receives a packet destined for a network for which it has no explicit route, the packet is forwarded to its default gateway.

The default gateway is typically the best route out of your network, usually in the direction of your ISP. An example of a router that uses a default gateway is shown in **Figure 3.9**.

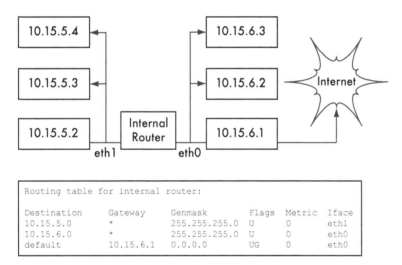

```
Routing table for internal router:

Destination      Gateway      Genmask         Flags   Metric   Iface
10.15.5.0        *            255.255.255.0   U       0        eth1
10.15.6.0        *            255.255.255.0   U       0        eth0
default          10.15.6.1    0.0.0.0         UG      0        eth0
```

Figure 3.9: When no explicit route exists to a particular destination, a host uses the default gateway entry in its routing table.

Routes can be updated manually, or can dynamically react to network outages and other events. Some examples of popular dynamic routing protocols are RIP, OSPF, BGP, and OLSR. Configuring dynamic routing is beyond the scope of this book, but for further reading on the subject, see the resources in **Appendix A**.

Network Address Translation (NAT)

In order to reach hosts on the Internet, RFC1918 addresses must be converted to global, publicly routable IP addresses. This is achieved using a technique known as **Network Address Translation**, or **NAT**. A NAT device is a router that manipulates the addresses of packets instead of simply forwarding them. On a NAT router, the Internet connection uses one (or more) globally routed IP addresses, while the private network uses an IP address from the RFC1918 private address range. The NAT router allows the global address(es) to be shared with all of the inside users, who all use private addresses. It converts the packets from one form of addressing to the other as the packets pass through it. As far as the network users can tell, they are directly connected to the Internet and require no special software or drivers. They simply use the NAT router as their default gateway, and address packets as they normally would. The NAT router translates outbound packets to use the global IP address as they leave the network, and translates them back again as they are received from the Internet.

The major consequence of using NAT is that machines from the Internet cannot easily reach servers within the organization without setting up explicit forwarding rules on the router. Connections initiated from within the private address space generally have no trouble, although some applications (such as Voice over IP and some VPN software) can have difficulty dealing with NAT.

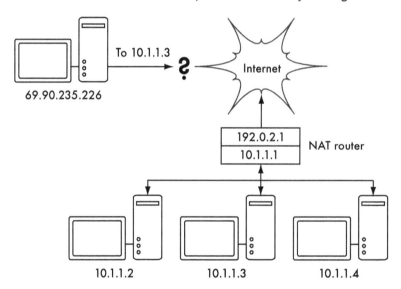

Figure 3.10: Network Address Translation allows you to share a single IP address with many internal hosts, but can make it difficult for some services to work properly.

Depending on your point of view, this can be considered a bug (since it makes it harder to set up two-way communication) or a feature (since it effectively provides a "free" firewall for your entire organization). RFC1918 addresses should be filtered on the edge of your network to prevent accidental or malicious RFC1918 traffic entering or leaving your network. While NAT performs some firewall-like functions, it is not a replacement for a real firewall.

Internet Protocol Suite

Machines on the Internet use the Internet Protocol (IP) to reach each other, even when separated by many intermediary machines. There are a number of protocols that are run in conjunction with IP that provide features as critical to normal operations as IP itself. Every packet specifies a protocol number which identifies the packet as one of these protocols. The most commonly used protocols are the **Transmission Control Protocol** (**TCP**, number 6), **User Datagram Protocol** (**UDP**, number 17), and the **Internet Control Message Protocol** (**ICMP**, number 1). Taken as a group, these protocols (and others) are known as the **Internet Protocol Suite**, or simply **TCP/IP** for short.

The TCP and UDP protocols introduce the concept of port numbers. Port numbers allow multiple services to be run on the same IP address, and still be distinguished from each other. Every packet has a source and destination port number. Some port numbers are well defined standards, used to reach well known services such as email and web servers. For example, web servers normally *listen* on TCP port 80, and SMTP email servers listen on TCP port 25. When we say that a service "listens" on a port (such as port 80), we mean that it will accept packets that use its IP as the destination IP address, and 80 as the destination port. Servers usually do not care about the source IP or source port, although sometimes they will use them to establish the identity of the other side. When sending a response to such packets, the server will use its own IP as the source IP, and 80 as the source port.

When a client connects to a service, it may use any source port number on its side which is not already in use, but it must connect to the proper port on the server (e.g. 80 for web, 25 for email). TCP is a **session oriented** protocol with guaranteed delivery and transmission control features (such as detection and mitigation of network congestion, retries, packet reordering and reassembly, etc.). UDP is designed for **connectionless** streams of information, and does not guarantee delivery at all, or in any particular order.

The ICMP protocol is designed for debugging and maintenance on the Internet. Rather than port numbers, it has **message types**, which are also numbers. Different message types are used to request a simple response from another computer (echo request), notify the sender of another packet of a possible routing loop (time exceeded), or inform the sender that a packet that could not be delivered due to firewall rules or other problems (destination unreachable).

By now you should have a solid understanding of how computers on the network are addressed, and how information flows on the network between them. Now let's take a brief look at the physical hardware that implements these network protocols.

Ethernet

Ethernet is the name of the most popular standard for connecting together computers on a **Local Area Network** (**LAN**). It is sometimes used to connect individual computers to the Internet, via a router, ADSL modem, or wireless device. However, if you connect a single computer to the Internet, you may not use Ethernet at all. The name comes from the physical concept of the ether, the medium which was once supposed to carry light waves through free space. The official standard is called IEEE 802.3.

The most common Ethernet standard is called 100baseT. This defines a data rate of 100 megabits per second, running over twisted pair wires, with modular RJ-45 connectors on the end. The network topology is a star, with switches or hubs at the center of each star, and end nodes (devices and additional switches) at the edges.

MAC addresses

Every device connected to an Ethernet network has a unique MAC address, assigned by the manufacturer of the network card. Its function is like that of an IP address, since it serves as a unique identifier that enables devices to talk to each other. However, the scope of a MAC address is limited to a broadcast domain, which is defined as all the computers connected together by wires, hubs, switches, and bridges, but not crossing routers or Internet gateways. MAC addresses are never used directly on the Internet, and are not transmitted across routers.

Hubs

Ethernet **hubs** connect multiple twisted-pair Ethernet devices together. They work at the physical layer (the lowest or first layer). They repeat the signals received by each port out to all of the other ports. Hubs can therefore be considered to be simple repeaters. Due to this design, only one port can successfully transmit at a time. If two devices transmit at the same time, they corrupt each other's transmissions, and both must back off and retransmit their packets later. This is known as a **collision**, and each host remains responsible for detecting collisions during transmission, and retransmitting its own packets when needed.

When problems such as excessive collisions are detected on a port, some hubs can disconnect (**partition**) that port for a while to limit its impact on the rest of the network. While a port is partitioned, devices attached to it cannot communicate with the rest of the network. Hub-based networks are generally more robust than coaxial Ethernet (also known as 10base2 or ThinNet), where misbehaving devices can disable the entire segment. But hubs are limited in their usefulness, since they can easily become points of congestion on busy networks.

Switches

A **switch** is a device which operates much like a hub, but provides a dedicated (or **switched**) connection between ports. Rather than repeating all traffic on every port, the switch determines which ports are communicating directly and temporarily connects them together. Switches generally provide much better performance than hubs, especially on busy networks with many computers. They are not much more expensive than hubs, and are replacing them in many situations.

Switches work at the data link layer (the second layer), since they interpret and act upon the MAC address in the packets they receive. When a packet arrives at a port on a switch, it makes a note of the source MAC address, which it associates with that port. It stores this information in an internal **MAC table**. The switch then looks up the destination MAC address in its MAC table, and transmits the packet on the matching port. If the destination MAC address is not found in the MAC table, the packet is then sent to all of the connected interfaces. If the destination port matches the incoming port, the packet is filtered and is not forwarded.

Hubs vs. Switches

Hubs are considered to be fairly unsophisticated devices, since they inefficiently rebroadcast all traffic on every port. This simplicity introduces both a performance penalty and a security issue. Overall performance is slower, since the available bandwidth must be shared between all ports. Since all traffic is seen by all ports, any host on the network can easily monitor all of the network traffic.

Switches create virtual connections between receiving and transmitting ports. This yields better performance because many virtual connections can be made simultaneously. More expensive switches can switch traffic by inspecting packets at higher levels (at the transport or application layer), allow the creation of VLANs, and implement other advanced features.

A hub can be used when repetition of traffic on all ports is desirable; for example, when you want to explicitly allow a monitoring machine to see all of the traffic on the network. Most switches provide **monitor port** functionality that enables repeating on an assigned port specifically for this purpose.

Hubs were once cheaper than switches. However, the price of switches have reduced dramatically over the years. Therefore, old network hubs should be replaced whenever possible with new switches.

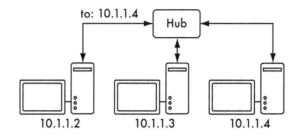

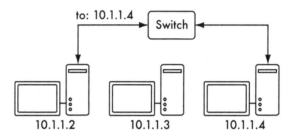

Figure 3.11: A hub simply repeats all traffic on every port, while a switch makes a temporary, dedicated connection between the ports that need to communicate.

Both hubs and switches may offer **managed** services. Some of these services include the ability to set the link speed (10baseT, 100baseT, 1000baseT, full or half duplex) per port, enable triggers to watch for network events (such as changes in MAC address or malformed packets), and usually include **port counters** for easy bandwidth accounting. A managed switch that provides upload and download byte counts for every physical port can greatly simplify network monitoring. These services are typically available via SNMP, or they may be accessed via telnet, ssh, a web interface, or a custom configuration tool.

Routers and firewalls

While hubs and switches provide connectivity on a local network segment, a router's job is to forward packets between different network segments. A router typically has two or more physical network interfaces. It may include support for different types of network media, such as Ethernet, ATM, DSL, or dial-up. Routers can be dedicated hardware devices (such as Cisco or Juniper routers) or they can be made from a standard PC with multiple network cards and appropriate software.

Routers sit at the **edge** of two or more networks. By definition, they have one connection to each network, and as border machines they may take on other responsibilities as well as routing. Many routers have **firewall** capabilities that provide a mechanism to filter or redirect packets that do not fit security or access policy requirements. They may also provide Network Address Translation (NAT) services.

Routers vary widely in cost and capabilities. The lowest cost and least flexible are simple, dedicated hardware devices, often with NAT functionality, used to share an Internet connection between a few computers. The next step up is a software router, which consists of an operating system running on a standard PC with multiple network interfaces. Standard operating systems such as Microsoft Windows, Linux, and BSD are all capable of routing, and are much more flexible than the low-cost hardware devices. However, they suffer from the same problems as conventional PCs, with high power consumption, a large number of complex and potentially unreliable parts, and more involved configuration.

The most expensive devices are high-end dedicated hardware routers, made by companies like Cisco and Juniper. They tend to have much better performance, more features, and higher reliability than software routers on PCs. It is also possible to purchase technical support and maintenance contracts for them.

Most modern routers offer mechanisms to monitor and record performance remotely, usually via the Simple Network Management Protocol (SNMP), although the least expensive devices often omit this feature.

Other equipment

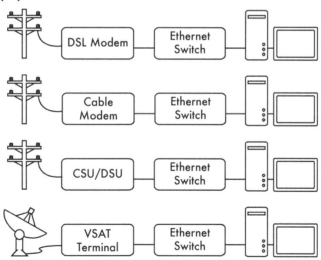

Figure 3.12: Many DSL modems, cable modems, CSU/DSUs, wireless access points, and VSAT terminals terminate at an Ethernet jack.

Each physical network has an associated piece of terminal equipment. For example, VSAT connections consist of a satellite dish connected to a terminal that either plugs into a card inside a PC, or ends at a standard Ethernet connection. DSL lines use a **DSL modem** that bridges the telephone line to a local device, either an Ethernet network or a single computer via USB. **Cable modems** bridge the television cable to Ethernet, or to an internal PC card bus. Some kinds of telecom circuit (such as a T1 or T3) use a CSU/DSU to bridge the circuit to a serial port or Ethernet. Standard dialup lines use modems to connect a computer to the telephone, usually via a plug-in card or serial port. And there are many different kinds of wireless networking equipment that connect to a variety of radios and antennas, but nearly always end at an Ethernet jack.

The functionality of these devices can vary significantly between manufacturers. Some provide mechanisms for monitoring performance, while others may not. Since your Internet connection ultimately comes from your ISP, you should follow their recommendations when choosing equipment that bridges their network to your Ethernet network.

Putting it all together

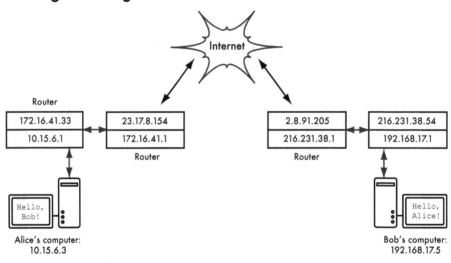

Figure 3.13: Internet networking. Each network segment has a router with two IP addresses, making it "link local" to two different networks. Packets are forwarded between routers until they reach their ultimate destination.

Once all network nodes have an IP address, they can send data packets to the IP address of any other node. Through the use of routing and forwarding, these packets can reach nodes on networks that are not physically connected to the originating node. This process describes much of what "happens" on the Internet.

In this example, you can see the path that the packets take as Alice chats with Bob using an instant messaging service. Each dotted line represents an

Ethernet cable, a wireless link, or any other kind of physical network. The cloud symbol is commonly used to stand in for "The Internet", and represents any number of intervening IP networks. Neither Alice nor Bob need to be concerned with how those networks operate, as long as the routers forward IP traffic towards the ultimate destination. If it weren't for Internet protocols and the cooperation of everyone on the net, this kind of communication would be impossible.

Designing the physical network

It may seem odd to talk about the "physical" network when building wireless networks. After all, where is the physical part of the network? In wireless networks, the physical medium we use for communication is obviously electromagnetic energy. But in the context of this chapter, the physical network refers to the mundane topic of where to put things. How do you arrange the equipment so that you can reach your wireless clients? Whether they fill an office building or stretch across many miles, wireless networks are naturally arranged in these three logical configurations: ***point-to-point links***, ***point-to-multipoint links***, and ***multipoint-to-multipoint clouds***. While different parts of your network can take advantage of all three of these configurations, any individual link will fall into one of these topologies.

Point-to-point

Point-to-point links typically provide an Internet connection where such access isn't otherwise available. One side of a point-to-point link will have an Internet connection, while the other uses the link to reach the Internet. For example, a university may have a fast frame relay or VSAT connection in the middle of campus, but cannot afford such a connection for an important building just off campus. If the main building has an unobstructed view of the remote site, a point-to-point connection can be used to link the two together. This can augment or even replace existing dial-up links. With proper antennas and clear line of sight, reliable point-to-point links in excess of thirty kilometers are possible.

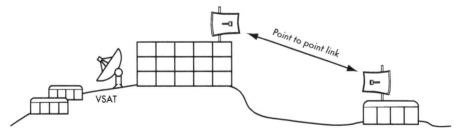

Figure 3.14: A point-to-point link allows a remote site to share a central Internet connection.

Of course, once a single point-to-point connection has been made, more can be used to extend the network even further. If the remote building in our example is at the top of a tall hill, it may be able to see other important locations that can't be seen directly from the central campus. By installing another point-to-point link at the remote site, another node can join the network and make use of the central Internet connection.

Point-to-point links don't necessarily have to involve Internet access. Suppose you have to physically drive to a remote weather monitoring station, high in the hills, in order to collect the data which it records over time. You could connect the site with a point-to-point link, allowing data collection and monitoring to happen in realtime, without the need to actually travel to the site. Wireless networks can provide enough bandwidth to carry large amounts of data (including audio and video) between any two points that have a connection to each other, even if there is no direct connection to the Internet.

Point-to-multipoint

The next most commonly encountered network layout is **point-to-multipoint**. Whenever several nodes[2] are talking to a central point of access, this is a point-to-multipoint application. The typical example of a point-to-multipoint layout is the use of a wireless **access point** that provides a connection to several laptops. The laptops do not communicate with each other directly, but must be in range of the access point in order to use the network.

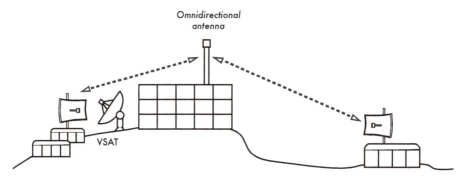

Figure 3.15: The central VSAT is now shared by multiple remote sites. All three sites can also communicate directly at speeds much faster than VSAT.

Point-to-multipoint networking can also apply to our earlier example at the university. Suppose the remote building on top of the hill is connected to the central campus with a point-to-point link. Rather than setting up several point-to-point links to distribute the Internet connection, a single antenna could be used that is visible from several remote buildings. This is a classic

---

2. A **node** is any device capable of sending and receiving data on a network. Access points, routers, computers, and laptops are all examples of nodes.

example of a wide area *point* (remote site on the hill) *to multipoint* (many buildings in the valley below) connection.

Note that there are a number of performance issues with using point-to-multipoint over very long distance, which will be addressed later in this chapter. Such links are possible and useful in many circumstances, but don't make the classic mistake of installing a single high powered radio tower in the middle of town and expecting to be able to serve thousands of clients, as you would with an FM radio station. As we will see, two-way data networks behave very differently than broadcast radio.

Multipoint-to-multipoint

The third type of network layout is *multipoint-to-multipoint*, which is also referred to as an *ad-hoc* or *mesh* network. In a multipoint-to-multipoint network, there is no central authority. Every node on the network carries the traffic of every other as needed, and all nodes communicate with each other directly.

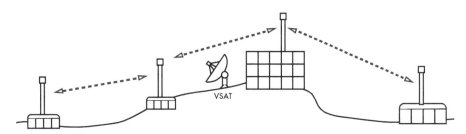

Figure 3.16: A multipoint-to-multipoint mesh. Every point can reach each other at very high speed, or use the central VSAT connection to reach the Internet.

The benefit of this network layout is that even if none of the nodes are in range of a central access point, they can still communicate with each other. Good mesh network implementations are self-healing, which means that they automatically detect routing problems and fix them as needed. Extending a mesh network is as simple as adding more nodes. If one of the nodes in the "cloud" happens to be an Internet gateway, then that connection can be shared among all of the clients.

Two big disadvantages to this topology are increased complexity and lower performance. Security in such a network is also a concern, since every participant potentially carries the traffic of every other. Multipoint-to-multipoint networks tend to be difficult to troubleshoot, due to the large number of changing variables as nodes join and leave the network. Multipoint-to-multipoint clouds typically have reduce capacity compared to point-to-point or point-to-multipoint networks, due to the additional overhead of managing the network routing and increased contention in the radio spectrum.

Nevertheless, mesh networks are useful in many circumstances. We will see an example of how to build a multipoint-to-multipoint mesh network using a routing protocol called OLSR later in this chapter.

Use the technology that fits

All of these network designs can be used to complement each other in a large network, and can obviously make use of traditional wired networking techniques whenever possible. It is a common practice, for example, to use a long distance wireless link to provide Internet access to a remote location, and then set up an access point on the remote side to provide local wireless access. One of the clients of this access point may also act as a mesh node, allowing the network to spread organically between laptop users who all ultimately use the original point-to-point link to access the Internet.

Now that we have a clear idea of how wireless networks are typically arranged, we can begin to understand how communication is possible over such networks.

802.11 wireless networks

Before packets can be forwarded and routed to the Internet, layers one (the physical) and two (the data link) need to be connected. Without link local connectivity, network nodes cannot talk to each other and route packets.

To provide physical connectivity, wireless network devices must operate in the same part of the radio spectrum. As we saw in **Chapter 2**, this means that 802.11a radios will talk to 802.11a radios at around 5 GHz, and 802.11b/g radios will talk to other 802.11b/g radios at around 2.4 GHz. But an 802.11a device cannot interoperate with an 802.11b/g device, since they use completely different parts of the electromagnetic spectrum.

More specifically, wireless cards must agree on a common channel. If one 802.11b radio card is set to channel 2 while another is set to channel 11, then the radios cannot communicate with each other.

When two wireless cards are configured to use the same protocol on the same radio channel, then they are ready to negotiate data link layer connectivity. Each 802.11a/b/g device can operate in one of four possible modes:

1. **Master mode** (also called **AP** or **infrastructure mode**) is used to create a service that looks like a traditional access point. The wireless card creates a network with a specified name (called the **SSID**) and channel, and offers network services on it. While in master mode, wireless cards manage all communications related to the network (authenticating wire-

less clients, handling channel contention, repeating packets, etc.) Wireless cards in master mode can only communicate with cards that are associated with it in managed mode.

2. ***Managed mode*** is sometimes also referred to as ***client*** mode. Wireless cards in managed mode will join a network created by a master, and will automatically change their channel to match it. They then present any necessary credentials to the master, and if those credentials are accepted, they are said to be ***associated*** with the master. Managed mode cards do not communicate with each other directly, and will only communicate with an associated master.

3. ***Ad-hoc mode*** creates a multipoint-to-multipoint network where there is no single master node or AP. In ad-hoc mode, each wireless card communicates directly with its neighbors. Nodes must be in range of each other to communicate, and must agree on a network name and channel.

4. ***Monitor mode*** is used by some tools (such as **Kismet**, see **Chapter 6**) to passively listen to all radio traffic on a given channel. When in monitor mode, wireless cards transmit no data. This is useful for analyzing problems on a wireless link or observing spectrum usage in the local area. Monitor mode is not used for normal communications.

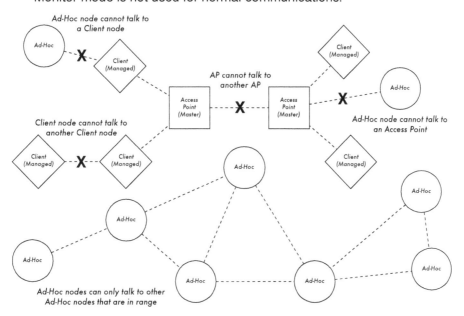

Figure 3.17: APs, Clients, and Ad-Hoc nodes.

When implementing a point-to-point or point-to-multipoint link, one radio will typically operate in master mode, while the other(s) operate in managed mode. In a multipoint-to-multipoint mesh, the radios all operate in ad-hoc mode so that they can communicate with each other directly.

It is important to keep these modes in mind when designing your network layout. Remember that managed mode clients cannot communicate with each other directly, so it is likely that you will want to run a high repeater site in master or ad-hoc mode. As we will see later in this chapter, ad-hoc is more flexible but has a number of performance issues as compared to using the master / managed modes.

Mesh networking with OLSR

Most WiFi networks operate in infrastructure mode - they consist of an access point somewhere (with a radio operating in master mode), attached to a DSL line or other large scale wired network. In such a **hotspot** the access point usually acts as a master station that is distributing Internet access to its clients, which operate in managed mode. This topology is similar to a mobile phone (GSM) service. Mobile phones connect to a base station - without the presence of such a base station mobiles can't communicate with each other. If you make a joke call to a friend that is sitting on the other side of the table, your phone sends data to the base station of your provider that may be a mile away - the base station then sends data back to the phone of your friend.

WiFi cards in managed mode can't communicate directly, either. Clients - for example, two laptops on the same table - have to use the access point as a relay. Any traffic between clients connected to an access point has to be sent twice. If client A and C communicate, client A sends data to the access point B, and then the access point will retransmit the data to client C. A single transmission may have a speed of 600 kByte/sec (thats about the maximum speed you could achieve with 802.11b) in our example - thus, because the data has to be repeated by the access point before it reaches its target, the effective speed between both clients will be only 300 kByte/sec.

In ad-hoc mode there is no hierarchical master-client relationship. Nodes can communicate directly as long as they are within the range of their wireless interfaces. Thus, in our example both computers could achieve full speed when operating ad-hoc, under ideal circumstances.

The disadvantage to ad-hoc mode is that clients do not repeat traffic destined for other clients. In the access point example, if two clients A and C can't directly "see" each other with their wireless interfaces, they still can communicate as long as the AP is in the wireless range of both clients.

Ad-hoc nodes do not repeat by default, but they can effectively do the same if **routing** is applied. Mesh networks are based on the strategy that every mesh-enabled node acts as a relay to extend coverage of the wireless network. The more nodes, the better the radio coverage and range of the mesh cloud.

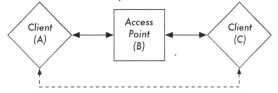

Clients A and C are in range of Access Point B but not each other.
Access Point B will relay traffic between the two nodes.

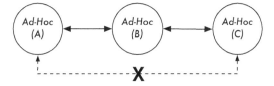

In the same setting, Ad-Hoc nodes A and C can communicate
with node B, but not with each other.

Figure 3.18: Access point B will relay traffic between clients A and C. In Ad-Hoc mode, node B will not relay traffic between A and C by default.

There is one big tradeoff that must be mentioned at this point. If the device only uses one radio interface, the available bandwidth is significantly reduced every time traffic is repeated by intermediate nodes on the way from A to B. Also, there will be interference in transmission due to nodes sharing the same channel. Thus, cheap ad-hoc mesh networks can provide good radio coverage on the last mile(s) of a community wireless network at the cost of speed-- especially if the density of nodes and transmit power is high.

If an ad-hoc network consists of only a few nodes that are up and running at all time, don't move and always have stable radio links - a long list of ifs - it is possible to write individual routing tables for all nodes by hand.

Unfortunately, those conditions are rarely met in the real world. Nodes can fail, WiFi enabled devices roam around, and interference can make radio links unusable at any time. And no one wants to update several routing tables by hand if one node is added to the network. By using routing protocols that automatically maintain individual routing tables in all nodes involved, we can avoid these issues. Popular routing protocols from the wired world (such as OSPF) do not work well in such an environment because they are not designed to deal with lossy links or rapidly changing topology.

Mesh routing with olsrd

The Optimized Link State Routing Daemon - olsrd - from *olsr.org* is a routing application developed for routing in wireless networks. We will concentrate on this routing software for several reasons. It is a open-source project that supports Mac OS X, Windows 98, 2000, XP, Linux, FreeBSD, OpenBSD and

NetBSD. Olsrd is available for access points that run Linux like the Linksys WRT54G, Asus Wl500g, AccessCube or Pocket PCs running Familiar Linux, and ships standard on Metrix kits running Pyramid. Olsrd can handle multiple interfaces and is extensible with plug-ins. It supports IPv6 and it is actively developed and used by community networks all over the world.

Note that there are several implementations of Optimized Link State Routing, which began as an IETF-draft written at INRIA France. The implementation from *olsr.org* started as a master thesis of Andreas Toennesen at UniK University. Based on practical experience of the free networking community, the routing daemon was modified. Olsrd now differs significantly from the original draft because it includes a mechanism called Link Quality Extension that measures the packet loss between nodes and calculates routes according to this information. This extension breaks compatibility to routing daemons that follow the INRIA draft. The olsrd available from *olsr.org* can be configured to behave according to the IETF draft that lacks this feature - but there is no reason to disable Link Quality Extension unless compliance with other implementations is required.

Theory

After olsrd is running for a while, a node knows about the existence of every other node in the mesh cloud and which nodes may be used to route traffic to them. Each node maintains a routing table covering the whole mesh cloud. This approach to mesh routing is called ***proactive routing***. In contrast, ***reactive routing*** algorithms seek routes only when it is necessary to send data to a specific node.

There are pros and cons to proactive routing, and there are many other ideas about how to do mesh routing that may be worth mentioning. The biggest advantage of proactive routing is that you know who is out there and you don't have to wait until a route is found. Higher protocol traffic overhead and more CPU load are among the disadvantages. In Berlin, the Freifunk community is operating a mesh cloud where olsrd has to manage more than 100 interfaces. The average CPU load caused by olsrd on a Linksys WRT54G running at 200 MHz is about 30% in the Berlin mesh. There is clearly a limit to what extent a proactive protocol can scale - depending on how many interfaces are involved and how often the routing tables are updated. Maintaining routes in a mesh cloud with static nodes takes less effort than a mesh with nodes that are constantly in motion, since the routing table has to be updated less often.

Mechanism

A node running olsrd is constantly broadcasting 'Hello' messages at a given interval so neighbors can detect it's presence. Every node computes a statistic how many 'Hellos' have been lost or received from each neighbor -

thereby gaining information about the topology and link quality of nodes in the neighborhood. The gained topology information is broadcasted as topology control messages (TC messages) and forwarded by neighbors that olsrd has chosen to be multipoint relays.

The concept of multipoint relays is a new idea in proactive routing that came up with the OLSR draft. If every node rebroadcasts topology information that it has received, unnecessary overhead can be generated. Such transmissions are redundant if a node has many neighbors. Thus, an olsrd node decides which neighbors are favorable multipoint relays that should forward its topology control messages. Note that multipoint relays are only chosen for the purpose of forwarding TC messages. Payload is routed considering all available nodes.

Two other message types exist in OLSR that announce information: whether a node offers a gateway to other networks (HNA messages) or has multiple interfaces (MID messages). There is not much to say about what this messages do apart from the fact that they exist. HNA messages make olsrd very convenient when connecting to the Internet with a mobile device. When a mesh node roams around it will detect gateways into other networks and always choose the gateway that it has the best route to. However, olsrd is by no means bullet proof. If a node announces that it is an Internet gateway - which it isn't because it never was or it is just offline at the moment - the other nodes will nevertheless trust this information. The pseudo-gateway is a black hole. To overcome this problem, a dynamic gateway plugin was written. The plugin will automatically detect at the gateway if it is actually connected and whether the link is still up. If not, olsrd ceases to send false HNA messages. It is highly recommended to build and use this plugin instead of statically enabling HNA messages.

Practice

Olsrd implements IP-based routing in a userland application - installation is pretty easy. Installation packages are available for OpenWRT, AccessCube, Mac OS X, Debian GNU/Linux and Windows. OLSR is a standard part of Metrix Pyramid. If you have to compile from source, please read the documentation that is shipped with the source package. If everything is configured properly all you have to do is start the olsr program.

First of all, it must be ensured that every node has a unique statically assigned IP-Address for each interface used for the mesh. It is not recommended (nor practicable) to use DHCP in an IP-based mesh network. A DHCP request will not be answered by a DHCP server if the node requesting DHCP needs a multihop link to connect to it, and applying dhcp relay throughout a mesh is likely impractical. This problem could be solved by using IPv6, since there is plenty of space available to generate a unique IP from the MAC address of each card involved (as suggested in "IPv6 Stateless Address Autoconfiguration in large mobile ad hoc networks" by K. Weniger and M. Zitterbart, 2002).

A wiki-page where every interested person can choose an individual IPv4 address for each interface the olsr daemon is running on may serve the purpose quite well. There is just not an easy way to automate the process if IPv4 is used.

The broadcast address should be 255.255.255.255 on mesh interfaces in general as a convention. There is no reason to enter the broadcast address explicitly, since olsrd can be configured to override the broadcast addresses with this default. It just has to be ensured that settings are the same everywhere. Olsrd can do this on its own. When a default olsrd configuration file is issued, this feature should be enabled to avoid confusion of the kind "why can't the other nodes see my machine?!?"

Now configure the wireless interface. Here is an example command how to configure a WiFi card with the name wlan0 using Linux:

```
iwconfig wlan0 essid olsr.org mode ad-hoc channel 10 rts 250 frag 256
```

Verify that the wireless part of the WiFi card has been configured so it has an ad-hoc connection to other mesh nodes within direct (single hop) range. Make sure the interface joins the same wireless channel, uses the same wireless network name ESSID (Extended Service Set IDentifier) and has the same Cell-ID as all other WiFi-Cards that build the mesh. Many WiFi cards or their respective drivers do not comply with the 802.11 standard for ad-hoc networking and may fail miserably to connect to a cell. They may be unable to connect to other devices on the same table, even if they are set up with the correct channel and wireless network name. They may even confuse other cards that behave according to the standard by creating their own Cell-ID on the same channel with the same wireless network name. WiFi cards made by Intel that are shipped with Centrino Notebooks are notorious for doing this.

You can check this out with the command **iwconfig** when using GNU-Linux. Here is the output on my machine:

```
wlan0 IEEE 802.11b  ESSID:"olsr.org"
 Mode:Ad-Hoc  Frequency:2.457 GHz  Cell: 02:00:81:1E:48:10
 Bit Rate:2 Mb/s    Sensitivity=1/3
 Retry min limit:8   RTS thr=250 B    Fragment thr=256 B
 Encryption key:off
 Power Management:off
 Link Quality=1/70  Signal level=-92 dBm  Noise level=-100 dBm
 Rx invalid nwid:0  Rx invalid crypt:28  Rx invalid frag:0
 Tx excessive retries:98024 Invalid misc:117503 Missed beacon:0
```

It is important to set the 'Request To Send' threshold value RTS for a mesh. There will be collisions on the radio channel between the transmissions of nodes on the same wireless channel, and RTS will mitigate this. RTS/CTS adds a handshake before each packet transmission to make sure that the channel is clear. This adds overhead, but increases performance in case of hidden nodes - and hidden nodes are the default in a mesh! This parameter sets the size of the smallest packet (in bytes) for which the node sends RTS. The RTS threshold value must be smaller than the IP-Packet size and the 'Fragmentation threshold' value - here set to 256 - otherwise it will be disabled. TCP is very sensitive to collisions, so it is important to switch RTS on.

Fragmentation allows to split an IP packet in a burst of smaller fragments transmitted on the medium. This adds overhead, but in a noisy environment this reduces the error penalty and allows packets to get through interference bursts. Mesh networks are very noisy because nodes use the same channel and therefore transmissions are likely to interfere with each other. This parameter sets the maximum size before a data packet is split and sent in a burst - a value equal to the maximum IP packet size disables the mechanism, so it must be smaller than the IP packet size. Setting fragmentation threshold is recommended.

Once a valid IP-address and netmask is assigned and the wireless interface is up, the configuration file of olsrd must be altered in order that olsrd finds and uses the interfaces it is meant to work on.

For Mac OS-X and Windows there are nice GUI's for configuration and monitoring of the daemon available. Unfortunately this tempts users that lack background knowledge to do stupid things - like announcing black holes. On BSD and Linux the configuration file **/etc/olsrd.conf** has to be edited with a text editor.

A simple olsrd.conf

It is not practical to provide a complete configuration file here. These are some essential settings that should be checked.

```
UseHysteresis          no
TcRedundancy           2
MprCoverage            3
LinkQualityLevel       2
LinkQualityWinSize     20

LoadPlugin "olsrd_dyn_gw.so.0.3"
{
    PlParam    "Interval"   "60"
    PlParam    "Ping"       "151.1.1.1"
    PlParam    "Ping"       "194.25.2.129"
}

Interface "ath0" "wlan0" {
 Ip4Broadcast 255.255.255.255
}
```

There are many more options available in the **olsrd.conf**, but these basic options should get you started. After these steps have been done, olsrd can be started with a simple command in a terminal:

```
olsrd -d 2
```

I recommend to run it with the debugging option -d 2 when used on a work-station, especially for the first time. You can see what olsrd does and monitor how well the links to your neighbors are. On embedded devices the debug level should be 0 (off), because debugging creates a lot of CPU load.

The output should look something like this:

```
--- 19:27:45.51 ---------------------------------------------- DIJKSTRA

192.168.120.1:1.00 (one-hop)
192.168.120.3:1.00 (one-hop)

--- 19:27:45.51 ---------------------------------------------- LINKS

IP address      hyst   LQ     lost   total  NLQ    ETX
192.168.120.1   0.000  1.000  0      20     1.000  1.00
192.168.120.3   0.000  1.000  0      20     1.000  1.00

--- 19:27:45.51 ---------------------------------------------- NEIGHBORS

IP address      LQ     NLQ    SYM   MPR   MPRS  will
192.168.120.1   1.000  1.000  YES   NO    YES   3
192.168.120.3   1.000  1.000  YES   NO    YES   6

--- 19:27:45.51 ---------------------------------------------- TOPOLOGY

Source IP addr   Dest IP addr    LQ     ILQ    ETX
192.168.120.1    192.168.120.17  1.000  1.000  1.00
192.168.120.3    192.168.120.17  1.000  1.000  1.00
```

Using OLSR on Ethernet and multiple interfaces

It is not necessary to have a wireless interface to test or use olsrd - although that is what olsrd is designed for. It may as well be used on any NIC. WiFi-interfaces don't have to operate always in ad-hoc mode to form a mesh when mesh nodes have more than one interface. For dedicated links it may be a very good option to have them running in infrastructure mode. Many WiFi cards and drivers are buggy in ad-hoc mode, but infrastructure mode works fine - because everybody expects at least this feature to work. Ad-hoc mode has not had many users so far, so the implementation of the ad-hoc mode was done sloppily by many manufacturers. With the rising popularity of mesh networks, the driver situation is improving now.

Many people use olsrd on wired and wireless interfaces - they don't think about network architecture. They just connect antennas to their WiFi cards, connect cables to their Ethernet cards, enable olsrd to run on all computers and all interfaces and fire it up. That is quite an abuse of a protocol that was designed to do wireless networking on lossy links - but - why not?

They expect olsrd to solve every networking problem. Clearly it is not necessary to send 'Hello' messages on a wired interface every two seconds - but it works. This should not be taken as a recommendation - it is just amazing what people do with such a protocol and that they have such success with it. In fact the idea of having a protocol that does everything for newbies that want to have a small to medium sized routed LAN is very appealing.

Plugins

A number of plugins are available for olsrd. Check out the *olsr.org* website for a complete list. Here a little HOWTO for the network topology visualization plugin **olsrd_dot_draw**.

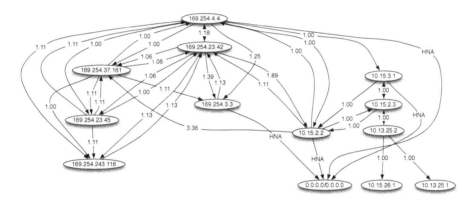

Figure 3.19: An automatically generated OLSR network topology.

Often it is very good for the understanding of a mesh network to have the ability to show the network topology graphically. **olsrd_dot_draw** outputs the topology in the dot file format on TCP port 2004. The graphviz tools can then be used to draw the graphs.

Installing the dot_draw Plugin

Compile the olsr plugins separately and install them. To load the plugin add the following lines to **/etc/olsrd.conf**. The parameter "accept" specifies which host is accepted to view the Topology Information (currently only one) and is "localhost" by default. The parameter "port" specifies the TCP port.

```
LoadPlugin "olsrd_dot_draw.so.0.3"
{
      PlParam "accept" "192.168.0.5"
      PlParam "port" "2004"
}
```

Then restart olsr and check if you get output on TCP Port 2004

```
telnet localhost 2004
```

After a while you should get some text output.

Now you can save the output graph descriptions and run the tools **dot** or **neato** form the graphviz package to get images.

Bruno Randolf has written a small perl script which continuously gets the topology information from olsrd and displays it using the graphviz and Image-Magick tools.

First install the following packages on your workstation:

- graphviz, *http://www.graphviz.org/*

- ImageMagick, *http://www.imagemagick.org/*

Download the script at: *http://meshcube.org/nylon/utils/olsr-topology-view.pl*

Now you can start the script with **./olsr-topology-view.pl** and view the topology updates in near-realtime.

Troubleshooting

As long as the WiFi-cards can 'see' each other directly with their radios, doing a ping will work whether olsrd is running or not. This works because the large netmasks effectively make every node link-local, so routing issues are side-stepped at the first hop. This should be checked first if things do not seem to work as expected. Most headaches people face with WiFi in Ad-Hoc mode are caused by the fact that the ad-hoc mode in drivers and cards are implemented sloppily. If it is not possible to ping nodes directly when they are in range it is most likely a card/driver issue, or your network settings are wrong.

If the machines can ping each other, but olsrd doesn't find routes, then the IP-addresses, netmask and broadcast address should be checked.

Finally, are you running a firewall? Make sure it doesn't block UDP port 698.

Estimating capacity

Wireless links can provide significantly greater *throughput* to users than traditional Internet connections, such as VSAT, dialup, or DSL. Throughput is also referred to as *channel capacity*, or simply *bandwidth* (although this term is unrelated to radio bandwidth). It is important to understand that a wireless device's listed speed (the *data rate*) refers to the rate at which the radios can exchange symbols, not the usable throughput you will observe. As mentioned earlier, a single 802.11g link may use 54 Mbps radios, but it will only provide up to 22 Mbps of actual throughput. The rest is overhead that the radios need in order to coordinate their signals using the 802.11g protocol.

Note that throughput is a measurement of bits over time. 22 Mbps means that in any given second, up to 22 megabits can be sent from one end of the link to the other. If users attempt to push more than 22 megabits through the link, it will take longer than one second. Since the data can't be sent immediately, it is put in a *queue*, and transmitted as quickly as possible. This backlog of data increases the time needed for the most recently queued bits to the traverse the link. The time that it takes for data to traverse a link is called *latency*, and high latency is commonly referred to as *lag*. Your link will eventually send all of the queued traffic, but your users will likely complain as the lag increases.

How much throughput will your users really need? It depends on how many users you have, and how they use the wireless link. Various Internet applications require different amounts of throughput.

Application	BW / User	Notes
Text messaging / IM	< 1 kbps	As traffic is infrequent and asynchronous, IM will tolerate high latency.
Email	1 to 100 kbps	As with IM, email is asynchronous and intermittent, so it will tolerate latency. Large attachments, viruses, and spam significantly add to bandwidth usage. Note that web email services (such as Yahoo or Hotmail) should be considered as web browsing, not as email.
Web browsing	50 - 100+ kbps	Web browsers only use the network when data is requested. Communication is asynchronous, so a fair amount of lag can be tolerated. As web browsers request more data (large images, long downloads, etc.) bandwidth usage will go up significantly.

Application	BW / User	Notes
Streaming audio	96 - 160 kbps	Each user of a streaming audio service will use a constant amount of relatively large bandwidth for as long as it plays. It can tolerate some transient latency by using large buffers on the client. But extended periods of lag will cause audio "skips" or outright session failures.
Voice over IP (VoIP)	24 - 100+ kbps	As with streaming audio, VoIP commits a constant amount of bandwidth to each user for the duration of the call. But with VoIP, the bandwidth is used roughly equally in both directions. Latency on a VoIP connection is immediate and annoying to users. Lag greater than a few milliseconds is unacceptable for VoIP.
Streaming video	64 - 200+ kbps	As with streaming audio, some intermittent latency is avoided by using buffers on the client. Streaming video requires high throughput and low latency to work properly.
Peer-to-peer file-sharing applications (BitTorrent, KaZaA, Gnutella, eDonkey, etc.)	0 - infinite Mbps	While peer to peer applications will tolerate any amount of latency, they tend to use up all available throughput by transmitting data to as many clients as possible, as quickly as possible. Use of these applications will cause latency and throughput problems for all other network users unless you use careful bandwidth shaping.

To estimate the necessary throughput you will need for your network, multiply the expected number of users by the sort of application they will probably use. For example, 50 users who are chiefly browsing the web will likely consume 2.5 to 5 Mbps or more of throughput at peak times, and will tolerate some latency. On the other hand, 50 simultaneous VoIP users would require 5 Mbps or more of throughput **in both directions** with absolutely no latency. Since 802.11g wireless equipment is *half duplex* (that is, it only transmits or receives, never both at once) you should accordingly double the required throughput, for a total of **10 Mbps**. Your wireless links must provide that capacity every second, or conversations will lag.

Since all of your users are unlikely to use the connection at precisely the same moment, it is common practice to *oversubscribe* available throughput by some factor (that is, allow more users than the maximum available bandwidth can support). Oversubscribing by a factor of 2 to 5 is quite common. In all likelihood, you will oversubscribe by some amount when building your network infrastructure. By carefully monitoring throughput throughout your network, you will be able to plan when to upgrade various parts of the network, and how much additional resources will be needed.

Expect that no matter how much capacity you supply, your users will eventually find applications that will use it all. As we'll see at the end of this chapter, using bandwidth shaping techniques can help mitigate some latency problems. By using bandwidth shaping, web caching, and other techniques, you can significantly reduce latency and increase overall network throughput.

To get a feeling for the lag felt on very slow connections, the ICTP has put together a bandwidth simulator. It will simultaneously download a web page at full speed and at a reduced rate that you choose. This demonstration gives you an immediate understanding of how low throughput and high latency reduce the usefulness of the Internet as a communications tool. It is available at *http://wireless.ictp.trieste.it/simulator/*

Link planning

A basic communication system consists of two radios, each with its associated antenna, the two being separated by the path to be covered. In order to have a communication between the two, the radios require a certain minimum signal to be collected by the antennas and presented to their input socket. Determining if the link is feasible is a process called *link budget* calculation. Whether or not signals can be passed between the radios depends on the quality of the equipment being used and on the diminishment of the signal due to distance, called *path loss*.

Calculating the link budget

The power available in an 802.11 system can be characterized by the following factors:

- **Transmit Power**. It is expressed in milliwatts or in dBm. Transmit Power ranges from 30mW to 200mW or more. TX power is often dependent on the transmission rate. The TX power of a given device should be specified in the literature provided by the manufacturer, but can sometimes be difficult to find. Online databases such as the one provided by SeattleWireless (*http://www.seattlewireless.net/HardwareComparison*) may help.

- **Antenna Gain**. Antennas are passive devices that create the effect of amplification by virtue of their physical shape. Antennas have the same characteristics when receiving and transmitting. So a 12 dBi antenna is simply a 12 dBi antenna, without specifying if it is in transmission or reception mode. Parabolic antennas have a gain of 19-24 dBi, omnidirectional antennas have 5-12 dBi, sectorial antennas have roughly a 12-15 dBi gain.

- **Minimum Received Signal Level,** or simply, the sensitivity of the receiver. The minimum RSL is always expressed as a negative dBm (- dBm) and is the lowest power of signal the radio can distinguish. The minimum RSL is dependent upon rate, and as a general rule the lowest rate (1 Mbps) has the greatest sensitivity. The minimum will be typically in the range of -75 to -95 dBm. Like TX power, the RSL specifications should be provided by the manufacturer of the equipment.

- **Cable Losses**. Some of the signal's energy is lost in the cables, the connectors and other devices, going from the radios to the antennas. The loss depends on the type of cable used and on its length. Signal loss for short coaxial cables including connectors is quite low, in the range of 2-3 dB. It is better to have cables as short as possible.

When calculating the path loss, several effects must be considered. One has to take into account the *free space loss*, *attenuation* and *scattering*. Signal power is diminished by geometric spreading of the wavefront, commonly known as free space loss. Ignoring everything else, the further away the two radios, the smaller the received signal is due to free space loss. This is independent from the environment, depending only on the distance. This loss happens because the radiated signal energy expands as a function of the distance from the transmitter.

Using decibels to express the loss and using 2.45 GHz as the signal frequency, the equation for the free space loss is

$$L_{fsl} = 40 + 20*\log(r)$$

where L_{fsl} is expressed in dB and r is the distance between the transmitter and receiver, in meters.

The second contribution to the path loss is given by attenuation. This takes place as some of the signal power is absorbed when the wave passes through solid objects such as trees, walls, windows and floors of buildings. Attenuation can vary greatly depending upon the structure of the object the signal is passing through, and it is very difficult to quantify. The most convenient way to express its contribution to the total loss is by adding an "allowed loss" to the free space. For example, experience shows that trees add 10 to 20 dB of loss per tree in the direct path, while walls contribute 10 to 15 dB depending upon the construction.

Along the link path, the RF energy leaves the transmitting antenna and energy spreads out. Some of the RF energy reaches the receiving antenna directly, while some bounces off the ground. Part of the RF energy which bounces off the ground reaches the receiving antenna. Since the reflected signal has a longer way to travel, it arrives at the receiving antenna later than the direct signal. This effect is called **multipath**, or signal dispersion. In some cases reflected signals add together and cause no problem. When they add together out of phase, the received signal is almost worthless. In some cases, the signal at the receiving antenna can be zeroed by the reflected signals. This is known as extreme fading, or **nulling**. There is a simple technique that is used to deal with multipath, called **antenna diversity**. It consists of adding a second antenna to the radio. Multipath is in fact a very location-specific phenomenon. If two signals add out of phase at one location, they will not add destructively at a second, nearby location. If there are two antennas, at least one of them should be able to receive a usable signal, even if the other is receiving a distorted one. In commercial devices, antenna switching diversity is used: there are multiple antennas on multiple inputs, with a single receiver. The signal is thus received through only one antenna at a time. When transmitting, the radio uses the antenna last used for reception. The distortion given by multipath degrades the ability of the receiver to recover the signal in a manner much like signal loss. A simple way of applying the effects of scattering in the calculation of the path loss is to change the exponent of the distance factor of the free space loss formula. The exponent tends to increase with the range in an environment with a lot of scattering. An exponent of 3 can be used in an outdoor environment with trees, while one of 4 can be used for an indoor environment.

When free space loss, attenuation, and scattering are combined, the path loss is:

```
L(dB) = 40 + 10*n*log(r) + L(allowed)
```

For a rough estimate of the link feasibility, one can evaluate just the free space loss. The environment can bring further signal loss, and should be considered for an exact evaluation of the link. The environment is in fact a very important factor, and should never be neglected.

To evaluate if a link is feasible, one must know the characteristics of the equipment being used and evaluate the path loss. Note that when performing this calculation, you should only add the TX power of one side of the link. If you are using different radios on either side of the link, you should calculate the path loss twice, once for each direction (using the appropriate TX power for each calculation). Adding up all the gains and subtracting all the losses gives

```
  TX Power Radio 1
+ Antenna Gain Radio 1
- Cable Losses Radio 1
+ Antenna Gain Radio 2
- Cable Losses Radio 2
_____

  = Total Gain
```

Subtracting the Path Loss from the Total Gain:

```
        Total Gain
      - Path Loss
      ─────────────
= Signal Level at one side of the link
```

If the resulting signal level is greater than the minimum received signal level, then the link is feasible! The received signal is powerful enough for the radios to use it. Remember that the minimum RSL is always expressed as a negative dBm, so -56 dBm is greater than -70 dBm. On a given path, the variation in path loss over a period of time can be large, so a certain margin (difference between the signal level and the minimum received signal level) should be considered. This margin is the amount of signal above the sensitivity of radio that should be received in order to ensure a stable, high quality radio link during bad weather and other atmospheric disturbances. A margin of 10 to 15 dB is fine. To give some space for attenuation and multipath in the received radio signal, a margin of 20dB should be safe enough.

Once you have calculated the link budget in one direction, repeat the calculation for the other direction. Substitute the transmit power for that of the second radio, and compare the result against the minimum received signal level of the first radio.

Example link budget calculation

As an example, we want to estimate the feasibility of a 5 km link, with one access point and one client radio. The access point is connected to an omni-directional antenna with 10 dBi gain, while the client is connected to a sectorial antenna with 14 dBi gain. The transmitting power of the AP is 100mW (or 20 dBm) and its sensitivity is -89 dBm. The transmitting power of the client is 30mW (or 15 dBm) and its sensitivity is -82 dBm. The cables are short, with a loss of 2dB at each side.

Adding up all the gains and subtracting all the losses for the AP to client link gives:

```
    20 dBm (TX Power Radio 1)
  + 10 dBi (Antenna Gain Radio 1)
  -  2 dB  (Cable Losses Radio 1)
  + 14 dBi (Antenna Gain Radio 2)
  -  2 dB  (Cable Losses Radio 2)
  ───────────
    40 dB = Total Gain
```

The path loss for a 5 km link, considering only the free space loss is:

```
Path Loss = 40 + 20log(5000) = 113 dB
```

Subtracting the path loss from the total gain

```
40 dB - 113 dB = -73 dB
```

Since -73 dB is greater than the minimum receive sensitivity of the client radio (-82 dBm), the signal level is just enough for the client radio to be able to hear the access point. There is only 9 dB of margin (82 dB - 73 dB) which will likely work fine in fair weather, but may not be enough to protect against extreme weather conditions.

Next we calculate the link from the client back to the access point:

```
  15 dBm (TX Power Radio 2)
+ 14 dBi (Antenna Gain Radio 2)
-  2 dB  (Cable Losses Radio 2)
+ 10 dBi (Antenna Gain Radio 1)
-  2 dB  (Cable Losses Radio 1)
  _____

  35 dB = Total Gain
```

Obviously, the path loss is the same on the return trip. So our received signal level on the access point side is:

```
35 dB - 113 dB = -78 dB
```

Since the receive sensitivity of the AP is -89dBm, this leaves us 11dB of fade margin (89dB - 78dB). Overall, this link will probably work but could use a bit more gain. By using a 24dBi dish on the client side rather than a 14dBi sectorial antenna, you will get an additional 10dBi of gain on both directions of the link (remember, antenna gain is reciprocal). A more expensive option would be to use higher power radios on both ends of the link, but note that adding an amplifier or higher powered card to one end generally does not help the overall quality of the link.

Online tools can be used to calculate the link budget. For example, the Green Bay Professional Packet Radio's Wireless Network Link Analysis (*http://my.athenet.net/~multiplx/cgi-bin/wireless.main.cgi*) is an excellent tool. The Super Edition generates a PDF file containing the Fresnel zone and radio path graphs. The calculation scripts can even be downloaded from the website and installed locally.

The Terabeam website also has excellent calculators available online (*http://www.terabeam.com/support/calculations/index.php*).

Tables for calculating link budget

To calculate the link budget, simply approximate your link distance, then fill in the following tables:

Free Space Path Loss at 2.4 GHz

Distance (m)	100	500	1,000	3,000	5,000	10,000
Loss (dB)	80	94	100	110	113	120

For more path loss distances, see **Appendix C**.

Antenna Gain:

Radio 1 Antenna	+ Radio 2 Antenna	= Total Antenna Gain

Losses:

Radio 1 + Cable Loss (dB)	Radio 2 + Cable Loss (dB)	Free Space Path Loss (dB)	= Total Loss (dB)

Link Budget for Radio 1 → Radio 2:

Radio 1 TX Power	+ Antenna Gain	- Total Loss	= Signal	> Radio 2 Sensitivity

Link Budget for Radio 2 → Radio 1:

Radio 2 TX Power	+ Antenna Gain	- Total Loss	= Signal	> Radio 1 Sensitivity

If the received signal is greater than the minimum received signal strength in both directions of the link, as well as any noise received along the path, then the link is possible.

Link planning software

While calculating a link budget by hand is straightforward, there are a number of tools available that will help automate the process. In addition to calculating free space loss, these tools will take many other relevant factors into account as well (such as tree absorption, terrain effects, climate, and even estimating path loss in urban areas). In this section, we will discuss two free tools that are useful for planning wireless links: Green Bay Professional Packet Radio's online interactive network design utilities, and RadioMobile.

Interactive design CGIs

The Green Bay Professional Packet Radio group (GBPRR) has made a variety of very useful link planning tools available for free online. You can browse these tools online at *http://www.qsl.net/n9zia/wireless/page09.html* . Since the tools are available online, they will work with any device that has a web browser and Internet access.

We will look at the first tool, **Wireless Network Link Analysis**, in detail. You can find it online at *http://my.athenet.net/~multiplx/cgi-bin/wireless.main.cgi*.

To begin, enter the channel to be used on the link. This can be specified in MHz or GHz. If you don't know the frequency, consult the table in **Appendix B**. Note that the table lists the channel's center frequency, while the tool asks for the highest transmitted frequency. The difference in the ultimate result is minimal, so feel free to use the center frequency instead. To find the highest transmitted frequency for a channel, just add 11MHz to the center frequency.

Next, enter the details for the transmitter side of the link, including the transmission line type, antenna gain, and other details. Try to fill in as much data as you know or can estimate. You can also enter the antenna height and elevation for this site. This data will be used for calculating the antenna tilt angle.   For calculating Fresnel zone clearance, you will need to use GBPRR's Fresnel Zone Calculator.

The next section is very similar, but includes information about the other end of the link. Enter all available data in the appropriate fields.

Finally, the last section describes the climate, terrain, and distance of the link. Enter as much data as you know or can estimate. Link distance can be calculated by specifying the latitude and longitude of both sites, or entered by hand.

Now, click the Submit button for a detailed report about the proposed link. This includes all of the data entered, as well as the projected path loss, error rates, and uptime. These numbers are all completely theoretical, but will give you a rough idea of the feasibility of the link.   By adjusting values on the form, you can play "what-if?" to see how changing various parameters will affect the connection.

In addition to the basic link analysis tool, GBPRR provides a "super edition" that will produce a PDF report, as well as a number of other very useful tools (including the Fresnel Zone Calculator, Distance & Bearing Calculator, and Decibel Conversion Calculator to name just a few). Source code to most of the tools is provided as well.

RadioMobile

Radio Mobile is a tool for the design and simulation of wireless systems. It predicts the performance of a radio link by using information about the equipment and a digital map of the area.   It is public domain software that runs on Windows, or using Linux and the Wine emulator.

Radio Mobile uses a ***digital terrain elevation model*** for the calculation of coverage, indicating received signal strength at various points along the path. It automatically builds a profile between two points in the digital map showing the coverage area and first Fresnel zone. During the simulation, it checks for line of sight and calculates the Path Loss, including losses due to obstacles. It is possible to create networks of different topologies, including net master/ slave, point-to-point, and point-to-multipoint. The software calculates the coverage area from the base station in a point-to-multipoint system. It works for systems having frequencies from 100 kHz to 200 GHz. ***Digital elevation maps*** (***DEM***) are available for free from several sources, and are available for most of the world. DEMs do not show coastlines or other readily identifiable landmarks, but they can easily be combined with other kinds of data (such as aerial photos or topographical charts) in several layers to obtain a more useful and readily recognizable representation. You can digitize your own maps and combine them with DEMs. The digital elevation maps can be merged with scanned maps, satellite photos and Internet map services (such as Google Maps) to produce accurate prediction plots.

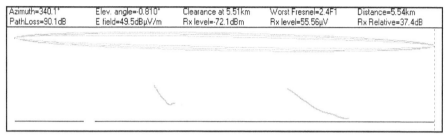

Azimuth=340.1°	Elev. angle=-0.810°	Clearance at 5.51km	Worst Fresnel=2.4F1	Distance=5.54km
PathLoss=90.1dB	E field=49.5dBµV/m	Rx level=-72.1dBm	Rx level=55.56µV	Rx Relative=37.4dB

Figure 3.20: Link feasibility, including Fresnel zone and line of sight estimate, using RadioMobile.

The main Radio Mobile webpage, with examples and tutorials, is available at: *http://www.cplus.org/rmw/english1.html*

RadioMobile under Linux

Radio Mobile will also work using Wine under Ubuntu Linux. While the application runs, some button labels may run beyond the frame of the button and can be hard to read.

We were able to make Radio Mobile work with Linux using the following environment:

• IBM Thinkpad x31

• Ubuntu Breezy (v5.10), *http://www.ubuntu.com/*

• Wine version 20050725, from the Ubuntu Universe repository

There are detailed instructions for installing RadioMobile on Windows at *http://www.cplus.org/rmw/english1.html*. You should follow all of the steps except for step 1 (since it is difficult to extract a DLL from the VBRUN60SP6.EXE file under Linux). You will either need to copy the MSVBVM60.DLL file from a Windows machine that already has the Visual Basic 6 run-time environment installed, or simply Google for MSVBVM60.DLL, and download the file.

Now continue with step 2 at from the above URL, making sure to unzip the downloaded files in the same directory into which you have placed the downloaded DLL file. Note that you don't have to worry about the stuff after step 4; these are extra steps only needed for Windows users.

Finally, you can start Wine from a terminal with the command:

```
# wine RMWDLX.exe
```

You should see RadioMobile running happily in your XWindows session.

Avoiding noise

The unlicensed ISM and U-NII bands represent a very tiny piece of the known electromagnetic spectrum. Since this region can be utilized without paying license fees, many consumer devices use it for a wide range of applications. Cordless phones, analog video senders, Bluetooth, baby monitors, and even microwave ovens compete with wireless data networks for use of the very limited 2.4 GHz band. These signals, as well as other local wireless networks, can cause significant problems for long range wireless links. Here are some steps you can use to reduce reception of unwanted signals.

- **Increase antenna gain on both sides of a point-to-point link.** Antennas not only add gain to a link, but their increased directionality tends to reject noise from areas around the link. Two high gain dishes that are pointed at each other will reject noise from directions that are outside the path of the link. Using omnidirectional antennas will receive noise from all directions.

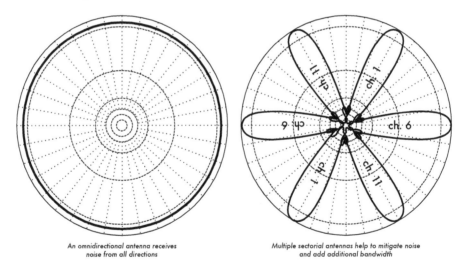

An omnidirectional antenna receives   Multiple sectorial antennas help to mitigate noise
noise from all directions   and add additional bandwidth

Figure 3.21: A single omnidirectional antenna vs. multiple sectorials.

- **Use sectorials instead of using an omnidirectional.** By making use of several sectorial antennas, you can reduce the overall noise received at a distribution point. By staggering the channels used on each sectorial, you can also increase the available bandwidth to your clients.

- **Don't use an amplifier.** As we will see in **Chapter 4**, amplifiers can make interference issues worse by indiscriminately amplifying all received signals, including sources of interference. Amplifiers also cause interference problems for other nearby users of the band.

- **Use the best available channel.** Remember that 802.11b/g channels are 22 MHz wide, but are only separated by 5MHz. Perform a site survey, and select a channel that is as far as possible from existing sources of interference. Remember that the wireless landscape can change at any time as people add new devices (cordless phones, other networks, etc.) If your link suddenly has trouble sending packets, you may need to perform another site survey and pick a different channel.

- **Use smaller hops and repeaters, rather than a single long distance shot.** Keep your point-to-point links as short as possible. While it may be possible to create a 12 km link that cuts across the middle of a city, you will likely have all kinds of interference problems. If you can break that link into two or three shorter hops, the link will likely be more stable. Obviously this isn't possible on long distance rural links where power and mounting structures are unavailable, but noise problems are also unlikely in those settings.

- **If possible, use 5.8 GHz, 900MHz, or another unlicensed band**. While this is only a short term solution, there is currently far more consumer equipment installed in the field that uses 2.4 GHz. Using 802.11a or a 2.4 GHz to 5.8 GHz step-up device will let you avoid this congestion altogether. If you can find it, some old 802.11 equipment uses unlicensed spectrum at 900MHz (unfortunately at much lower bit rates). Other technologies, such as Ronja (*http://ronja.twibright.com/*) use optical technology for short distance, noise-free links.

- **If all else fails, use licensed spectrum**. There are places where all available unlicensed spectrum is effectively used. In these cases, it may make sense to spend the additional money for proprietary equipment that uses a less congested band. For long distance point-to-point links that require very high throughput and maximum uptime, this is certainly an option. Of course, these features come at a much higher price tag compared to unlicensed equipment.

To identify sources of noise, you need tools that will show you what is happening in the air at 2.4 GHz. We will see some examples of these tools in **Chapter 6**.

Repeaters

The most critical component to building long distance network links is *line of sight* (often abbreviated as *LOS*). Terrestrial microwave systems simply cannot tolerate large hills, trees, or other obstacles in the path of a long distance link. You must have a clear idea of the lay of the land between two points before you can determine if a link is even possible.

But even if there is a mountain between two points, remember that obstacles can sometimes be turned into assets. Mountains may block your signal, but assuming power can be provided they also make very good *repeater* sites.

Repeaters are nodes that are configured to rebroadcast traffic that is not destined for the node itself. In a mesh network, every node is a repeater. In a traditional infrastructure network, nodes must be configured to pass along traffic to other nodes.

A repeater can use one or more wireless devices. When using a single radio (called a *one-arm repeater*), overall efficiency is slightly less than half of the available bandwidth, since the radio can either send or receive data, but never both at once. These devices are cheaper, simpler, and have lower power requirements. A repeater with two (or more) radio cards can operate all radios at full capacity, as long as they are each configured to use non-overlapping channels. Of course, repeaters can also supply an Ethernet connection to provide local connectivity.

Repeaters can be purchased as a complete hardware solution, or easily assembled by connecting two or more wireless nodes together with Ethernet cable. When planning to use a repeater built with 802.11 technology, remember that nodes must be configured for master, managed, or ad-hoc mode. Typically, both radios in a repeater are configured for master mode, to allow multiple clients to connect to either side of the repeater. But depending on your network layout, one or more devices may need to use ad-hoc or even client mode.

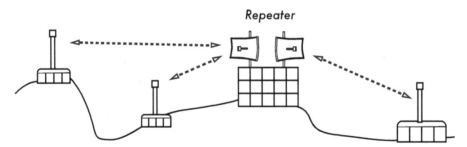

Figure 3.22: The repeater forwards packets over the air between nodes that have no direct line of sight.

Typically, repeaters are used to overcome obstacles in the path of a long distance link. For example, there may be buildings in your path, but those buildings contain people. Arrangements can often be worked out with building owners to provide bandwidth in exchange for roof rights and electricity. If the building owner isn't interested, tenants on high floors may be able to be persuaded to install equipment in a window.

If you can't go over or through an obstacle, you can often go around it. Rather than using a direct link, try a multi-hop approach to avoid the obstacle.

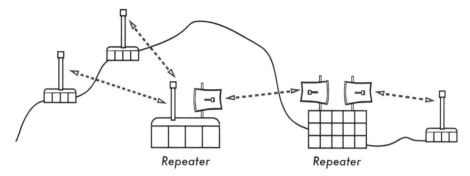

Figure 3.23: *No power was available at the top of the hill, but it was circumvented by using multiple repeater sites around the base.*

Finally, you may need to consider going backwards in order to go forwards. If there is a high site available in a different direction, and that site can see beyond the obstacle, a stable link can be made via an indirect route.

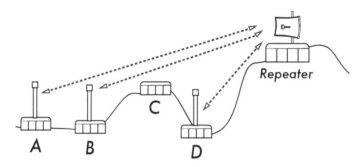

Figure 3.24: *Site D could not make a clean link to site A or B, since site C is in the way and is not hosting a node. By installing a high repeater, nodes A, B, and D can communicate with each other. Note that traffic from node D actually travels further away from the rest of the network before the repeater forwards it along.*

Repeaters in networks remind me of the "six degrees of separation" principle. This idea says that no matter who you are looking for, you need only contact five intermediaries before finding the person. Repeaters in high places can "see" a great deal of intermediaries, and as long as your node is in range of the repeater, you can communicate with any node the repeater can reach.

Traffic optimization

Bandwidth is measured as the amount of bits transmitted over a time interval. This means that over time, bandwidth available on any link approaches infinity. Unfortunately, for any given period of time, the bandwidth provided by any given network connection is not infinite. You can always download (or upload) as much traffic as you like; you need only wait long enough.   Of course, human users are not as patient as computers, and are not willing to wait an infinite amount of time for their information to traverse the network. For this reason, bandwidth must be managed and prioritized much like any other limited resource.

You will significantly improve response time and maximize available throughput by eliminating unwanted and redundant traffic from your network. This section describes a few common techniques for making sure that your network carries only the traffic that must traverse it. For a more thorough discussion of the complex subject of bandwidth optimization, see the free book *How to Accelerate Your Internet* (*http://bwmo.net/*).

Web caching

A web proxy server is a server on the local network that keeps copies of recently retrieved or often used web pages, or parts of pages. When the next person retrieves these pages, they are served from the local proxy server instead of from the Internet. This results in significantly faster web access in most cases, while reducing overall Internet bandwidth usage. When a proxy server is implemented, the administrator should also be aware that some pages are not cacheable-- for example, pages that are the output of server-side scripts, or other dynamically generated content.

The apparent loading of web pages is also affected. With a slow Internet link, a typical page begins to load slowly, first showing some text and then displaying the graphics one by one. In a network with a proxy server, there could be a delay when nothing seems to happen, and then the page will load almost at once. This happens because the information is sent to the computer so quickly that it spends a perceptible amount of time rendering the page. The overall time it takes to load the whole page might take only ten seconds (whereas without a proxy server, it may take 30 seconds to load the page gradually). But unless this is explained to some impatient users, they may say the proxy server has made things slower. It is usually the task of the network administrator to deal with user perception issues like these.

Proxy server products

There are a number of web proxy servers available. These are the most commonly used software packages:

- **Squid**. Open source Squid is the de facto standard at universities. It is free, reliable, easy to use and can be enhanced (for example, adding content filtering and advertisement blocking). Squid produces logs that can be analyzed using software such as Awstats, or Webalizer, both of which are open source and produce good graphical reports. In most cases, it is easier to install as part of the distribution than to download it from *http://www.squid-cache.org/* (most Linux distributions such as Debian, as well as other versions of Unix such as NetBSD and FreeBSD come with Squid). A good Squid configuration guide can be found on the Squid Users Guide Wiki at *http://www.deckle.co.za/squid-users-guide/*.

- **Microsoft Proxy server 2.0.** Not available for new installations because it has been superseded by Microsoft ISA server and is no longer supported. It is nonetheless used by some institutions, although it should perhaps not be considered for new installations.

- **Microsoft ISA server.** ISA server is a very good proxy server program, that is arguably too expensive for what it does. However, with academic discounts it may be affordable to some institutions. It produces its own graphical reports, but its log files can also be analyzed with popular analyzer software such as Sawmill (*http://www.sawmill.net/*). Administrators at a site with MS ISA Server should spend sufficient time getting the configuration right; otherwise MS ISA Server can itself be a considerable bandwidth user. For example, a default installation can easily consume more bandwidth than the site has used before, because popular pages with short expiry dates (such as news sites) are continually being refreshed. Therefore it is important to get the pre-fetching settings right, and to configure pre-fetching to take place mainly overnight. ISA Server can also be tied to content filtering products such as WebSense. For more information, see: *http://www.microsoft.com/isaserver/* and *http://www.isaserver.org/* .

Preventing users from bypassing the proxy server

While circumventing Internet censorship and restrictive information access policy may be a laudable political effort, proxies and firewalls are necessary tools in areas with extremely limited bandwidth. Without them, the stability and usability of the network are threatened by legitimate users themselves. Techniques for bypassing a proxy server can be found at *http://www.antiproxy.com/* . This site is useful for administrators to see how their network measures up against these techniques.

To enforce use of the caching proxy, you might consider simply setting up a network access policy and trusting your users. In the layout below, the administrator has to trust that his users will not bypass the proxy server.

In this case the administrator typically uses one of the following techniques:

- **Not giving out the default gateway address through DCHP.** This may work for a while, but some network-savvy users who want to bypass the proxy might find or guess the default gateway address. Once that happens, word tends to spread about how to bypass the proxy.

- **Using domain or group policies.** This is very useful for configuring the correct proxy server settings for Internet Explorer on all computers in the domain, but is not very useful for preventing the proxy from being by-passed, because it depends on a user logging on to the NT domain. A user with a Windows 95/98/ME computer can cancel his log-on and then bypass the proxy, and someone who knows a local user password on his Windows NT/2000/XP computer can log on locally and do the same.

- **Begging and fighting with users.** This approach, while common, is never an optimal situation for a network administrator.

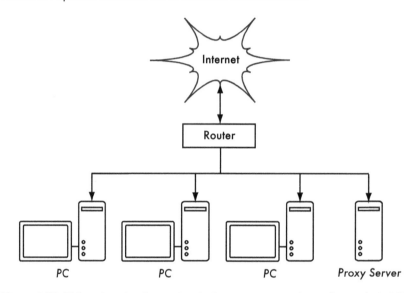

Figure 3.25: This network relies on trusted users to properly configure their PCs to use the proxy server.

The only way to ensure that proxies cannot be bypassed is by using the correct network layout, by using one of the three techniques described below.

Firewall

A more reliable way to ensure that PCs don't bypass the proxy can be implemented using the firewall. The firewall can be configured to allow only the proxy server to make HTTP requests to the Internet. All other PCs are blocked, as shown in **Figure 3.26**.

Relying on a firewall may or may not be sufficient, depending on how the firewall is configured. If it only blocks access from the campus LAN to port 80 on web servers, there will be ways for clever users to find ways around it. Additionally, they will be able to use other bandwidth hungry protocols such as BitTorrent or Kazaa.

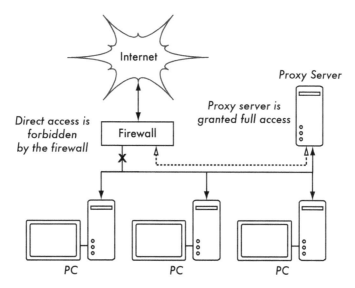

Figure 3.26: The firewall prevents PCs from accessing the Internet directly, but allows access via the proxy server.

Two network cards

Perhaps the most reliable method is to install two network cards in the proxy server and connect the campus network to the Internet as shown below. In this way, the network layout makes it physically impossible to reach the Internet without going through the proxy server.

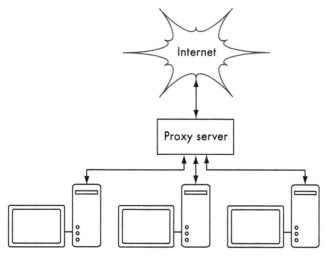

Figure 3.27: The only route to the Internet is through the proxy.

The proxy server in this diagram should not have IP forwarding enabled, unless the administrators knows exactly what they want to let through.

One big advantage to this design is that a technique known as **transparent proxying** can be used. Using a transparent proxy means that users' web requests are automatically forwarded to the proxy server, without any need to manually configure web browsers to use it. This effectively forces all web traffic to be cached, eliminates many chances for user error, and will even work with devices that do not support use of a manual proxy. For more details about configuring a transparent proxy with Squid, see:

- *http://www.squid-cache.org/Doc/FAQ/FAQ-17.html*

- *http://tldp.org/HOWTO/TransparentProxy.html*

Policy-based routing

One way to prevent bypassing of the proxy using Cisco equipment is with policy routing. The Cisco router transparently directs web requests to the proxy server. This technique is used at Makerere University. The advantage of this method is that, if the proxy server is down, the policy routes can be temporarily removed, allowing clients to connect directly to the Internet.

Mirroring a website

With permission of the owner or web master of a site, the whole site can be mirrored to a local server overnight, if it is not too large. This is something that might be considered for important websites that are of particular interest to the organization or that are very popular with web users. This may have some use, but it has some potential pitfalls. For example, if the site that is mirrored contains CGI scripts or other dynamic content that require interactive input from the user, this would cause problems. An example is a website that requires people to register online for a conference. If someone registers online on a mirrored server (and the mirrored script works), the organizers of the site will not have the information that the person registered.

Because mirroring a site may infringe copyright, this technique should only be used with permission of the site concerned. If the site runs **rsync**, the site could be mirrored using rsync. This is likely the fastest and most efficient way to keep site contents synchronized. If the remote web server is not running rsync, the recommended software to use is a program called **wget**. It is part of most versions of Unix/Linux. A Windows version can be found at *http://xoomer.virgilio.it/hherold/*, or in the free Cygwin Unix tools package (*http://www.cygwin.com/*).

A script can be set up to run every night on a local web server and do the following:

- Change directory to the web server document root: for example, **/var/www/** on Unix, or **C:\Inetpub\wwwroot** on Windows.

- Mirror the website using the command:

```
wget --cache=off -m http://www.python.org
```

The mirrored website will be in a directory **www.python.org**. The web server should now be configured to serve the contents of that directory as a name-based virtual host. Set up the local DNS server to fake an entry for this site. For this to work, client PCs should be configured to use the local DNS server(s) as the primary DNS. (This is advisable in any case, because a local caching DNS server speeds up web response times).

Pre-populate the cache using wget

Instead of setting up a mirrored website as described in the previous section, a better approach is to populate the proxy cache using an automated process. This method has been described by J. J. Eksteen and J. P. L. Cloete of the CSIR in Pretoria, South Africa, in a paper entitled **Enhancing International World Wide Web Access in Mozambique Through the Use of Mirroring and Caching Proxies**. In this paper (available at *http://www.isoc.org/inet97/ans97/cloet.htm*) they describe how the process works:

> "*An automatic process retrieves the site's home page and a specified number of extra pages (by recursively following HTML links on the retrieved pages) through the use of a proxy. Instead of writing the retrieved pages onto the local disk, the mirror process discards the retrieved pages. This is done in order to conserve system resources as well as to avoid possible copyright conflicts. By using the proxy as intermediary, the retrieved pages are guaranteed to be in the cache of the proxy as if a client accessed that page. When a client accesses the retrieved page, it is served from the cache and not over the congested international link. This process can be run in off-peak times in order to maximize bandwidth utilization and not to compete with other access activities.*"

The following command (scheduled to run at night once every day or week) is all that is needed (repeated for every site that needs pre-populating).

```
wget --proxy-on --cache=off --delete after -m http://www.python.org
```

These options enable the following:

- **-m**: Mirrors the entire site. wget starts at *www.python.org* and follows all hyperlinks, so it downloads all subpages.

- **--proxy-on**: Ensures that wget makes use of the proxy server. This might not be needed in set-ups where a transparent proxy is employed.

- **--cache=off**: Ensures that fresh content is retrieved from the Internet, and not from the local proxy server.

- **--delete after**: Deletes the mirrored copy. The mirrored content remains in the proxy cache if there is sufficient disk space, and the proxy server caching parameters are set up correctly.

In addition, wget has many other options; for example, to supply a password for websites that require them. When using this tool, Squid should be configured with sufficient disk space to contain all the pre-populated sites and more (for normal Squid usage involving pages other than the pre-populated ones). Fortunately, disk space is becoming ever cheaper and disk sizes are far larger than ever before. However, this technique can only be used with a few selected sites. These sites should not be too big for the process to finish before the working day starts, and an eye should be kept on disk space.

Cache hierarchies

When an organization has more than one proxy server, the proxies can share cached information among them. For example, if a web page exists in server A's cache, but not in the cache of server B, a user connected via server B might get the cached object from server A via server B. *Inter-Cache Protocol* (*ICP*) and *Cache Array Routing Protocol* (*CARP*) can share cache information. CARP is considered the better protocol. Squid supports both protocols, and MS ISA Server supports CARP. For more information, see *http://squid-docs.sourceforge.net/latest/html/c2075.html*. This sharing of cached information reduces bandwidth usage in organizations where more than one proxy is used.

Proxy specifications

On a university campus network, there should be more than one proxy server, both for performance and also for redundancy reasons. With today's cheaper and larger disks, powerful proxy servers can be built, with 50 GB or more disk space allocated to the cache. Disk performance is important, therefore the fastest SCSI disks would perform best (although an IDE based cache is better than none at all). RAID or mirroring is not recommended.

It is also recommended that a separate disk be dedicated to the cache. For example, one disk could be for the cache, and a second for the operating system and cache logging. Squid is designed to use as much RAM as it can get, because when data is retrieved from RAM it is much faster than when it comes from the hard disk. For a campus network, RAM memory should be 1GB or more:

- Apart from the memory required for the operating system and other applications, Squid requires 10 MB of RAM for every 1 GB of disk cache. Therefore, if there is 50 GB of disk space allocated to caching, Squid will require 500 MB extra memory.

- The machine would also require 128 MB for Linux and 128 MB for Xwindows.

- Another 256 MB should be added for other applications and in order that everything can run easily. Nothing increases a machine's performance as much as installing a large amount of memory, because this reduces the need to use the hard disk. Memory is thousands of times faster than a hard disk. Modern operating systems keep frequently accessed data in memory if there is enough RAM available. But they use the page file as an extra memory area when they don't have enough RAM.

DNS caching and optimization

Caching-only DNS servers are not authoritative for any domains, but rather just cache results from queries asked of them by clients. Just like a proxy server that caches popular web pages for a certain time, DNS addresses are cached until their **time to live** (**TTL**) expires. This will reduce the amount of DNS traffic on your Internet connection, as the DNS cache may be able to satisfy many of the queries locally. Of course, client computers must be configured to use the caching-only name server as their DNS server. When all clients use this server as their primary DNS server, it will quickly populate a cache of IP addresses to names, so that previously requested names can quickly be resolved. DNS servers that are authoritative for a domain also act as cache name-address mappings of hosts resolved by them.

Bind (named)

Bind is the de facto standard program used for name service on the Internet. When Bind is installed and running, it will act as a caching server (no further configuration is necessary). Bind can be installed from a package such as a Debian package or an RPM. Installing from a package is usually the easiest method. In Debian, type

```
apt-get install bind9
```

In addition to running a cache, Bind can also host authoritative zones, act as a slave to authoritative zones, implement split horizon, and just about everything else that is possible with DNS.

dnsmasq

One alternative caching DNS server is **dnsmasq**. It is available for BSD and most Linux distributions, or from *http://www.thekelleys.org.uk/dnsmasq/*. The big advantage of dnsmasq is flexibility: it easily acts as both a caching DNS proxy and an authoritative source for hosts and domains, without complicated zone file configuration. Updates can be made to zone data without even restarting the service. It can also serve as a DHCP server, and will integrate DNS service with DHCP host requests. It is very lightweight, stable, and extremely flexible. Bind is likely a better choice for very large networks (more than a couple of hundred nodes), but the simplicity and flexibility of dnsmasq makes it attractive for small to medium sized networks.

Windows NT

To install the DNS service on Windows NT4: select Control Panel → Network → Services → Add → Microsoft DNS server. Insert the Windows NT4 CD when prompted.   Configuring a caching-only server in NT is described in Knowledge Base article 167234. From the article:

> "*Simply install DNS and run the Domain Name System Manager. Click on DNS in the menu, select New Server, and type in the IP address of your computer where you have installed DNS. You now have a caching-only DNS server.*"

Windows 2000

Install DNS service: Start → Settings → Control Panel → Add/Remove Software.   In Add/Remove Windows Components, select Components → Networking Services → Details → Domain Name System (DNS).   Then start the DNS MMC (Start → Programs → Administrative Tools → DNS) From the Action menu select "Connect To Computer..." In the Select Target Computer window, enable "The following computer:" and enter the name of a DNS server you want to cache. If there is a . [dot] in the DNS manager (this appears by default), this means that the DNS server thinks it is the root DNS server of the Internet. It is certainly not. Delete the . [dot] for anything to work.

Split DNS and a mirrored server

The aim of split DNS (also known as **split horizon**) is to present a different view of your domain to the inside and outside worlds. There is more than one way to do split DNS; but for security reasons, it's recommended that you have two separate internal and external content DNS servers (each with different databases).

Split DNS can enable clients from a campus network to resolve IP addresses for the campus domain to local RFC1918 IP addresses, while the rest of the

Internet resolves the same names to different IP addresses. This is achieved by having two zones on two different DNS servers for the same domain.

One of the zones is used by internal network clients and the other by users on the Internet. For example, in the network below the user on the Makerere campus gets *http://www.makerere.ac.ug/* resolved to 172.16.16.21, whereas a user elsewhere on the Internet gets it resolved to 195.171.16.13.

The DNS server on the campus in the above diagram has a zone file for *makerere.ac.ug* and is configured as if it is authoritative for that domain. In addition, it serves as the DNS caching server for the Makerere campus, and all computers on the campus are configured to use it as their DNS server.

The DNS records for the campus DNS server would look like this:

```
makerere.ac.ug
www CNAME      webserver.makerere.ac.ug
ftp CNAME      ftpserver.makerere.ac.ug
mail CNAME     exchange.makerere.ac.ug
mailserver     A    172.16.16.21
webserver      A    172.16.16.21
ftpserver      A    172.16.16.21
```

But there is another DNS server on the Internet that is actually authoritative for the *makerere.ac.ug* domain. The DNS records for this external zone would look like this:

```
makerere.ac.ug
www A 195.171.16.13
ftp A 195.171.16.13
mail   A 16.132.33.21
       MX mail.makerere.ac.ug
```

Split DNS is not dependent on using RFC 1918 addresses. An African ISP might, for example, host websites on behalf of a university but also mirror those same websites in Europe. Whenever clients of that ISP access the website, it gets the IP address at the African ISP, and so the traffic stays in the same country. When visitors from other countries access that website, they get the IP address of the mirrored web server in Europe. In this way, international visitors do not congest the ISP's VSAT connection when visiting the university's website. This is becoming an attractive solution, as web hosting close to the Internet backbone has become very cheap.

Internet link optimization

As mentioned earlier, network throughput of up to 22 Mbps can be achieved by using standard, unlicensed 802.11g wireless gear. This amount of bandwidth will likely be at least an order of magnitude higher than that provided by your Internet link, and should be able to comfortably support many simultaneous Internet users.

But if your primary Internet connection is through a VSAT link, you will encounter some performance issues if you rely on default TCP/IP parameters. By optimizing your VSAT link, you can significantly improve response times when accessing Internet hosts.

TCP/IP factors over a satellite connection

A VSAT is often referred to as a ***long fat pipe network***. This term refers to factors that affect TCP/IP performance on any network that has relatively large bandwidth, but high latency. Most Internet connections in Africa and other parts of the developing world are via VSAT. Therefore, even if a university gets its connection via an ISP, this section might apply if the ISP's connection is via VSAT. The high latency in satellite networks is due to the long distance to the satellite and the constant speed of light. This distance adds about 520 ms to a packet's round-trip time (RTT), compared to a typical RTT between Europe and the USA of about 140 ms.

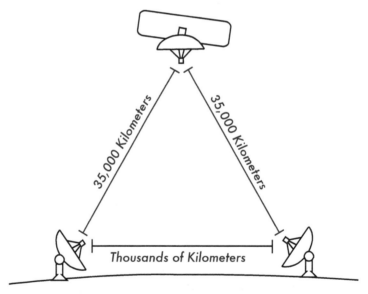

Figure 3.28: Due to the speed of light and long distances involved, a single ping packet can take more than 520 ms to be acknowledged over a VSAT link.

The factors that most significantly impact TCP/IP performance are **long RTT**, **large bandwidth delay product**, and **transmission errors**.

Generally speaking, operating systems that support modern TCP/IP implementations should be used in a satellite network. These implementations support the RFC 1323 extensions:

- The *window scale* option for supporting large TCP window sizes (larger than 64KB).

- *Selective acknowledgment* (*SACK*) to enable faster recovery from transmission errors.

- Timestamps for calculating appropriate RTT and retransmission timeout values for the link in use.

Long round-trip time (RTT)

Satellite links have an average RTT of around 520ms to the first hop. TCP uses the slow-start mechanism at the start of a connection to find the appropriate TCP/IP parameters for that connection. Time spent in the slow-start stage is proportional to the RTT, and for a satellite link it means that TCP stays in slow-start mode for a longer time than would otherwise be the case. This drastically decreases the throughput of short-duration TCP connections. This is can be seen in the way that a small website might take surprisingly long to load, but when a large file is transferred acceptable data rates are achieved after a while.

Furthermore, when packets are lost, TCP enters the congestion-control phase, and owing to the higher RTT, remains in this phase for a longer time, thus reducing the throughput of both short- and long-duration TCP connections.

Large bandwidth-delay product

The amount of data in transit on a link at any point of time is the product of bandwidth and the RTT. Because of the high latency of the satellite link, the bandwidth-delay product is large. TCP/IP allows the remote host to send a certain amount of data in advance without acknowledgment. An acknowledgment is usually required for all incoming data on a TCP/IP connection. However, the remote host is always allowed to send a certain amount of data without acknowledgment, which is important to achieve a good transfer rate on large bandwidth-delay product connections. This amount of data is called the *TCP window size*. The window size is usually 64KB in modern TCP/IP implementations.

On satellite networks, the value of the bandwidth-delay product is important. To utilize the link fully, the window size of the connection should be equal to the bandwidth-delay product. If the largest window size allowed is 64KB, the maximum theoretical throughput achievable via satellite is (window size) / RTT, or 64KB / 520 ms. This gives a maximum data rate of 123 KB/s, which is 984 kbps, regardless of the fact that the capacity of the link may be much greater.

Each TCP segment header contains a field called *advertised window*, which specifies how many additional bytes of data the receiver is prepared to accept. The advertised window is the receiver's current available buffer size.

The sender is not allowed to send more bytes than the advertised window. To maximize performance, the sender should set its send buffer size and the receiver should set its receive buffer size to no less than the bandwidth-delay product. This buffer size has a maximum value of 64KB in most modern TCP/IP implementations.

To overcome the problem of TCP/IP stacks from operating systems that don't increase the window size beyond 64KB, a technique known as **TCP acknowledgment spoofing** can be used (see Performance Enhancing Proxy, below).

Transmission errors

In older TCP/IP implementations, packet loss is always considered to have been caused by congestion (as opposed to link errors). When this happens, TCP performs congestion avoidance, requiring three duplicate ACKs or slow start in the case of a timeout. Because of the long RTT value, once this congestion-control phase is started, TCP/IP on satellite links will take a longer time to return to the previous throughput level. Therefore errors on a satellite link have a more serious effect on the performance of TCP than over low latency links. To overcome this limitation, mechanisms such as **Selective Acknowledgment** (**SACK**) have been developed. SACK specifies exactly those packets that have been received, allowing the sender to retransmit only those segments that are missing because of link errors.

The Microsoft Windows 2000 TCP/IP Implementation Details White Paper states

> "*Windows 2000 introduces support for an important performance feature known as Selective Acknowledgment (SACK). SACK is especially important for connections using large TCP window sizes.*"

SACK has been a standard feature in Linux and BSD kernels for quite some time. Be sure that your Internet router and your ISP's remote side both support SACK.

Implications for universities

If a site has a 512 kbps connection to the Internet, the default TCP/IP settings are likely sufficient, because a 64 KB window size can fill up to 984 kbps. But if the university has more than 984 kbps, it might in some cases not get the full bandwidth of the available link due to the "long fat pipe network" factors discussed above. What these factors really imply is that they prevent a single machine from filling the entire bandwidth. This is not a bad thing during the day, because many people are using the bandwidth. But if, for example, there are large scheduled downloads at night, the administrator might want those downloads to make use of the full bandwidth, and the "long fat pipe network" factors might be an obstacle. This may also become critical if a significant amount of your network traffic routes through a single tunnel or VPN connection to the other end of the VSAT link.

Administrators might consider taking steps to ensure that the full bandwidth can be achieved by tuning their TCP/IP settings. If a university has implemented a network where all traffic has to go through the proxy (enforced by network layout), then the only machines that make connections to the Internet will be the proxy and mail servers.

For more information, see *http://www.psc.edu/networking/perf_tune.html* .

Performance-enhancing proxy (PEP)

The idea of a Performance-enhancing proxy is described in RFC 3135 (see *http://www.ietf.org/rfc/rfc3135*), and would be a proxy server with a large disk cache that has RFC 1323 extensions, among other features. A laptop has a TCP session with the PEP at the ISP. That PEP, and the one at the satellite provider, communicate using a different TCP session or even their own proprietary protocol. The PEP at the satellite provider gets the files from the web server. In this way, the TCP session is split, and thus the link characteristics that affect protocol performance (long fat pipe factors) are overcome (by TCP acknowledgment spoofing, for example). Additionally, the PEP makes use of proxying and pre-fetching to accelerate web access further.

Such a system can be built from scratch using Squid, for example, or purchased "off the shelf" from a number of vendors.

More information

While bandwidth optimization is a complex and often difficult subject, the techniques in this chapter should help reduce obvious sources of wasted bandwidth. To make the best possible use of available bandwidth, you will need to define a good access policy, set up comprehensive monitoring and analysis tools, and implement a network architecture that enforces desired usage limits.

For more information about bandwidth optimization, see the free book *How to Accelerate Your Internet* (*http://bwmo.net/*).

4

Antennas & Transmission Lines

The transmitter that generates the RF[1] power to drive the antenna is usually located at some distance from the antenna terminals. The connecting link between the two is the **RF transmission line**. Its purpose is to carry RF power from one place to another, and to do this as efficiently as possible. From the receiver side, the antenna is responsible for picking up any radio signals in the air and passing them to the receiver with the minimum amount of distortion, so that the radio has its best chance to decode the signal. For these reasons, the RF cable has a very important role in radio systems: it must maintain the integrity of the signals in both directions.

There are two main categories of transmission lines: cables and waveguides. Both types work well for efficiently carrying RF power at 2.4 GHz.

Cables

RF cables are, for frequencies higher than HF, almost exclusively coaxial cables (or **coax** for short, derived from the words "of common axis"). Coax cables have a core **conductor** wire surrounded by a non-conductive material called **dielectric**, or simply **insulation**. The dielectric is then surrounded by an encompassing shielding which is often made of braided wires. The dielectric prevents an electrical connection between the core and the shielding. Finally, the coax is protected by an outer casing which is generally made

---

1. Radio Frequency. See chapter two for discussion of electromagnetic waves.

from a PVC material. The inner conductor carries the RF signal, and the outer shield prevents the RF signal from radiating to the atmosphere, and also prevents outside signals from interfering with the signal carried by the core. Another interesting fact is that high frequency electrical signal always travels along the outer layer of a conductor: the larger the central conductor, the better signal will flow. This is called the "skin effect".

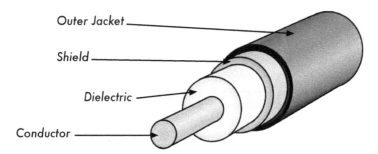

Figure 4.1: Coaxial cable with jacket, shield, dielectric, and core conductor.

Even though the coaxial construction is good at containing the signal on the core wire, there is some resistance to the electrical flow: as the signal travels down the core, it will fade away. This fading is known as ***attenuation***, and for transmission lines it is measured in decibels per meter (***dB/m***). The rate of attenuation is a function of the signal frequency and the physical construction of the cable itself. As the signal frequency increases, so does its attenuation. Obviously, we need to minimize the cable attenuation as much as possible by keeping the cable very short and using high quality cables.

Here are some points to consider when choosing a cable for use with microwave devices:

1. "The shorter the better!" The first rule when you install a piece of cable is to try to keep it as short as possible. The power loss is not linear, so doubling the cable length means that you are going to lose much more than twice the power. In the same way, reducing the cable length by half gives you more than twice the power at the antenna. The best solution is to place the transmitter as close as possible to the antenna, even when this means placing it on a tower.

2. "The cheaper the worse!" The second golden rule is that any money you invest in buying a **good quality** cable is a bargain. Cheap cables are intended to be used at low frequencies, such as VHF. Microwaves require the highest quality cables available. All other options are nothing but a dummy load[2].

---

2. A dummy load is a device that dissipates RF energy without radiating it. Think of it as a heat sink that works at radio frequencies.

3. Always avoid RG-58. It is intended for thin Ethernet networking, CB or VHF radio, not for microwave.

4. Always avoid RG-213. It is intended for CB and HF radio. In this case the cable diameter does not imply a high quality, or low attenuation.

5. Whenever possible, use **Heliax** (also called "Foam") cables for connecting the transmitter to the antenna. When Heliax is unavailable, use the best rated LMR cable you can find. Heliax cables have a solid or tubular center conductor with a corrugated solid outer conductor to enable them to flex. Heliax can be built in two ways, using either air or foam as a dielectric. Air dielectric Heliax is the most expensive and guarantees the minimum loss, but it is very difficult to handle. Foam dielectric Heliax is slightly more lossy, but is less expensive and easier to install. A special procedure is required when soldering connectors in order to keep the foam dielectric dry and uncorrupted. LMR is a brand of coax cable available in various diameters that works well at microwave frequencies. LMR-400 and LMR-600 are a commonly used alternative to Heliax.

6. Whenever possible, use cables that are pre-crimped and tested in a proper lab. Installing connectors to cable is a tricky business, and is difficult to do properly even with the proper tools. Unless you have access to equipment that can verify a cable you make yourself (such as a spectrum analyzer and signal generator, or time domain reflectometer), troubleshooting a network that uses homemade cable can be difficult.

7. Don't abuse your transmission line. Never step over a cable, bend it too much, or try to unplug a connector by pulling directly the cable. All of those behaviors may change the mechanical characteristic of the cable and therefore its impedance, short the inner conductor to the shield, or even break the line. Those problems are difficult to track and recognize and can lead to unpredictable behavior on the radio link.

Waveguides

Above 2 GHz, the wavelength is short enough to allow practical, efficient energy transfer by different means. A waveguide is a conducting tube through which energy is transmitted in the form of electromagnetic waves. The tube acts as a boundary that confines the waves in the enclosed space. The Faraday cage effect prevents electromagnetic effects from being evident outside the guide. The electromagnetic fields are propagated through the waveguide by means of reflections against its inner walls, which are considered perfect conductors. The intensity of the fields is greatest at the center along the X dimension, and must diminish to zero at the end walls because the existence of any field parallel to the walls at the surface would cause an infinite current to flow in a perfect conductor. Waveguides, of course, cannot carry RF in this fashion.

The X, Y and Z dimensions of a rectangular waveguide can be seen in the following figure:

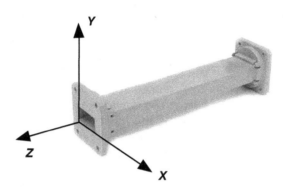

Figure 4.2: The X, Y, and Z dimensions of a rectangular waveguide.

There are an infinite number of ways in which the electric and magnetic fields can arrange themselves in a waveguide for frequencies above the low cutoff frequency. Each of these field configurations is called a **mode**. The modes may be separated into two general groups. One group, designated **TM** (Transverse Magnetic), has the magnetic field entirely transverse to the direction of propagation, but has a component of the electric field in the direction of propagation. The other type, designated **TE** (Transverse Electric) has the electric field entirely transverse, but has a component of magnetic field in the direction of propagation.

The mode of propagation is identified by the group letters followed by two subscript numerals. For example, TE 10, TM 11, etc. The number of possible modes increases with the frequency for a given size of guide, and there is only one possible mode, called the **dominant mode**, for the lowest frequency that can be transmitted. In a rectangular guide, the critical dimension is X. This dimension must be more than 0.5 λ at the lowest frequency to be transmitted. In practice, the Y dimension usually is made about equal to 0.5 X to avoid the possibility of operation in other than the dominant mode. Cross-sectional shapes other than the rectangle can be used, the most important being the circular pipe. Much the same considerations apply as in the rectangular case. Wavelength dimensions for rectangular and circular guides are given in the following table, where X is the width of a rectangular guide and r is the radius of a circular guide. All figures apply to the dominant mode.

Type of guide	Rectangular	Circular
Cutoff wavelength	2X	3.41r
Longest wavelength transmitted with little attenuation	1.6X	3.2r
Shortest wavelength before next mode becomes possible	1.1X	2.8r

Energy may be introduced into or extracted from a waveguide by means of either an electric or magnetic field. The energy transfer typically happens through a coaxial line. Two possible methods for coupling to a coaxial line are using the inner conductor of the coaxial line, or through a loop. A probe which is simply a short extension of the inner conductor of the coaxial line can be oriented so that it is parallel to the electric lines of force. A loop can be arranged so that it encloses some of the magnetic lines of force. The point at which maximum coupling is obtained depends upon the mode of propagation in the guide or cavity. Coupling is maximum when the coupling device is in the most intense field.

If a waveguide is left open at one end, it will radiate energy (that is, it can be used as an antenna rather than as a transmission line). This radiation can be enhanced by flaring the waveguide to form a pyramidal horn antenna. We will see an example of a practical waveguide antenna for WiFi later in this chapter.

Cable Type	Core	Dielectric	Shield	Jacket
RG-58	0.9 mm	2.95 mm	3.8 mm	4.95 mm
RG-213	2.26 mm	7.24 mm	8.64 mm	10.29 mm
LMR-400	2.74 mm	7.24 mm	8.13 mm	10.29 mm
3/8" LDF	3.1 mm	8.12 mm	9.7 mm	11 mm

Here is a table contrasting the sizes of various common transmission lines. Choose the best cable you can afford with the lowest possible attenuation at the frequency you intend to use for your wireless link.

Connectors and adapters

Connectors allow a cable to be connected to another cable or to a component of the RF chain. There are a wide variety of fittings and connectors designed to go with various sizes and types of coaxial lines. We will describe some of the most popular ones.

BNC connectors were developed in the late 40s. BNC stands for Bayonet Neill Concelman, named after the men who invented it: Paul Neill and Carl Concelman. The BNC product line is a miniature quick connect / disconnect connector. It features two bayonet lugs on the female connector, and mating is achieved with only a quarter turn of the coupling nut. BNC's are ideally suited for cable termination for miniature to subminiature coaxial cable (RG-58 to RG-179, RG-316, etc.) They have acceptable performance up to few GHz. They are most commonly found on test equipment and 10base2 coaxial Ethernet cables.

TNC connectors were also invented by Neill and Concelman, and are a threaded variation of the BNC. Due to the better interconnect provided by the threaded connector, TNC connectors work well through about 12 GHz. TNC stands for Threaded Neill Concelman.

Type N (again for Neill, although sometimes attributed to "Navy") connectors were originally developed during the Second World War. They are usable up to 18 Ghz, and very commonly used for microwave applications. They are available for almost all types of cable. Both the plug / cable and plug / socket joints are waterproof, providing an effective cable clamp.

SMA is an acronym for SubMiniature version A, and was developed in the 60s. SMA connectors are precision, subminiature units that provide excellent electrical performance up to 18 GHz. These high-performance connectors are compact in size and mechanically have outstanding durability.

The *SMB* name derives from SubMiniature B, and it is the second subminiature design. The SMB is a smaller version of the SMA with snap-on coupling. It provides broadband capability through 4 GHz with a snap-on connector design.

MCX connectors were introduced in the 80s. While the MCX uses identical inner contact and insulator dimensions as the SMB, the outer diameter of the plug is 30% smaller than the SMB. This series provides designers with options where weight and physical space are limited. MCX provides broadband capability though 6 GHz with a snap-on connector design.

In addition to these standard connectors, most WiFi devices use a variety of proprietary connectors. Often, these are simply standard microwave connectors with the center conductor parts reversed, or the thread cut in the opposite direction. These parts are often integrated into a microwave system using a short jumper called a **pigtail** that converts the non-standard connector into something more robust and commonly available. Some of these connectors include:

RP-TNC. This is a TNC connector with the genders reversed. These are most commonly found on Linksys equipment, such as the WRT54G.

U.FL (also known as **MHF**). The U.FL is a patented connector made by Hirose, while the MHF is a mechanically equivalent connector. This is possibly the smallest microwave connector currently in wide use. The U.FL / MHF is typically used to connect a mini-PCI radio card to an antenna or larger connector (such as an N or TNC).

The **MMCX** series, which is also called a MicroMate, is one of the smallest RF connector line and was developed in the 90s. MMCX is a micro-miniature connector series with a lock-snap mechanism allowing for 360 degrees rotation enabling flexibility. MMCX connectors are commonly found on PCMCIA radio cards, such as those manufactured by Senao and Cisco.

MC-Card connectors are even smaller and more fragile than MMCX. They have a split outer connector that breaks easily after just a few interconnects. These are commonly found on Lucent / Orinoco / Avaya equipment.

Adapters, which are also called coaxial adapters, are short, two-sided connectors which are used to join two cables or components which cannot be connected directly. Adapters can be used to interconnect devices or cables with different types. For example, an adapter can be used to connect an SMA connector to a BNC. Adapters may also be used to fit together connectors of the same type, but which cannot be directly joined because of their gender.

Figure 4.3: An N female barrel adapter.

For example a very useful adapter is the one which enables to join two Type N connectors, having socket (female) connectors on both sides.

Choosing the proper connector

1. "The gender question." Virtually all connectors have a well defined gender consisting of either a pin (the "male" end) or a socket (the "female" end). Usually cables have male connectors on both ends, while RF devices (i.e. transmitters and antennas) have female connectors. Devices such as directional couplers and line-through measuring devices may have both male and female connectors. Be sure that every male connector in your system mates with a female connector.

2. "Less is best!" Try to minimize the number of connectors and adapters in the RF chain. Each connector introduces some additional loss (up to a few dB for each connection, depending on the connector!)

3. "Buy, don't build!" As mentioned earlier, buy cables that are already terminated with the connectors you need whenever possible. Soldering connectors is not an easy task, and to do this job properly is almost impossible for small connectors as U.FL and MMCX. Even terminating "Foam" cables is not an easy task.

4. Don't use BNC for 2.4 GHz or higher. Use N type connectors (or SMA, SMB, TNC, etc.)

5. Microwave connectors are precision-made parts, and can be easily damaged by mistreatment. As a general rule, you should rotate the outer sleeve to tighten the connector, leaving the rest of the connector (and cable) stationary. If other parts of the connector are twisted while tightening or loosening, damage can easily occur.

6. Never step over connectors, or drop connectors on the floor when disconnecting cables (this happens more often than what you may imagine, especially when working on a mast over a roof).

7. Never use tools like pliers to tighten connectors. Always use your hands. When working outside, remember that metals expand at high temperatures and reduce their size at low temperatures: a very tightened connector in the summer can bind or even break in winter.

Antennas & radiation patterns

Antennas are a very important component of communication systems. By definition, an antenna is a device used to transform an RF signal traveling on a conductor into an electromagnetic wave in free space. Antennas demonstrate a property known as *reciprocity*, which means that an antenna will maintain the same characteristics regardless if whether it is transmitting or receiving. Most antennas are resonant devices, which operate efficiently over a relatively narrow frequency band. An antenna must be tuned to the same frequency band of the radio system to which it is connected, otherwise the reception and the transmission will be impaired. When a signal is fed into an antenna, the antenna will emit radiation distributed in space in a certain way. A graphical representation of the relative distribution of the radiated power in space is called a **radiation pattern**.

Antenna term glossary

Before we talk about specific antennas, there are a few common terms that must be defined and explained:

Input Impedance

For an efficient transfer of energy, the **impedance** of the radio, antenna, and transmission cable connecting them must be the same. Transceivers and their transmission lines are typically designed for 50Ω impedance. If the antenna has an impedance different than 50Ω, then there is a mismatch and an impedance matching circuit is required. When any of these components are mismatched, transmission efficiency suffers.

Return loss

Return loss is another way of expressing mismatch. It is a logarithmic ratio measured in dB that compares the power reflected by the antenna to the power that is fed into the antenna from the transmission line. The relationship between SWR and return loss is the following:

$$\text{Return Loss (in dB)} = 20\log_{10} \frac{SWR}{SWR-1}$$

While some energy will always be reflected back into the system, a high return loss will yield unacceptable antenna performance.

Bandwidth

The **bandwidth** of an antenna refers to the range of frequencies over which the antenna can operate correctly. The antenna's bandwidth is the number of Hz for which the antenna will exhibit an SWR less than 2:1.

The bandwidth can also be described in terms of percentage of the center frequency of the band.

$$\text{Bandwidth} = 100 \times \frac{F_H - F_L}{F_C}$$

...where F_H is the highest frequency in the band, F_L is the lowest frequency in the band, and F_C is the center frequency in the band.

In this way, bandwidth is constant relative to frequency. If bandwidth   was expressed in absolute units of frequency, it would be different depending upon the center frequency. Different types of antennas have different bandwidth limitations.

Directivity and Gain

Directivity is the ability of an antenna to focus energy in a particular direction when transmitting, or to receive energy from a particular direction when receiving. If a wireless link uses fixed locations for both ends, it is possible to use antenna directivity to concentrate the radiation beam in the wanted direction. In a mobile application where the transceiver is not fixed, it may be impossible to predict where the transceiver will be, and so the antenna should ideally radiate as well as possible in all directions. An omnidirectional antenna is used in these applications.

Gain is not a quantity which can be defined in terms of a physical quantity such as the Watt or the Ohm, but it is a dimensionless ratio. Gain is given in reference to a standard antenna. The two most common reference antennas are the **isotropic antenna** and the **resonant half-wave dipole antenna**. The isotropic antenna radiates equally well in all directions. Real isotropic antennas do not exist, but they provide useful and simple theoretical antenna patterns with which to compare real antennas. Any real antenna will radiate more energy in some directions than in others. Since antennas cannot create energy, the total power radiated is the same as an isotropic antenna. Any additional energy radiated in the directions it favors is offset by equally less energy radiated in all other directions.

The gain of an antenna in a given direction is the amount of energy radiated in that direction compared to the energy an isotropic antenna would radiate in the same direction when driven with the same input power. Usually we are only interested in the maximum gain, which is the gain in the direction in which the antenna is radiating most of the power. An antenna gain of 3 dB compared to an isotropic antenna would be written as **3 dBi**. The resonant half-wave dipole can be a useful standard for comparing to other antennas at one frequency or over a very narrow band of frequencies. To compare the dipole to an antenna over a range of frequencies requires a number of dipoles of different lengths. An antenna gain of 3 dB compared to a dipole antenna would be written as **3 dBd**.

The method of measuring gain by comparing the antenna under test against a known standard antenna, which has a calibrated gain, is technically known as a **gain transfer** technique. Another method for measuring gain is the 3 antennas method, where the transmitted and received power at the antenna terminals is measured between three arbitrary antennas at a known fixed distance.

Radiation Pattern

The **radiation pattern** or **antenna pattern** describes the relative strength of the radiated field in various directions from the antenna, at a constant distance. The radiation pattern is a reception pattern as well, since it also describes the receiving properties of the antenna. The radiation pattern is three-dimensional, but usually the measured radiation patterns are a two-dimensional slice of the three-dimensional pattern, in the horizontal or vertical planes. These pattern measurements are presented in either a **rectangular** or a **polar** format. The following figure shows a rectangular plot presentation of a typical ten-element Yagi. The detail is good but it is difficult to visualize the antenna behavior in different directions.

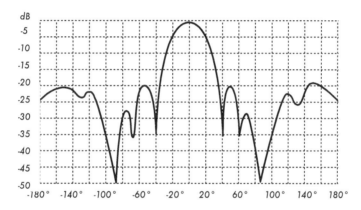

Figure 4.4: A rectangular plot of a yagi radiation pattern.

Polar coordinate systems are used almost universally. In the polar-coordinate graph, points are located by projection along a rotating axis (radius) to an intersection with one of several concentric circles. The following is a polar plot of the same 10 element Yagi antenna.

Polar coordinate systems may be divided generally in two classes: **linear** and **logarithmic**. In the linear coordinate system, the concentric circles are equally spaced, and are graduated. Such a grid may be used to prepare a linear plot of the power contained in the signal. For ease of comparison, the equally spaced concentric circles may be replaced with appropriately placed circles representing the decibel response, referenced to 0 dB at the outer edge of the plot. In this kind of plot the minor lobes are suppressed. Lobes with peaks more than 15 dB or so below the main lobe disappear because of their small size. This grid enhances plots in which the antenna has a high directivity and small minor lobes. The voltage of the signal, rather than the power, can also be plotted on a linear coordinate system. In this case, too, the directivity is enhanced and the minor lobes suppressed, but not in the same degree as in the linear power grid.

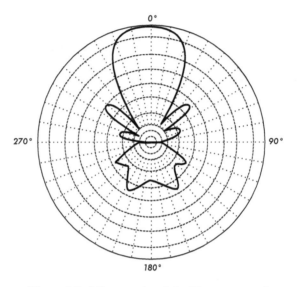

Figure 4.5: A linear polar plot of the same yagi.

In the logarithmic polar coordinate system the concentric grid lines are spaced periodically according to the logarithm of the voltage in the signal. Different values may be used for the logarithmic constant of periodicity, and this choice will have an effect on the appearance of the plotted patterns. Generally the 0 dB reference for the outer edge of the chart is used. With this type of grid, lobes that are 30 or 40 dB below the main lobe are still distinguishable. The spacing between points at 0 dB and at -3 dB is greater than the spacing between -20 dB and -23 dB, which is greater than the spacing between -50 dB and -53 dB. The spacing thus correspond to the relative significance of such changes in antenna performance.

A modified logarithmic scale emphasizes the shape of the major beam while compressing very low-level (>30 dB) sidelobes towards the center of the pattern. This is shown in **Figure 4.6**.

There are two kinds of radiation pattern: ***absolute*** and ***relative***. Absolute radiation patterns are presented in absolute units of field strength or power. Relative radiation patterns are referenced in relative units of field strength or power. Most radiation pattern measurements are relative to the isotropic antenna, and the gain transfer method is then used to establish the absolute gain of the antenna.

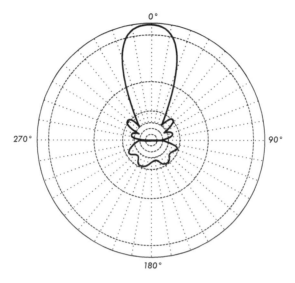

Figure 4.6: The logarithmic polar plot

The radiation pattern in the region close to the antenna is not the same as the pattern at large distances. The term near-field refers to the field pattern that exists close to the antenna, while the term far-field refers to the field pattern at large distances. The far-field is also called the radiation field, and is what is most commonly of interest. Ordinarily, it is the radiated power that is of interest, and so antenna patterns are usually measured in the far-field region. For pattern measurement it is important to choose a distance sufficiently large to be in the far-field, well out of the near-field. The minimum permissible distance depends on the dimensions of the antenna in relation to the wavelength. The accepted formula for this distance is:

$$r_{min} = \frac{2d^2}{\lambda}$$

where r_{min} is the minimum distance from the antenna, d is the largest dimension of the antenna, and λ is the wavelength.

Beamwidth

An antenna's **beamwidth** is usually understood to mean the half-power beamwidth. The peak radiation intensity is found, and then the points on either side of the peak which represent half the power of the peak intensity are located. The angular distance between the half power points is defined as the beamwidth. Half the power expressed in decibels is -3dB, so the half power beamwidth is sometimes referred to as the 3dB beamwidth. Both horizontal and vertical beamwidth are usually considered.

Assuming that most of the radiated power is not divided into sidelobes, then the directive gain is inversely proportional to the beamwidth: as the beamwidth decreases, the directive gain increases.

Sidelobes

No antenna is able to radiate all the energy in one preferred direction. Some is inevitably radiated in other directions. These smaller peaks are referred to as **sidelobes**, commonly specified in dB down from the main lobe.

Nulls

In an antenna radiation pattern, a **null** is a zone in which the effective radiated power is at a minimum. A null often has a narrow directivity angle compared to that of the main beam. Thus, the null is useful for several purposes, such as suppression of interfering signals in a given direction.

Polarization

Polarization is defined as the orientation of the electric field of an electromagnetic wave. Polarization is in general described by an ellipse. Two special cases of elliptical polarization are **linear polarization** and **circular polarization**. The initial polarization of a radio wave is determined by the antenna.

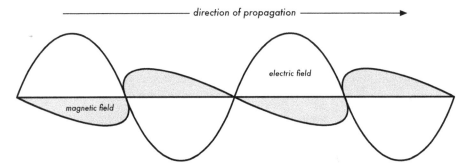

Figure 4.7: The electrical wave is perpendicular to magnetic wave, both of which are perpendicular to the direction of propagation.

With linear polarization, the electric field vector stays in the same plane all the time. The electric field may leave the antenna in a vertical orientation, a horizontal orientation, or at some angle between the two. **Vertically polarized** radiation is somewhat less affected by reflections over the transmission path. Omnidirectional antennas always have vertical polarization. With **horizontal polarization**, such reflections cause variations in received signal strength. Horizontal antennas are less likely to pick up man-made interference, which ordinarily is vertically polarized.

In circular polarization the electric field vector appears to be rotating with circular motion about the direction of propagation, making one full turn for each RF cycle. This rotation may be right-hand or left-hand. Choice of polarization is one of the design choices available to the RF system designer.

Polarization Mismatch

In order to transfer maximum power between a transmit and a receive antenna, both antennas must have the same spatial orientation, the same polarization sense, and the same axial ratio.

When the antennas are not aligned or do not have the same polarization, there will be a reduction in power transfer between the two antennas. This reduction in power transfer will reduce the overall system efficiency and performance.

When the transmit and receive antennas are both linearly polarized, physical antenna misalignment will result in a polarization mismatch loss, which can be determined using the following formula:

$$\text{Loss (dB)} = 20 \log (\cos \theta)$$

...where θ is the difference in alignment angle between the two antennas. For 15° the loss is approximately 0.3dB, for 30° we lose 1.25dB, for 45° we lose 3dB and for 90° we have an infinite loss.

In short, the greater the mismatch in polarization between a transmitting and receiving antenna, the greater the apparent loss. In the real world, a 90° mismatch in polarization is quite large but not infinite. Some antennas, such as yagis or can antennas, can be simply rotated 90° to match the polarization of the other end of the link. You can use the polarization effect to your advantage on a point-to-point link. Use a monitoring tool to observe interference from adjacent networks, and rotate one antenna until you see the lowest received signal. Then bring your link online and orient the other end to match polarization. This technique can sometimes be used to build stable links, even in noisy radio environments.

Front-to-back ratio

It is often useful to compare the ***front-to-back ratio*** of directional antennas. This is the ratio of the maximum directivity of an antenna to its directivity in the opposite direction. For example, when the radiation pattern is plotted on a relative dB scale, the front-to-back ratio is the difference in dB between the level of the maximum radiation in the forward direction and the level of radiation at 180 degrees.

This number is meaningless for an omnidirectional antenna, but it gives you an idea of the amount of power directed forward on a very directional antenna.

Types of Antennas

A classification of antennas can be based on:

• **Frequency and size**. Antennas used for HF are different from antennas used for VHF, which in turn are different from antennas for microwave. The wavelength is different at different frequencies, so the antennas must be different in size to radiate signals at the correct wavelength. We are particularly interested in antennas working in the microwave range, especially in the 2.4 GHz and 5 GHz frequencies. At 2.4 GHz the wavelength is 12.5 cm, while at 5 GHz it is 6 cm.

• **Directivity.** Antennas can be omnidirectional, sectorial or directive. *Omnidirectional antennas* radiate roughly the same pattern all around the antenna in a complete 360° pattern. The most popular types of omnidirectional antennas are the *dipole* and the *ground plane*. *Sectorial antennas* radiate primarily in a specific area. The beam can be as wide as 180 degrees, or as narrow as 60 degrees. *Directional* or *directive antennas* are antennas in which the beamwidth is much narrower than in sectorial antennas. They have the highest gain and are therefore used for long distance links. Types of directive antennas are the Yagi, the biquad, the horn, the helicoidal, the patch antenna, the parabolic dish, and many others.

• **Physical construction.** Antennas can be constructed in many different ways, ranging from simple wires, to parabolic dishes, to coffee cans.

When considering antennas suitable for 2.4 GHz WLAN use, another classification can be used:

• **Application**. Access points tend to make point-to-multipoint networks, while remote links are point-to-point. Each of these suggest different types of antennas for their purpose. Nodes that are used for multipoint access will likely use omni antennas which radiate equally in all directions, or sectorial antennas which focus into a small area. In the point-to-point case, antennas are used to connect two single locations together. Directive antennas are the primary choice for this application.

A brief list of common type of antennas for the 2.4 GHz frequency is presented now, with a short description and basic information about their characteristics.

1/4 wavelength ground plane

The 1/4 wavelength ground plane antenna is very simple in its construction and is useful for communications when size, cost and ease of construction are important. This antenna is designed to transmit a vertically polarized signal. It consists of a   1/4 wave element as half-dipole and three or four 1/4 wavelength ground elements bent 30 to 45 degrees down. This set of   elements, called radials, is known as a ground plane.

Figure 4.8: Quarter wavelength ground plane antenna.

This is a simple and effective antenna that can capture a signal equally from all directions. To increase the gain, the signal can be flattened out to take away focus from directly above and below, and providing more focus on the horizon. The vertical beamwidth represents the degree of flatness in the focus. This is useful in a Point-to-Multipoint situation, if all the other antennas are also at the same height. The gain of this antenna is in the order of 2 - 4 dBi.

Yagi antenna

A basic Yagi consists of a certain number of straight elements, each measuring approximately half wavelength. The driven or active element of a Yagi is the equivalent of a center-fed, half-wave dipole antenna. Parallel to the driven element, and approximately 0.2 to 0.5 wavelength on either side of it, are straight rods or wires called reflectors and directors, or simply passive elements. A reflector is placed behind the driven element and is slightly longer than half wavelength; a director is placed in front of the driven element and is slightly shorter than half wavelength. A typical Yagi has one reflector and one or more directors. The antenna propagates electromagnetic field energy in the direction running from the driven element toward the directors, and is most sensitive to incoming electromagnetic field energy in this same direction. The more directors a Yagi has, the greater the gain. As more directors are added to a Yagi, it therefore becomes longer. Following is the photo of a Yagi antenna with 6 directors and one reflector.

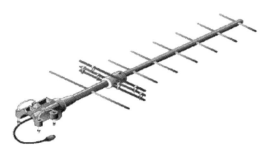

Figure 4.9: A Yagi antenna.

Yagi antennas are used primarily for Point-to-Point links, have a gain from 10 to 20 dBi and a horizontal beamwidth of 10 to 20 degrees.

Horn

The horn antenna derives its name from the characteristic flared appearance. The flared portion can be square, rectangular, cylindrical or conical. The direction of maximum radiation corresponds with the axis of the horn. It is easily fed with a waveguide, but can be fed with a coaxial cable and a proper transition.

Figure 4.10: Feed horn made from a food can.

Horn antennas are commonly used as the active element in a dish antenna. The horn is pointed toward the center of the dish reflector. The use of a horn, rather than a dipole antenna or any other type of antenna, at the focal point of the dish minimizes loss of energy around the edges of the dish reflector. At 2.4 GHz, a simple horn antenna made with a tin can has a gain in the order of 10 - 15 dBi.

Parabolic Dish

Antennas based on parabolic reflectors are the most common type of directive antennas when a high gain is required. The main advantage is that they can be made to have gain and directivity as large as required. The main disadvantage is that big dishes are difficult to mount and are likely to have a large windage.

Figure 4.11: A solid dish antenna.

Dishes up to one meter are usually made from solid material. Aluminum is frequently used for its weight advantage, its durability and good electrical characteristics. Windage increases rapidly with dish size and soon becomes a severe problem. Dishes which have a reflecting surface that uses an open mesh are frequently used. These have a poorer front-to-back ratio, but are safer to use and easier to build. Copper, aluminum, brass, galvanized steel and iron are suitable mesh materials.

BiQuad

The BiQuad antenna is simple to build and offers good directivity and gain for Point-to-Point communications. It consists of a two squares of the same size of 1/4 wavelength as a radiating element and of a metallic plate or grid as reflector. This antenna has a beamwidth of about 70 degrees and a gain in the order of 10-12 dBi. It can be used as stand-alone antenna or as feeder for a Parabolic Dish. The polarization is such that looking at the antenna from the front, if the squares are placed side by side the polarization is vertical.

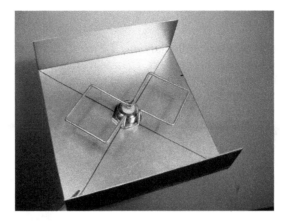

Figure 4.12: The BiQuad.

Other Antennas

Many other types of antennas exist and new ones are created following the advances in technology.

- Sector or Sectorial antennas: they are widely used in cellular telephony infrastructure and are usually built adding a reflective plate to one or more phased dipoles. Their horizontal beamwidth can be as wide as 180 degrees, or as narrow as 60 degrees, while the vertical is usually much narrower. Composite antennas can be built with many Sectors to cover a wider horizontal range (multisectorial antenna).

- Panel or Patch antennas: they are solid flat panels used for indoor coverage, with a gain up to 20 dB.

Reflector theory

The basic property of a perfect parabolic reflector is that it converts a spherical wave irradiating from a point source placed at the focus into a plane wave. Conversely, all the energy received by the dish from a distant source is reflected to a single point at the focus of the dish. The position of the focus, or focal length, is given by:

$$f = \frac{D^2}{16 \times c}$$

...where D is the dish diameter and c is the depth of the parabola at its center.

The size of the dish is the most important factor since it determines the maximum gain that can be achieved at the given frequency and the resulting beamwidth. The gain and beamwidth obtained are given by:

$$\text{Gain} = \frac{(\pi \times D)^2}{\lambda^2} \times n$$

$$\text{Beamwidth} = \frac{70 \lambda}{D}$$

...where D is the dish diameter and n is the efficiency. The efficiency is determined mainly by the effectiveness of illumination of the dish by the feed, but also by other factors. Each time the diameter of a dish is doubled, the gain is four times, or 6 dB, greater. If both stations double the size of their dishes, signal strength can be increased of 12 dB, a very substantial gain. An efficiency of 50% can be assumed when hand-building the antenna.

The ratio f / D (focal length/diameter of the dish) is the fundamental factor governing the design of the feed for a dish. The ratio is directly related to the beamwidth of the feed necessary to illuminate the dish effectively. Two dishes of the same diameter but different focal lengths require different design of feed if both are to be illuminated efficiently. The value of 0.25 corresponds to the common focal-plane dish in which the focus is in the same plane as the rim of the dish.

Amplifiers

As mentioned earlier, antennas do not actually create power. They simply direct all available power into a particular pattern. By using a ***power amplifier***, you can use DC power to augment your available signal. An amplifier connects between the radio transmitter and the antenna, and has an additional lead that connects to a power source. Amplifiers are available that work at 2.4 GHz, and can add several Watts of power to your transmission. These devices sense when an attached radio is transmitting, and quickly power up and amplify the signal. They then switch off again when transmission ends. When receiving, they also add amplification to the signal before sending it to the radio.

Unfortunately, simply adding amplifiers will not magically solve all of your networking problems. We do not discuss power amplifiers at length in this book because there are a number of significant drawbacks to using them:

- **They are expensive**. Amplifiers must work at relatively wide bandwidths at 2.4 GHz, and must switch quickly enough to work for Wi-Fi applications.

These amplifiers do exist, but they tend to cost several hundred dollars per unit.

- **You will need at least two**. Whereas antennas provide reciprocal gain that benefits both sides of a connection, amplifiers work best at amplifying a transmitted signal. If you only add an amplifier to one end of a link with insufficient antenna gain, it will likely be able to be heard but will not be able to hear the other end.

- **They provide no additional directionality.** Adding antenna gain provides both gain and directionality benefits to both ends of the link. They not only improve the available amount of signal, but tend to reject noise from other directions. Amplifiers blindly amplify both desired and interfering signals, and can make interference problems worse.

- **Amplifiers generate noise for other users of the band.** By increasing your output power, you are creating a louder source of noise for other users of the unlicensed band. This may not be much of an issue today in rural areas, but it can cause big problems in populated areas. Conversely, adding antenna gain will improve your link and can actually decrease the noise level for your neighbors.

- **Using amplifiers probably isn't legal.** Every country imposes power limits on use of unlicensed spectrum. Adding an antenna to a highly amplified signal will likely cause the link to exceed legal limits.

Using amplifiers is often compared to the inconsiderate neighbor who wants to listen to the radio outside their home, and so turns it up to full volume. They might even "improve" reception by pointing their speakers out the window. While they may now be able to hear the radio, so must everyone else on the block. This approach may scale to exactly one user, but what happens when the neighbors decide to do the same thing with their radios? Using amplifiers for a wireless link causes roughly the same effect at 2.4 GHz. Your link may "work better" for the moment, but you will have problems when other users of the band decide to use amplifiers of their own.

By using higher gain antennas rather than amplifiers, you avoid all of these problems. Antennas cost far less than amps, and can improve a link simply by changing the antenna on one end. Using more sensitive radios and good quality cable also helps significantly on long distance shots. These techniques are unlikely to cause problems for other users of the band, and so we recommend pursuing them before adding amplifiers.

Practical antenna designs

The cost of 2.4 GHz antennas has fallen dramatically since the introduction of 802.11b. Innovative designs use simpler parts and fewer materials to achieve impressive gain with relatively little machining. Unfortunately, availability of good antennas is still limited in many areas of the world, and importing them can be prohibitively expensive. While actually designing an antenna can be a complex and error-prone process, constructing antennas from locally available components is very straightforward, and can be a lot of fun. We present four practical antenna designs that can be built for very little money.

USB dongle as dish feed

Possibly the simplest antenna design is the use of a parabola to direct the output of a USB wireless device (known in networking circles as a ***USB dongle***). By placing the internal dipole antenna present in USB wireless dongles at the focus of a parabolic dish, you can provide significant gain without the need to solder or even open the wireless device itself. Many kinds of parabolic dishes will work, including satellite dishes, television antennas, and even metal cookware (such as a wok, round lid, or strainer). As a bonus, inexpensive and lossless USB cable is then used to feed the antenna, eliminating the need for expensive coaxial cable or Heliax.

To build a USB dongle parabolic, you will need to find the orientation and location of the dipole inside the dongle. Most devices orient the dipole to be parallel with the short edge of the dongle, but some will mount the dipole perpendicular to the short edge. You can either open the dongle and look for yourself, or simply try the dongle in both positions to see which provides more gain.

To test the antenna, point it at an access point several meters away, and connect the USB dongle to a laptop. Using the laptop's client driver or a tool such as Netstumbler (see **Chapter 6**), observe the received signal strength of the access point. Now, slowly move the dongle in relation to the parabolic while watching the signal strength meter. You should see a significant improvement in gain (20 dB or more) when you find the proper position. The proper position will vary depending on the shape of the parabola and the construction of the USB dongle. Try various positions while watching your signal strength meter until you find the optimum location.

Once the best location is found, securely fix the dongle in place. You will need to waterproof the dongle and cable if the antenna is used outdoors. Use a silicone compound or a piece of PVC tubing to seal the electronics against the weather. Many USB-fed parabolic designs and ideas are documented online at *http://www.usbwifi.orcon.net.nz/* .

Collinear omni

This antenna is very simple to build, requiring just a piece of wire, an N socket and a square metallic plate. It can be used for indoor or outdoor point-to-multipoint short distance coverage. The plate has a hole drilled in the middle to accommodate an N type chassis socket that is screwed into place. The wire is soldered to the center pin of the N socket and has coils to separate the active phased elements. Two versions of the antenna are possible: one with two phased elements and two coils and another with four phased elements and four coils. For the short antenna the gain will be around 5 dBi, while the long one with four elements will have 7 to 9 dBi of gain. We are going to describe how to build the long antenna only.

Parts list and tools required

- One screw-on N-type female connector
- 50 cm of copper or brass wire of 2 mm of diameter
- 10x10 cm or greater square metallic plate

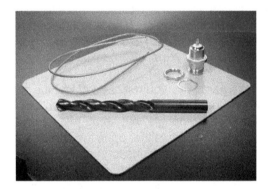

Figure 4.13: 10 cm x 10 cm aluminum plate.

- Ruler
- Pliers
- File
- Soldering iron and solder
- Drill with a set of bits for metal (including a 1.5 cm diameter bit)
- A piece of pipe or a drill bit with a diameter of 1 cm
- Vice or clamp
- Hammer
- Spanner or monkey wrench

Construction

1. Straighten the wire using the vice.

Figure 4.14: Make the wire as straight as you can.

2. With a marker, draw a line at 2.5 cm starting from one end of the wire. On this line, bend the wire at 90 degrees with the help of the vice and of the hammer.

Figure 4.15: Gently tap the wire to make a sharp bend.

3. Draw another line at a distance of 3.6 cm from the bend. Using the vice and the hammer, bend once again the wire over this second line at 90 degrees, in the opposite direction to the first bend but in the same plane. The wire should look like a 'Z'.

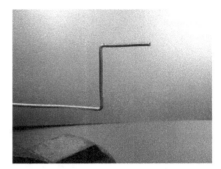

Figure 4.16: Bend the wire into a "Z" shape.

4. We will now twist the 'Z' portion of the wire to make a coil with a diameter of 1 cm. To do this, we will use the pipe or the drill bit and curve the wire around it, with the help of the vice and of the pliers.

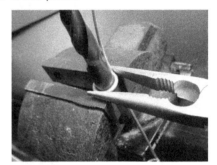

Figure 4.17: Bend the wire around the drill bit to make a coil.

The coil will look like this:

Figure 4.18: The completed coil.

5. You should make a second coil at a distance of 7.8 cm from the first one. Both coils should have the same turning direction and should be placed on the same side of the wire. Make a third and a fourth coil following the

same procedure, at the same distance of 7.8 cm one from each other. Trim the last phased element at a distance of 8.0 cm from the fourth coil.

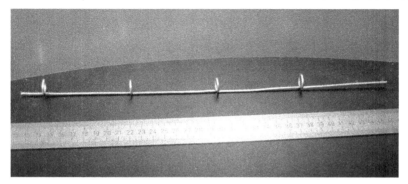

Figure 4.19: Try to keep it as straight possible.

If the coils have been made correctly, it should now be possible to insert a pipe through all the coils as shown.

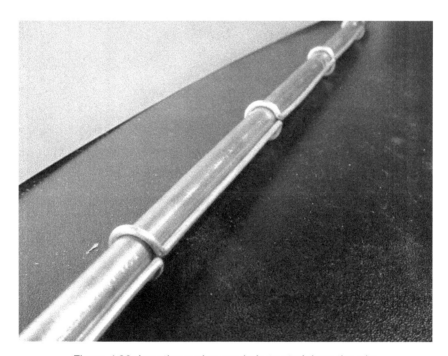

Figure 4.20: Inserting a pipe can help to straighten the wire.

6. With a marker and a ruler, draw the diagonals on the metallic plate, finding its center. With a small diameter drill bit, make a pilot hole at the center of the plate. Increase the diameter of the hole using bits with an increasing diameter.

Figure 4.21: Drilling the hole in the metal plate.

The hole should fit the N connector exactly. Use a file if needed.

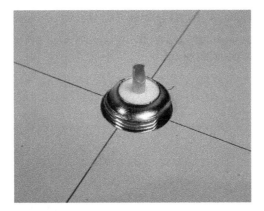

Figure 4.22: The N connector should fit snugly in the hole.

7. To have an antenna impedance of 50 Ohms, it is important that the visible surface of the internal insulator of the connector (the white area around the central pin) is at the same level as the surface of the plate. For this reason, cut 0.5 cm of copper pipe with an external diameter of 2 cm, and place it between the connector and the plate.

Figure 4.23: Adding a copper pipe spacer helps to match the impedance of the antenna to 50 Ohms.

8. Screw the nut to the connector to fix it firmly on the plate using the spanner.

Figure 4.24: Secure the N connector tightly to the plate.

9. Smooth with the file the side of the wire which is 2.5 cm long, from the first coil. Tin the wire for around 0.5 cm at the smoothed end helping yourself with the vice.

Figure 4.25: Add a little solder to the end of the wire to "tin" it prior to soldering.

10. With the soldering iron, tin the central pin of the connector. Keeping the wire vertical with the pliers, solder its tinned side in the hole of the central pin. The first coil should be at 3.0 cm from the plate.

Figure 4.26: The first coil should start 3.0 cm from the surface of the plate.

11. We are now going to stretch the coils extending the total vertical length of the wire. Using the use the vice and the pliers, you should pull the cable so that the final length of the coil is of 2.0 cm.

Figure 4.27: Stretching the coils. Be very gentle and try not to scrape the surface of the wire with the pliers.

12. Repeat the same procedure for the other three coils, stretching their length to 2.0 cm.

Figure 4.28: Repeat the stretching procedure for all of the remaining coils.

13. At the end the antenna should measure 42.5 cm from the plate to the top.

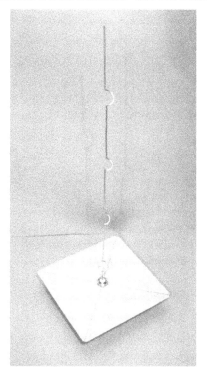

Figure 4.29: The finished antenna should be 42.5 cm from the plate to the end of the wire.

14. If you have a spectrum analyzer with a tracking generator and a directional coupler, you can check the curve of the reflected power of the antenna. The picture below shows the display of the spectrum analyzer.

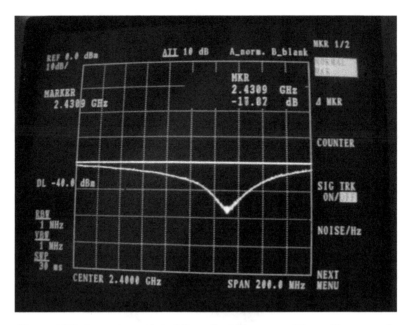

Figure 4.30: A spectrum plot of the reflected power of the collinear omni.

If you intend to use this antenna outside, you will need to weatherproof it. The simplest method is to enclose the whole thing in a large piece of PVC pipe closed with caps. Cut a hole at the bottom for the transmission line, and seal the antenna shut with silicone or PVC glue.

Cantenna

The waveguide antenna, sometimes called a Cantenna, uses a tin can as a waveguide and a short wire soldered on an N connector as a probe for coaxial-cable-to-waveguide transition. It can be easily built at just the price of the connector, recycling a food, juice, or other tin can. It is a directional antenna, useful for short to medium distance point-to-point links. It may be also used as a feeder for a parabolic dish or grid.

Not all cans are good for building an antenna because there are dimensional constraints.

1. The acceptable values for the diameter D of the feed are between 0.60 and 0.75 wavelength in air at the design frequency. At 2.44 GHz the wavelength λ is 12.2 cm, so the can diameter should be in the range of 7.3 - 9.2 cm.

2. The length L of the can preferably should be at least 0.75 λ_G , where λ_G is the guide wavelength and is given by:

$$\lambda_G = \frac{\lambda}{\text{sqrt}(1\ -\ (\lambda\ /\ 1.706D)^2)}$$

For D = 7.3 cm, we need a can of at least 56.4 cm, while for D = 9.2 cm we need a can of at least 14.8 cm. Generally the smaller the diameter, the longer the can should be. For our example, we will use oil cans that have a diameter of 8.3 cm and a height of about 21 cm.

3. The probe for coaxial cable to waveguide transition should be positioned at a distance S from the bottom of the can, given by:

$$S\ =\ 0.25\ \lambda_G$$

Its length should be 0.25 λ, which at 2.44 GHz corresponds to 3.05 cm.

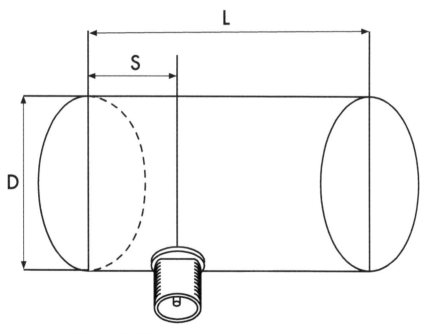

Figure 4.31: Dimensional constraints on the cantenna

The gain for this antenna will be in the order of 10 to 14 dBi, with a beam-width of around 60 degrees.

Figure 4.32: The finished cantenna.

Parts list

- one screw-on N-type female connector
- 4 cm of copper or brass wire of 2 mm of diameter
- an oil can of 8.3 cm of diameter and 21 cm of height

Figure 4.33: Parts needed for the can antenna.

Tools required

- Can opener
- Ruler
- Pliers
- File
- Soldering iron
- Solder
- Drill with a set of bits for metal (with a 1.5 cm diameter bit)
- Vice or clamp
- Spanner or monkey wrench
- Hammer
- Punch

Construction

1. With the can opener, carefully remove the upper part of the can.

Figure 4.34: Be careful of sharp edges when opening the can.

The circular disk has a very sharp edge. Be careful when handling it! Empty the can and wash it with soap. If the can contained pineapple, cookies, or some other tasty treat, have a friend serve the food.

2. With the ruler, measure 6.2 cm from the bottom of the can and draw a point. Be careful to measure from the inner side of the bottom. Use a punch (or a small drill bit or a Phillips screwdriver) and a hammer to mark the point. This makes it easier to precisely drill the hole. Be careful not to

change the shape of the can doing this by inserting a small block of wood or other object in the can before tapping it.

Figure 4.35: Mark the hole before drilling.

3. With a small diameter drill bit, make a hole at the center of the plate. Increase the diameter of the hole using bits with an increasing diameter. The hole should fit exactly the N connector. Use the file to smooth the border of the hole and to remove the painting around it in order to ensure a better electrical contact with the connector.

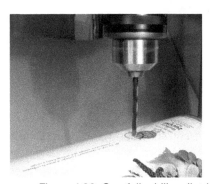 

Figure 4.36: Carefully drill a pilot hole, then use a larger bit to finish the job.

4. Smooth with the file one end of the wire. Tin the wire for around 0.5 cm at the same end helping yourself with the vice.

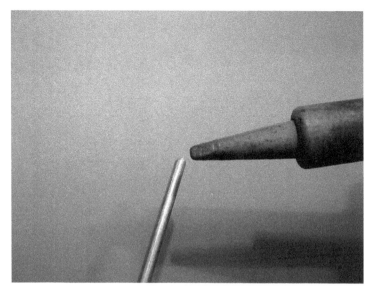

Figure 4.37: Tin the end of the wire before soldering.

5. With the soldering iron, tin the central pin of the connector. Keeping the wire vertical with the pliers, solder its tinned side in the hole of the central pin.

Figure 4.38: Solder the wire to the gold cup on the N connector.

6. Insert a washer and gently screw the nut onto the connector. Trim the wire at 3.05 cm measured from the bottom part of the nut.

Figure 4.39: The length of the wire is critical.

7. Unscrew the nut from the connector, leaving the washer in place. Insert the connector into the hole of the can. Screw the nut on the connector from inside the can.

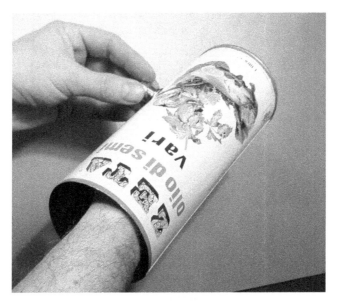

Figure 4.40: Assemble the antenna.

8. Use the pliers or the monkey wrench to screw firmly the nut on the connector. You are done!

Figure 4.41: Your finished cantenna.

As with the other antenna designs, you should make a weatherproof enclosure for the antenna if you wish to use it outdoors. PVC works well for the can antenna. Insert the entire can in a large PVC tube, and seal the ends with caps and glue. You will need to drill a hole in the side of the tube to accommodate the N connector on the side of the can.

Cantenna as dish feed

As with the USB dongle parabolic, you can use the cantenna design as a feeder for significantly higher gain. Mount the can on the parabolic with the opening of the can pointed at the center of the dish. Use the technique described in the USB dongle antenna example (watching signal strength changes over time) to find the optimum location of the can for the dish you are using.

By using a well-built cantenna with a properly tuned parabolic, you can achieve an overall antenna gain of 30dBi or more. As the size of the parabolic increases, so does the potential gain and directivity of the antenna. With very large parabolas, you can achieve significantly higher gain.

For example, in 2005, a team of college students successfully established a link from Nevada to Utah in the USA. The link crossed a distance of over 200 kilometers! The wireless enthusiasts used a 3.5 meter satellite dish to establish an 802.11b link that ran at 11 Mbps, without using an amplifier. Details about this achievement can be found at *http://www.wifi-shootout.com/*

NEC2

NEC2 stands for **Numerical Electromagnetics Code** (version 2) and is a free antenna modeling package. NEC2 lets you build an antenna model in 3D, and then analyzes the antenna's electromagnetic response. It was developed more than ten years ago and has been compiled to run on many different computer systems. NEC2 is particularly effective for analyzing wire-grid models, but also has some surface patch modeling capability.

The antenna design is described in a text file, and then the model is built using this text description. An antenna described in NEC2 is given in two parts: its **structure** and a sequence of **controls**. The structure is simply a numerical description of where the different parts of the antenna are located, and how the wires are connected up. The controls tell NEC where the RF source is connected. Once these are defined, the transmitting antenna is then modeled. Because of the reciprocity theorem the transmitting gain pattern is the same as the receiving one, so modeling the transmission characteristics is sufficient to understand the antenna's behavior completely.

A frequency or range of frequencies of the RF signal must be specified. The next important element is the character of the ground. The conductivity of the earth varies from place to place, but in many cases it plays a vital role in determining the antenna gain pattern.

To run NEC2 on Linux, install the NEC2 package from the URL below. To launch it, type **nec2** and enter the input and output filenames. It is also worth installing the **xnecview** package for structure verification and radiation pattern plotting. If all went well you should have a file containing the output. This can be broken up into various sections, but for a quick idea of what it represents a gain pattern can be plotted using xnecview. You should see the expected pattern, horizontally omnidirectional, with a peak at the optimum angle of takeoff. Windows and Mac versions are also available.

The advantage of NEC2 is that we can get an idea of how the antenna works before building it, and how we can modify the design in order to get the maximum gain. It is a complex tool and requires some research to learn how to use it effectively, but it is an invaluable tool for antenna designers.

NEC2 is available from *http://www.nec2.org/*

Online documentation can be obtained from the "Unofficial NEC Home Page" at *http://www.nittany-scientific.com/nec/* .

5

Networking Hardware

In the last couple of years, an unprecedented surge in interest in wireless networking hardware has brought a huge variety of inexpensive equipment to the market. So much variety, in fact, that it would be impossible to catalog every available component. In this chapter, we'll look at the sort of features and attributes that are desirable in a wireless component, and see several examples of commercial and DIY gear that has worked well in the past.

Wired wireless

With a name like "wireless", you may be surprised at how many wires are involved in making a simple point-to-point link. A wireless node consists of many components, which must all be connected to each other with appropriate cabling. You obviously need at least one computer connected to an Ethernet network, and a wireless router or bridge attached to the same network. Radio components need to be connected to antennas, but along the way they may need to interface with an amplifier, lightning arrestor, or other device. Many components require power, either via an AC mains line or using a DC transformer. All of these components use various sorts of connectors, not to mention a wide variety of cable types and thicknesses.

Now multiply those cables and connectors by the number of nodes you will bring online, and you may well be wondering why this stuff is referred to as "wireless". The diagram on the next page will give you some idea of the cabling required for a typical point-to-point link. Note that this diagram is not to scale, nor is it necessarily the best choice of network design. But it will introduce you to many common interconnects and components that you will likely encounter in the real world.

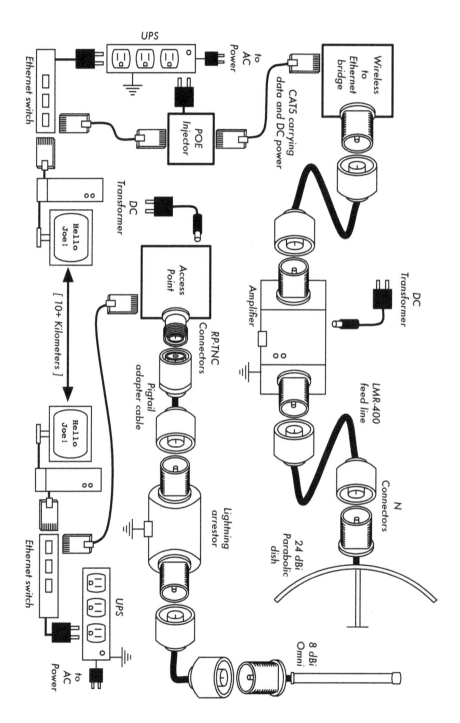

Figure 5.1: Component interconnects.

While the actual components used will vary from node to node, every installation will incorporate these parts:

1. An existing computer or network connected to an Ethernet switch.

2. A device that connects that network to a wireless device (a wireless router, bridge, or repeater).

3. An antenna that is connected via feed line, or is integrated into the wireless device itself.

4. Electrical components consisting of power supplies, conditioners, and lightning arrestors.

The actual selection of hardware should be determined by establishing the requirements for the project, determining the available budget, and verifying that the project is feasible using the available resources (including providing for spares and ongoing maintenance costs). As discussed in **Chapter 1**, establishing the scope of your project is critical before any purchasing decisions are made.

Choosing wireless components

Unfortunately, in a world of competitive hardware manufacturers and limited budgets, the price tag is the single factor that usually receives the most attention. The old saying that "you get what you pay for" often holds true when buying high tech equipment, but should not be considered an absolute truth. While the price tag is an important part of any purchasing decision, it is vital to understand precisely what you get for your money so you can make a choice that fits your needs.

When comparing wireless equipment for use in your network, be sure to consider these variables:

- **Interoperability.** Will the equipment you are considering work with equipment from other manufacturers? If not, is this an important factor for this segment of your network? If the gear in question supports an open protocol (such as 802.11b/g), then it will likely interoperate with equipment from other sources.

- **Range.** As we saw in **Chapter 4**, range is not something inherent in a particular piece of equipment. A device's range depends on the antenna connected to it, the surrounding terrain, the characteristics of the device at the other end of the link, and other factors. Rather than relying on a semi-fictional "range" rating supplied by the manufacturer, it is more useful to know the *transmission power* of the radio as well as the *antenna gain* (if an antenna is included). With this information, you can calculate the theoretical range as described in **Chapter 3**.

- **Radio sensitivity.** How sensitive is the radio device at a given bit rate? The manufacturer should supply this information, at least at the fastest and slowest speeds. This can be used as a measure of the quality of the hardware, as well as allow you to complete a link budget calculation. As we saw in **Chapter 3**, a lower number is better for radio sensitivity.

- **Throughput.** Manufacturers consistently list the highest possible bit rate as the "speed" of their equipment. Keep in mind that the radio symbol rate (eg. 54 Mbps) is never the actual throughput rating of the device (eg. about 22 Mbps for 802.11g). If throughput rate information is not available for the device you are evaluating, a good rule of thumb is to divide the device "speed" by two, and subtract 20% or so. When in doubt, perform throughput testing on an evaluation unit before committing to purchasing a large amount of equipment that has no official throughput rating.

- **Required accessories.** To keep the initial price tag low, vendors often leave out accessories that are required for normal use. Does the price tag include all power adapters? (DC supplies are typically included; power over Ethernet injectors typically are not. Double-check input voltages as well, as equipment is often provided with a US-centric power supply). What about pigtails, adapters, cables, antennas, and radio cards? If you intend to use it outdoors, does the device include a weatherproof case?

- **Availability.** Will you be able to easily replace failed components? Can you order the part in large quantity, should your project require it? What is the projected life span of this particular product, both in terms of useful running time in-the-field and likely availability from the vendor?

- **Other factors.** Be sure that other needed features are provided for to meet your particular needs. For example, does the device include an external antenna connector? If so, what type is it? Are there user or throughput limits imposed by software, and if so, what is the cost to increase these limits? What is the physical form factor of the device? How much power does it consume? Does it support POE as a power source? Does the device provide encryption, NAT, bandwidth monitoring tools, or other features critical to the intended network design?

By answering these questions first, you will be able to make intelligent buying decisions when it comes time to choose networking hardware. It is unlikely that you will be able to answer every possible question before buying gear, but if you prioritize the questions and press the vendor to answer them before committing to a purchase, you will make the best use of your budget and build a network of components that are well suited to your needs.

Commercial vs. DIY solutions

Your network project will almost certainly consist of components purchased from vendors as well as parts that are sourced or even fabricated locally. This is a basic economic truth in most areas of the world. At this stage of human technology, global distribution of information is quite trivial compared to global distribution of goods. In many regions, importing every component needed to build a network is prohibitively expensive for all but the largest budgets. You can save considerable money in the short term by finding local sources for parts and labor, and only importing components that must be purchased.

Of course, there is a limit to how much work can be done by any individual or group in a given amount of time. To put it another way, by importing technology, you can exchange money for equipment that can solve a particular problem in a comparatively short amount of time. The art of building local telecommunications infrastructure lies in finding the right balance of money to effort needed to be expended to solve the problem at hand.

Some components, such as radio cards and antenna feed line, are likely far too complex to consider having them fabricated locally. Other components, such as antennas and towers, are relatively simple and can be made locally for a fraction of the cost of importing. Between these extremes lie the communication devices themselves.

By using off-the-shelf radio cards, motherboards, and other components, you can build devices that provide features comparable (or even superior) to most commercial implementations. Combining open hardware platforms with open source software can yield significant "bang for the buck" by providing custom, robust solutions for very low cost.

This is not to say that commercial equipment is inferior to a do-it-yourself solution. By providing so-called "turn-key solutions", manufacturers not only save development time, but they can also allow relatively unskilled people to install and maintain equipment. The chief strengths of commercial solutions are that they provide **support** and a (usually limited) **equipment warranty**. They also provide a **consistent platform** that tends to lead to very stable, often interchangeable network installations.

If a piece of equipment simply doesn't work or is difficult to configure or troubleshoot, a good manufacturer will assist you. Should the equipment fail in normal use (barring extreme damage, such as a lightning strike) then the manufacturer will typically replace it. Most will provide these services for a limited time as part of the purchase price, and many offer support and warranty for an extended period for a monthly fee. By providing a consistent platform, it is simple to keep spares on hand and simply "swap out" equipment that fails in the field, without the need for a technician to configure equipment on-site. Of course, all of this comes at comparatively higher initial cost for the equipment compared to off-the-shelf components.

From a network architect's point of view, the three greatest hidden risks when choosing commercial solutions are **vendor lock-in**, **discontinued product lines**, and **ongoing licensing costs**.

It can be costly to allow the lure of ill-defined new "features" drive the development of your network. Manufacturers will frequently provide features that are incompatible with their competition by design, and then issue marketing materials to convince you that you simply cannot live without them (regardless of whether the feature contributes to the solution of your communications problem). As you begin to rely on these features, you will likely decide to continue purchasing equipment from the same manufacturer in the future. This is the essence of vendor lock-in. If a large institution uses a significant amount of proprietary equipment, it is unlikely that they will simply abandon it to use a different vendor. Sales teams know this (and indeed, some rely on it) and use vendor lock-in as a strategy for price negotiations.

When combined with vendor lock-in, a manufacturer may eventually decide to discontinue a product line, regardless of its popularity. This ensures that customers, already reliant on the manufacturer's proprietary features, will purchase the newest (and nearly always more expensive) model. The long term effects of vendor lock-in and discontinued products are difficult to estimate when planning a networking project, but should be kept in mind.

Finally, if a particular piece of equipment uses proprietary computer code, you may need to license use of that code on an ongoing basis. The cost of these licenses may vary depending on features provided, number of users, connection speed, or other factors. If the license fee is unpaid, some equipment is designed to simply stop working until a valid, paid-up license is provided! Be sure that you understand the terms of use for any equipment you purchase, including ongoing licensing fees.

By using generic equipment that supports open standards and open source software, you can avoid some of these pitfalls. For example, it is very difficult to become locked-in to a vendor that uses open protocols (such as TCP/IP over 802.11a/b/g). If you encounter a problem with the equipment or the vendor, you can always purchase equipment from a different vendor that will interoperate with what you have already purchased. It is for these reasons that we recommend using proprietary protocols and licensed spectrum **only** in cases where the open equivalent (such as 802.11a/b/g) is not technically feasible.

Likewise, while individual products can always be discontinued at any time, you can limit the impact this will have on your network by using generic components. For example, a particular motherboard may become unavailable on the market, but you may have a number of PC motherboards on hand that will perform effectively the same task. We will see some examples of how to use these generic components to build a complete wireless node later in this chapter.

Obviously, there should be no ongoing licensing costs involved with open source software (with the exception of a vendor providing extended support or some other service, without charging for the use of the software itself). There have occasionally been vendors who capitalize on the gift that open source programmers have given to the world by offering the code for sale on an ongoing licensed basis, thereby violating the terms of distribution set forth by the original authors. It would be wise to avoid such vendors, and to be suspicious of claims of "free software" that come with an ongoing license fee.

The disadvantage of using open source software and generic hardware is clearly the question of support. As problems with the network arise, you will need to solve those problems for yourself. This is often accomplished by consulting free online resources and search engines, and applying code patches directly. If you do not have team members who are competent and dedicated to designing a solution to your communications problem, then it can take a considerable amount of time to get a network project off the ground. Of course, there is never a guarantee that simply "throwing money at the problem" will solve it either. While we provide many examples of how to do much of the work yourself, you may find this work very challenging. You will need to find the balance of commercial solutions and the do-it-yourself approach that works for project.

In short, always define the scope of your network first, identify the resources you can bring to bear on the problem, and allow the selection of equipment to naturally emerge from the results. Consider commercial solutions as well as open components, while keeping in mind the long-term costs of both.

When considering which equipment to use, always remember to compare the expected useful distance, reliability, and throughput, in addition to the price. Be sure to include any ongoing license fees when calculating the overall cost of the equipment. And finally, make sure that the radios you purchase operate in an unlicensed band where you are installing them, or if you must use licensed spectrum, that you have budget and permission to pay for the appropriate licenses.

Professional lightning protection

Lightning is a natural predator of wireless equipment. There are two different ways lightning can strike or damage equipment: direct hits or induction hits. Direct hits happen when lightning actually hits the tower or antenna. Induction hits are caused when lightning strikes near the tower. Imagine a negatively charged lightning bolt. Since like charges repel each other, that bolt will cause the electrons in the cables to move away from the strike, creating current on the lines. This can be much more current than the sensitive radio equipment can handle. Either type of strike will usually destroy unprotected equipment.

Figure 5.2: A tower with a heavy copper grounding wire.

Protecting wireless networks from lightning is not an exact science, and there is no guarantee that a lightning strike will not happen, even if every single precaution is taken. Many of the methods used will help prevent both direct and induction strikes. While it is not necessary to use every single lightning protection method, using more methods will help further protect the equipment. The amount of lightning historically observed within a service area will be the biggest guide to how much needs to be done.

Start at the very bottom of the tower. Remember, the bottom of the tower is below the ground. After the tower foundation is laid, but before the hole is backfilled, a ring of heavy braided ground wire should have been installed with the lead extending above ground surfacing near a tower leg. The wire should be American Wire Gauge (AWG) #4 or thicker. In addition, a backup ground or earthing rod should be driven into the ground, and a ground wire run from the rod to the lead from the buried ring.

It is important to note that not all steel conducts electricity the same way. Some types of steel act as better electrical conductors then others, and different surface coatings can also affect how tower steel handles electrical current. Stainless steel is one of the worst conductors, and rust proof coatings like galvanizing or paint lessen the conductivity of the steel. For this reason, a braided ground wire is run from the bottom of the tower all the way to the top. The bottom needs to be properly attached to the leads from both the ring and the backup ground rod. The top of the tower should have a lightning rod attached, and the top of that needs to be pointed. The finer and sharper the point, the more effective the rod will be. The braided ground wire from the bottom needs to be terminated at this grounding rod. It is very important to be sure that the ground wire is connected to the actual metal. Any sort of coating, such as paint, must be removed before the wire is attached. Once the connection is made, the exposed area can be repainted, covering the wire and connectors if necessary to save the tower from rust and other corrosion.

The above solution details the installation of the basic grounding system. It provides protection for the tower itself from direct hits, and installs the base system to which everything else will connect.

The ideal protection for indirect induction lightning strikes are gas tube arrestors at both ends of the cable. These arrestors need to be grounded directly to the ground wire installed on the tower if it is at the high end. The bottom end needs to be grounded to something electrically safe, like a ground plate or a copper pipe that is consistently full of water. It is important to make sure that the outdoor lightning arrestor is weatherproofed. Many arresters for coax cables are weatherproofed, while many arresters for CAT5 cable are not.

In the event that gas arrestors are not being used, and the cabling is coax based, then attaching one end of a wire to the shield of the cable and the other to the ground wire installed on the towers will provide some protection. This can provide a path for induction currents, and if the charge is weak enough, it will not affect the conductor wire of the cable. While this method is by no means as good of protection as using the gas arrestors, it is better then doing nothing at all.

Building an access point from a PC

Unlike consumer operating systems (such as Microsoft Windows), the GNU/Linux operating system gives a network administrator the potential for full access to the networking stack. One can access and manipulate network packets at any level from the data-link layer through the application layer. Routing decisions can be made based on any information contained in a network packet, from the routing addresses and ports to the contents of the data segment. A Linux-based access point can act as a router, bridge, firewall, VPN concentrator, application server, network monitor, or virtually any other networking role you can think of. It is freely available software, and requires no licensing fees. GNU/Linux is a very powerful tool that can fill a broad variety of roles in a network infrastructure.

Adding a wireless card and Ethernet device to a PC running Linux will give you a very flexible tool that can help you deliver bandwidth and manage your network for very little cost. The hardware could be anything from a recycled laptop or desktop machine to an embedded computer, such as a Linksys WRT54G or Metrix networking kit.

In this section we will see how to configure Linux in the following configurations:

• As a wireless access point with Masquerading/NAT and a wired connection to the Internet (also referred to as a wireless gateway).

• As a wireless access point that acts as a transparent bridge. The bridge can be used either as a simple access point, or as a repeater with 2 radios.

Consider these recipes as a starting point. By building on these simple examples, you can create a server that fits precisely into your network infrastructure.

Prerequisites

Before proceeding, you should already be familiar with Linux from a users perspective, and be capable of installing the Gnu/Linux distribution of your choice. A basic understanding of the command line interface (terminal) in Linux is also required.

You will need a computer with one or more wireless cards already installed, as well as a standard Ethernet interface. These examples use a specific card and driver, but there are a number of different cards that should work equally well. Wireless cards based on the Atheros and Prism chipsets work particularly well. These examples are based on Ubuntu Linux version 5.10 (Breezy Badger), with a wireless card that is supported by the HostAP or MADWiFi drivers. For more information about these drivers, see *http://hostap.epitest.fi/* and *http://madwifi.org/* .

The following software is required to complete these installations. It should be provided in your Linux distribution:

- Wireless Tools (iwconfig, iwlist commands)

- iptables firewall

- dnsmasq (caching DNS server and DHCP server)

The CPU power required depends on how much work needs to be done beyond simple routing and NAT. For many applications, a 133MHz 486 is perfectly capable of routing packets at wireless speeds. If you intend to use a lot of encryption (such as WEP or a VPN server), then you will need something faster. If you also want to run a caching server (such as Squid) then you will need a computer with plenty of fast disk space and RAM. A typical router that is only performing NAT will operate will with as little as 64MB of RAM and storage.

When building a machine that is intended to be part of your network infrastructure, keep in mind that hard drives have a limited lifespan compared to most other components. You can often use solid state storage, such as a flash disk, in place of a hard drive. This could be a USB flash drive (assuming your PC will boot from USB), or a Compact Flash card using a CF to IDE adapter. These adapters are quite inexpensive, and will make a CF card appear act like standard IDE hard drive. They can be used in any PC that supports IDE hard drives. Since they have no moving parts, they will operate for many years through a much wider range of temperatures than a hard disk will tolerate.

Scenario 1: Masquerading access point

This is the simplest of the scenarios, and is especially useful in situations where you want a single access point for an office setting. This is easiest in a situation where:

1. There is an existing dedicated firewall and gateway running Linux, and you just want to add a wireless interface.

2. You have an old refurbished computer or laptop available, and prefer to use that as an access point.

3. You require more power in terms of monitoring, logging and/or security than most commercial access points provide, but don't want to splurge on an enterprise access point.

4. You would like a single machine to act as 2 access points (and firewall) so that you can offer both a secure network access to the intranet, as well as open access to guests.

Initial setup

Start of with an already configured computer running GNU/Linux. This could be an Ubuntu Server installation, or Fedora Core. The computer must have at least 2 interfaces for this to work, and at least one of these interfaces should be wireless. The rest of this description assumes that your cabled Ethernet port (eth0) is connected to the Internet, and that there is a wireless interface (wlan0) that will provide the access point functionality.

To find out if your chipset supports master mode, try the following command as root:

```
# iwconfig wlan0 mode Master
```

...replacing wlan0 with the name of your interface.

If you get an error message, then your wireless card doesn't support access point mode. You can still try the same setup in Ad-hoc mode, which is supported by all chipsets. This requires that you to set all the laptops that are connecting to this "access point" into Ad-hoc mode as well, and may not work quite the way you are expecting. It is usually better to find a wireless card that will support AP mode. See the HostAP and MADWiFi websites mentioned earlier for a list of supported cards.

Before continuing, make sure dnsmasq is installed on your machine. You can use the graphical package manager of your distribution to install it. In Ubuntu you can simply run the following as root:

```
# apt-get install dnsmasq
```

Setting up the interfaces

Set up your server so that eth0 is connected to the Internet. Use the graphical configuration tool that came with your distribution.

If your Ethernet network uses DHCP, you could try the following command as root:

```
# dhclient eth0
```

You should receive an IP address and default gateway. Next, set your wireless interface to Master mode and give it a name of your choice:

```
# iwconfig wlan0 essid "my network" mode Master enc off
```

The **enc off** switch turns off WEP encryption. To enable WEP, add a hex-key string of the correct length:

```
# iwconfig wlan0 essid "my network" mode Master enc 1A2B3C4D5E
```

Alternately, you can use a readable string by starting with "s:"

```
# iwconfig wlan0 essid "my network" mode Master enc "s:apple"
```

Now give your wireless interface an IP address in a private subnet, but make sure it is not the same subnet as that of your Ethernet adapter:

```
# ifconfig wlan0 10.0.0.1 netmask 255.255.255.0 broadcast 10.0.0.255 up
```

Setting up masquerading in the kernel

In order for us to be able to translate addresses between the two interfaces on the computer, we need to enable masquerading (NAT) in the linux kernel. First we load the relevant kernel module:

```
# modprobe ipt_MASQUERADE
```

Now we will flush all existing firewall rules to ensure that the firewall is not blocking us from forwarding packets between the two interfaces. If you have an existing firewall running, make sure you know how to restore the existing rules later before proceeding.

```
# iptables -F
```

Enable the NAT functionality between the two interfaces

```
# iptables -t nat -A POSTROUTING -o eth0 -j MASQUERADE
```

Finally we need to enable the kernel to forward packets between interfaces:

```
# echo 1 > /proc/sys/net/ipv4/ip_forward
```

On Debian-based Linux distributions such as Ubuntu, this change can also be made by editing the file **/etc/network/options**, and be sure that **ip_forward** is set to **yes**:

```
ip_forward=yes
```

and then restarting the network interfaces with:

```
# /etc/init.d/network restart
```

or

```
# /etc/init.d/networking restart
```

Setting up the DHCP server

At this point we actually should have a working access point. It can be tested by connecting to the wireless network "my network" with a separate machine and giving that machine an address in the same address range as our wireless interface on the server (10.0.0.0/24 if you followed the examples). If you have enabled WEP, be sure to use the same key that you specified on the AP.

In order to make it easier for people to connect to the server without knowing the IP address range, we will set up a DHCP server to automatically hand out addresses to wireless clients.

We use the program dnsmasq for this purpose. As the name indicates, it provides a caching DNS server as well as a DHCP server. This program was developed especially for use with firewalls performing NAT. Having a caching DNS server is especially helpful if your Internet connection is a high-latency and/or low-bandwidth connection, such as a VSAT or dial-up. It means that many DNS queries can be resolved locally, saving a lot of traffic on the Internet connection, and also making the connection feel noticeably faster for those connecting.

Install dnsmasq with your distributions package manager. If dnsmasq is not available as a package, download the source code and install it manually. It is available from *http://www.thekelleys.org.uk/dnsmasq/doc.html*.

All that is required for us to run dnsmasq is to edit a few lines of the dnsmasq configuration file, **/etc/dnsmasq.conf**.

The configuration file is well commented, and has many options for various types of configuration. To get the basic DHCP server up and running we just need to uncomment and/or edit two lines.

Find the lines that starts:

```
interface=
```

...and make sure it reads:

```
interface=wlan0
```

...changing wlan0 to match name of your wireless interface. Then find the line that starts with:

```
#dhcp-range=
```

Uncomment the line and edit it to suit the match addresses being used, i.e.

```
dhcp-range=10.0.0.10,10.0.0.110,255.255.255.0,6h
```

Then save the file and start dnsmasq:

```
# /etc/init.d/dnsmasq start
```

That's it, you should now be able to connect to the server as an access point, and get an IP address using DHCP. This should let you connect to the Internet through the server.

Adding extra security: Setting up a Firewall

Once this is set up and tested, you can add extra firewall rules using whatever firewall tool is included in your distribution. Some typical front-ends for setting up firewall rules include:

- *firestarter* - a graphical client for Gnome, which requires that your server is running Gnome

- *knetfilter* – a graphical client for KDE, which requires that your server is running KDE

- *Shorewall* – a set of scripts and configuration files that will make it easier to setup an iptables firewall. There are also frontends for shorewall, such as webmin-shorewall

- *fwbuilder* - a powerful, but slightly complex graphical tool that will let you create iptables scripts on a machine separate from your server, and then transfer them to the server later. This does not require you to be running a graphical desktop on the server, and is a strong option for the security conscious.

Once everything is configured properly, make sure that all settings are reflected in the system startup scripts. This way, your changes will continue to work should the machine need to be rebooted.

Scenario 2: Transparent Bridging access point

This scenario can either be used for a two-radio repeater, or for an access point connected to an Ethernet. We use a bridge instead of routing when we want both interfaces on the access point to share the same subnet. This can be particularly useful in networks with multiple access points where we prefer to have a single, central firewall and perhaps authentication server. Because all clients share the same subnet they, can easily be managed with a single DHCP server and firewall without the need for DHCP relay.

For example, you could setup a server as the first scenario, but use two wired Ethernet interfaces instead of one wired and one wireless. One interface would be your Internet connection, and the other would connect to a switch. Then connect as many access points as you require to the same switch, set them up as transparent bridges, and everyone will pass through the same firewall and use the same DHCP server.

The simplicity of bridging comes at a cost of efficiency. Since all clients share the same subnet, broadcast traffic will be repeated throughout the network. This is usually fine for small networks, but as the number of clients increases, more wireless bandwidth will be wasted on broadcast network traffic.

Initial setup

The initial setup for a bridging access point is similar to that of a masquerading access point, without the requirement of dnsmasq. Follow the initial setup instructions from the previous example.

In addition, the **bridge-utils** package is required for bridging. This package exists for Ubuntu and other Debian-based distributions, as well as for Fedora Core. Make sure it is installed and that the command **brctl** is available before proceeding.

Setting up the Interfaces

On Ubuntu or Debian the network interfaces are configured by editing the file **/etc/network/interfaces**.

Add a section like the following, but change the names of interfaces and the IP addresses accordingly. The IP address and netmask must match that of your existing network. This example assumes you are building a wireless repeater with two wireless interfaces, wlan0 and wlan1. The wlan0 interface will be a client to the "office" network, and wlan1 will create a network called "repeater".

Add the following to **/etc/network/interfaces**:

```
auto br0
iface br0 inet static
  address 192.168.1.2
  network 192.168.1.0
  netmask 255.255.255.0
  broadcast 192.168.1.255
  gateway 192.168.1.1
  pre-up ifconfig wlan 0 0.0.0.0 up
  pre-up ifconfig wlan1 0.0.0.0 up
  pre-up iwconfig wlan0 essid "office" mode Managed
  pre-up iwconfig wlan1 essid "repeater" mode Master
  bridge_ports wlan0 wlan1
  post-down ifconfig wlan1 down
  post-down ifconfig wlan0 down
```

Comment out any other sections in the file that refer to wlan0 or wlan1 to make sure that they don't interfere with our setup.

This syntax for setting up bridges via the **interfaces** file is specific to Debian-based distributions, and the details of actually setting up the bridge are handled by a couple of scripts: **/etc/network/if-pre-up.d/bridge** and **/etc/network/if-post-down.d/bridge**. The documentation for these scripts is found in **/usr/share/doc/bridge-utils/**.

If those scripts don't exist on your distribution (such as Fedora Core), here is an alternative setup for **/etc/network/interfaces** which will achieve the same thing with only marginally more hassle:

```
iface br0 inet static
  pre-up ifconfig wlan 0 0.0.0.0 up
  pre-up ifconfig wlan1 0.0.0.0 up
  pre-up iwconfig wlan0 essid "office" mode Managed
  pre-up iwconfig wlan1 essid "repeater" mode Master
  pre-up brctl addbr br0
  pre-up brctl addif br0 wlan0
  pre-up brctl addif br0 wlan1
  post-down ifconfig wlan1 down
  post-down ifconfig wlan0 down
  post-down brctl delif br0 wlan0
  post-down brctl delif br0 wlan1
  post-down brctl delbr br0
```

Starting the bridge

Once the bridge is defined as an interface, starting the bridge is as simple as typing:

```
# ifup -v br0
```

The "-v" means verbose output and will give you information to what is going on.

On Fedora Core (i.e. non-debian distributions) you still need to give your bridge interface an ip address and add a default route to the rest of the network:

```
#ifconfig br0 192.168.1.2 netmask 255.255.255.0 broadcast 192.168.1.255
#route add default gw 192.168.1.1
```

You should now be able to connect a wireless laptop to this new access point, and connect to the Internet (or at least to the rest of your network) through this box.

Use the **brctl** command to see what your bridge is doing:

```
# brctl show br0
```

Scenario 1 & 2 the easy way

Instead of setting up your computer as an access point from scratch, you may wish to use a dedicated Linux distribution that is specially tailored for this purpose. These distributions can make the job as simple as booting from a particular CD on a computer with a wireless interface. See the following section, "Wireless-friendly operating systems" for more information.

As you can see, it is straightforward to provide access point services from a standard Linux router. Using Linux gives you significantly more control over how packets are routed through your network, and allows for features that simply aren't possible on consumer grade access point hardware.

For example, you could start with either of the above two examples and implement a private wireless network where users are authenticated using a standard web browser. Using a captive portal such as Chillispot, wireless users can be checked against credentials in an existing database (say, a Windows domain server accessible via RADIUS). This arrangement could allow for preferential access to users in the database, while providing a very limited level of access for the general public.

Another popular application is the prepaid commercial model. In this model, users must purchase a ticket before accessing the network. This ticket provides a password that is valid for a limited amount of time (typically one day). When the ticket expires, the user must purchase another. This ticketing feature is only available on relatively expensive commercial networking equipment, but can be implemented using free software such as Chillispot and phpMyPrePaid. We will see more about captive portal technology and ticketing systems in the **Authentication** section in **Chapter 6**.

Wireless-friendly operating systems

There are a number of open source operating system that provide useful tools for working with wireless networks. These are intended to be used on repurposed PCs or other networking hardware (rather than on a laptop or server) and are fine-tuned for building wireless networks. Some of these projects include:

- **Freifunk**. Based on the OpenWRT project (*http://openwrt.org/*), the Freifunk firmware brings easy OLSR support to MIPS-based consumer access points, such as the Linksys WRT54G / WRT54GS / WAP54G, Siemens SE505, and others. By simply flashing one of these APs with the Freifunk firmware, you can rapidly build a self-forming OLSR mesh. Freifunk is not currently available for x86 architecture machines. It is maintained by Sven Ola of the Freifunk wireless group in Berlin. You can download the firmware from *http://www.freifunk.net/wiki/FrelfunkFirmware* .

- **Pyramid Linux**. Pyramid is a Linux distribution for use on embedded platforms that evolved out of the venerable Pebble Linux platform. It supports several different wireless cards, and has a simple web interface for configuring networking interfaces, port forwarding, WifiDog, and OLSR. Pyramid is distributed and maintained by Metrix Communication LLC, and is available at *http://pyramid.metrix.net/*.

- **m0n0wall**. Based on FreeBSD, m0n0wall is a very tiny but complete firewall package that provides AP services. It is configured from a web interface and the entire system configuration is stored in a single XML file. Its tiny size (less than 6MB) makes it attractive for use in very small embedded systems. Its goal is to provide a secure firewall, and as such does not include userspace tools (it is not even possible to log into the machine over the network). Despite this limitation, it is a popular choice for wireless networkers, particularly those with a background in FreeBSD. You can download m0n0wall from *http://www.m0n0.ch/* .

All of these distributions are designed to fit in machines with limited storage. If you are using a very large flash disk or hard drive, you can certainly install a more complete OS (such as Ubuntu or Debian) and use the machine as a router or access point. It will likely take a fair amount of development time to be sure all needed tools are included, without installing unnecessary packages. By using one of these projects as a starting point for building a wireless node, you will save yourself considerable time and effort.

The Linksys WRT54G

One of the most popular consumer access points currently on the market is the Linksys WRT54G. This access point features two external RP-TNC antenna connectors, a four port Ethernet switch, and an 802.11b/g radio. It is configured through a simple web interface. While it is not designed as an outdoor solution, it can be installed in a large sprinkler box or plastic tub for relatively little cost. As of this writing, the WRT54G sells for about $60.

Back in 2003, network hackers realized that the firmware that shipped with the WRT54G was actually a version of Linux. This led to a tremendous interest in building custom firmware that extended the capabilities of the router significantly. Some of these new features include client radio mode support, captive portals, and mesh networking. Some popular alternative firmware packages for the WRT54G are DD-Wrt (*http://www.dd-wrt.com/*), OpenWRT (*http://openwrt.org/*), Tomato (*http://www.polarcloud.com/tomato*) and Freifunk (*http://www.freifunk.net/*).

Unfortunately, in the fall of 2005, Linksys released version 5 of the WRT54G. This hardware revision eliminated some RAM and flash storage on the motherboard, making it very difficult to run Linux (it ships with VxWorks, a much smaller operating system that does not allow easy customization). Linksys also released the WRT54GL, which is essentially the WRT54G v4 (which runs Linux) with a slightly bigger price tag.

A number of other Linksys access points also run Linux, including the WRT54GS and WAP54G. While these also have relatively low price tags, the hardware specifications may change at any time. It is difficult to know which hardware revision is used without opening the packaging, making it risky to purchase them at a retail store and practically impossible to order online. While the WRT54GL is guaranteed to run Linux, Linksys has made it known that it does not expect to sell this model in large volume, and it is unclear how long it will be offered for sale.

Fortunately, wireless hackers have now been able to install custom firmware on the notoriously difficult WRT54G version 5 and 6, and the latest revisions as well(v7 and v8). For details on getting alternate firmware installed on a v5 or v6 access point see: *http://www.scorpiontek.org/portal/content/view/27/36/*

For more information about the current state of Linksys wireless router hacking, see *http://linksysinfo.org/*

DD-WRT

One popular alternate firmware for the Linksys family of access point hardware is DD-WRT (*http://www.dd-wrt.com/*). It includes several useful features, including radio client mode, adjustable transmission power, various captive portals, QoS support, and much more. It uses an intuitive web-based configuration tool (unencrypted or via HTTPS), and also provides SSH and telnet access.

Several versions of the firmware are available from the DD-WRT website. The general procedure for upgrading is to download the version of the firmware appropriate for your hardware, and upload it via the router's "firmware update" feature. Specific installation details vary according to the hardware version of your router. In addition to Linksys hardware, DD-WRT will run on Buffalo, ASUS, the La Fonera, and other access points.

For specific instructions for your hardware, see the installation guide on the DD-WRT wiki at *http://www.dd-wrt.com/wiki/index.php/Installation.* The default login for a fresh DD-WRT installation is **root** with the password **admin**.

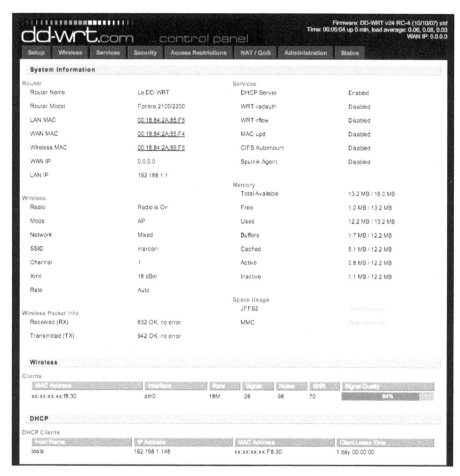

Figure 5.3: The DD-WRT (v23) control panel

6
Security & Monitoring

In a traditional wired network, access control is very straightforward: If a person has physical access to a computer or network hub, they can use (or abuse) the network resources. While software mechanisms are an important component of network security, limiting physical access to the network devices is the ultimate access control mechanism. Simply put, if all terminals and network components are only accessible to trusted individuals, the network can likely be trusted.

The rules change significantly with wireless networks. While the apparent range of your access point may seem to be just a few hundred meters, a user with a high gain antenna may be able to make use of the network from several blocks away. Should an unauthorized user be detected, is impossible to simply "trace the cable" back to the user's location. Without transmitting a single packet, a nefarious user can even log all network data to disk. This data can later be used to launch a more sophisticated attack against the network. Never assume that radio waves simply "stop" at the edge of your property line.

It is usually unreasonable to completely trust all users of the network, even on wired networks. Disgruntled employees, uneducated network users, and simple mistakes on the part of honest users can cause significant harm to network operations. As the network architect, your goal is to facilitate private communication between legitimate users of the network. While a certain amount of access control and authentication is necessary in any network, you have failed in your job if legitimate users find it difficult to use the network to communicate.

There's an old saying that the only way to completely secure a computer is to unplug it, lock it in a safe, destroy the key, and bury the whole thing in concrete. While such a system might be completely "secure", it is useless for communication. When you make security decisions for your network, remember that above all else, the network exists so that its users can communicate with each other. Security considerations are important, but should not get in the way of the network's users.

Physical security

When installing a network, you are building an infrastructure that people depend on. Security measures exist to ensure that the network is reliable. For many installations, outages often occur due to human tampering, whether accidental or not. Networks have physical components, such as wires and boxes, which are easily disturbed. In many installations, people will not understand the purpose of the installed equipment, or curiosity may lead them to experiment. They may not realize the importance of a cable connected to a port. Someone may unplug an Ethernet cable so that they can connect their laptop for 5 minutes, or move a switch because it is in their way. A plug might be removed from a power bar because someone needs that receptacle. Assuring the physical security of an installation is paramount. Signs and labels will only be useful to those who can read your language. Putting things out of the way and limiting access is the best means to assure that accidents and tinkering do not occur.

In less developed economies, proper fasteners, ties, or boxes will not be as easy to find. You should be able to find electrical supplies that will work just as well. Custom enclosures are also easy to manufacture and should be considered essential to any installation. It is often economical to pay a mason to make holes and install conduit. Where this would be an expensive option in the developed world, this type of labour intensive activity can be affordable in Southern countries. PVC can be embedded in cement walls for passing cable from room to room. This avoids the need to smash new holes every time a cable needs to be passed. Plastic bags can be stuffed into the conduit around the cables for insulation.

Small equipment should be mounted on the wall and larger equipment should be put in a closet or in a cabinet.

Switches

Switches, hubs or interior access points can be screwed directly onto a wall with a wall plug. It is best to put this equipment as high as possible to reduce the chance that someone will touch the device or its cables.

Cables

At the very least, cables should be hidden and fastened. It is possible to find plastic cable conduit that can be used in buildings. If you cannot find it, simple cable attachments can be nailed into the wall to secure the cable. This will make sure that the cable doesn't hang where it can be snagged, pinched or cut.

It is preferable to bury cables, rather than to leave them hanging across a yard. Hanging wires might be used for drying clothes, or be snagged by a ladder, etc. To avoid vermin and insects, use plastic electrical conduit. The marginal expense will be well worth the trouble. The conduit should be buried about 30 cm deep, or below the frost level in cold climates. It is worth the extra investment of buying larger conduit than is presently required, so that future cables can be run through the same tubing. Consider labeling buried cable with a "call before you dig" sign to avoid future accidental outages.

Power

It is best to have power bars locked in a cabinet. If that is not possible, mount the power bar under a desk, or on the wall and use duct tape (or gaffer tape, a strong adhesive tape) to secure the plug into the receptacle. On the UPS and power bar, do not leave any empty receptacles. Tape them if necessary. People will have the tendency to use the easiest receptacle, so make these critical ones difficult to use. If you do not, you might find a fan or light plugged into your UPS; though it is nice to have light, it is nicer to keep your server running!

Water

Protect your equipment from water and moisture. In all cases make sure that your equipment, including your UPS is at least 30 cm from the ground, to avoid damage from flooding. Also try to have a roof over your equipment, so that water and moisture will not fall onto it. In moist climates, it is important that the equipment has proper ventilation to assure that moisture can be exhausted. Small closets need to have ventilation, or moisture and heat can degrade or destroy your gear.

Masts

Equipment installed on a mast is often safe from thieves. Nevertheless, to deter thieves and to keep your equipment safe from winds it is good to over-engineer mounts. Painting equipment a dull white or grey color reflects the sun and makes it look plain and uninteresting. Panel antennas are often preferred because they are much more subtle and less interesting than dishes. Any installation on walls should be high enough to require a ladder to reach. Try choosing well-lit but not prominent places to put equipment. Also avoid antennae that resemble television antennae, as those are items that will attract interest by thieves, where a wifi antenna will be useless to the average thief.

Threats to the network

One critical difference between Ethernet and wireless is that wireless networks are built on a **shared medium**. They more closely resemble the old network hubs than modern switches, in that every computer connected to the network can "see" the traffic of every other user. To monitor all network traffic on an access point, one can simply tune to the channel being used, put the network card into monitor mode, and log every frame. This data might be directly valuable to an eavesdropper (including data such as email, voice data, or online chat logs). It may also provide passwords and other sensitive data, making it possible to compromise the network even further. As we'll see later in this chapter, this problem can be mitigated by the use of encryption.

Another serious problem with wireless networks is that its users are relatively **anonymous**. While it is true that every wireless device includes a unique MAC address that is supplied by the manufacturer, these addresses can often be changed with software. Even when the MAC address is known, it can be very difficult to judge where a wireless user is physically located. Multipath effects, high-gain antennas, and widely varying radio transmitter characteristics can make it impossible to determine if a malicious wireless user is sitting in the next room or is in an apartment building a mile away.

While unlicensed spectrum provides a huge cost savings to the user, it has the unfortunate side effect that **denial of service** (**DoS**) attacks are trivially simple. By simply turning on a high powered access point, cordless phone, video transmitter, or other 2.4 GHz device, a malicious person could cause significant problems on the network. Many network devices are vulnerable to other forms of denial of service attacks as well, such as disassociation flooding and ARP table overflows.

Here are several categories of individuals who may cause problems on a wireless network:

- **Unintentional users**. As more wireless networks are installed in densely populated areas, it is common for laptop users to accidentally associate to the wrong network. Most wireless clients will simply choose any available wireless network when their preferred network is unavailable. The user may then make use of this network as usual, completely unaware that they may be transmitting sensitive data on someone else's network. Malicious people may even take advantage of this by setting up access points in strategic locations, to try to attract unwitting users and capture their data.

The first step in avoiding this problem is educating your users, and stressing the importance of connecting only to known and trusted networks. Many wireless clients can be configured to only connect to trusted networks, or to ask permission before joining a new network. As we will see later in this chapter, users can safely connect to open public networks by using strong encryption.

• **War drivers**. The "war driving" phenomenon draws its name from the popular 1983 hacker film, "War Games". War drivers are interested in finding the physical location of wireless networks. They typically drive around with a laptop, GPS, and omnidirectional antenna, logging the name and location of any networks they find. These logs are then combined with logs from other war drivers, and are turned into graphical maps depicting the wireless "footprint" of a particular city.

The vast majority of war drivers likely pose no direct threat to networks, but the data they collect might be of interest to a network cracker. For example, it might be obvious that an unprotected access point detected by a war driver is located inside a sensitive building, such as a government or corporate office. A malicious person could use this information to illegally access the network there. Arguably, such an AP should never have been set up in the first place, but war driving makes the problem all the more urgent. As we will see later in this chapter, war drivers who use the popular program NetStumbler can be detected with programs such as Kismet. For more information about war driving, see sites such as *http://www.wifimaps.com/, http://www.nodedb.com/,* or *http://www.netstumbler.com/* .

• **Rogue access points**. There are two general classes of rogue access points: those incorrectly installed by legitimate users, and those installed by malicious people who intend to collect data or do harm to the network. In the simplest case, a legitimate network user may want better wireless coverage in their office, or they might find security restrictions on the corporate wireless network too difficult to comply with. By installing an inexpensive consumer access point without permission, the user opens the entire network up to potential attacks from the inside. While it is possible to scan for unauthorized access points on your wired network, setting a clear policy that prohibits them is very important.

The second class of rogue access point can be very difficult to deal with. By installing a high powered AP that uses the same ESSID as an existing network, a malicious person can trick people into using their equipment, and log or even manipulate all data that passes through it. Again, if your users are trained to use strong encryption, this problem is significantly reduced.

• **Eavesdroppers**. As mentioned earlier, eavesdropping is a very difficult problem to deal with on wireless networks. By using a passive monitoring tool (such as Kismet), an eavesdropper can log all network data from a great distance away, without ever making their presence known. Poorly encrypted data can simply be logged and cracked later, while unencrypted data can be easily read in real time.

If you have difficulty convincing others of this problem, you might want to demonstrate tools such as Etherpeg (*http://www.etherpeg.org/*) or Driftnet (*http://www.ex-parrot.com/~chris/driftnet/*). These tools watch a wireless network for graphical data, such as GIF and JPEG files. While other users are browsing the Internet, these tools simply display all graphics found in a graphical collage. I often use tools such as this as a demonstration when lecturing on wireless security. While you can tell a user that their email is vulnerable without encryption, nothing drives the message home like showing them the pictures they are looking at in their web browser.

Again, while it cannot be completely prevented, proper application of strong encryption will discourage eavesdropping.

This introduction is intended to give you an idea of the problems you are up against when designing a wireless network. Later in this chapter, we will look at tools and techniques that will help you to mitigate these problems.

Authentication

Before being granted access to network resources, users should first be **authenticated**. In an ideal world, every wireless user would have an identifier that is unique, unchangeable, and cannot be impersonated by other users. This turns out to be a very difficult problem to solve in the real world.

The closest feature we have to a unique identifier is the MAC address. This is the 48-bit number assigned by the manufacturer to every wireless and Ethernet device. By employing *mac filtering* on our access points, we can authenticate users based on their MAC address. With this feature, the access point keeps an internal table of approved MAC addresses. When a wireless user tries to associate to the access point, the MAC address of the client must be on the approved list, or the association will be denied. Alternately, the AP may keep a table of known "bad" MAC addresses, and permit all devices that are not on the list.

Unfortunately, this is not an ideal security mechanism. Maintaining MAC tables on every device can be cumbersome, requiring all client devices to have their MAC addresses recorded and uploaded to the APs. Even worse, MAC addresses can often be changed in software. By observing MAC addresses in use on a wireless network, a determined attacker can *spoof* (impersonate) an approved MAC address and successfully associate to the AP. While MAC filtering will prevent unintentional users and even most curious individuals from accessing the network, MAC filtering alone cannot prevent attacks from determined attackers.

MAC filters are useful for temporarily limiting access from misbehaving clients. For example, if a laptop has a virus that sends large amounts of spam or other traffic, its MAC address can be added to the filter table to stop the traffic immediately. This will buy you time to track down the user and fix the problem.

Another popular authentication feature of wireless the so-called *closed network*. In a typical network, APs will broadcast their ESSID many times per second, allowing wireless clients (as well as tools such as NetStumbler) to find the network and display its presence to the user. In a closed network, the AP does not beacon the ESSID, and users must know the full name of the network before the AP will allow association. This prevents casual users from discovering the network and selecting it in their wireless client.

There are a number of drawbacks to this feature. Forcing users to type in the full ESSID before connecting to the network is error prone and often leads to support calls and complaints. Since the network isn't obviously present in site survey tools like NetStumbler, this can prevent your networks from showing up on war driving maps. But it also means that other network builders cannot easily find your network either, and specifically won't know that you are already using a given channel. A conscientious neighbor may perform a site survey, see no nearby networks, and install their own network on the same channel you are using. This will cause interference problems for both you and your neighbor.

Finally, using closed networks ultimately adds little to your overall networks security. By using passive monitoring tools (such as Kismet), a skilled user can detect frames sent from your legitimate clients to the AP. These frames necessarily contain the network name. A malicious user can then use this name to associate to the access point, just like a normal user would.

Encryption is probably the best tool we have for authenticating wireless users. Through strong encryption, we can uniquely identify a user in a manner that is very difficult to spoof, and use that identity to determine further network access. Encryption also has the benefit of adding a layer of privacy by preventing eavesdroppers from easily watching network traffic.

The most widely employed encryption method on wireless networks is *WEP encryption*. WEP stands for *wired equivalent privacy*, and is supported by virtually all 802.11a/b/g equipment. WEP uses a shared 40-bit key to encrypt data between the access point and client. The key must be entered on the APs as well as on each of the clients. With WEP enabled, wireless clients cannot associate with the AP until they use the correct key. An eavesdropper listening to a WEP-enabled network will still see traffic and MAC addresses, but the data payload of each packet is encrypted. This provides a fairly good authentication mechanism while also adding a bit of privacy to the network.

WEP is definitely not the strongest encryption solution available. For one thing, the WEP key is shared between all users. If the key is compromised (say, if one user tells a friend what the password is, or if an employee is let go) then changing the password can be prohibitively difficult, since all APs and client devices need to be changed. This also means that legitimate users of the network can still eavesdrop on each others' traffic, since they all know the shared key.

The key itself is often poorly chosen, making offline cracking attempts feasible. Even worse, the implementation of WEP itself is broken in many access points, making it even easier to crack some networks. While manufacturers have implemented a number of extensions to WEP (such as longer keys and fast rotation schemes), these extensions are not part of the standard, and generally will not interoperate between equipment from different manufacturers. By upgrading to the most recent firmware for all of your wireless devices, you can prevent some of the early attacks found in WEP.

WEP can still be a useful authentication tool. Assuming your users can be trusted not to give away the password, you can be fairly sure that your wireless clients are legitimate. While WEP cracking is possible, it is beyond the skill of most users. WEP is quite useful for securing long distance point-to-point links, even on generally open networks. By using WEP on such a link, you will discourage others from associating to the link, and they will likely use other available APs instead. Think of WEP as a handy "keep out" sign for your network. Anyone who detects the network will see that a key is required, making it clear that they are not welcome to use it.

WEPs greatest strength is its interoperability. In order to comply with the 802.11 standards, all wireless devices support basic WEP. While it isn't the strongest method available, it is certainly the most commonly implemented encryption feature. We will look at other more advanced encryption techniques later in this chapter.

For more details about the state of WEP encryption, see these papers:

* http://www.isaac.cs.berkeley.edu/isaac/wep-faq.html
* http://www.cs.umd.edu/~waa/wireless.pdf
* http://www.crypto.com/papers/others/rc4_ksaproc.ps

Another data-link layer authentication protocol is **Wi-Fi Protected Access**, or **WPA**. WPA was created specifically to deal with the known problems with WEP mentioned earlier. It provides a significantly stronger encryption scheme, and can use a shared private key, unique keys assigned to each user, or even SSL certificates to authenticate both the client and the access point. Authentication credentials are checked using the 802.1X protocol, which can consult a third party database such as RADIUS. Through the use of *Temporal Key Integrity Protocol* (*TKIP*), keys can be rotated quickly over time, further reducing the likelihood that a particular session can be cracked. Overall, WPA provides significantly better authentication and privacy than standard WEP.

WPA requires fairly recent access point hardware and up-to-date firmware on all wireless clients, as well as a substantial amount of configuration. If you are installing a network in a setting where you control the entire hardware platform, WPA can be ideal. By authenticating both clients and APs, it solves the rogue access point problem and provides many significant advantages over WEP. But in most network settings where the vintage of hardware is mixed and the knowledge of wireless users is limited, WPA can be a nightmare to install. It is for this reason that most sites continue to use WEP, if encryption is used at all.

Captive portals

One common authentication tool used on wireless networks is the *captive portal*. A captive portal uses a standard web browser to give a wireless user the opportunity to present login credentials. It can also be used to present information (such as an Acceptable Use Policy) to the user before granting further access. By using a web browser instead of a custom program for authentication, captive portals work with virtually all laptops and operating systems. Captive portals are typically used on open networks with no other authentication methods (such as WEP or MAC filters).

To begin, a wireless user opens their laptop and selects the network. Their computer requests a DHCP lease, which is granted. They then use their web browser to go to any site on the Internet.

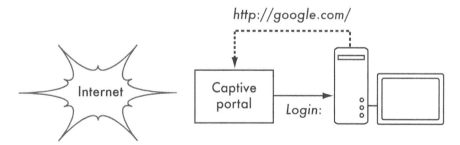

Figure 6.1: The user requests a web page and is redirected.

Instead of receiving the requested page, the user is presented with a login screen. This page can require the user to enter a user name and password, simply click a "login" button, type in numbers from a pre-paid ticket, or enter any other credentials that the network administrators require. The user then enters their credentials, which are checked by the access point or another server on the network. All other network access is blocked until these credentials are verified.

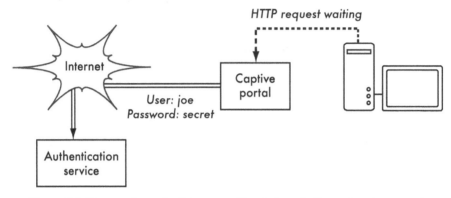

Figure 6.2: The user's credentials are verified before further network access is granted. The authentication server can be the access point itself, another machine on the local network, or a server anywhere on the Internet.

Once authenticated, the user is permitted to access network resources, and is typically redirected to the site they originally requested.

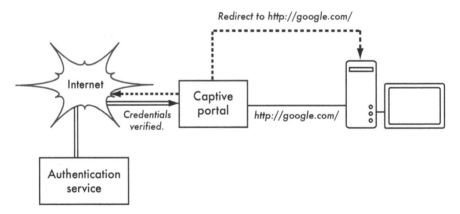

Figure 6.3: After authenticating, the user is permitted to access the rest of the network.

Captive portals provide no encryption for the wireless users, instead relying on the MAC and IP address of the client as a unique identifier. Since this is not necessarily very secure, many implementations will require the user to re-authenticate periodically. This can often be automatically done by minimizing a special pop-up browser window when the user first logs in.

Since they do not provide strong encryption, captive portals are not a very good choice for networks that need to be locked down to only allow access from trusted users. They are much more suited to cafes, hotels, and other public access locations where casual network users are expected.

In public or semi-public network settings, encryption techniques such as WEP and WPA are effectively useless. There is simply no way to distribute public or shared keys to members of the general public without compromising the security of those keys. In these settings, a simple application such as a captive portal provides a level of service somewhere between completely open and completely closed.

Popular hotspot projects

- Chillispot (*http://www.chillispot.info/*). Chillispot is a captive portal designed to authenticate against an existing user credentials database, such as RADUIS. Combined with the application phpMyPrePaid, pre-paid ticket based authentication can be implemented very easily You can download phpMyPrePaid from *http://sourceforge.net/projects/phpmyprepaid/*.

- WiFi Dog (*http://www.wifidog.org/*). WiFi Dog provides a very complete captive portal authentication package in very little space (typically under 30kb). From a user's perspective, it requires no pop-up or javascript support, allowing it to work on a wider variety of wireless devices.

- m0n0wall (*http://m0n0.ch/wall/*). m0n0wall is a complete embedded operating system based on FreeBSD. It includes a captive portal with RADIUS support, as well as a PHP web server.

- NoCatSplash (*http://nocat.net/download/NoCatSplash/*) provides a customizable splash page to your users, requiring them to click a "login" button before using the network. This is useful for identifying the operators of the network and displaying rules for network access. It provides a very easy solution in situations where you need to provide users of an open network with information and an acceptable use policy.

Privacy

Most users are blissfully unaware that their private email, chat conversations, and even passwords are often sent "in the clear" over dozens of untrusted networks before arriving at their ultimate destination on the Internet. However mistaken they may be, users still typically have some expectation of privacy when using computer networks.

Privacy can be achieved, even on untrusted networks such as public access points and the Internet. The only proven effective method for protecting privacy is the use of strong ***end-to-end encryption***.

Encryption techniques such as WEP and WPA attempt to address the privacy issue at layer two, the data-link layer. This does protect against eavesdroppers listening in on the wireless connection, but this protection ends at the access point. If the wireless client uses insecure protocols (such as POP or simple SMTP for receiving and sending email), then users beyond the AP can still log the session and see the sensitive data. As mentioned earlier, WEP also suffers from the fact that it uses a shared private key. This means that legitimate wireless users can eavesdrop on each other, since they all know the private key.

By using encryption to the remote end of the connection, users can neatly sidestep the entire problem. These techniques work well even on untrusted public networks, where eavesdroppers are listening and possibly even manipulating data coming from the access point.

To ensure data privacy, good end-to-end encryption should provide the following features:

- **Verified authentication of the remote end**. The user should be able to know without a doubt that the remote end is who it claims to be. Without authentication, a user could give sensitive data to anyone claiming to be the legitimate service.

- **Strong encryption methods**. The encryption algorithm should stand up to public scrutiny, and not be easily decrypted by a third party. There is no security in obscurity, and strong encryption is even stronger when the algorithm is widely known and subject to peer review. A good algorithm with a suitably large and protected key can provide encryption that is unlikely to be broken by any effort in our lifetimes using current technology.

- **Public key cryptography**. While not an absolute requirement for end-to-end encryption, the use of public key cryptography instead of a shared key can ensure that an individual's data remains private, even if the key of another user of the service is compromised. It also solves certain problems with distributing keys to users over untrusted networks.

- **Data encapsulation**. A good end-to-end encryption mechanism protects as much data as possible. This can range from encrypting a single email transaction to encapsulation of all IP traffic, including DNS lookups and other supporting protocols. Some encryption tools simply provide a secure channel that other applications can use. This allows users to run any program they like and still have the protection of strong encryption, even if the programs themselves don't support it.

Be aware that laws regarding the use of encryption vary widely from place to place. Some countries treat encryption as munitions, and may require a permit, escrow of private keys, or even prohibit its use altogether. Before implementing any solution that involves encryption, be sure to verify that use of this technology is permitted in your local area.

In the following sections, we'll take a look at some specific tools that can provide good protection for your users' data.

SSL

The most widely available end-to-end encryption technology is **Secure Sockets Layer**, known simply as **SSL**. Built into virtually all web browsers, SSL uses public key cryptography and a trusted **public key infrastructure** (**PKI**) to secure data communications on the web. Whenever you visit a web URL that starts with https, you are using SSL.

The SSL implementation built into web browsers includes a collection of certificates from trusted sources, called **certificate authorities** (**CA**). These certificates are cryptographic keys that are used to verify the authenticity of websites. When you browse to a website that uses SSL, the browser and the server first exchange certificates. The browser then verifies that the certificate provided by the server matches its DNS host name, that it has not expired, and that it is signed by a trusted certificate authority. The server optionally verifies the identity of the browser's certificate. If the certificates are approved, the browser and server then negotiate a master session key using the previously exchanged certificates to protect it. That key is then used to encrypt all communications until the browser disconnects. This kind of data encapsulation is known as a **tunnel**.

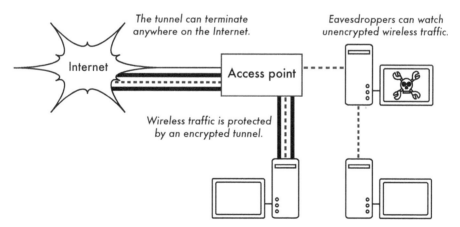

Figure 6.4: Eavesdroppers must break strong encryption to monitor traffic over an encrypted tunnel. The conversation inside the tunnel is identical to any other unencrypted conversation.

The use of certificates with a PKI not only protects the communication from eavesdroppers, but also prevents so-called **man-in-the-middle** (**MITM**) attacks. In a man-in-the-middle attack, a malicious user intercepts all communication between the browser and the server. By presenting counterfeit certificates to both the browser and the server, the malicious user could carry on two simultaneous encrypted sessions. Since the malicious user knows the secret on both connections, it is trivial to observe and manipulate data passing between the server and the browser.

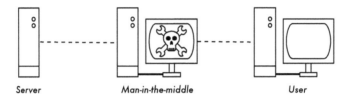

Server   Man-in-the-middle   User

Figure 6.5: The man-in-the-middle effectively controls everything the user sees, and can record and manipulate all traffic. Without a public key infrastructure to verify the authenticity of keys, strong encryption alone cannot protect against this kind of attack.

Use of a good PKI prevents this kind of attack. In order to be successful, the malicious user would have to present a certificate to the client that is signed by a trusted certificate authority. Unless a CA has been compromised (very unlikely) or the user is tricked into accepting the forged certificate, then such an attack is not possible. This is why it is vitally important that users understand that ignoring warnings about expired or improper certificates is very dangerous, especially when using wireless networks. By clicking the "ignore" button when prompted by their browser, users open themselves up to many potential attacks.

SSL is not only used for web browsing. Insecure email protocols such as IMAP, POP, and SMTP can be secured by wrapping them in an SSL tunnel. Most modern email clients support IMAPS and POPS (secure IMAP and POP) as well as SSL/TLS protected SMTP. If your email server does not provide SSL support, you can still secure it with SSL using a package like Stunnel (*http://www.stunnel.org/*). SSL can be used to effectively secure just about any service that runs over TCP.

SSH

Most people think of SSH as a secure replacement for **telnet**, just as **scp** and **sftp** are the secure counterparts of **rcp** and **ftp**. But SSH is much more than encrypted remote shell. Like SSL, it uses strong public key cryptography to verify the remote server and encrypt data. Instead of a PKI, it uses a key fingerprint cache that is checked before a connection is permitted. It can use passwords, public keys, or other methods for user authentication.

Many people do not know that SSH can also act as a general purpose encrypting tunnel, or even an encrypting web proxy. By first establishing an

SSH connection to a trusted location near (or even on) a remote server, in-secure protocols can be protected from eavesdropping and attack.

While this technique may be a bit advanced for many users, network archi-tects can use SSH to encrypt traffic across untrusted links, such as wireless point-to-point links. Since the tools are freely available and run over stan-dard TCP, any educated user can implement SSH connections for them-selves, providing their own end-to-end encryption without administrator inter-vention.

OpenSSH (*http://openssh.org/*) is probably the most popular implementation on Unix-like platforms. Free implementations such as Putty (*http://www.putty.nl/*) and WinSCP (*http://winscp.net/*) are available for Windows. OpenSSH will also run on Windows under the Cygwin package (*http://www.cygwin.com/*). These examples will assume that you are using a recent version of OpenSSH.

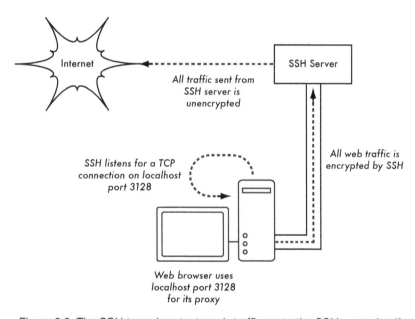

Figure 6.6: The SSH tunnel protects web traffic up to the SSH server itself.

To establish an encrypted tunnel from a port on the local machine to a port on the remote side, use the **-L** switch. For example, suppose you want to forward web proxy traffic over an encrypted link to the squid server at *squid.example.net*. Forward port 3128 (the default proxy port) using this command:

```
ssh -fN -g -L3128:squid.example.net:3128 squid.example.net
```

The **-fN** switches instruct ssh to fork into the background after connecting. The **-g** switch allows other users on your local segment to connect to the local machine and use it for encryption over the untrusted link. OpenSSH will use a public key for authentication if you have set one up, or it will prompt you for your password on the remote side. You can then configure your web browser to connect to localhost port 3128 as its web proxy service. All web traffic will then be encrypted before transmission to the remote side.

SSH can also act as a dynamic SOCKS4 or SOCKS5 proxy. This allows you to create an encrypting web proxy, without the need to set up squid. Note that this is not a caching proxy; it simply encrypts all traffic.

```
ssh -fN -D 8080 remote.example.net
```

Configure your web browser to use SOCKS4 or SOCKS5 on local port 8080, and away you go.

SSH can encrypt data on any TCP port, including ports used for email. It can even compress the data along the way, which can decrease latency on low capacity links.

```
ssh -fNCg -L110:localhost:110 -L25:localhost:25 mailhost.example.net
```

The **-C** switch turns on compression. You can add as many port forwarding rules as you like by specifying the **-L** switch multiple times. Note that in order to bind to a local port less than 1024, you must have root privileges on the local machine.

These are just a few examples of the flexibility of SSH. By implementing public keys and using the ssh forwarding agent, you can automate the creation of encrypted tunnels throughout your wireless network, and protect your communications with strong encryption and authentication.

OpenVPN

OpenVPN is a free, open source VPN implementation built on SSL encryption. There are OpenVPN client implementations for a wide range of operating systems, including Linux, Windows 2000/XP and higher, OpenBSD, FreeBSD, NetBSD, Mac OS X, and Solaris. Being a VPN, it encapsulates all traffic (including DNS and all other protocols) in an encrypted tunnel, not just a single TCP port. Most people find it considerably easier to understand and configure than IPSEC.

OpenVPN also has some disadvantages, such as fairly high latency. Some amount of latency is unavoidable since all encryption/decryption is done in user space, but using relatively new computers on either end of the tunnel can minimize this. While it can use traditional shared keys, OpenVPN really shines when used with SSL certificates and a certificate authority. OpenVPN has many advantages that make it a good option for providing end-to-end security.

Some of these reasons include:

• It is based on a proven, robust encryption protocol (SSL and RSA)

• It is relatively easy to configure

• It functions across many different platforms

• It is well documented

• It's free and open source.

OpenVPN needs to connect to a single TCP or UDP port on the remote side. Once established, it can encapsulate all data down to the Networking layer, or even down to the Data-Link layer, if your solution requires it. You can use it to create robust VPN connections between individual machines, or simply use it to connect network routers over untrusted wireless networks.

VPN technology is a complex field, and is a bit beyond the scope of this section to go into more detail. It is important to understand how VPNs fit into the structure of your network in order to provide the best possible protection without opening up your organization to unintentional problems. There are many good online resources that deal with installing OpenVPN on a server and client, we recommend this article from Linux Journal: *http://www.linuxjournal.com/article/7949* as well as the official HOWTO: *http://openvpn.net/howto.html*

Tor & Anonymizers

The Internet is basically an open network based on trust. When you connect to a web server across the Internet, your traffic passes through many different routers, owned by a great variety of institutions, corporations and individuals. In principle, any one of these routers has the ability to look closely at your data, seeing the source and destination addresses, and quite often also the actual content of the data. Even if your data is encrypted using a secure protocol, it is possible for your Internet provider to monitor the amount of data transferred, as well as the source and destination of that data. Often this is enough to piece together a fairly complete picture of your activities on-line.

Privacy and anonymity are important, and closely linked to each other. There are many valid reasons to consider protecting your privacy by ***anonymizing*** your network traffic. Suppose you want to offer Internet connectivity to your local community by setting up a number of access points for people to connect to. Whether you charge them for their access or not, there is always the risk that people use the network for something that is not legal in your country or region. You could plead with the legal system that this particular illegal action was not performed by yourself, but could have been performed by anyone connecting to your network. The problem is neatly sidestepped if it were technically infeasible to determine where your traffic was actually headed. And what about on-line censorship? Publishing web pages anonymously may also be necessary to avoid government censorship.

There are tools that allow you to anonymize your traffic in relatively easy ways. The combination of **Tor** (*http://www.torproject.org/*) and **Privoxy** (*http://www.privoxy.org/*) is a powerful way to run a local proxy server that will pass your Internet traffic through a number of servers all across the net, making it very difficult to follow the trail of information. Tor can be run on a local PC, under Microsoft Windows, Mac OSX, Linux and a variety of BSD's, where it anonymizes traffic from the browser on that particular machine. Tor and Privoxy can also be installed on a gateway server, or even a small embedded access point (such as a Linksys WRT54G) where they provides anonymity to all network users automatically.

Tor works by repeatedly bouncing your TCP connections across a number of servers spread throughout the Internet, and by wrapping routing information in a number of encrypted layers (hence the term **onion routing**), that get peeled off as the packet moves across the network. This means that, at any given point in the network, the source and destination addresses cannot be linked together. This makes traffic analysis extremely difficult.

The need for the Privoxy privacy proxy in connection with Tor is due to the fact that name server queries (DNS queries) in most cases are not passed through the proxy server, and someone analyzing your traffic would easily be able to see that you were trying to reach a specific site (say *google.com*) by the fact that you sent a DNS query to translate google.com to the appropriate IP address. Privoxy connects to Tor as a SOCKS4a proxy, which uses hostnames (not IP addresses) to get your packets to the intended destination.

In other words, using Privoxy with Tor is a simple and effective way to prevent traffic analysis from linking your IP address with the services you use online. Combined with secure, encrypted protocols (such as those we have seen in this chapter), Tor and Privoxy provide a high level of anonymity on the Internet.

Network Monitoring

Network monitoring is the use of logging and analysis tools to accurately determine traffic flows, utilization, and other performance indicators on a network. Good monitoring tools give you both hard numbers and graphical aggregate representations of the state of the network. This helps you to visualize precisely what is happening, so you know where adjustments may be needed. These tools can help you answer critical questions, such as:

- What are the most popular services used on the network?

- Who are the heaviest network users?

- What other wireless channels are in use in my area?

- Are users installing wireless access points on my private wired network?

- At what time of the day is the network most utilized?

- What sites do your users frequent?

- Is the amount of inbound or outbound traffic close to our available network capacity?

- Are there indications of an unusual network situation that is consuming bandwidth or causing other problems?

- Is our Internet Service Provider (ISP) providing the level of service that we are paying for? This should be answered in terms of available bandwidth, packet loss, latency, and overall availability.

And perhaps the most important question of all:

- Do the observed traffic patterns fit our expectations?

Let's look at how a typical system administrator can make good use of network monitoring tools.

An effective network monitoring example

For the purposes of example, let's assume that we are in charge of a network that has been running for three months. It consists of 50 computers and three servers: email, web, and proxy servers. While initially things are going well, users begin to complain of slow network speeds and an increase in spam emails. As time goes on, computer performance slows to a crawl (even when not using the network), causing considerable frustration in your users.

With frequent complaints and very low computer usage, the Board is questioning the need for so much network hardware. The Board also wants evidence that the bandwidth they are paying for is actually being used. As the network administrator, you are on the receiving end of these complaints. How can you diagnose the sudden drop in network and computer performance and also justify the network hardware and bandwidth costs?

Monitoring the LAN (local traffic)

To get an idea of exactly what is causing the slow down, you should begin by looking at traffic on the local LAN. There are several advantages to monitoring local traffic:

• Troubleshooting is greatly simplified.

• Viruses can be detected and eliminated.

• Malicious users can be detected and dealt with.

• Network hardware and resources can be justified with real statistics.

Assume that all of the switches support the **Simple Network Management Protocol** (**SNMP**). SNMP is an application-layer protocol designed to facilitate the exchange of management information between network devices. By assigning an IP address to each switch, you are able to monitor all the interfaces on that switch, observing the entire network from a single point. This is much easier than enabling SNMP on all computers in a network.

By using a free tool such as MRTG (see **Page 190**), you can monitor each port on the switch and present data graphically, as an aggregate average over time. The graphs are accessible from the web, so you are able to view the graphs from any machine at anytime.

With MRTG monitoring in place, it becomes obvious that the internal LAN is swamped with far more traffic than the Internet connection can support, even when the lab is unoccupied. This is a pretty clear indication that some of the computers are infested with a network virus. After installing good anti-virus and anti-spyware software on all of the machines, the internal LAN traffic settles down to expected levels. The machines run much more quickly, spam emails are reduced, and the users' morale quickly improves.

Monitoring the WAN (external traffic)

In addition to watching the traffic on the internal LAN, you need to demonstrate that the bandwidth the organization is paying for is actually what they are getting from their ISP. You can achieve this by monitoring **external traffic**.

External traffic is generally classified as anything sent over a **Wide Area Network** (**WAN**). Anything received from (or sent to) a network other than your internal LAN also qualifies as external traffic. The advantages of monitoring external traffic include:

• Internet bandwidth costs are justified by showing actual usage, and whether that usage agrees with your ISP's bandwidth charges.

- Future capacity needs are estimated by watching usage trends and predicting likely growth patterns.

- Intruders from the Internet are detected and filtered before they can cause problems.

Monitoring this traffic is easily done with the use of MRTG on an SNMP enabled device, such as a router. If your router does not support SNMP, then you can add a switch between your router and your ISP connection, and monitor the port traffic just as you would with an internal LAN.

Detecting Network Outages

With monitoring tools in place, you now have an accurate measurement of how much bandwidth the organization is using. This measurement should agree with your ISP's bandwidth charges. It can also indicate the actual throughput of your connection if you are using close to your available capacity at peak times. A "flat top" graph is a fairly clear indication that you are operating at full capacity. **Figure 6.7** shows flat tops in peak outbound traffic in the middle of every day except Sunday.

It is clear that your current Internet connection is overutilized at peak times, causing network lag. After presenting this information to the Board, you can make a plan for further optimizing your existing connection (by upgrading your proxy server and using other techniques in this book) and estimate how soon you will need to upgrade your connection to keep up with the demand. This is also an excellent time to review your operational policy with the Board, and discuss ways to bring actual usage in line with that policy.

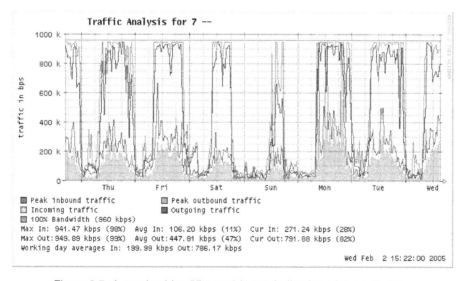

Figure 6.7: A graph with a "flat top" is one indication of overutilization.

Later in the week, you receive an emergency phone call in the evening. Apparently, no one in the lab can browse the web or send email. You rush to the lab and hastily reboot the proxy server, with no results. Browsing and email are still broken. You then reboot the router, but there is still no success. You continue eliminating the possible fault areas one by one until you realize that the network switch is off - a loose power cable is to blame. After applying power, the network comes to life again.

How can you troubleshoot such an outage without such time consuming trial and error? Is it possible to be notified of outages as they occur, rather than waiting for a user to complain? One way to do this is to use a program such as *Nagios* that continually polls network devices and notifies you of outages. Nagios will report on the availability of various machines and services, and will alert you to machines that have gone down. In addition to displaying the network status graphically on a web page, it will send notifications via SMS or email, alerting you immediately when problems arise.

With good monitoring tools in place, you will be able to justify the cost of equipment and bandwidth by effectively demonstrating how it is being used by the organization. You are notified automatically when problems arise, and you have historical statistics of how the network devices are performing. You can check the current performance against this history to find unusual behavior, and head off problems before they become critical. When problems do come up, it is simple to determine the source and nature of the problem. Your job is easier, the Board is satisfied, and your users are much happier.

Monitoring your network

Managing a network without monitoring is similar to driving a vehicle without a speedometer or a fuel gauge, with your eyes closed. How do you know how fast you are going? Is the car consuming fuel as efficiently as promised by the dealers? If you do an engine overhaul several months later, is the car any faster or more efficient than it was before?

Similarly, how can you pay for an electricity or water bill without seeing your monthly usage from a meter? You must have an account of your network bandwidth utilization in order to justify the cost of services and hardware purchases, and to account for usage trends.

There are several benefits to implementing a good monitoring system for your network:

1. **Network budget and resources are justified.** Good monitoring tools can demonstrate without a doubt that the network infrastructure (bandwidth, hardware, and software) is suitable and able to handle the requirements of network users.

2. **Network intruders are detected and filtered.** By watching your network traffic, you can detect attackers and prevent access to critical internal servers and services.

3. **Network viruses are easily detected.** You can be alerted to the presence of network viruses, and take appropriate action before they consume Internet bandwidth and destabilize your network

4. **Troubleshooting of network problems is greatly simplified.** Rather than attempting "trial and error" to debug network problems, you can be instantly notified of specific problems. Some kinds of problems can even be repaired automatically.

5. **Network performance can be highly optimized.**   Without effective monitoring, it is impossible to fine tune your devices and protocols to achieve the best possible performance.

6. **Capacity planning is much easier.** With solid historical performance records, you do not have to "guess" how much bandwidth you will need as your network grows.

7. **Proper network usage can be enforced.** When bandwidth is a scarce resource, the only way to be fair to all users is to ensure that the network is being used for its intended purpose.

Fortunately, network monitoring does not need to be an expensive undertaking. There are many freely available open source tools that will show you exactly what is happening on your network in considerable detail. This section will help you identify many invaluable tools and how best to use them.

The dedicated monitoring server

While monitoring services can be added to an existing network server, it is often desirable to dedicate one machine (or more, if necessary) to network monitoring. Some applications (such as *ntop*) require considerable resources to run, particularly on a busy network. But most logging and monitoring programs have modest RAM and storage requirements, typically with little CPU power required. Since open source operating systems (such as Linux or BSD) make very efficient use of hardware resources, this makes it possible to build a very capable monitoring server from recycled PC parts. There is usually no need to purchase a brand new server to relegate to monitoring duties.

The exception to this rule is in very large installations. If your network includes more than a few hundred nodes, or if you consume more than 50 Mbps of Internet bandwidth, you will likely need to split up monitoring duties between a few dedicated machines. This depends largely on exactly what you want to monitor. If you are attempting to account for all services accessed per MAC address, this will consume considerably more resources than simply measuring network flows on a switch port. But for the majority of installations, a single dedicated monitoring machine is usually enough.

While consolidating monitoring services to a single machine will streamline administration and upgrades, it can also ensure better ongoing monitoring. For example, if you install monitoring services on a web server, and that web server develops problems, then your network may not be monitored until the problem is resolved.

To a network administrator, the data collected about network performance is nearly as important as the network itself. Your monitoring should be robust and protected from service outages as well as possible. Without network statistics, you are effectively blind to problems with the network.

Where does the server fit in my network?

If you are only interested in collecting network flow statistics from a router, you can do this from just about anywhere on the LAN. This provides simple feedback about utilization, but cannot give you comprehensive details about usage patterns. **Figure 6.8** shows a typical MRTG graph generated from the Internet router. While the inbound and outbound utilization are clear, there is no detail about which computers, users, or protocols are using bandwidth.

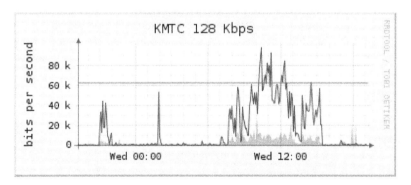

Figure 6.8: Polling the edge router can show you the overall network utilization, but you cannot break the data down further into machines, services, and users.

For more detail, the dedicated monitoring server must have access to everything that needs to be watched. Typically, this means it must have access to the entire network. To monitor a WAN connection, such as the Internet link to your ISP, the monitoring server must be able to see the traffic passing through the edge router. To monitor a LAN, the monitoring server is typically connected to a **monitor port** on the switch. If multiple switches are used in an installation, the monitoring server may need a connection to all of them. That connection can either be a physical cable, or if your network switches support it, a VLAN specifically configured for monitoring traffic.

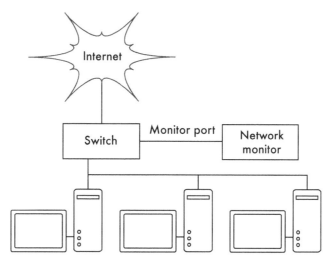

Figure 6.9: Use the monitor port on your switch to observe traffic crossing all of the network ports.

If monitor port functionality is not available on your switch, the monitoring server may be installed between your internal LAN and the Internet. While this will work, it introduces a single point of failure for the network, as the network will fail if the monitoring server develops a problem. It is also a potential performance bottleneck, if the server cannot keep up with the demands of the network.

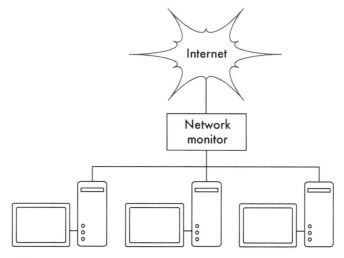

Figure 6.10: By inserting a network monitor between the LAN and your Internet connection, you can observe all network traffic.

A better solution is to use a simple network hub (not a switch) which connects the monitoring machine to the internal LAN, external router, and the monitoring machine. While this does still introduce an additional point of failure to the network (since the entire network will be unreachable if the hub dies), hubs are generally considered to be much more reliable than routers. They are also very easily replaced should they fail.

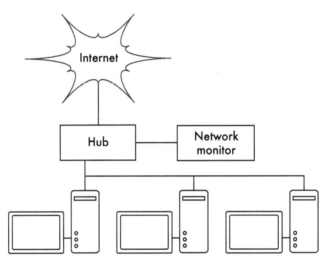

Figure 6.11: If your switch does not provide monitor port functionality, you can insert a network hub between your Internet router and the LAN, and connect the monitoring server to the hub.

Once your monitoring server is in place, you are ready to start collecting data.

What to monitor

It is possible to plot just about any network event and watch its value on a graph over time. Since every network is slightly different, you will have to decide what information is important in order to gauge the performance of your network.

Here are some important indicators that many network administrators will typically track.

Wireless statistics

- Received signal and noise from all backbone nodes
- Number of associated stations
- Detected adjacent networks and channels
- Excessive retransmissions

- Radio data rate, if using automatic rate scaling

Switch statistics

- Bandwidth usage per switch port
- Bandwidth usage broken down by protocol
- Bandwidth usage broken down by MAC address
- Broadcasts as a percentage of total packets
- Packet loss and error rate

Internet statistics

- Internet bandwidth use by host and protocol
- Proxy server cache hits
- Top 100 sites accessed
- DNS requests
- Number of inbound emails / spam emails / email bounces
- Outbound email queue size
- Availability of critical services (web servers, email servers, etc.).
- Ping times and packet loss rates to your ISP
- Status of backups

System health statistics

- Memory usage
- Swap file usage
- Process count / zombie processes
- System load
- Uninterruptible Power Supply (UPS) voltage and load
- Temperature, fan speed, and system voltages
- Disk SMART status
- RAID array status

You should use this list as a suggestion of where to begin. As your network matures, you will likely find new key indicators of network performance, and you should of course track those as well. There are many freely available tools that will show you as much detail as you like about what is happening on your network. You should consider monitoring the availability of any resource where unavailability would adversely affect your network users.

For example, your users may dial into modems on your site to gain remote access to your network. If all the modems are used, or if any are faulty, then users will be denied access and will probably complain. You can predict and avoid such problems by monitoring the number of available modems, and provisioning extra capacity before you run out.

Don't forget to monitor the monitoring machine itself, for example its CPU usage and disk space, in order to receive advance warning if it becomes overloaded or faulty. A monitoring machine that is low on resources can affect your ability to monitor the network effectively.

Types of monitoring tools

We will now look at several different classes of monitoring tools. *Network detection* tools listen for the beacons sent by wireless access points, and display information such as the network name, received signal strength, and channel. *Spot check* tools are designed for troubleshooting and normally run interactively for short periods of time. A program such as `ping` may·be considered an active spot check tool, since it generates traffic by polling a particular machine. Passive spot check tools include *protocol analyzers*, which inspect every packet on the network and provide complete detail about any network conversation (including source and destination addresses, protocol information, and even application data). *Trending* tools perform unattended monitoring over long periods, and typically plot the results on a graph. *Real-time monitoring* tools perform similar monitoring, but notify administrators immediately if they detect a problem. *Throughput testing* tools tell you the actual bandwidth available between two points on a network. *Intrusion detection* tools watch for undesirable or unexpected network traffic, and take appropriate action (typically denying access and/or notifying a network administrator). Finally, *benchmarking* tools estimate the maximum performance of a service or network connection.

Network detection

The simplest wireless monitoring tools simply provide a list of available networks, along with basic information (such as signal strength and channel). They let you quickly detect nearby networks and determine if they are in range or are causing interference.

- **The built-in client.** All modern operating systems provide built-in support for wireless networking. This typically includes the ability to scan for available networks, allowing the user to choose a network from a list. While virtually all wireless devices are guaranteed to have a simple scanning utility, functionality can vary widely between implementations. These tools are typically only useful for configuring a computer in a home or office setting. They tend to provide little information apart from network names and the available signal to the access point currently in use.

- **Netstumbler** (*http://www.netstumbler.com/*). This is the most popular tool for detecting wireless networks using Microsoft Windows. It supports a variety of wireless cards, and is very easy to use. It will detect open and encrypted networks, but cannot detect "closed" wireless networks. It also features a signal/noise meter that plots radio receiver data as a graph over time. It also integrates with a variety of GPS devices, for logging precise location and signal strength information. This makes Netstumbler a handy tool to have for an informal site survey.

- **Ministumbler** (*http://www.netstumbler.com/*). From the makers of Netstumbler, Ministumbler provides much of the same functionality as the Windows version, but works on the Pocket PC platform. Ministumbler is handy to run on a handheld PDA with a wireless card for detecting access points in the field.

- **Macstumbler** (*http://www.macstumbler.com/*). While not directly related to the Netstumbler, Macstumbler provides much of the same functionality but for the Mac OS X platform. It works with all Apple Airport cards.

- **Wellenreiter** (*http://www.wellenreiter.net/*). Wellenreiter is a nice graphical wireless network detector for Linux. It requires Perl and GTK, and supports Prism2, Lucent, and Cisco wireless cards.

Spot check tools

What do you do when the network breaks? If you can't access a web page or email server, and clicking the reload button doesn't fix the problem, then you'll need to be able to isolate the exact location of the problem. These tools will help you to determine just where a connection problem exists.

This section is simply an introduction to commonly used troubleshooting tools. For more discussion of common network problems and how to diagnose them, see **Chapter 9, Troubleshooting**.

ping

Just about every operating system (including Windows, Mac OS X, and of course Linux and BSD) includes a version of the **ping** utility. It uses ICMP packets to attempt to contact a specified host, and tells you how long it takes to get a response.

Knowing what to ping is just as important as knowing how to ping. If you find that you cannot connect to a particular service in your web browser (say, *http://yahoo.com/*), you could try to ping it:

```
$ ping yahoo.com
PING yahoo.com (66.94.234.13): 56 data bytes
64 bytes from 66.94.234.13: icmp_seq=0 ttl=57 time=29.375 ms
64 bytes from 66.94.234.13: icmp_seq=1 ttl=56 time=35.467 ms
64 bytes from 66.94.234.13: icmp_seq=2 ttl=56 time=34.158 ms
^C
--- yahoo.com ping statistics ---
3 packets transmitted, 3 packets received, 0% packet loss
round-trip min/avg/max/stddev = 29.375/33.000/35.467/2.618 ms
```

Hit control-C when you are finished collecting data. If packets take a long time to come back, there may be network congestion. If return ping packets have an unusually low **Time To Live** (**TTL**), you may have routing problems between your machine and the remote end. But what if the ping doesn't return any data at all? If you are pinging a name instead of an IP address, you may be running into DNS problems.

Try pinging an IP address on the Internet. If you can't reach it, it's a good idea to see if you can ping your default router:

```
$ ping 69.90.235.230
PING 69.90.235.230 (69.90.235.230): 56 data bytes
64 bytes from 69.90.235.230: icmp_seq=0 ttl=126 time=12.991 ms
64 bytes from 69.90.235.230: icmp_seq=1 ttl=126 time=14.869 ms
64 bytes from 69.90.235.230: icmp_seq=2 ttl=126 time=13.897 ms
^C
--- 216.231.38.1 ping statistics ---
3 packets transmitted, 3 packets received, 0% packet loss
round-trip min/avg/max/stddev = 12.991/13.919/14.869/0.767 ms
```

If you can't ping your default router, then chances are you won't be able to get to the Internet either. If you can't even ping other IP addresses on your local LAN, then it's time to check your connection. If you're using Ethernet, is it plugged in? If you're using wireless, are you connected to the proper wireless network, and is it in range?

Network debugging with ping is a bit of an art, but it is useful to learn. Since you will likely find ping on just about any machine you will work on, it's a good idea to learn how to use it well.

traceroute and mtr

http://www.bitwizard.nl/mtr/. As with ping, traceroute is found on most operating systems (it's called **tracert** in some versions of Microsoft Windows). By running traceroute, you can find the location of problems between your computer and any point on the Internet:

```
$ traceroute -n google.com
traceroute to google.com (72.14.207.99), 64 hops max, 40 byte packets
 1   10.15.6.1    4.322 ms   1.763 ms   1.731 ms
 2   216.231.38.1   36.187 ms   14.648 ms   13.561 ms
 3   69.17.83.233   14.197 ms   13.256 ms   13.267 ms
 4   69.17.83.150   32.478 ms   29.545 ms   27.494 ms
 5   198.32.176.31   40.788 ms   28.160 ms   28.115 ms
 6   66.249.94.14   28.601 ms   29.913 ms   28.811 ms
 7   172.16.236.8   2328.809 ms   2528.944 ms   2428.719 ms
 8   * * *
```

The **-n** switch tells traceroute not to bother resolving names in DNS, and makes the trace run more quickly. You can see that at hop seven, the round trip time shoots up to more than two seconds, while packets seem to be discarded at hop eight. This might indicate a problem at that point in the network. If this part of the network is in your control, it might be worth starting your troubleshooting effort there.

My TraceRoute (**mtr**) is a handy program that combines ping and traceroute into a single tool. By running mtr, you can get an ongoing average of latency and packet loss to a single host, instead of the momentary snapshot that ping and traceroute provide.

```
                          My traceroute  [v0.69]
tesla.rob.swn (0.0.0.0)          (tos=0x0 psize=64 bitpatSun Jan  8 20:01:26 2006
Keys:  Help    Display mode    Restart statistics    Order of fields    quit
                                 Packets                 Pings
Host                             Loss%   Snt    Last   Avg   Best   Wrst StDev
1. gremlin.rob.swn               0.0%     4     1.9   2.0   1.7    2.6   0.4
2. er1.sea1.speakeasy.net        0.0%     4    15.5  14.0  12.7   15.5   1.3
3. 220.ge-0-1-0.cr2.sea1.speakeasy.   0.0%  4   11.0  11.7  10.7   14.0   1.6
4. fe-0-3-0.cr2.sfo1.speakeasy.net    0.0%  4   36.0  34.7  28.7   38.1   4.1
5. bas1-m.pao.yahoo.com          0.0%     4    27.9  29.6  27.9   33.0   2.4
6. so-1-1-0.pat1.dce.yahoo.com   0.0%     4    89.7  91.0  89.7   93.0   1.4
7. ae1.p400.msr1.dcn.yahoo.com   0.0%     4    91.2  93.1  90.8   99.2   4.1
8. ge5-2.bas1-m.dcn.yahoo.com    0.0%     4    89.3  91.0  89.3   93.4   1.9
9. w2.rc.vip.dcn.yahoo.com       0.0%     3    91.2  93.1  90.8   99.2   4.1
```

The data will be continuously updated and averaged over time. As with ping, you should hit control-C when you are finished looking at the data. Note that you must have root privileges to run mtr.

While these tools will not revel precisely what is wrong with the network, they can give you enough information to know where to continue troubleshooting.

Protocol analyzers

Network protocol analyzers provide a great deal of detail about information flowing through a network, by allowing you to inspect individual packets. For wired networks, you can inspect packets at the data-link layer or above. For wireless networks, you can inspect information all the way down to individual 802.11 frames. Here are several popular (and free) network protocol analyzers:

Kismet

http://www.kismetwireless.net/.   Kismet is a powerful wireless protocol analyzer for many platforms including Linux, Mac OS X, and even the embedded
OpenWRT Linux distribution. It works with any wireless card that supports
passive monitor mode. In addition to basic network detection, Kismet will
passively log all 802.11 frames to disk or to the network in standard PCAP
format, for later analysis with tools like Ethereal. Kismet also features associated client information, AP hardware fingerprinting, Netstumbler detection,
and GPS integration.

Since it is a passive network monitor, it can even detect "closed" wireless
networks by analyzing traffic sent by wireless clients. You can run Kismet on
several machines at once, and have them all report over the network back to
a central user interface. This allows for wireless monitoring over a large area,
such as a university or corporate campus.

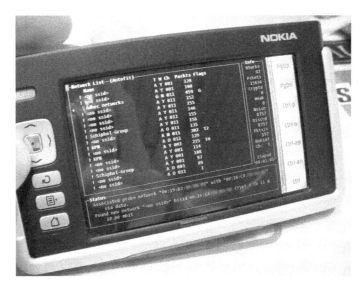

Figure 6.12: Kismet running on a Nokia 770 Internet Tablet

Since Kismet uses the radio card's passive monitor mode, it does all of this
without transmitting any data. Kismet is an invaluable tool for diagnosing
wireless network problems.

KisMAC

http://kismac.macpirate.ch/.   Exclusively for the Mac OS X platform, KisMAC
does much of what Kismet can do, but with a slick Mac OS X graphical interface.   It is a passive scanner that will log data to disk in PCAP format com-
patible with Wireshark.   It supports passive scanning with AirportExtreme
cards as well as a variety of USB wireless adapters.

tcpdump

http://www.tcpdump.org/. **tcpdump** is a command-line tool for monitoring network traffic. It does not have all the bells and whistles of wireshark but it does use fewer resources. Tcpdump can capture and display all network protocol information down to the link layer. It can show all of the packet headers and data received, or just the packets that match particular criteria. Packets captured with tcpdump can be loaded into wireshark for visual analysis and further diagnostics. This is very useful if you wish to monitor an interface on a remote system and bring the file back to your local machine for analysis. The tcpdump tool is available as a standard tool in Unix derivatives (Linux, BSD, and Mac OS X). There is also a Windows port called **WinDump** available at *http://www.winpcap.org/windump/*.

Wireshark

http://www.wireshark.org/. Formerly known as **Ethereal**, Wireshark is a free network protocol analyzer for Unix and Windows. It is billed as "The World's Most Popular Network Protocol Analyzer."

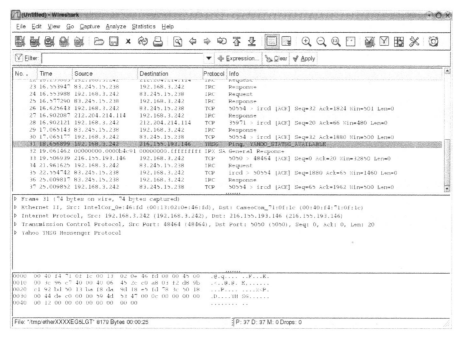

Figure 6.13: Wireshark (formerly Ethereal) is a powerful network protocol analyzer that can show you as much detail as you like about any packet.

Wireshark allows you to examine data from a live network or from a capture file on disk, and interactively browse and sort the captured data. Both summary and detailed information is available for each packet, including the full header and data portions. Wireshark has several powerful features, including a rich display filter language and the ability to view the reconstructed stream of a TCP session.

It can be daunting to use for first time users or those that are not familiar with the OSI layers. It is typically used to isolate and analyze specific traffic to or from an IP address, but it can be also used as a general purpose fault finding tool. For example, a machine infected with a network worm or virus can be identified by looking for the machine that is send out the same sort of TCPIP packets to large groups of IP addresses.

Trending tools

Trending tools are used to see how your network is used over a long period of time. They work by periodically monitoring your network activity, and displaying a summary in a human-readable form (such as a graph). Trending tools collect data as well as analyze and report on it.

Below are some examples of trending tools. Some of them need to be used in conjunction with each other, as they are not stand-alone programs.

MRTG

http://oss.oetiker.ch/mrtg/. The **Multi Router Traffic Grapher** (**MRTG**) monitors the traffic load on network links using SNMP. MRTG generates graphs that provide a visual representation of inbound and outbound traffic. These are typically displayed on a web page.

MRTG can be a little confusing to set up, especially if you are not familiar with SNMP. But once it is installed, MRTG requires virtually no maintenance, unless you change something on the system that is being monitored (such as its IP address).

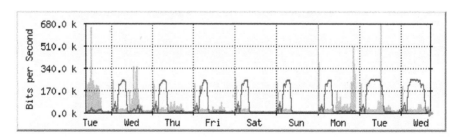

Figure 6.14: MRTG is probably the most widely installed network flow grapher.

RRDtool

http://oss.oetiker.ch/rrdtool/. **RRD** is short for **Round Robin Database**. RRD is a database that stores information in a very compact way that does not expand over time. **RRDtool** refers to a suite of tools that allow you to create and modify RRD databases, as well as generate useful graphs to present the data. It is used to keep track of time-series data (such as network bandwidth, machine room temperature, or server load average) and can display that data as an average over time.

Note that RRDtool itself does not contact network devices to retrieve data. It is merely a database manipulation tool. You can use a simple wrapper script (typically in shell or Perl) to do that work for you. RRDtool is also used by many full featured front-ends that present you with a friendly web interface for configuration and display. RRD graphs give you more control over display options and the number of items available on a graph as compared to MRTG.

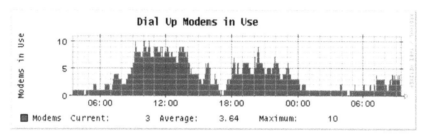

Figure 6.15: RRDtool gives you a lot of flexibility in how your collected network data may be displayed.

RRDtool is included in virtually all modern Linux distributions, and can be downloaded from *http://oss.oetiker.ch/rrdtool/*.

ntop

http://www.ntop.org/. For historical traffic analysis and usage, you will certainly want to investigate **ntop**. This program builds a detailed real-time report on observed network traffic, displayed in your web browser. It integrates with rrdtool, and makes graphs and charts visually depicting how the network is being used. On very busy networks, ntop can use a lot of CPU and disk space, but it gives you extensive insight into how your network is being used. It runs on Linux, BSD, Mac OS X, and Windows.

Some of its more useful features include:

- Traffic display can be sorted by various criteria (source, destination, protocol, MAC address, etc.).
- Traffic statistics grouped by protocol and port number
- An IP traffic matrix which shows connections between machines
- Network flows for routers or switches that support the NetFlow protocol
- Host operating system identification

- P2P traffic identification

- Numerous graphical charts

- Perl, PHP, and Python API

Ntop is available from *http://www.ntop.org/* and is available for most operating systems. It is often included in many of the popular Linux distributions, including RedHat, Debian, and Ubuntu. While it can be left running to collect historical data, ntop can be fairly CPU intensive, depending on the amount of traffic observed. If you are going to run it for long periods you should monitor the CPU utilization of the monitoring machine.

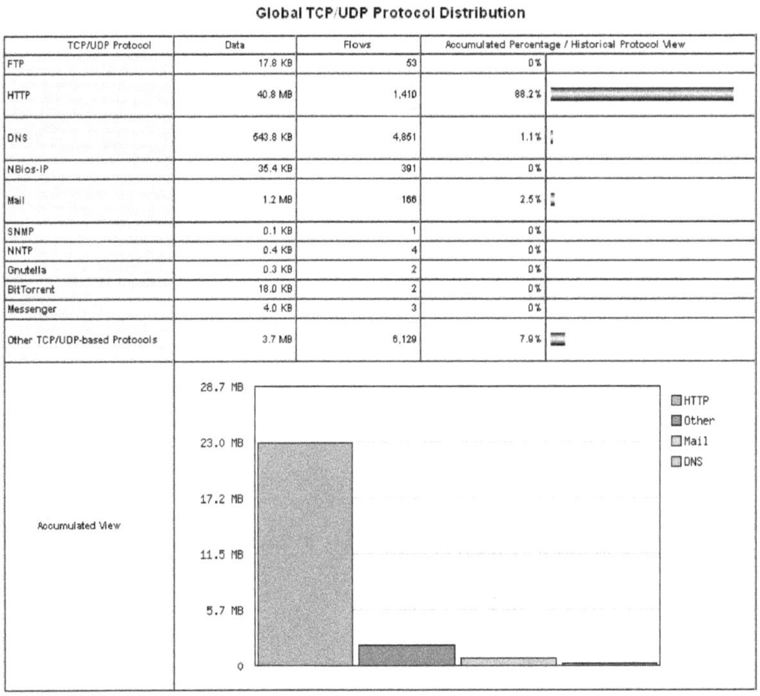

Global TCP/UDP Protocol Distribution

TCP/UDP Protocol	Data	Flows	Accumulated Percentage / Historical Protocol View
FTP	17.8 KB	53	0%
HTTP	40.8 MB	1,410	88.2%
DNS	643.8 KB	4,851	1.1%
NBios-IP	35.4 KB	391	0%
Mail	1.2 MB	166	2.5%
SNMP	0.1 KB	1	0%
NNTP	0.4 KB	4	0%
Gnutella	0.3 KB	2	0%
BitTorrent	16.0 KB	2	0%
Messenger	4.0 KB	3	0%
Other TCP/UDP-based Protocols	3.7 MB	6,129	7.9%

Figure 6.16: ntop displays a wealth of information about how your network is utilized by various clients and servers.

The main disadvantage of ntop is that it does not provide instantaneous information, only long-term totals and averages. This can make it difficult to use to diagnose a problem that starts suddenly.

Cacti

http://www.cacti.net/. **Cacti** is a front-end for RRDtool. It stores all of the necessary information to create graphs in a MySQL database. The front-end is written in PHP. Cacti does the work of maintaining graphs, data sources, and handles the actual data gathering. There is support for SNMP devices, and custom scripts can easily be written to poll virtually any conceivable network event.

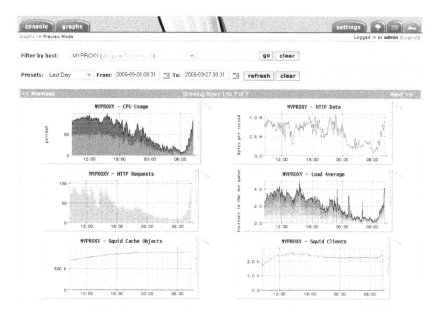

Figure 6.17: Cacti can manage the polling of your network devices, and can build very complex and informative visualizations of network behavior.

Cacti can be somewhat confusing to configure, but once you work through the documentation and examples, it can yield very impressive graphs. There are hundreds of templates for various systems available on the cacti website, and the code is under rapid development.

NetFlow

NetFlow is a protocol for collecting IP traffic information invented by Cisco. From the Cisco website:

> *Cisco IOS NetFlow efficiently provides a key set of services for IP applications, including network traffic accounting, usage-based network billing, network planning, security, Denial of Service monitoring capabilities, and network monitoring. NetFlow provides valuable information about network users and applications, peak usage times, and traffic routing.*

Cisco routers can generate NetFlow information which is available from the router in the form of UDP packets. NetFlow is also less CPU-intensive on Cisco routers than using SNMP. It also provides more granular information than SNMP, letting you get a more detailed picture of port and protocol usage.

This information is collected by a NetFlow collector that stores and presents the data as an aggregate over time. By analyzing flow data, one can build a picture of traffic flow and traffic volume in a network or on a connection. There are several commercial and free NetFlow collectors available. Ntop is one free tool that can act as a NetFlow collector and probe. Another is Flowc (see below).

It can also be desirable to use Netflow as a spot check tool, by just looking at a quick snapshot of data during a network crisis. Think of NetFlow as an alternative to SNMP for Cisco devices. For more information about NetFlow, see *http://en.wikipedia.org/wiki/Netflow* .

Flowc

http://netacad.kiev.ua/flowc/. **Flowc** is an open source NetFlow collector (see NetFlow above). It is lightweight and easy to configure. Flowc uses a MySQL database to store aggregated traffic information. Therefore, it is possible to generate your own reports from the data using SQL, or use the included report generators. The built-in report generators produce reports in HTML, plain text or a graphical format.

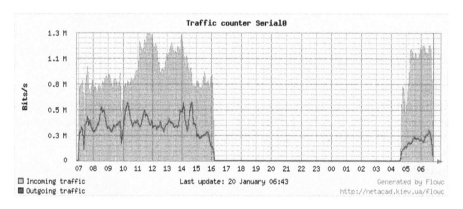

Figure 6.18: A typical flow chart generated by Flowc.

The large gap in data probably indicates a network outage. Trending tools typically will not notify you of outages, but merely log the occurrence. To be notified when network problems occur, use a realtime monitoring tool such as Nagios (see **Page 200**).

SmokePing

http://oss.oetiker.ch/smokeping/. **SmokePing** is a deluxe latency measurement tool written in Perl. It can measure, store and display latency, latency distribution and packet loss all on a single graph. SmokePing uses RRDtool for data storage, and can draw very informative graphs that present up to the minute information on the state of your network connection.

It is very useful to run SmokePing on a host with good connectivity to your entire network. Over time, trends are revealed that can point to all sorts of network problems. Combined with MRTG (see **Page 190**) or Cacti (see **Page 192**), you can observe the effect that network congestion has on packet loss and latency. SmokePing can optionally send alerts when certain conditions are met, such as when excessive packet loss is seen on a link for an extended period of time. An example of SmokePing in action is shown in **Figure 6.19**.

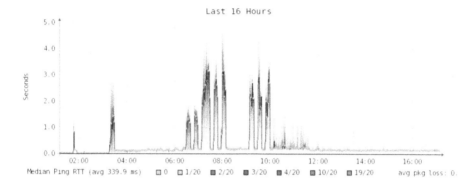

Figure 6.19: SmokePing can simultaneously display packet loss and latency spreads in a single graph.

EtherApe

http://etherape.sourceforge.net/. **EtherApe** displays a graphical representation of network traffic. Hosts and links change size depending on the amount of traffic sent and received. The colors change to represent the protocol most used. As with wireshark and tcpdump, data can be captured "off the wire" from a live network connection or read from a tcpdump capture file.

EtherApe doesn't show quite as much detail as ntop, but its resource requirements are much lighter.

iptraf

http://iptraf.seul.org/. **IPTraf** is a lightweight but powerful LAN monitor. It has an ncurses interface and runs in a command shell. IPTraf takes a moment to measure observed traffic, and then displays various network statistics including TCP and UDP connections, ICMP and OSPF information, traffic flows, IP checksum errors, and more. It is a simple to use program that uses minimal system resources.

While it does not keep historical data, it is very useful for displaying an instantaneous usage report.

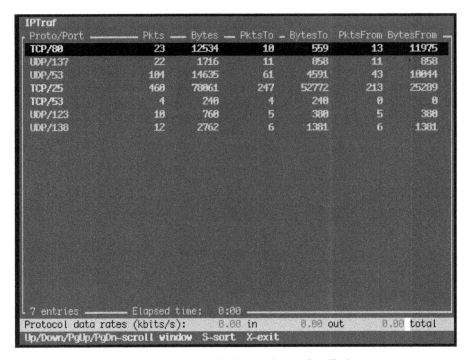

Figure 6.20: iptraf's statistical breakdown of traffic by port.

Argus

http://qosient.com/argus/. **Argus** stands for **Audit Record Generation and Utilization System**. Argus is also the name of the mythological Greek god who had hundreds of eyes.

From the Argus website:

> *Argus generates flow statistics such as connectivity, capacity, demand, loss, delay, and jitter on a per transaction basis. Argus can be used to analyze and report on the contents of packet capture files or it can run as a continuous monitor, examining data from a live interface; generating an audit log of all the network activity seen in the packet stream. Argus can be deployed to monitor individual end-systems, or an entire enterprises network activity. As a continuous monitor, Argus provides both push and pull data handling models, to allow flexible strategies for collecting network audit data. Argus data clients support a range of operations, such as sorting, aggregation, archival and reporting.*

Argus consists of two parts: a master collector that reads packets from a network device, and a client that connects to the master and displays the usage statistics. Argus runs on BSD, Linux, and most other UNIX systems.

NeTraMet

http://freshmeat.net/projects/netramet/. **NeTraMet** is another popular flow analysis tool. Like Argus, NeTraMet consists of two parts: a collector that gathers statistics via SNMP, and a manager that specifies which flows should be watched. Flows are specified using a simple programming language that define the addresses used on either end, and can include Ethernet, IP, protocol information, or other identifiers. NeTraMet runs on DOS and most UNIX systems, including Linux and BSD.

Throughput testing

How fast can the network go? What is the actual usable capacity of a particular network link? You can get a very good estimate of your throughput capacity by flooding the link with traffic and measuring how long it takes to transfer the data.

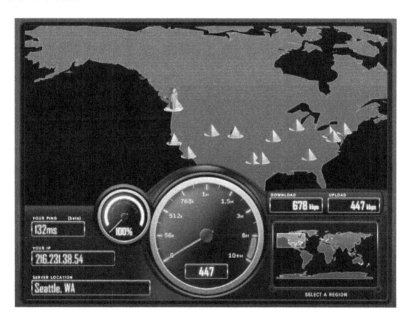

Figure 6.21: Tools such as this one from SpeedTest.net are pretty, but don't always give you an accurate picture of network performance.

While there are web pages available that will perform a "speed test" in your browser (such as *http://www.dslreports.com/stest* or *http://speedtest.net/*), these tests are increasingly inaccurate as you get further from the testing source. Even worse, they do not allow you to test the speed of a given link, but only the speed of your link to a particular site on the Internet. Here are a few tools that will allow you to perform throughput testing on your own networks.

ttcp

http://ftp.arl.mil/ftp/pub/ttcp/.   Now a standard part of most Unix-like systems, **ttcp** is a simple network performance testing tool.   One instance is run on either side of the link you want to test.   The first node runs in receive mode, and the other transmits:

```
node_a$ ttcp -r -s

node_b$ ttcp -t -s node_a
ttcp-t: buflen=8192, nbuf=2048, align=16384/0, port=5001  tcp -> node_a
ttcp-t: socket
ttcp-t: connect
ttcp-t: 16777216 bytes in 249.14 real seconds = 65.76 KB/sec +++
ttcp-t: 2048 I/O calls, msec/call = 124.57, calls/sec = 8.22
ttcp-t: 0.0user 0.2sys 4:09real 0% 0i+0d 0maxrss 0+0pf 7533+0csw
```

After collecting data in one direction, you should reverse the transmit and receive partners to test the link in the other direction.   It can test UDP as well as TCP streams, and can alter various TCP parameters and buffer lengths to give the network a good workout. It can even use a user-supplied data stream instead of sending random data.   Remember that the speed readout is in kilobytes, not kilobits. Multiply the result by 8 to find the speed in kilobits per second.

The only real disadvantage to ttcp is that it hasn't been developed in years. Fortunately, the code has been released in the public domain and is freely available. Like ping and traceroute, ttcp is found as a standard tool on many systems.

iperf

http://dast.nlanr.net/Projects/Iperf/.   Much like ttcp, **iperf** is a commandline tool for estimating the throughput of a network connection. It supports many of the same features as ttcp, but uses a "client" and "server" model instead of a "receive" and "transmit" pair. To run iperf, launch a server on one side and a client on the other:

```
node_a$ iperf -s

node_b$ iperf -c node_a
------------------------------------------------------------
Client connecting to node_a, TCP port 5001
TCP window size: 16.0 KByte (default)
------------------------------------------------------------
[  5] local 10.15.6.1 port 1212 connected with 10.15.6.23 port 5001
[ ID] Interval       Transfer     Bandwidth
[  5]  0.0-11.3 sec   768 KBytes   558 Kbits/sec
```

The server side will continue to listen and accept client connections on port 5001 until you hit control-C to kill it. This can make it handy when running multiple test runs from a variety of locations.

The biggest difference between ttcp and iperf is that iperf is under active development, and has many new features (including IPv6 support). This makes it a good choice as a performance tool when building new networks.

bing

http://fgouget.free.fr/bing/index-en.shtml. Rather than flood a connection with data and see how long the transfer takes to complete, **Bing** attempts to estimate the available throughput of a point-to-point connection by analyzing round trip times for various sized ICMP packets. While it is not always as accurate as a flood test, it can provide a good estimate without transmitting a large number of bytes.

Since bing works using standard ICMP echo requests, so it can estimate available bandwidth without the need to run a special client on the other end, and can even attempt to estimate the throughput of links outside your network. Since it uses relatively little bandwidth, bing can give you a rough idea of network performance without running up the charges that a flood test would certainly incur.

Realtime tools

It is desirable to find out when people are trying to break into your network, or when some part of the network has failed. Because no system administrator can be monitoring a network all the time, there are programs that constantly monitor the status of the network and can send alerts when notable events occur. The following are some open source tools that can help perform this task.

Snort

Snort (*http://www.snort.org/*) is a packet sniffer and logger which can be used as a lightweight network intrusion detection system. It features rule-based logging and can perform protocol analysis, content searching, and packet matching. It can be used to detect a variety of attacks and probes, such as stealth port scans, CGI attacks, SMB probes, OS fingerprinting attempts, and many other kinds of anomalous traffic patterns. Snort has a real-time alert capability that can notify administrators about problems as they occur with a variety of methods.

Installing and running Snort is not trivial, and depending on the amount of network traffic, will likely require a dedicated monitoring machine with considerable resources. Fortunately, Snort is very well documented and has a strong user community. By implementing a comprehensive Snort rule set, you can identify unexpected behavior that would otherwise mysteriously eat up your Internet bandwidth.

See *http://snort.org/docs/* for an extensive list of installation and configuration resources.

Apache: mod_security

ModSecurity (*http://www.modsecurity.org/*) is an open source intrusion detection and prevention engine for web applications. This kind of security tool is also known as a *web application firewall*. ModSecurity increases web application security by protecting web applications from known and unknown attacks. It can be used on its own, or as a module in the Apache web server (*http://www.apache.org/*).

There are several sources for updated mod_security rules that help protect against the latest security exploits. One excellent resource is GotRoot, which maintains a huge and frequently updated repository of rules:

http://gotroot.com/tiki-index.php?page=mod_security+rules

Web application security is important in defending against attacks on your web server, which could result in the theft of valuable or personal data, or in the server being used to launch attacks or send spam to other Internet users. As well as being damaging to the Internet as a whole, such intrusions can seriously reduce your available bandwidth.

Nagios

Nagios (*http://nagios.org/*) is a program that monitors hosts and services on your network, notifying you immediately when problems arise. It can send notifications via email, SMS, or by running a script, and will send notifications to the relevant person or group depending on the nature of the problem. Nagios runs on Linux or BSD, and provides a web interface to show up-to-the-minute system status.

Nagios is extensible, and can monitor the status of virtually any network event. It performs checks by running small scripts at regular intervals, and checks the results against an expected response. This can yield much more sophisticated checks than a simple network probe. For example, ping (**page 185**) may tell you that a machine is up, and nmap may report that a TCP port responds to requests, but Nagios can actually retrieve a web page or make a database request, and verify that the response is not an error.

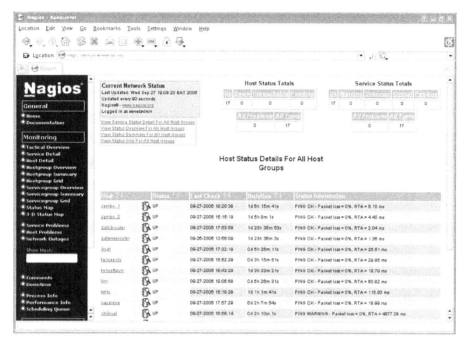

Figure 6.22: Nagios keeps you informed the moment a network fault or service outage occurs.

Nagios can even notify you when bandwidth usage, packet loss, machine room temperature, or other network health indicator crosses a particular threshold. This can give you advance warning of network problems, often allowing you to respond to the problem before users have a chance to complain.

Zabbix

Zabbix (*http://www.zabbix.org/*) is an open source realtime monitoring tool that is something of a hybrid between Cacti and Nagios. It uses a SQL database for data storage, has its own graph rendering package, and performs all of the functions you would expect from a modern realtime monitor (such as SNMP polling and instant notification of error conditions). Zabbix is released under the GNU General Public License.

Other useful tools

There are thousands of free network monitoring tools that fill very specialized needs. Here are a few of our favorites that don't quite fit into the above categories.

Driftnet and Etherpeg.

These tools decode graphical data (such as GIF and JPEG files) and display them as a collage. As mentioned earlier, tools such as these are of limited use in troubleshooting problems, but are very valuable for demonstrating the insecurity of unencrypted protocols. **Etherpeg** is available from *http://www.etherpeg.org/*, and **Driftnet** can be downloaded at *http://www.ex-parrot.com/~chris/driftnet/*.

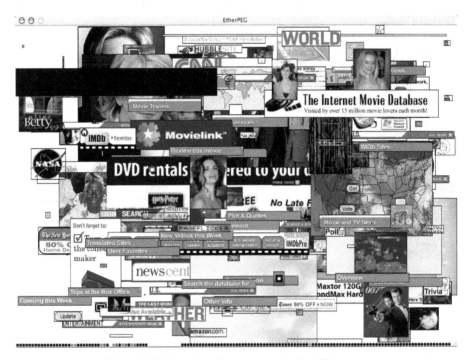

Figure 6.23: A web collage generated by Etherpeg.

ngrep

Ngrep provides most of GNU grep's pattern matching features, but applies them to network traffic. It currently recognizes IPv4 and IPv6, TCP, UDP, ICMP, IGMP, PPP, SLIP, FDDI, Token Ring, and much more. As it makes extensive use of regular expression matches, it is a tool suited to advanced users or those that have a good knowledge of regular expressions.

But you don't necessarily need to be a regex expert to be able to make basic use of ngrep. For example, to view all packets that contain the string GET (presumably HTTP requests), try this:

```
# ngrep -q GET
```

Pattern matches can be constrained further to match particular protocols, ports, or other criteria using BPF filters. This is the filter language used by common packet sniffing tools, such as tcpdump and snoop.   To view GET or POST strings sent to destination port 80, use this command line:

```
# ngrep -q 'GET|POST' port 80
```

By using ngrep creatively, you can detect anything from virus activity to spam email. You can download ngrep at *http://ngrep.sourceforge.net/*.

What is normal?

If you are looking for a definitive answer as to what your traffic patterns **should** look like, you are going to be disappointed. There is no absolute right answer to this question, but given some work you can determine what is normal for your network. While every environment is different, some of the factors that can influence the appearance of your traffic patterns are:

• The capacity of your Internet connection

• The number of users that have access to the network

• The social policy (byte charging, quotas, honor system, etc.).

• The number, types, and level of services offered

• The health of the network (presence of viruses, excessive broadcasts, routing loops, open email relays, denial of service attacks, etc.).

• The competence of your computer users

• The location and configuration of control structures (firewalls, proxy servers, caches, and so on)

This is not a definitive list, but should give you an idea of how a wide range of factors can affect your bandwidth patterns. With this in mind, let's look at the topic of baselines.

Establishing a baseline

Since every environment is different, you need to determine for yourself what your traffic patterns look like under normal situations. This is useful because it allows you to identify changes over time, either sudden or gradual. These changes may in turn indicate a problem, or a potential future problem, with your network.

For example, suppose that your network grinds to a halt, and you are not sure of the cause. Fortunately, you have decided to keep a graph of broadcasts as a percentage of the overall network traffic. If this graph shows a sudden increase in the amount of broadcast traffic, it may mean that your network has been infected with a virus. Without an idea of what is "normal" for your network (a baseline), you would not be able to see that the number of broadcasts had increased, only that it was relatively high, which may not indicate a problem.

Baseline graphs and figures are also useful when analyzing the effects of changes made to the network. It is often very useful to experiment with such changes by trying different possible values. Knowing what the baseline looks like will show you whether your changes have improved matters, or made them worse.

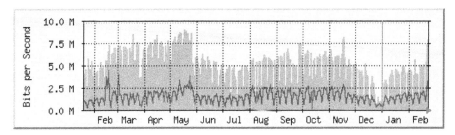

Figure 6.24: By collecting data over a long period of time, you can predict the growth of your network and make changes before problems develop.

In **Figure 6.24**, we can see the effect the implementation of delay pools has made on Internet utilization around the period of May. If we did not keep a graph of the line utilization, we would never know what the effect of the change over the long term was. When watching a total traffic graph after making changes, don't assume that just because the graph does not change radically that your efforts were wasted. You might have removed frivolous usage from your line only to have it replaced by genuine legitimate traffic. You could then combine this baseline with others, say the top 100 sites accessed or the average utilization by your top twenty users, to determine if habits have simply changed. As we will see later, MRTG, RRDtool, and Cacti are excellent tools you can use to keep a baseline.

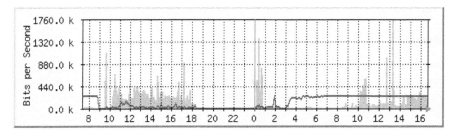

Figure 6.25: The traffic trend at Aidworld logged over a single day.

Figure 6.25 shows traffic on an Aidworld firewall over a period of 24 hours. There is nothing apparently wrong with this graph, but users were complaining about slow Internet access.

Figure 6.26 shows that the upload bandwidth use (dark area) was higher during working hours on the last day than on previous days. A period of heavy upload usage started every morning at 03:00, and was normally finished by 09:00, but on the last day it was still running at 16:30. Further investigation revealed a problem with the backup software, which ran at 03:00 every day.

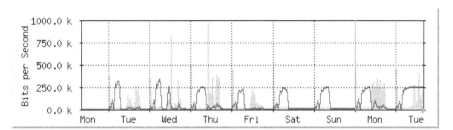

Figure 6.26: The same network logged over an entire week reveals a problem with backups, which caused unexpected congestion for network users.

Figure 6.27 shows measurements of latency on the same connection as measured by a program called SmokePing. The position of the dots shows the average latency, while the gray smoke indicates the distribution of latency (jitter). The color of the dots indicates the number of lost packets. This graph over a period of four hours does not help to identify whether there are any problems on the network.

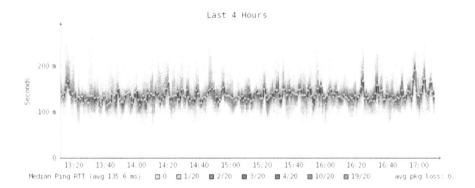

Figure 6.27: Four hours of jitter and packet loss.

The next graph (**Figure 6.28**) shows the same data over a period of 16 hours. This indicates that the values in the graph above are close to the normal level (baseline), but that there were significant increases in latency at several times during the early morning, up to 30 times the baseline value. This indicates that additional monitoring should be performed during these early morning periods to establish the cause of the high latency, which is probably heavy traffic of some kind.

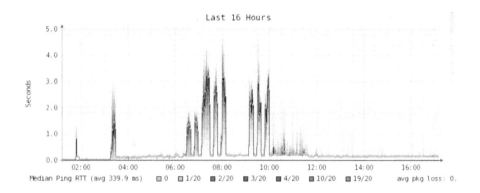

Figure 6.28: A higher spread of jitter is revealed in the 16 hour log.

Figure 6.29 shows that Tuesday was significantly worse than Sunday or Monday for latency, especially during the early morning period. This might indicate that something has changed on the network.

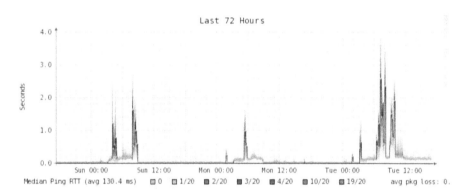

Figure 6.29: Zooming out to the week long view reveals a definite repetition of increased latency and packet loss in the early morning hours.

How do I interpret the traffic graph?

In a basic network flow graph (such as that generated by the network monitor MRTG), the green area indicates **inbound traffic**, while the blue line indicates **outbound traffic**. Inbound traffic is traffic that originates from another network (typically the Internet) and is addressed to a computer inside your network. Outbound traffic is traffic that originates from your network, and is addressed to a computer somewhere on the Internet. Depending on what sort of network environment you have, the graph will help you understand how your network is actually being used. For example, monitoring of servers usually reveals larger amounts of outbound traffic as the servers respond to requests (such as sending mail or serving web pages), while monitoring client machines might reveal higher amounts of inbound traffic to the machines as they receive data from the servers.

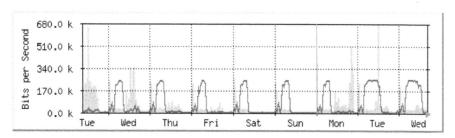

Figure 6.30: The classic network flow graph. The dark area represents inbound traffic, while the line represents outbound traffic. The repeating arcs of outbound traffic show when the nightly backups have run.

Traffic patterns will vary with what you are monitoring. A router will normally show more incoming traffic than outgoing traffic as users download data from the Internet. An excess of outbound bandwidth that is not transmitted by your network servers may indicate a peer-to-peer client, unauthorized server, or even a virus on one or more of your clients. There are no set metrics that indicate what outgoing traffic to incoming traffic should look like. It is up to you to establish a baseline to understand what normal network traffic patterns look like on your network.

Detecting network overload

Figure 6.31 shows traffic on an overloaded Internet connection.

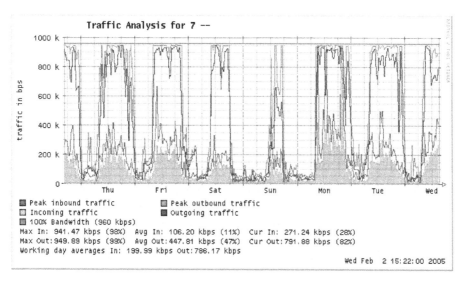

Figure 6.31: Flat-topped graphs indicate that a line is using the maximum available bandwidth, and is overutilized during these times.

The most apparent sign of overloading is the flat tops on outbound traffic during the middle of every day. Flat tops may indicate overloading, even if they are well below the maximum theoretical capacity of the link. In this case it may indicate that you are not getting as much bandwidth from your service provider as you expect.

Measuring 95th percentile

The 95th percentile is a widely used mathematical calculation to evaluate regular and sustained utilization of a network pipe. Its value shows the highest consumption of traffic for a given period. Calculating the 95th percentile means that 95% of the time the usage is below a certain amount, and 5% of the time usage is above that amount. The 95th percentile is a good value to use to show the bandwidth that is actually used at least 95% of the time.

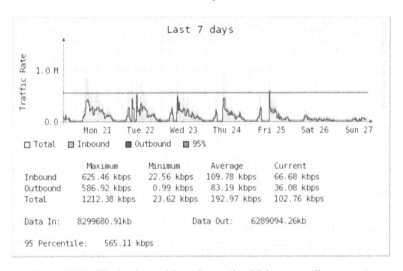

Figure 6.32: The horizontal line shows the 95th percentile amount.

MRTG and Cacti will calculate the 95th Percentile for you. This is a sample graph of a 960 kbps connection. The 95th percentile came to 945 kbps after discarding the highest 5% of traffic.

Monitoring RAM and CPU usage

By definition, servers provide critical services that should always be available. Servers receive and respond to client machine requests, providing access to services that are the whole point of having a network in the first place. Therefore, servers must have sufficient hardware capabilities to accommodate the work load. This means they must have adequate RAM, storage, and processing power to accommodate the number of client requests. Otherwise, the server will take longer to respond, or in the worst case, may be incapable of responding at all. Since hardware resources are finite, it is important to keep track of how system resources are being used. If a core server (such as a proxy server or email server) is overwhelmed by requests, access times become slow. This is often perceived by users as a network problem.

There are several programs that can be used to monitor resources on a server. The simplest method on a Windows machine is to access the Task Manager using the **Ctrl Alt + Del** keys, and then click on the Performance tab. On a Linux or BSD box, you can type **top** in a terminal window. To keep historical logs of such performance, MRTG or RRDtool (on **Page 190**) can also be used.

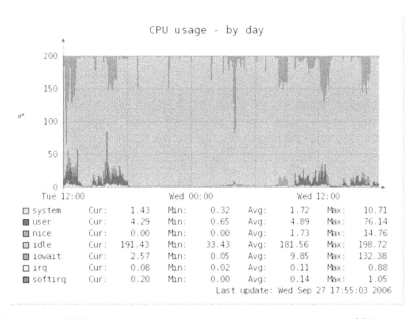

Figure 6.33: RRDtool can show arbitrary data, such as memory and CPU usage, expressed as an average over time.

Mail servers require adequate space, as some people may prefer to leave their email messages on the server for long periods of time. The messages can accumulate and fill the hard disk, especially if quotas are not in use. If the disk or partition used for mail storage fills up, the mail server cannot receive mail. If that disk is also used by the system, all kinds of system problems may occur as the operating system runs out of swap space and temporary storage.

File servers need to be monitored, even if they have large disks. Users will find a way to fill any size disk more quickly than you might think. Disk usage can be enforced through the use of quotas, or by simply monitoring usage and telling people when they are using too much. Nagios (see **Page 200**) can notify you when disk usage, CPU utilization, or other system resources cross a critical threshold.

If a machine becomes unresponsive or slow, and measurements show that a system resource is being heavily used, this may be an indication that an upgrade is required. If processor usage constantly exceeds 60% of the total, it may be time to upgrade the processor. Slow speeds could also be as a result of insufficient RAM. Be sure to check the overall usage of CPU, RAM, and disk space before deciding to upgrade a particular component.

A simple way to check whether a machine has insufficient RAM is to look at the hard disk light. When the light is on constantly, it usually means that the machine is constantly swapping large amounts of data to and from the disk. This is known as **thrashing**, and is extremely bad for performance. It can usually be fixed by investigating which process is using the most RAM, and killing or reconfiguring that process. Failing that, the system needs more RAM.

You should always determine whether it is more cost effective to upgrade an individual component or purchase a whole new machine. Some computers are difficult or impossible to upgrade, and it often costs more to replace individual components than to replace the entire system. Since the availability of parts and systems varies widely around the world, be sure to weigh the cost of parts vs. whole systems, including shipping and taxes, when determining the cost of upgrading.

7

Solar Power

This chapter provides an introduction to the components of a ***standalone photovoltaic system***. The word standalone refers to the fact that the system works without any connection to an established power grid. In this chapter, we will present the basic concepts of the generation and storage of photovoltaic solar energy. We will also provide a method for designing a functional solar system with limited access to information and resources.

This chapter only discusses the use of solar energy for the direct production of electricity (***photovoltaic solar energy***). Solar energy can also be used to heat fluids (***thermal solar energy***) which can then be used as a heat source or to turn a turbine to generate electricity. Thermal solar energy systems are beyond the scope of this chapter.

Solar energy

A photovoltaic system is based on the ability of certain materials to convert the radiant energy of the sun into electrical energy. The total amount of solar energy that lights a given area is known as ***irradiance*** (***G***) and it is measured in ***watts per square meter*** (***W/m^2***). The instantaneous values are normally averaged over a period of time, so it is common to talk about total irradiance per hour, day or month.

Of course, the precise amount of radiation that arrives at the surface of the Earth cannot be predicted with high precision, due to natural weather variations. Therefore it is necessary to work with statistical data based on the "solar history" of a particular place. This data is gathered by a weather station over a long period and is available from a number of sources, as tables or databases. In most cases, it can be difficult to find detailed information about a specific area, and you will need to work with approximate values.

A few organizations have produced maps that include average values of daily global irradiation for different regions. These values are known as **peak sun hours** or **PSH**s. You can use the PSH value for your region to simplify your calculations. One unit of "peak sun" corresponds to a radiation of 1000 Watts per square meter. If we find that certain area has 4 PSH in the worst of the months, it means that in that month we should not expect a daily irradiation bigger than 4000 W/m² (day). The peak sun hours are an easy way to represent the worst case average of irradiation per day.

Low resolution PSH maps are available from a number of online sources, such as *http://www.solar4power.com/solar-power-global-maps.html*. For more detailed information, consult a local solar energy vendor or weather station.

What about wind power?

It is possible to use a wind generator in place of solar panels when an autonomous system is being designed for installation on a hill or mountain. To be effective, the average wind speed over the year should be at least 3 to 4 meter per second, and the wind generator should be 6 meters higher than other objects within a distance of 100 meters. A location far away from the coast usually lacks sufficient wind energy to support a wind powered system.

Generally speaking, photovoltaic systems are more reliable than wind generators, as sunlight is more available than consistent wind in most places. On the other hand, wind generators are able to charge batteries even at night, as long as there is sufficient wind. It is of course possible to use wind in conjunction with solar power to help cover times when there is extended cloud cover, or when there is insufficient wind.

For most locations, the cost of a good wind generator is not justified by the meager amount of power it will add to the overall system. This chapter will therefore focus on the use of solar panels for generating electricity.

Photovoltaic system components

A basic photovoltaic system consists of four main components: the **solar panel**, the **batteries**, the **regulator**, and the **load**. The panels are responsible for collecting the energy of the sun and generating electricity. The battery stores the electrical energy for later use. The regulator ensures that panel and battery are working together in an optimal fashion. The load refers to any device that requires electrical power, and is the sum of the consumption of all electrical equipment connected to the system. It is important to remember that solar panels and batteries use **direct current** (**DC**).

If the range of operational voltage of your equipment does not fit the voltage supplied by your battery, it will also be necessary to include some type of **converter**. If the equipment that you want to power uses a different DC voltage than the one supplied by the battery, you will need to use a **DC/DC converter**. If some of your equipment requires AC power, you will need to use a **DC/AC converter**, also known as an **inverter**.

Every electrical system should also incorporate various safety devices in the event that something goes wrong. These devices include proper wiring, circuit breakers, surge protectors, fuses, ground rods, lighting arrestors, etc.

The solar panel

The **solar panel** is composed of solar cells that collect solar radiation and transform it into electrical energy. This part of the system is sometimes referred to as a **solar module** or **photovoltaic generator**. **Solar panel arrays** can be made by connecting a set of panels in series and/or parallel in order to provide the necessary energy for a given load. The electrical current supplied by a solar panel varies proportionally to the solar radiation. This will vary according to climatological conditions, the hour of the day, and the time of the year.

Figure 7.1: A solar panel

Several technologies are used in the manufacturing of solar cells. The most common is crystalline silicon, and can be either monocrystalline or polycrystalline. Amorphous silicon can be cheaper but is less efficient at converting solar energy to electricity. With a reduced life expectancy and a 6 to 8% transformation efficiency, amorphous silicon is typically used for low power equipment, such as portable calculators. New solar technologies, such as silicon ribbon and thin film photovoltaics, are currently under development. These technologies promise higher efficiencies but are not yet widely available.

The battery

The **battery** stores the energy produced by the panels that is not immediately consumed by the load. This stored energy can then be used during periods of low solar irradiation. The battery component is also sometimes called the **accumulator**. Batteries store electricity in the form of chemical energy. The most common type of batteries used in solar applications are **maintenance-free lead-acid batteries**, also called **recombinant** or **VRLA** (**valve regulated lead acid**) batteries.

Figure 7.2: A 200 Ah lead-acid battery. The negative terminal was broken due to weight on the terminals during transportation.

Aside from storing energy, sealed lead-acid batteries also serve two important functions:

• They are able to provide an instantaneous power superior to what the array of panels can generate. This instantaneous power is needed to start some appliances, such as the motor of a refrigerator or a pump.

• They determine the operating voltage of your installation.

For a small power installation and where space constraints are important, other type of batteries (such as NiCd, NiMh, or Li-ion) can be used. These types of batteries need a specialized charger/regulator and cannot directly replace lead-acid batteries.

The regulator

The **regulator** (or more formally, the **solar power charge regulator**) assures that the battery is working in appropriate conditions. It avoids **overcharging** or **overdischarging** the battery, both of which are very detrimental to the life of the battery. To ensure proper charging and discharging of the battery, the regulator maintains knowledge of the **state of charge** (**SoC**) of the battery. The SoC is estimated based on the actual voltage of the battery. By measuring the battery voltage and being programmed with the type of storage technology used by the battery, the regulator can know the precise points where the battery would be overcharged or excessively discharged.

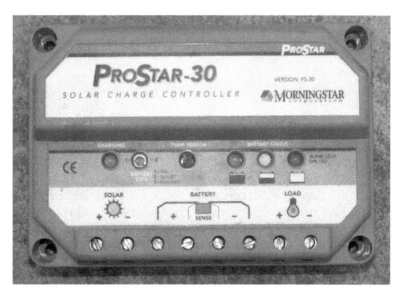

Figure 7.3: A 30 Amp solar charge controller

The regulator can include other features that add valuable information and security control to the equipment. These features include ammeters, voltmeters, measurement of ampere-hour, timers, alarms, etc. While convenient, none of these features are required for a working photovoltaic system.

The converter

The electricity provided by the panel array and battery is DC at a fixed voltage. The voltage provided might not match what is required by your load. A **direct/alternating (DC/AC) converter**, also known as **inverter**, converts the DC current from your batteries into AC. This comes at the price of losing some energy during the conversion. If necessary, you can also use converters to obtain DC at voltage level other than what is supplied by the batteries. **DC/DC converters** also lose some energy during the conversion. For optimal operation, you should design your solar-powered system to match the generated DC voltage to match the load.

Figure 7.4: An 800 Watt DC/AC converter (power inverter)

The load

The **load** is the equipment that consumes the power generated by your energy system. The load may include wireless communications equipment, routers, workstations, lamps, TV sets, VSAT modems, etc. Although it is not possible to precisely calculate the exact total consumption of your equipment, it is vital to be able to make a good estimate. In this type of system it is absolutely necessary to use efficient and low power equipment to avoid wasting energy.

Putting it all together

The complete photovoltaic system incorporates all of these components. The solar panels generate power when solar energy is available. The regulator ensures the most efficient operation of the panels and prevents damage to the batteries. The battery bank stores collected energy for later use. Converters and inverters adapt the stored energy to match the requirements of your load. Finally, the load consumes the stored energy to do work. When all of the components are in balance and are properly maintained, the system will support itself for years.

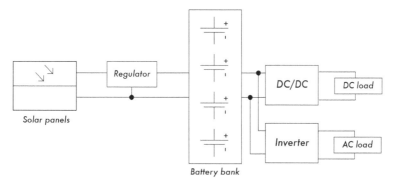

Figure 7.5: A solar installation with DC and AC loads

We will now examine each of the individual components of the photovoltaic system in greater detail.

The solar panel

An individual solar panel is made of many solar cells. The cells are electrically connected to provide a particular value of current and voltage. The individual cells are properly encapsulated to provide isolation and protection from humidity and corrosion.

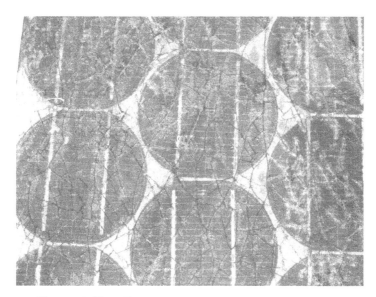

Figure 7.6: The effect of water and corrosion in a solar panel

There are different types of modules available on the market, depending on the power demands of your application. The most common modules are composed of 32 or 36 solar cells of crystalline silicon. These cells are all of equal size, wired in series, and encapsulated between glass and plastic material, using a polymer resin (EVA) as a thermal insulator. The surface area of the module is typically between 0.1 and 0.5 m². Solar panels usually have two electrical contacts, one positive and one negative.

Some panels also include extra contacts to allow the installation of **bypass diodes** across individual cells. Bypass diodes protect the panel against a phenomenon known as "hot-spots". A hot-spot occurs when some of the cells are in shadow while the rest of the panel is in full sun. Rather than producing energy, shaded cells behave as a load that dissipates energy. In this situation, shaded cells can see a significant increase in temperature (about 85 to 100°C.) Bypass diodes will prevent hot-spots on shaded cells, but reduce the maximum voltage of the panel. They should only be used when shading is unavoidable. It is a much better solution to expose the entire panel to full sun whenever possible.

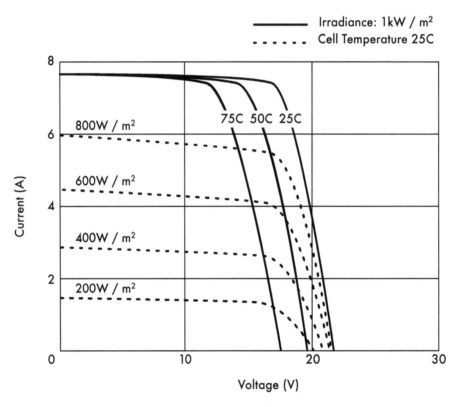

Figure 7.7: Different IV Curves. The current (A) changes with the irradiance, and the voltage (V) changes with the temperature.

The electrical performance of a solar module its represented by the **IV characteristic curve**, which represents the current that is provided based on the voltage generated for a certain solar radiation.

The curve represents all the possible values of voltage-current. The curves depend on two main factors: the temperature and the solar radiation received by the cells. For a given solar cell area, the current generated is directly proportional to solar irradiance (G), while the voltage reduces slightly with an increase of temperature. A good regulator will try to maximize the amount of energy that a panel provides by tracking the point that provides maximum power (V x I). The maximum power corresponds to the knee of the IV curve.

Solar Panel Parameters

The main parameters that characterize a photovoltaic panel are:

1. **SHORT CIRCUIT CURRENT** (I_{SC}): the maximum current provided by the panel when the connectors are short circuited.

2. **OPEN CIRCUIT VOLTAGE** (V_{OC}): the maximum voltage that the panel provides when the terminals are not connected to any load (an open circuit). This value is normally 22 V for panels that are going to work in 12 V systems, and is directly proportional to the number of cells connected in series.

3. **MAXIMUM POWER POINT** (P_{max}): the point where the power supplied by the panel is at maximum, where $P_{max} = I_{max} \times V_{max}$. The maximum power point of a panel is measured in Watts (W) or peak Watts (W_p). It is important not to forget that in normal conditions the panel will not work at peak conditions, as the voltage of operation is fixed by the load or the regulator. Typical values of V_{max} and I_{max} should be a bit smaller than the I_{SC} and V_{OC}

4. **FILL FACTOR** (FF): the relation between the maximum power that the panel can actually provide and the product $I_{SC} \cdot V_{OC}$. This gives you an idea of the quality of the panel because it is an indication of the type of IV characteristic curve. The closer FF is to 1, the more power a panel can provide. Common values usually are between 0.7 and 0.8.

5. **EFFICIENCY** (h): the ratio between the maximum electrical power that the panel can give to the load and the power of the solar radiation (P_L) incident on the panel. This is normally around 10-12%, depending on the type of cells (monocrystalline, polycrystalline, amorphous or thin film).

Considering the definitions of point of maximum power and the fill factor we see that:

$$h = P_{max} \; / \; P_L \; = FF \; \cdot \; I_{SC} \; \cdot \; V_{OC} \; / \; P_L$$

The values of I_{SC}, V_{OC}, I_{Pmax} and V_{Pmax} are provided by the manufacturer and refer to standard conditions of measurement with irradiance G = 1000 W/m², at sea-level, for a temperature of cells of T_c = 25°C.

The panel parameters values change for other conditions of irradiance and temperature. Manufacturers will sometimes include graphs or tables with values for conditions different from the standard. You should check the performance values at the panel temperatures that are likely to match your particular installation.

Be aware that two panels can have the same W_p but very different behavior in different operating conditions. When acquiring a panel, it is important to verify, if possible, that their parameters (at least, I_{SC} and V_{OC}) match the values promised by the manufacturer.

Panel parameters for system sizing

To calculate the number of panels required to cover a given load, you just need to know the current and voltage at the point of maximum power: I_{Pmax} and V_{Pmax}.

You should always be aware that the panel is not going to perform under perfect conditions as the load or regulation system is not always going to work at the point of maximum power of the panel. You should assume a loss of efficiency of 5% in your calculations to compensate for this.

Interconnection of panels

A **solar panel array** is a collection of solar panels that are electrically interconnected and installed on some type of support structure. Using a solar panel array allows you to generate greater voltage and current than is possible with a single solar panel. The panels are interconnected in such a way that the voltage generated is close to (but greater than) the level of voltage of the batteries, and that the current generated is sufficient to feed the equipment and to charge the batteries.

Connecting solar panels in series increases the generated voltage. Connecting panels in parallel increases the current. The number of panels used should be increased until the amount of power generated slightly exceeds the demands of your load.

It is very important that all of the panels in your array are as identical as possible. In an array, you should use panels of the same brand and characteristics because any difference in their operating conditions will have a big impact on the health and performance of your system. Even panels that have identical performance ratings will usually display some variance in their characteristics due to manufacturing processes. The actual operating characteristics of two panels from the same manufacturer can vary by as much as ±10%.

Whenever possible, it is a good idea to test the real-world performance of individual panels to verify their operating characteristics before assembling them into an array.

Figure 7.8: Interconnection of panels in parallel. The voltage remains constant while the current duplicates. (Photo: Fantsuam Foundation, Nigeria)

How to choose a good panel

One obvious metric to use when shopping for solar panels is to compare the ratio of the nominal peak power (W_p) to the price. This will give you a rough idea of the cost per Watt for different panels. But there are a number of other considerations to keep in mind as well.

If you are going to install solar panels in geographical areas where soiling (from dust, sand, or grit) will likely be a problem, consider purchasing panels with a low affinity for soil retention. These panels are made of materials that increase the likelihood that the panel will be automatically cleaned by wind and rain.

Always check the mechanical construction of each panel. Verify that the glass is hardened and the aluminum frame is robust and well built. The solar cells inside the panel can last for more than 20 years, but they are very fragile and the panel must protect them from mechanical hazards. Look for the manufacturer's quality guarantee in terms of expected power output and mechanical construction.

Finally, be sure that the manufacturer provides not only the nominal peak power of the panel (W_p) but also the variation of the power with irradiation and temperature. This is particularly important when panels are used in arrays, as variations in the operating parameters can have a big impact on the quality of power generated and the useful lifetime of the panels.

The battery

The battery "hosts" a certain reversible chemical reaction that stores electrical energy that can later be retrieved when needed. Electrical energy is transformed into chemical energy when the battery is being charged, and the reverse happens when the battery is discharged.

A battery is formed by a set of elements or **cells** arranged in series. Lead-acid batteries consist of two submerged lead electrodes in an electrolytic solution of water and sulfuric acid. A potential difference of about 2 volts takes place between the electrodes, depending on the instantaneous value of the charge state of the battery. The most common batteries in photovoltaic solar applications have a nominal voltage of 12 or 24 volts. A 12 V battery therefore contains 6 cells in series.

The battery serves two important purposes in a photovoltaic system: to provide electrical energy to the system when energy is not supplied by the array of solar panels, and to store excess energy generated by the panels whenever that energy exceeds the load. The battery experiences a cyclical process of charging and discharging, depending on the presence or absence of sunlight. During the hours that there is sun, the array of panels produces electrical energy. The energy that is not consumed immediately it is used to charge the battery. During the hours of absence of sun, any demand of electrical energy is supplied by the battery, thereby discharging it.

These cycles of charge and discharge occur whenever the energy produced by the panels does not match the energy required to support the load. When there is sufficient sun and the load is light, the batteries will charge. Obviously, the batteries will discharge at night whenever any amount of power is required. The batteries will also discharge when the irradiance is insufficient to cover the requirements of the load (due to the natural variation of climatological conditions, clouds, dust, etc.)

If the battery does not store enough energy to meet the demand during periods without sun, the system will be exhausted and will be unavailable for consumption. On the other hand, the oversizing the system (by adding far too many panels and batteries) is expensive and inefficient. When designing a stand-alone system we need to reach a compromise between the cost of components and the availability of power from the system. One way to do this is to estimate the required **number of days of autonomy**. In the case of a telecommunications system, the number of days of autonomy depends on its critical function within your network design. If the equipment is going to serve as repeater and is part of the backbone of your network, you will likely want to design your photovoltaic system with an autonomy of up to 5-7 days. On the other hand, if the solar system is responsible for a providing energy to client equipment you can probably reduce number of days of autonomy to two or three. In areas with low irradiance, this value may need to be increased even more. In any case, you will always have to find the proper balance between cost and reliability.

Types of batteries

Many different battery technologies exist, and are intended for use in a variety of different applications. The most suitable type for photovoltaic applications is the **stationary battery**, designed to have a fixed location and for scenarios where the power consumption is more or less irregular. "Stationary" batteries can accommodate deep discharge cycles, but they are not designed to produce high currents in brief periods of time.

Stationary batteries can use an electrolyte that is alkaline (such as Nickel-Cadmium) or acidic (such as Lead-Acid). Stationary batteries based on Nickel-Cadmium are recommended for their high reliability and resistance whenever possible. Unfortunately, they tend to be much more expensive and difficult to obtain than sealed lead-acid batteries.

In many cases when it is difficult to find local, good and cheap stationary batteries (importing batteries is not cheap), you will be forced to use batteries targeted to the automobile market.

Using car batteries

Automobile batteries are not well suited for photovoltaic applications as they are designed to provide a substantial current for just few seconds (when starting then engine) rather than sustaining a low current for long period of time. This design characteristic of car batteries (also called **traction batteries**) results in an shortened effective life when used in photovoltaic systems. Traction batteries can be used in small applications where low cost is the most important consideration, or when other batteries are not available.

Traction batteries are designed for vehicles and electric wheelbarrows. They are cheaper than stationary batteries and can serve in a photovoltaic installation, although they require very frequent maintenance. These batteries should never be deeply discharged, because doing so will greatly reduce their ability to hold a charge. A truck battery should not discharged by more than 70% of its total capacity. This means that you can only use a maximum of 30% of a lead-acid battery's nominal capacity before it must be recharged.

You can extend the life of a lead-acid battery by using distilled water. By using a densimeter or hydrometer, you can measure the density of the battery's electrolyte. A typical battery has specific gravity of 1.28. Adding distilled water and lowering the density to 1.2 can help reduce the anode's corrosion, at a cost of reducing the overall capacity of the battery. If you adjust the density of battery electrolyte, you **must** use distilled water, as tap water or well water will permanently damage the battery.

States of charge

There are two special state of charge that can take place during the cyclic charge and discharge of the battery. They should both be avoided in order to preserve the useful life of the battery.

Overcharge

Overcharge takes place when the battery arrives at the limit of its capacity. If energy is applied to a battery beyond its point of maximum charge, the electrolyte begins to break down. This produces bubbles of oxygen and hydrogen, in a process is known as **gasification**. This results in a loss of water, oxidation on the positive electrode, and in extreme cases, a danger of explosion.

On the other hand, the presence of gas avoids the stratification of the acid. After several continuous cycles of charge and discharge, the acid tends to concentrate itself at the bottom of the battery thereby reducing the effective capacity. The process of gasification agitates the electrolyte and avoids stratification.

Again, it is necessary to find a compromise between the advantages (avoiding electrolyte stratification) and the disadvantages (losing water and production of hydrogen). One solution is to allow a slight overcharge condition every so often. One typical method is to allow a voltage of 2.35 to 2.4 Volts for each element of the battery every few days, at 25°C. The regulator should ensure a periodical and controlled overcharges.

Overdischarge

In the same way that there is a upper limit, there is also a lower limit to a battery's state of charge. Discharging beyond that limit will result in deterioration of the battery. When the effective battery supply is exhausted, the regulator prevents any more energy from being extracted from the battery. When the voltage of the battery reaches the minimum limit of 1.85 Volts per cell at 25°C, the regulator disconnects the load from the battery.

If the discharge of the battery is very deep and the battery remains discharged for a long time, three effects take place: the formation of crystallized sulfate on the battery plates, the loosening of the active material on the battery plate, and plate buckling. The process of forming stable sulfate crystals is called hard sulfation. This is particularly negative as it generates big crystals that do not take part in any chemical reaction and can make your battery unusable.

Battery Parameters

The main parameters that characterize a battery are:

. **Nominal Voltage**, V_{NBat}: the most common value being 12 V.

. **Nominal Capacity**, C_{NBat}: the maximum amount of energy that can be extracted from a fully charged battery. It is expressed in Ampere-hours (Ah) or Watt-hours (Wh). The amount of energy that can be obtained from a battery depends on the time in which the extraction process takes place. Discharging a battery over a long period will yield more energy compared to discharging the same battery over a short period. The capacity of a battery is therefore specified at different discharging times. For photovoltaic applications, this time should be longer than 100 hours (C100).

. **Maximum Depth of Discharge**, DoD_{max}: The depth of discharge is the amount of energy extracted from a battery in a single discharge cycle, expressed as a percentage. The life expectancy of a battery depends on how deeply it is discharged in each cycle. The manufacturer should provide graphs that relate the number of charge-discharge cycles to the life of the battery. As a general rule you should avoid discharging a deep cycle battery beyond 50%. Traction batteries should only be discharged by as little as 30%.

. **Useful Capacity**, C_{UBat}: It is the real (as in usable) capacity of a battery. It is equal to the product of the nominal capacity and the maximum DoD. For example, a stationary battery of nominal capacity (C100) of 120 Ah and depth of discharge of 70% has a useful capacity of (120 x 0.7) 84 Ah.

Measuring the state of charge of the battery

A sealed lead-acid battery of 12 V provides different voltages depending on its state of charge. When the battery is fully charged in an open circuit, the output voltage is about 12.8 V. The output voltage lowers quickly to 12.6 V when loads are attached. As the battery is providing constant current during operation, the battery voltage reduces linearly from 12.6 to 11.6 V depending on the state of charge. A sealed lead-acid batteries provides 95% of its energy within this voltage range. If we make the broad assumption that a fully loaded battery has a voltage of 12.6 V when "full" and 11.6 V when "empty", we can estimate that a battery has discharged 70% when it reaches a voltage of 11.9 V. These values are only a rough approximation since they depend on the life and quality of the battery, the temperature, etc.

State of Charge	12V Battery Voltage	Volts per Cell
100%	12.7	2.12
90%	12.5	2.08
80%	12.42	2.07
70%	12.32	2.05
60%	12.2	2.03
50%	12.06	2.01
40%	11.9	1.98
30%	11.75	1.96
20%	11.58	1.93
10%	11.31	1.89
0%	10.5	1.75

According to this table, and considering that a truck battery should not be discharged more than 20% to 30%, we can determine that the useful capacity of a truck 170 Ah truck battery is 34 Ah (20%) to 51 Ah (30%). Using the same table, we find that we should program the regulator to prevent the battery from discharging below 12.3 V.

Battery and regulator protection

Thermomagnetic circuit breakers or one time fuses must be used to protect the batteries and the installation from short circuit and malfunctions. There are two types of fuses: **slow blow**, and **quick blow**. Slow blow fuses should be used with inductive or capacitive loads where a high current can occur at power up. Slow blow fuses will allow a higher current than their rating to pass for a short time. Quick blow fuses will immediately blow if the current flowing through them is higher than their rating.

The regulator is connected to the battery and the loads, so two different kinds of protection needs to be considered. One fuse should be placed between the battery and the regulator, to protect the battery from short-circuit in case of regulator failure. A second fuse is needed to protect the regulator from excessive load current. This second fuse is normally integrated into the regulator itself.

Figure 7.9: A battery bank of 3600 Ah, currents reach levels of 45 A during charging

Every fuse is rated with a maximum current and a maximum usable voltage. The maximum current of the fuse should be 20% bigger than the maximum current expected. Even if the batteries carry a low voltage, a short circuit can lead to a very high current which can easily reach several hundred amperes. Large currents can cause fire, damage the equipment and batteries, and possibly cause electric shock to a human body

If a fuse breaks, never replace a fuse with a wire or a higher rated fuse. First determine the cause of the problem, then replace the fuse with another one which has the same characteristics.

Temperature effects

The ambient temperature has several important effects on the characteristics of a battery:

• The nominal capacity of a battery (that the manufacturer usually gives for 25°C) increases with temperature at the rate of about 1%/°C. But if the temperature is too high, the chemical reaction that takes place in the battery accelerates, which can cause the same type of oxidation that takes places during overcharging. This will obviously reduce the life expectancy of battery. This problem can be compensated partially in car batteries by using a low density of dissolution (a specific gravity of 1.25 when the battery is totally charged).

• As the temperature is reduced, the useful life of the battery increases. But if the temperature is too low, you run the the risk of freezing the electrolyte. The freezing temperature depends on the density of the solution, which is also related to the state of charge of the battery. The lower the density, the greater the risk of freezing. In areas of low temperatures, you should avoid deeply discharging the batteries (that is, DoD_{max} is effectively reduced.)

• The temperature also changes the relation between voltage and charge. It is preferable to use a regulator which adjusts the low voltage disconnect and reconnect parameters according to temperature. The temperature sensor of the regulator should be fixed to the battery using tape or some other simple method.

• In hot areas it is important to keep the batteries as cool as possible. The batteries must be stored in a shaded area and never get direct sunlight. It's also desirable to place the batteries on a small support to allow air to flow under them, thus increase the cooling.

How to choose a good battery

Choosing a good battery can be very challenging in developing regions. High capacity batteries are heavy, bulky and expensive to import. A 200 Ah battery weights around 50 kg (120 pounds) and it can not be transported as hand luggage. If you want long-life (as in > 5 years) and maintenance free batteries be ready to pay the price.

A good battery should always come with its technical specifications, including the capacity at different discharge rates (C20, C100), operating temperature, cut-off voltage points, and requirements for chargers.

The batteries must be free of cracks, liquid spillage or any sign of damage, and battery terminals should be free of corrosion. As laboratory tests are necessary to obtain complete data about real capacity and aging, expect lots of low quality batteries (including fakes) in the local markets. A typical price (not including transport and import tax) is $3-4 USD per Ah for 12 V lead-acid batteries.

Life expectancy versus number of cycles

Batteries are the only component of a solar system that should be amortized over a short period and regularly replaced. You can increase the useful lifetime of a battery by reducing the depth of discharge per cycle. Even deep cycle batteries will have an increased battery life if the the number of deep discharge (>30%) cycles is reduced.

If you completely discharge the battery every day, you will typically need to change it after less than one year. If you use only 1/3 of the capacity the battery, it can last more than 3 years. It can be cheaper to buy a battery with 3 times the capacity than to change the battery every year.

The power charge regulator

The power charge regulator is also known as charge controller, voltage regulator, charge-discharge controller or charge-discharge and load controller. The regulator sits between the array of panels, the batteries, and your equipment or loads.

Remember that the voltage of a battery, although always close to 2 V per cell, varies according to its state of charge. By monitoring the voltage of the battery, the regulator prevents overcharging or overdischarging.

Regulators used in solar applications should be connected in series: they disconnect the array of panels from the battery to avoid overcharging, and they disconnect the battery from the load to avoid overdischarging. The connection and disconnection is done by means of switches which can be of two types: electromechanical (relays) or solid state (bipolar transistor, MOSFET). Regulators should never be connected in parallel.

In order to protect the battery from gasification, the switch opens the charging circuit when the voltage in the battery reaches its high voltage disconnect (HVD) or cut-off set point. The low voltage disconnect (LVD) prevents the battery from overdischarging by disconnecting or shedding the load. To prevent continuous connections and disconnections the regulator will not connect back the loads until the battery reaches a low reconnect voltage (LRV).

Typical values for a 12 V lead-acid battery are:

Voltage Point	Voltage
LVD	11.5
LRV	12.6
Constant Voltage Regulated	14.3
Equalization	14.6
HVD	15.5

The most modern regulators are also able to automatically disconnect the panels during the night to avoid discharging of the battery. They can also periodically overcharge the battery to improve their life, and they may use a mechanism known as pulse width modulation (PWM) to prevent excessive gassing.

As the peak power operating point of the array of panels will vary with temperature and solar illumination, new regulators are capable of constantly tracking the maximum point of power of the solar array. This feature is known as maximum power point tracking (MPPT).

Regulator Parameters

When selecting a regulator for your system, you should at least know the **operating voltage** and the **maximum current** that the regulator can handle. The operating Voltage will be 12, 24, or 48 V. The maximum current must be 20% bigger than the current provided by the array of panels connected to the regulator.

Other features and data of interest include:

• Specific values for LVD, LRV and HVD.

• Support for temperature compensation. The voltage that indicates the state of charge of the battery vary with temperature. For that reason some regulators are able to measure the battery temperature and correct the different cut-off and reconnection values.

• Instrumentation and gauges. The most common instruments measure the voltage of the panels and batteries, the state of charge (SoC) or Depth of Discharge (DoD). Some regulators include special alarms to indicate that the panels or loads have been disconnected, LVD or HVD has been reached, etc.

Converters

The regulator provides DC power at a specific voltage. Converters and inverters are used to adjust the voltage to match the requirements of your load.

DC/DC Converters

DC/DC converters transform a continuous voltage to another continuous voltage of a different value. There are two conversion methods which can be used to adapt the voltage from the batteries: *linear conversion* and *switching conversion*.

Linear conversion lowers the voltage from the batteries by converting excess energy to heat. This method is very simple but is obviously inefficient. Switching conversion generally uses a magnetic component to temporarily store the energy and transform it to another voltage. The resulting voltage can be greater, less than, or the inverse (negative) of the input voltage.

The efficiency of a linear regulator decreases as the difference between the input voltage and the output voltage increases. For example, if we want to convert from 12 V to 6 V, the linear regulator will have an efficiency of only 50%. A standard switching regulator has an efficiency of at least 80%.

DC/AC Converter or Inverter

Inverters are used when your equipment requires AC power. Inverters chop and invert the DC current to generate a square wave that is later filtered to approximate a sine wave and eliminate undesired harmonics. Very few inverters actually supply a pure sine wave as output. Most models available on the market produce what is known as "modified sine wave", as their voltage output is not a pure sinusoid. When it comes to efficiency, modified sine wave inverters perform better than pure sinusoidal inverters.

Be aware that not all the equipment will accept a modified sine wave as voltage input. Most commonly, some laser printers will not work with a modified sine wave inverter. Motors will work, but they may consume more power than if they are fed with a pure sine wave. In addition, DC power supplies tend to warm up more, and audio amplifiers can emit a buzzing sound.

Aside from the type of waveform, some important features of inverters include:

- **Reliability in the presence of surges.** Inverters have two power ratings: one for continuous power, and a higher rating for peak power. They are capable of providing the peak power for a very short amount of time, as when starting a motor. The inverter should also be able to safely interrupt itself (with a circuit breaker or fuse) in the event of a short circuit, or if the requested power is too high.

- **Conversion efficiency.** Inverters are most efficient when providing 50% to 90% of their continuous power rating. You should select an inverter that most closely matches your load requirements. The manufacturer usually provides the performance of the inverter at 70% of its nominal power.

- **Battery charging.** Many inverters also incorporate the inverse function: the possibility of charging batteries in the presence of an alternative source of current (grid, generator, etc). This type of inverter is known as a charger/inverter.

- **Automatic fall-over.** Some inverters can switch automatically between different sources of power (grid, generator, solar) depending on what is available.

When using telecommunication equipment, it is best to avoid the use of DC/AC converters and feed them directly from a DC source. Most communications equipment can accept a wide range of input voltage.

Equipment or load

It should be obvious that as power requirements increase, the expense of the photovoltaic system also increases. It is therefore critical to match the size of the system as closely as possible to the expected load. When designing the system you must first make a realistic estimate of the maximum consumption. Once the installation is in place, the established maximum consumption must be respected in order to avoid frequent power failures.

Home Appliances

The use of photovoltaic solar energy is not recommended for heat-exchange applications (electrical heating, refrigerators, toasters, etc.) Whenever possible, energy should be used sparingly using low power appliances.

Here are some points to keep in mind when choosing appropriate equipment for use with a solar system:

- The photovoltaic solar energy is suitable for illumination. In this case, the use of halogen light bulbs or fluorescent lamps is mandatory. Although these lamps are more expensive, they have much better energy efficiency than incandescent light bulbs. LED lamps are also a good choice as they are very efficient and are fed with DC.

- It is possible to use photovoltaic power for appliances that require low and constant consumption (as in a typical case, the TV). Smaller televisions use less power than larger televisions. Also consider that a black-and-white TV consumes about half the power of a color TV.

- Photovoltaic solar energy is not recommended for any application that transforms energy into heat (thermal energy). Use solar heating or butane as alternative.

- Conventional automatic washing machines will work, but you should avoid the use of any washing programs that include centrifuged water heating.

- If you must use a refrigerators, it should consume as little power as possible. There are specialized refrigerators that work in DC, although their consumption can be quite high (around 1000 Wh/day).

The estimation of total consumption is a fundamental step in sizing your solar system. Here is a table that gives you a general idea of the power consumption that you can expect from different appliances.

Equipment	Consumption (Watts)
Portable computer	30-50
Low power lamp	6-10
WRAP router (one radio)	4-10
VSAT modem	15-30
PC (without LCD)	20-30
PC (with LCD)	200-300
Network Switch (16 port)	6-8

Wireless telecommunications equipment

Saving power by choosing the right gear saves a lot of money and trouble. For example , a long distance link doesn't necessarily need a strong amplifier that draws a lot of power. A Wi-Fi card with good receiver sensitivity and a fresnel zone that is at least 60% clear will work better than an amplifier, and save power consumption as well. A well known saying of radio amateurs applies here, too: The best amplifier is a good antenna. Further measures to reduce power consumption include throttling the CPU speed, reducing transmit power to the minimum value that is necessary to provide a stable link, increasing the length of beacon intervals, and switching the system off during times it is not needed.

Most autonomous solar systems work at 12 or 24 volts. Preferably, a wireless device that runs on DC voltage should be used, operating at the 12 Volts that most lead acid batteries provide. Transforming the voltage provided by the battery to AC or using a voltage at the input of the access point different from the voltage of the battery will cause unnecessary energy loss. A router or access point that accepts 8-20 Volts DC is perfect.

Most cheap access points have a switched mode voltage regulator inside and will work through such a voltage range without modification or becoming hot (even if the device was shipped with a 5 or 12 Volt power supply).

WARNING: Operating your access point with a power supply other than the one provided by your manufacturer will certainly void any warranty, and may cause damage to your equipment. While the following technique will typically work as described, remember that should you attempt it, you do so at your own risk.

Open your access point and look near the DC input for two relatively big capacitors and an inductor (a ferrite toroid with copper wire wrapped around it). If they are present then the device has a switched mode input, and the maximum input voltage should be somewhat below the voltage printed on the capacitors. Usually the rating of these capacitors is 16 or 25 volts. Be aware that an unregulated power supply has a ripple and may feed a much higher voltage into your access point than the typical voltage printed on it may suggest. So, connecting an unregulated power supply with 24 Volts to a device with 25 Volt-capacitors is not a good idea. Of course, opening your device will void any existing warranty. Do not try to operate an access point at higher voltage if it doesn't have a switched mode regulator. It will get hot, malfunction, or burn.

Equipment based on traditional Intel x86 CPUs are power hungry in comparison with RISC-based architectures as ARM or MIPS. One of the boards with lowest power consumptions is the Soekris platform that uses an AMD ElanSC520 processor. Another alternative to AMD (ElanSC or Geode SC1100) is the use of equipment with MIPS processors. MIPS processors have a better performance than an AMD Geode at the price of consuming between 20-30% of more energy.

The popular Linksys WRT54G runs at any voltage between 5 and 20 volts DC and draws about 6 Watts, but it has an Ethernet switch onboard. Having a switch is of course nice and handy - but it draws extra power. Linksys also offers a Wi-Fi access point called WAP54G that draws only 3 Watts and can run OpenWRT and Freifunk firmware. The 4G Systems Accesscube draws about 6 Watts when equipped with a single WiFi interface. If 802.11b is suffi-cient, mini-PCI cards with the Orinoco chipset perform very well while draw-ing a minimum amount of power.

Equipment	Consumption (Watts)
Linksys WRT54G (BCM2050 radio)	6
Linksys WAP54G (BCM2050 radio)	3
Orinoco WavePoint II ROR (30mW radio)	15
Soekris net4511 (no radio)	1.8
PC Engines WRAP.1E-1 (no radio)	2.04
Mikrotik Routerboard 532 (no radio)	2.3
Inhand ELF3 (no radio)	1.53
Senao 250mW radio	3
Ubiquiti 400mW radio	6

The amount of power required by wireless equipment depends not only on the architecture but on the number of network interfaces, radios, type of memory/storage and traffic. As a general rule, a wireless board of low con-sumption consumes 2 to 3 W, and a 200 mW radio card consumes as much as 3 W. High power cards (such as the 400 mW Ubiquity) consume around 6 W. A repeating station with two radios can range between 8 and 10 W.

Although the standard IEEE 802.11 incorporates a power saving mode (PS) mechanism, its benefit is not as good as you might hope. The main mecha-nism for energy saving is to allow stations to periodically put their wireless cards to "sleep" by means of a timing circuit. When the wireless card wakes up it verifies if a beacon exists, indicating pending traffic. The energy saving therefore only takes place in the client side, as the access point always needs to remain awake to send beacons and store traffic for the clients. Power saving mode may be incompatible between implementations from different manufacturers, which can cause unstable wireless connections. It is nearly always best to leave power saving mode disabled on all equipment, as the difficulties created will likely outweigh the meager amount of saved power.

Selecting the voltage

Most low power stand-alone systems use 12 V battery power as that is the most common operational voltage in sealed lead-acid batteries. When designing a wireless communication system you need to take into consideration the most efficient voltage of operation of your equipment. While the input voltage can accept a wide range of values, you need to ensure that the overall power consumption of the system is minimal.

Wiring

An important component of the installation is the wiring, as proper wiring will ensure efficient energy transfer. Some good practices that you should consider include:

- Use a screw to fasten the cable to the battery terminal. Loose connections will waste power.

- Spread Vaseline or mineral jelly on the battery terminals. Corroded connection have an increased resistance, resulting in loss.

- For low currents (<10 A) consider the use of Faston or Anderson power-pole connectors. For bigger currents, use metallic ring lugs.

Wire size is normally given in American Wire Gauge (AWG). During your calculations you will need to convert between AWG and mm² to estimate cable resistance. For example, an AWG #6 cable has a diameter of 4.11 mm and can handle up to 55 A. A conversion chart, including an estimate of resistance and current carrying capacity, is available in **Appendix D**. Keep in mind that the current carrying capacity can also vary depending on the type of insulation and application. When in doubt, consult the manufacturer for more information.

Orientation of the panels

Most of the energy coming from the sun arrives in straight line. The solar module will capture more energy if it is "facing" the sun, perpendicular to the straight line between the position of the installation and the sun. Of course, the sun's position is constantly changing relative to the earth, so we need to find an optimal position for our panels. The orientation of the panels is determined by two angles, the **azimuth a** and the **inclination** or **elevation ß**. The azimuth is the angle that measures the deviation with respect to the south in the northern hemisphere, and with respect to the north in the southern hemisphere. The inclination is the angle formed by the surface of the module and the horizontal plane.

Azimuth

You should have the module turned towards the terrestrial equator (facing south in the northern hemisphere, and north in the southern) so that during the day the panel catches the greatest possible amount of radiation (a = 0).

It is very important that no part of the panels are ever under shade!. Study the elements that surround the panel array (trees, buildings, walls, other panels, etc.) to be sure that they will not cast a shadow on the panels at any time of the day or year. It is acceptable to turn the panels ±20° towards the east or the west if needed (a = ±20°).

Inclination

Once you have fixed the azimuth, the parameter that is key in our calculations is the inclination of the panel, which we will express as the angle beta (ß). The maximum height that the sun reaches every day will vary, with the maximum on the day of the summer solstice and the minimum on the winter solstice. Ideally, the panels should track this variation, but this is usually not possible for cost reasons.

In installations with telecommunications equipment it is normal to install the panels at a fixed inclination. In most telecommunications scenarios the energy demands of the system are constant throughout the year. Providing for sufficient power during the "worst month" will work well for the rest of the year.

The value of ß should maximize the ratio between the offer and the demand of energy.

- For installations with consistent (or nearly consistent) consumption throughout the year, it is preferable to optimize the installation to capture the maximum radiation during "the winter" months. You should use the absolute value of the latitude of the place (angle F) increased by 10° (ß = I F I + 10 °).

- For installations with less consumptions during winter, the value of the latitude of the place can be used as the solar panel inclination. This way the system is optimized for the months of spring and autumn (ß = I F I).

- For installations that are only used during summer, you should use the absolute value of the latitude of the place (angle F) decreased by 10° (ß = I F I - 10°). The inclination of the panel should never be less than 15° to avoid the accumulation of dust and/or humidity on the panel. In areas where snow and ice occur, it is very important to protect the panels and to incline them an angle of 65° or greater.

If there is a considerable increase in consumption during the summer, you might consider arranging for two fixed inclinations, one position for the months of summer and another for the months of winter. This would require special support structures and a regular schedule for changing the position of the panels.

How to size your photovoltaic system

When choosing equipment to meet your power needs, you will need to determine the following, at a minimum:

- The number and type of solar panels required to capture enough solar energy to support your load.
- The minimum capacity of the battery. The battery will need to store enough energy to provide power at night and through days with little sun, and will determine your number of days of autonomy.
- The characteristics of all other components (the regulator, wiring, etc.) needed to support the amount of power generated and stored.

System sizing calculations are important, because unless the system components are balanced, energy (and ultimately, money) is wasted. For example, if we install more solar panels to produce more energy, the batteries should have enough capacity to store the additional energy produced. If the bank of batteries is too small and the load is not using the energy as it is generated, then energy must be thrown away. A regulator of a smaller amperage than needed, or one single cable that is too small, can be a cause of failure (or even fire) and render the installation unusable.

Never forget that the ability of the photovoltaic energy to produce and store electrical energy is limited. Accidentally leaving on a light bulb during the day can easily drain your reserves before nighttime, at which point no additional power will be available. The availability of "fuel" for photovoltaic systems (i.e. solar radiation) can be difficult to predict. In fact, it is never possible to be absolutely sure that a standalone system is going to be able to provide the necessary energy at any particular moment. Solar systems are designed for a certain consumption, and if the user exceeds the planned limits the provision of energy will fail.

The design method that we propose consists of considering the energy requirements, and based on them to calculate a system that works for the maximum amount of time so it is as reliable as possible. Of course, if more panels and batteries are installed, more energy will be able to be collected and stored. This increase of reliability will also have an increase in cost.

In some photovoltaic installations (such as the provision of energy for tele-communications equipment on a network backbone) the reliability factor is more important that the cost. In a client installation, low cost is likely going to be a the most important factor. Finding a balance between cost and reliability is not a easy task, but whatever your situation, you should be able to determine what it is expected from your design choices, and at what price.

The method we will use for sizing the system is known as the ***method of the worst month***. We simply calculate the dimensions of the standalone system so it will work in the month in which the demand for energy is greatest with respect to the available solar energy. It is the worst month of the year, as this month with have the largest ratio of demanded energy to available energy.

Using this method, ***reliability*** is taken into consideration by fixing the maximum number of days that the system can work without receiving solar radiation (that is, when all consumption is made solely at the expense of the energy stored in the battery.) This is known as the ***maximum number of days of autonomy*** (N), and can be thought of as the number of consecutive cloudy days when the panels do not collect any significant amount of energy.

When choosing N, it is necessary to know the climatology of the place, as well as the economic and social relevance of the installation. Will it be used to illuminate houses, a hospital, a factory, for a radio link, or for some other application? Remember that as N increases, so does the investment in equipment and maintenance. It is also important to evaluate all possible logistical costs of equipment replacement. It is not the same to change a discharged battery from an installation in the middle of a city versus one at the top a telecommunication tower that is several hours or days of walking distance.

Fixing the value of N it is not an easy task as there are many factors involved, and many of them cannot be evaluated easily. Your experience will play an important role in this part of the system sizing. One commonly used value for critical telecommunications equipment is N = 5, whereas for low cost client equipment it is possible to reduce the autonomy to N = 3.

In **Appendix E**, we have included several tables that will facilitate the collection of required data for sizing the system. The rest of this chapter will explain in detail what information you need to collect or estimate and how to use the method of the "worst month".

Data to collect

- **Latitude of the installation**. Remember to use a positive sign in the northern hemisphere and negative in the south.

- **Solar radiation data**. For the method of the "worst month" it is enough to know just twelve values, one for every month. The twelve numbers are the monthly average values of daily global irradiation on horizontal plane ($G_{dm}(0)$, in kWh/m² per day). The monthly value is the sum of the values of global irradiation for every day of the month, divided by the number of days of the month.

If you have the data in Joules (J), you can apply the following conversion:

$$1\ J = 2.78 \times 10^{-7}\ kWh$$

The irradiation data $G_{dm}(0)$ of many places of the world is gathered in tables and databases. You should check for this information from a weather station close to your implementation site, but do not be surprised if you cannot find the data in electronic format. It is a good idea to ask companies that install photovoltaic systems in the region, as their experience can be of great value.

Do not confuse "sun hours" with the number of "peak sun hours". The number of peak sun hours has nothing to do with the number of hours without clouds, but refers to the amount of daily irradiation. A day of 5 hours of sun without clouds does not necessary have those hours when the sun is at its zenith.

A peak sun hour is a normalized value of solar radiation of 1000 W/m² at 25 C. So when we refer to 5 peak sun hours, this implies a daily solar radiation of 5000 W/m².

Electrical characteristics of system components

The electrical characteristics of the components of your system should be provided by the manufacturer. It is advisable to make your our own measurements to check for any deviation from the nominal values. Unfortunately, deviation from promised values can be large and should be expected.

These are the minimum values that you need to gather before starting your system sizing:

Panels

You need to know the voltage V_{Pmax} and the current I_{Pmax} at the point of maximum power in standard conditions.

Batteries

Nominal capacity (for 100 hours discharge) C_{NBat}, operational voltage V_{NBat}, and either the maximum depth of discharge DoD_{max} or useful capacity C_{UBat}. You also need to know the type of battery that you plan to use, whether sealed lead-acid, gel, AGM, modified traction etc. The type of battery is important when deciding the cut-off points in the regulator.

Regulator

You need to know the nominal voltage V_{NReg}, and the maximum current that can operate I_{maxReg}.

DC/AC Converter/Inverter

If you are going to use a converter, you need to know the nominal voltage V_{NConv}, instantaneous power P_{IConv} and performance at 70% of maximum load H_{70}.

Equipment or load

It is necessary to know the nominal voltage V_{NC} and the nominal power of operation P_C for every piece of equipment powered by the system.

In order to know the total energy that our installation is going to consume, it is also very important to consider the average time each load will be used. Is it constant? Or will it be used daily, weekly, monthly or annually? Consider any changes in the usage that might impact the amount of energy needed (seasonal usage, training or school periods, etc.)

Other variables

Aside from the electrical characteristics of the components and load, it is necessary to decide on two more pieces of information before being able to size a photovoltaic system. These two decisions are the required number of days of autonomy and the operational voltage of the system.

N, number of days of autonomy

You need to decide on a value for N that will balance meteorological conditions with the type of installation and overall costs. It is impossible to give a concrete value of N that is valid for every installation, but the next table gives some recommended values. Take these values as a rough approximation, and consult with an experienced designer to reach a final decision.

Available Sunlight	Domestic Installation	Critical Installation
Very cloudy	5	10
Variable	4	8
Sunny	3	6

V_N, nominal voltage of the installation

The components of your system need to be chosen to operate at a nominal voltage V_N. This voltage is usually 12 or 24 Volts for small systems, and if the total power of consumption surpasses 3 kW, the voltage will be 48 V. The selection of V_N is not arbitrary, and depends on the availability of equipment.

- If the equipment allows it, try to fix the nominal voltage to 12 or 24 V. Many wireless communications boards accept a wide range of input voltage and can be used without a converter.

- If you need to power several types of equipment that work at different nominal voltages, calculate the voltage that minimizes the overall power consumption including the losses for power conversion in DC/DC and DC/AC converters.

Procedure of calculation

There are three main steps that need to be followed to calculate the proper size of a system:

1. **Calculate the available solar energy (the offer).** Based on statistical data of solar radiation, and the orientation and the optimal inclination of the solar panels, we calculate the solar energy available. The estimation of solar energy available is done in monthly intervals, reducing the statistical data to 12 values. This estimation is a good compromise between precision and simplicity.

2. **Estimate the required electrical energy (the demand).** Record the power consumption characteristics of the equipment chosen as well as estimated usage. Then calculate the electrical energy required on a monthly basis. You should consider the expected fluctuations of usage due to the variations between winter and summer, the rainy period / dry season, school / vacation periods, etc. The result will be 12 values of energy demand, one for each month of the year.

3. **Calculate the ideal system size (the result)**. With the data from the "worst month", when the relation between the solar demanded energy and the energy available is greatest, we calculate:

   - The current that the array of panels needs to provide, which will determine the minimum number of panels.

   - The necessary energy storage capacity to cover the minimum number of days of autonomy, which will determine the required number of batteries.

   - The required electrical characteristics of the regulator.

   - The length and the necessary sections of cables for the electrical connections.

Required current in the worst month

For each month you need to calculate the value of I_m, which is the maximum daily current that an array of panels operating at nominal voltage of V_N needs to provide, in a day with a irradiation of G_{dm} for month "m", for panels with an inclination of ß degrees..

The I_m(WORST MONTH) will be the largest value of I_m, and the system sizing is based on the data of that worth month. The calculations of $G_{dm}(ß)$ for a certain place can be made based on $G_{dm}(0)$ using computer software such as PVSYST (*http://www.pvsyst.com/*) or PVSOL (*http://www.solardesign.co.uk/*).

Due to losses in the regulator and batteries, and due to the fact that the panels do not always work at the point of maximum power, the required current I_{mMAX} is calculated as:

$$I_{mMAX} = 1.21 \ I_m \ (WORST \ MONTH)$$

Once you have determined the worst month, the value of I_{mMAX}, and the total energy that you require E_{TOTAL}(WORST MONTH) you can proceed to the final calculations. E_{TOTAL} is the sum of all DC and AC loads, in Watts. To calculate E_{TOTAL} see **Appendix E**.

Number of panels

By combining solar panels in series and parallel, we can obtain the desired voltage and current. When panels are connected in series, the total voltage is equal to the sum of the individual voltages of each module, while the current remains unchanged. When connecting panels in parallel, the currents are summed together while the voltage remains unchanged. It is very important, to use panels of nearly identical characteristics when building an array.

You should try to acquire panels with V_{Pmax} a bit bigger than the nominal voltage of the system (12, 24 or 48 V). Remember that you need to provide a few volts more than the nominal voltage of the battery in order to charge it. If it is not possible to find a single panel that satisfies your requirements, you need to connect several panels in series to reach your desired voltage. The number of panels in series N_{ps} is equal to the nominal voltage of the system divided by the voltage of a single panel, rounded up to the nearest integer.

$$N_{ps} = V_N \, / \, V_{Pmax}$$

In order to calculate the number of panels in parallel (N_{pp}), you need to divide the I_{mMAX} by the current of a single panel at the point of maximum power I_{pmax}, rounded up to the nearest integer.

$$N_{pp} = I_{mMAX} \, / \, I_{Pmax}$$

The total number of panels is the result of multiplying the number of panels in series (to set the voltage) by the number of panels in parallel (to set the current).

$$N_{TOTAL} = N_{ps} \times N_{pp}$$

Capacity of the battery or accumulator

The battery determines the overall voltage of the system and needs to have enough capacity to provide energy to the load when there is not enough solar radiation.

To estimate the capacity of our battery, we first calculate the required energy capacity of our system (necessary capacity, C_{NEC}). The necessary capacity depends on the energy available during the "worst month" and the desired number of days of autonomy (N).

$$C_{NEC} \, (Ah) = E_{TOTAL} (WORST \; MONTH) (Wh) \, / \, V_N(V) \times N$$

The nominal capacity of the battery C_{NOM} needs to be bigger than the C_{NEC} as we cannot fully discharge a battery. To calculate the size of the battery we need to consider the maximum depth of discharge (DoD) that the battery allows:

$$C_{NOM}(Ah) = C_{NEC}(Ah) \, / \, DoD_{MAX}$$

In order to calculate the number of batteries in series (N_{bs}), we divide the nominal voltage of our installation (V_N) by the nominal voltage of a single battery (V_{NBat}):

$$N_{bs} = V_N / V_{NBat}$$

Regulator

One important warning: always use regulators in series, never in parallel. If your regulator does not support the current required by your system, you will need to buy a new regulator with a larger working current.

For security reasons, a regulator needs to be able to operate with a current I_{maxReg} at least 20% greater than the maximum intensity that is provided by the array of panels:

$$I_{maxReg} = 1.2 \ N_{pp} \ I_{PMax}$$

DC/AC Inverter

The total energy needed for the AC equipment is calculated including all the losses that are introduced by the DC/AC converter or inverter. When choosing an inverter, keep in mind that the performance of the inverter varies according to the amount of requested power. An inverter has better performance characteristics when operating close to its rated power. Using a 1500 Watt inverter to power a 25 Watt load is extremely inefficient. In order to avoid this wasted energy, it is important to consider not the peak power of all your equipment, but the peak power of the equipment that is expected to operate simultaneously.

Cables

Once you know the numbers of panels and batteries, and type of regulators and inverters that you want to use, it is necessary to calculate the length and the thickness of the cables needed to connect the components together.

The **length** depends on the location of your the installation. You should try to minimize the length of the cables between the regulator, panels, and batteries. Using short cables will minimize lost power and cable costs.

The **thickness** is chosen is based on the length of the cable and the maximum current it must carry. The goal is to minimize voltage drops. In order to calculate the thickness S of the cable it is necessary to know:

- The maximum current I_{MC} that is going to circulate in the cable. In the case of the panel-battery subsystem, it is I_{mMAX} calculated for every month. In the battery-load subsystem it depends on the way that the loads are connected.

- The voltage drop (V_a-V_b) that we consider acceptable in the cable. The voltage drop that results of adding all possible individual drops is expressed as a percent of the nominal voltage of the installation. Typical maximum values are:

Component	Voltage Drop (% of V_N)
Panel Array -> Battery	1%
Battery -> Converter	1%
Main Line	3%
Main Line (Illumination)	3%
Main Line (Equipment)	5%

Typical acceptable voltage drops in cables

The section of the cable is determined by Ohm's Law:

$$S(mm^2) = r(\Omega mm^2/m)\, L(m)\ I_{mMAX}(A)/\ (V_a-V_b)(V)$$

where S is the section, r is resistivity (intrinsic property of the material: for copper, 0.01286 $\Omega mm^2/m$), and L the length.

S is chosen taking into consideration the cables available in the market. You should choose the immediately superior section to the one that is obtained from the formula. For security reasons that are some minimum values, for the cable that connects panels and battery, this is a minimum of 6 mm². For the other sections, that minimum is 4 mm².

Cost of a solar installation

While solar energy itself is free, the equipment needed to turn it into useful electric energy is not. You not only need to buy equipment to transform the solar energy in electricity and store it for use, but you must also replace and maintain various components of the system. The problem of equipment replacement is often overlooked, and a solar system is implemented without a proper maintenance plan.

In order to calculate the real cost of your installation, we include an illustrative example. The first thing to do it is to calculate the initial investment costs.

Description	Number	Unit Cost	Subtotal
60W Solar panel (about $4 / W)	4	$300	$1,200
30A Regulator	1	$100	$100
Wiring (meters)	25	$1 / meter	$25
50 Ah Deep cycle batteries	6	$150	$900
		Total:	$2,225

The calculation of our investment cost is relatively easy once the system has been dimensioned. You just need to add the price for each piece equipment and the labor cost to install and wire the equipments together. For simplicity, we do not include the costs of transport and installation but you should not overlook them.

To figure out how much a system will really cost to operate we must estimate how long each part will last and how often you must replace it. In accounting terminology this is known as ***amortization***. Our new table will look like this:

Description	#	Unit Cost	Subtotal	Lifetime (Years)	Yearly Cost
60W Solar panel	4	$300	$1,200	20	$60
30A Regulator	1	$100	$100	5	$20
Wiring (meters)	25	$1 / meter	$25	10	$2.50
50 Ah Deep cycle batteries	6	$150	$900	5	$180
		Total:	$2,225	Annual Cost:	$262.50

As you see, once the first investment has been done, an annual cost of $262.50 is expected. The annual cost is an estimation of the required capital per year to replace the system components once they reach the end of their useful life.

8

Building an Outdoor Node

There are many practical considerations when installing electronic equipment outdoors. Obviously, it has to be protected from the rain, wind, sun, and other harsh elements. Power needs to be provided, and the antenna should be mounted at a sufficient height. Without proper grounding, nearby lightning strikes, fluctuating mains power, and even a light winds in the proper climate can annihilate your wireless links. This chapter will give you some idea of the practical problems you will be up against when installing wireless equipment outdoors.

Waterproof enclosures

Suitable waterproof enclosures come in many varieties. Metal or plastic may be used to create a watertight container for outdoor embedded equipment.

Of course, equipment needs power to work, and will likely need to connect to an antenna and Ethernet cable. Each time you pierce a watertight enclosure, you provide another potential place for water to seep in.

The National Electrical Manufacturers Association (NEMA) provides guidelines for protection of electrical equipment from rain, ice, dust, and other contaminants. An enclosure with a rating of *NEMA 3* or better is suitable for outdoor use in a fair climate. A *NEMA 4X* or *NEMA 6* provides excellent protection, even from hose driven water and ice. For fixtures that pierce the body of an enclosure (such as cable glands and bulkhead connectors), the International Electrotechnical Commission (IEC) assigns an ingress protection (IP) rating. An ingress protection rating of *IP66* or *IP67* will protect these holes from very strong jets of water. A good outdoor enclosure should also provide UV protection to prevent breakdown of the seal from exposure to the sun, as well as to protect the equipment inside.

Of course, finding NEMA or IEC rated enclosures may be a challenge in your local area. Often, locally available parts can be repurposed for use as enclosures. Rugged plastic or metal sprinkler boxes, electrical conduit housings, or even plastic food containers can be used in a pinch. When piercing an enclosure, use quality gaskets or o-rings along with a cable gland to seal the opening. UV stabilized silicone compound or other sealant can be used for temporary installations, but remember that cables flex in the wind, and glued joints will eventually weaken and allow moisture to seep in.

You can greatly extend the life of a plastic enclosure by providing some protection from the sun. Mounting the box in the shade, either beneath existing equipment, solar panel, or thin sheet of metal specifically for this purpose, will add to the life span of the box as well as the equipment contained inside.

Before putting any piece of electronics in a sealed box, be sure that it has minimal heat dissipation requirements. If your motherboard requires a fan or large heat sink, remember that there will be no airflow, and your electronics will likely bake to death on the tower. Only use electronic components that are designed to be used in an embedded environment.

Providing power

Obviously, DC power can be provided by simply poking a hole in your enclosure and running a wire. If your enclosure is large enough (say, an outdoor electrical box) you could even wire an AC outlet inside the box. But manufacturers are increasingly supporting a very handy feature that eliminates the need for an additional hole in the box: *Power over Ethernet* (*POE*).

The 802.3af standard defines a method for supplying power to devices using the unused pairs in a standard Ethernet cable. Nearly 13 Watts of power can be provided safely on a CAT5 cable without interfering with data transmissions on the same wire. Newer 802.3af compliant Ethernet switches (called *end span injectors*) supply power directly to connected devices. End span switches can supply power on the same wires that are used for data (pairs 1-2 and 3-6) or on the unused wires (pairs 4-5 and 7-8). Other equipment, called *mid span injectors,* are inserted between Ethernet switches and the device to be powered. These injectors supply power on the unused pairs.

If your wireless router or CPE includes support for 802.3af, you could in theory simply connect it to an injector. Unfortunately, some manufacturers (notably Cisco) disagree on power polarity, and connecting mismatching gear can damage the injector and the equipment to be powered. Read the fine print and be sure that your injector and wireless equipment agree on which pins and polarity should be used for power.

If your wireless equipment doesn't support power over Ethernet, you can still use the unused pairs in a CAT5 cable to carry power. You can either use a **passive POE injector**, or simply build one yourself. These devices manually connect DC power to the unused wires on one end of the cable, and connect the other end directly to a barrel connector inserted in the device's power receptacle. A pair of passive POE devices can typically be purchased for under $20.

To make your own, you will need to find out how much power the device requires to operate, and provide at least that much current and voltage, plus enough to account for loss in the Ethernet run. You don't want to supply too much power, as the resistance of the small cable can present a fire hazard. Here is an online calculator that will help you calculate the voltage drop for a given run of CAT5 : *http://www.gweep.net/~sfoskett/tech/poecalc.html*

Once you know the proper power and electrical polarity needed to power your wireless gear, crimp a CAT5 cable only using the data wires (pairs 1-2 and 3-6). Then simply connect the transformer to pairs 4-5 (usually blue / blue-white) and 7-8 (brown / brown-white) on one end, and a matching barrel connector on the other.

Mounting considerations

In many cases, equipment can be located inside a building, provided there is a window with ordinary glass through which the beam can travel. Normal glass will introduce little attenuation, but tinted glass will introduce unacceptable attenuation. This greatly simplifies mounting, power, and weatherproofing problems, but is obviously only useful in populated areas.

When mounting antennas on towers, it is very important to use a stand off bracket, and not mount the antennas directly to the tower. These brackets help with many functions including antenna separation, antenna alignment and protection.

Stand off brackets need to be strong enough to support the weight of the antenna, and also hold it in place on windy days. Remember, antennas can act like small sails, and can put a lot of force on to their mounts in strong winds. When estimating wind resistance, the total surface of the antenna structure must be considered, as well as the distance from the center of the antenna to the point of attachment to the building. Large antennas such as solid dishes or high gain sectorial panels can have considerable wind load. Using a slotted or mesh parabolic, rather than a solid dish, will help reduce the wind load without much affect on antenna gain. Be sure that the mounting brackets and supporting structure are solid, or your antennas will become misaligned over time (or worse, fall off the tower entirely!)

Mounting brackets must have enough clearance from the tower to allow for aiming, but not too much clearance that the antennas become too hard to reach if any service or maintenance is required.

Figure 8.1: An antenna with a standoff bracket being lifted onto a tower.

The pipe on the standoff bracket that the antenna will be mounted on needs to be round. This way the antenna can be pivoted on the pipe for aiming. Secondly, the pipe must also be vertical. If it is being mounted on a tapered tower, the standoff bracket will have to be designed to allow for this. This can be done using different lengths of steel, or by using combinations of threaded rod and steel plates.

As the equipment will be outside for all of its service life, it is important to be sure that the steel used is weatherproofed. Stainless steel often has too high a price tag for tower installations. Hot galvanizing is preferred, but may not be available in some areas. Painting all steel with a good rust paint will also work. If paint is chosen, it will be important to plan a yearly inspection of the mount and repaint when necessary.

Guyed towers

A climbable guyed tower is an excellent choice for many installations, but for very tall structures a self supporting tower might be required.

When installing guyed towers, a pulley attached to the top of a pole will facilitate the tower installation. The pole will be secured to the lower section already in place, while the two tower sections are attached with an articulated joint. A rope passing through the pulley will facilitate the raising of the next section. After the cantilever section becomes vertical, bolt it to the lower section of the pole. The pole (called a gin pole in the trade) can then be removed, and the operation may be repeated, if required. Tighten the guy wires carefully, ensuring that you use the same tension at all suitable anchoring points. Chose the points so that the angles, as seen from the center of the tower, are as evenly spaced as possible.

Figure 8.2: A climbable guyed tower.

Self-supporting towers

Self supporting towers are expensive but sometimes needed, particularly when greater elevation is a requirement. This can be as simple as a heavy pole sunk into a concrete piling, or as complicated as a professional radio tower.

Figure 8.3: A simple self-supporting tower.

An existing tower can sometimes be used for subscribers, although AM transmitting station antennas should be avoided because the whole structure is active. FM station antennas are acceptable, provided that at least a few of meters of separation is kept between the antennas. Be aware that while adjacent transmitting antennas may not interfere with your wireless connection, high powered FM may interfere with your wired Ethernet cable. Whenever using a heavily populated antenna tower, be very scrupulous about proper grounding and consider using shielded cable.

Figure 8.4: A much more complicated tower.

Rooftop assemblies

Non-penetrating roof mount antenna assemblies can be used on flat roofs. These consist of a tripod mounted to a metal or wooden base. The base is then weighed down with bricks, sandbags, water jugs, or just about anything heavy. Using such a rooftop "sled" eliminates the need to pierce the roof with mounting bolts, avoiding potential leaks.

Figure 8.5: This metal base can be weighed down with sandbags, rocks, or water bottles to make a stable platform without penetrating a roof.

Wall mount or metal strap assemblies can be used on existing structures such as chimneys or the sides of a buildings. If the antennas have to be mounted more than about 4 meters above the rooftop, a climbable tower may be a better solution to allow easier access to the equipment and to prevent antenna movement during high winds.

Dissimilar metals

To minimize electrolytic corrosion when two different metals are in moist contact, their electrolytic potential should be as close as possible. Use dielectric grease on the connection between two metals of different type to prevent any electrolysis effect.

Copper should never touch galvanized material directly without proper joint protection. Water shedding from the copper contains ions that will wash away the galvanized (zinc) tower covering. Stainless steel can be used as a buffer material, but you should be aware that stainless steel is not a very good conductor. If it is used as a buffer between copper and galvanized metals, the surface area of the contact should be large and the stainless steel should be thin. Joint compound should also be used to cover the connection so water can not bridge between the dissimilar metals.

Protecting microwave connectors

Moisture leakage in connectors is likely the most observed cause of radio link failure. Be sure to tighten connectors firmly, but never use a wrench or other tool to do so. Remember that metals expand and contract as temperature changes, and an over-tightened connector can break in extreme weather changes.

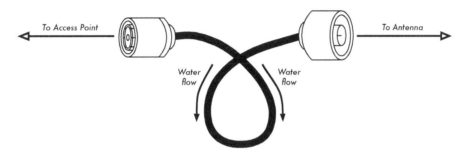

Figure 8.6: A drip loop forces rainwater away from your connectors.

Once tight, connectors should be protected by applying a layer of electrical tape, then a layer of sealing tape, and then another layer of electrical tape on top. The sealant protects the connector from water seepage, and the tape layer protects the sealant from ultraviolet (UV) damage. Cables should have an extra drip loop to prevent water from getting inside the transceiver.

Safety

Always use a harness securely attached to the tower when working at heights. If you have never worked on a tower, hire a professional to do it for you. Many countries require special training for people to be allowed to work on towers above a certain height.

Avoid working on towers during strong winds or storms. Always climb with a partner, and only when there is plenty of light. Tower work will likely take longer than you think it will. Remember that it is **extremely** hazardous to work in the dark. Give yourself plenty of time to complete the job long before the sun sets. If you run out of time, remember that the tower will be there in the morning, when you can start on the problem again after a good night's sleep.

Aligning antennas on a long distance link

To properly align antennas at a great distance, you will need some sort of visual feedback that shows you the instantaneous received power at the antenna feed. This lets you to make small changes to the antenna alignment while watching the feedback tool, ultimately stopping when the maximum received power has been found.

The ideal antenna alignment toolkit consists of a **signal generator** and a **spectrum analyzer**, preferably one of each at both ends of the link. By attaching a signal generator to one end of the link and a spectrum analyzer to the other, you can observe the received power and watch the effect of moving the antenna to various positions in real time. Once the maximum has been found on one end of a point to point link, the generator and analyzer can be swapped, and the process repeated for the other end.

The use of a signal generator is preferable to using the radio card itself, as the signal generator can generate a continuous carrier. A WiFi card transmits many discrete packets of information, switching the transmitter on and off very rapidly. This can be very difficult to find with a spectrum analyzer, particularly when operating in noisy areas.

Obviously, the cost of a calibrated signal generator and spectrum analyzer that works at 2.4 GHz (or even 5 GHz if using 802.11a) is well beyond the budget of most projects. Fortunately there are a number of inexpensive tools that can be used instead.

Inexpensive signal generator

There are many inexpensive transmitters that use the 2.4 GHz ISM band. For example, cordless phones, baby monitors, and miniature television transmitters all generate a continuous signal at 2.4 GHz. Television transmitters (sometimes called **video senders**) are particularly useful, since they often include an external SMA antenna connector and can be powered by a small battery.

Video senders usually include support for three or four channels. While these do not directly correspond to WiFi channels, they permit you to test the low, middle, or high end of the band.

For 5 GHz work, you can use a video sender in combination with a 2.4 GHz to 5 GHz converter. These devices accept a low power 2.4 GHz signal and emit high power 5 GHz signals. They are usually quite expensive ($300-$500 each) but will still likely be cheaper than a 5 GHz signal generator and spectrum analyzer.

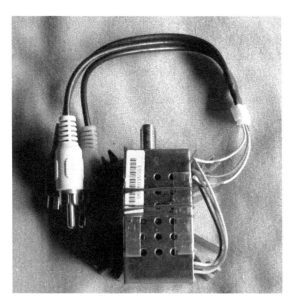

Figure 8.7: A 2.4 GHz video sender with an SMA antenna connector.

Whatever you choose for a signal source, you will need a way to display the received power level levels at the other end. While the cost of 2.4 GHz spectrum analyzers is slowly coming down, they still typically cost a few thousand dollars, even for used equipment.

Wi-Spy

The Wi-Spy is a USB spectrum analysis tool made by MetaGeek (*http://www.metageek.net/*). It features a very sensitive receiver in a small form factor (about the size of a USB thumb drive).

Figure 8.8: The Wi-Spy USB spectrum analyzer

The latest version of the Wi-Spy includes better dynamic range and an external antenna connector. It also comes with very good spectrum analysis software for Windows called Chanalyzer. It provides instantaneous, average, maximum, topographic, and spectral views.

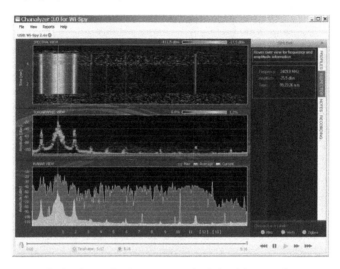

Figure 8.9: The distinctive spiked pattern to the left of the graph was caused by a high power 2.4 GHz television transmitter.

There is an excellent free software package for Mac OS X called EaKiu (*http://www.cookwareinc.com/EaKiu/*). In addition to the standard views, it also provides an animated 3D view, and adds support for multiple Wi-Spy devices.

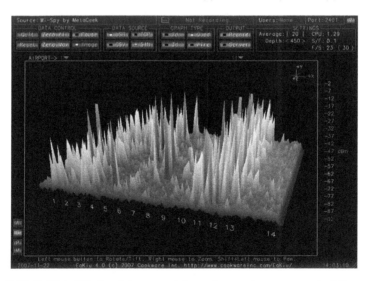

Figure 8.10: EaKiu's 3D view lets you rotate and zoom in on any part of the graph in real time. There is probably a WiFi network on channel 11, with other noise sources lower down in the band.

For Linux users, the Wi-Spy is supported by the Kismet Spectrum-Tools project (*http://kismetwireless.net/spectools/*). This package includes command line tools as well as a GUI built on GTK.

Other methods

Some wireless routers (such as the Mikrotik) provide an "antenna alignment tool" that shows you a moving bar representing the received power. When the bar is at the maximum, the antenna is aligned. With some routers, you can also enable an audio feedback mode. This causes the router to emit a loud tone, changing the pitch according to the received power.

If you don't have a spectrum analyzer, Wi-Spy, or a device that supports an antenna alignment mode, you will need to use the operating system to provide feedback about the wireless link quality. One simple method to do this in Linux is with a loop that continually calls **iwconfig**. For example:

```
wildnet:~# while :; do clear; iwconfig; sleep 1; done
```

This will show the state of all radio cards in the system, updating once every second. Note that this will only work on the client end of a link. On the access point (master mode) side, you should use the **iwspy** command to collect statistics for the MAC address of the client:

```
wildnet:~# iwspy ath0 00:15:6D:63:6C:3C
wildnet:~# iwspy
ath0      Statistics collected:
 00:15:6D:63:6C:3C : Quality=21/94  Signal=-74 dBm  Noise=-95 dBm
 Link/Cell/AP     : Quality=19/94  Signal=-76 dBm  Noise=-95 dBm
 Typical/Reference : Quality:0  Signal level:0  Noise level:0
```

You can then use a **while** loop (as in the previous example) to continually update the link status.

```
wildnet:~# while :; do clear; iwspy; sleep 1; done
```

Antenna alignment procedure

The key to successfully aligning antennas on a very long distance link is communication. If you change too many variables at once (say, one team starts wiggling an antenna while the other tries to take a signal strength reading), then the process will take all day and will probably end with misaligned antennas.

You will have two teams of people. Ideally, each team should have at least two people: one to take signal readings and communicate with the remote end, the other to manipulate the antenna. Keep these points in mind while working on long distance links.

1. **Test all equipment ahead of time.** You don't want to fiddle with settings once you're in the field. Before separating the equipment, power everything on, connect every antenna and pigtail, and make sure you can establish a connection between the devices. You should be able to return to this known good state by simply powering on the device, without having to log in or change any settings. Now is a good time to agree on antenna polarization (see **Chapter 2** if you don't understand what polarization means).

2. **Bring backup communications gear.** While mobile phones are usually good enough for working in cities, mobile reception can be bad or nonexistent in rural areas. Bring a high powered FRS or GMRS radio, or if your teams have amateur radio licenses, use a ham rig. Working at a distance can be very frustrating if you are constantly asking the other team "can you hear me now?" Pick your communication channels and test your radios (including the batteries) before separating.

3. **Bring a camera.** Take some time to document the location of each site, including surrounding landmarks and obstructions. This can be very useful later to determine the feasibility of another link to the location without having to travel there in person. If this is your first trip to the site, log the GPS coordinates and elevation as well.

4. **Start by estimating the proper bearing and elevation.** To begin, both teams should use triangulation (using GPS coordinates or a map) to get a rough idea of the direction to point. Use a compass to roughly align the antenna to the desired bearing. Large landmarks are also useful for pointing. If you can use binoculars to see the other end, all the better. Once you have made your guess, take a signal strength reading. If you are close enough and have made a good guess, you may already have signal.

5. **If all else fails, build your own landmark.** Some kinds of terrain make it difficult to judge the location of the other end of a link. If you are building a link in an area with few landmarks, a self-made landmark such as a kite, balloon, flood light, flare, or even smoke signal might help. You don't necessarily need a GPS to get an idea of where to point your antenna.

6. **Test signal in both directions, but only one at a time.** Once both ends have made their best guess, the end with the lowest gain antenna should make fix their antenna into position. Using a good monitoring tool (such as Kismet, Netstumbler, or a good built-in wireless client), the team with the highest gain antenna should slowly sweep it horizontally while watching the signal meter. Once the best position is found, try altering the elevation of the antenna. After the best possible position is found, lock the antenna firmly into place and signal the other team to begin slowly sweeping around. Repeat this process a couple of times until the best possible position for both antennas is found.

7. **Don't touch the antenna when taking a reading.** Your body will affect the radiation pattern of the antenna. Do not touch the antenna, and don't stand in the path of the shot, when taking signal strength readings. The same goes for the team on the other side of the link, too.

8. **Don't be afraid to push past the best received signal.** As we saw in chapter four, radiation patterns incorporate many smaller sidelobes of sensitivity, in addition to a much larger main lobe. If your received signal is mysteriously small, you may have found a sidelobe. Continue sweeping slowly beyond that lobe to see if you can find the main lobe.

9. **The antenna angle may look completely wrong.** The main lobe of an antenna often radiates slightly to one side or the other of the visual dead center of the antenna. Offset feed dishes will seem to be pointing too far down, or even directly at the ground. Don't worry about how the antenna looks; you are concerned with finding the best possible position to achieve the greatest possible received signal.

10. **Double-check polarization.** It can be frustrating to attempt aligning a dish only to discover that the other team is using the opposite polarization. Again, this should be agreed upon before leaving home base, but if a link stays stubbornly weak, a double check doesn't hurt.

11. **If nothing works, check all components one at a time.** Are the devices on both ends of the link powered on? Are all pigtails and connectors properly connected, with no damaged or suspect parts? As outlined in chapter eight, proper troubleshooting technique will save you time and frustration. Work slowly and communicate your status well with the other team.

By working methodically and communicating well, you can complete the job of aligning high gain antennas in just a short while. If done properly, it should be fun!

Surge and lightning protection

Power is the greatest challenge for most installations in the developing world. Where there are electrical networks, they are often poorly controlled, fluctuate dramatically and are susceptible to lightning. Proper surge protection is critical to not only protect your wireless equipment, but all of the equipment connected to it.

Fuses and circuit breakers

Fuses are critical, but very often neglected. In rural areas, and even in many urban areas of developing countries, fuses are difficult to find. Despite the added cost, it is always prudent to use circuit breakers instead. These may need to be imported, but shouldn't be overlooked. Too often, replaceable fuses are removed and pocket change is used instead. In a recent case, all of the electronic equipment at at rural radio station was destroyed when a lightning strike went through the circuit, without circuit breaker or even a fuse to protect it.

How to ground

Proper grounding doesn't have to be a complicated job. When grounding, you are trying to accomplish two things: provide a short-circuit for a lightning strike, and provide a circuit for excess energy to be dissipated.

The first step is to protect equipment from a direct or near direct lightning hit, while the second provides a path to dissipate excess energy that would otherwise cause a build-up of static electricity. Static can cause significant degradation to signal quality, particularly on sensitive receivers (VSATs for example). Providing the short-circuit is simple. The installer simply needs to make the shortest path from the highest conductive surface (a lightning rod) to the ground. When a strike hits the rod, the energy will travel the shortest path and thus by-pass the equipment. This ground should be able to handle high-voltage (i.e. you need thick gauge wire, like 8 gauge braided copper).

To ground the equipment, mount a lightning rod above the equipment on a tower or other structure. Then use a thick gauge conductive wire to connect the rod to something that itself is well grounded. Underground copper pipes can be very well grounded (depending on their depth, the moisture, salinity, amount of metal and organic content of the soil). In many sites in West Africa, pipes aren't yet in the ground, and previous grounding equipment is often inadequate due to ill-conductive soil (typical of seasonally arid, tropical soils). There are three easy ways to measure the efficiency of your ground:

1. The least accurate is to simply plug a good quality UPS or power strip into the circuit that has a ground detect indicator (a LED light). This LED is lit by energy that is being diffused to the ground circuit. An effective ground will dissipate small amounts of energy to the ground. Some people actually use this to pirate a bit of free light, as this energy does not turn an electrical counter!

2. Take a light socket and a low-wattage bulb (30 Watts), connect one wire to the ground wire and the second to the hot wire. If the ground is working, the bulb should shine slightly.

3. The more sophisticated way is to simply measure the impedance between the positive circuit and the ground.

If your ground is not efficient you will need to bury a grounding stake deeper (where the soil is more moist, has more organic matter and metals) or you need to make the ground more conductive. A common approach where there is little soil is to dig a hole that is 1 meter in diameter and 2 meters deep. Drop in a highly conductive piece of metal that has some mass to it. This is sometimes called a ***plomb***, which literally means lead but can be any heavy piece of metal weighing 50 kg or more, such as an iron anvil or steel wheel. Then fill the hole with charcoal and mix in salt, then top with soil. Soak the area, and the charcoal and salt will diffuse around the hole and make a conductive area surrounding your plomb, improving the efficiency of the ground.

If radio cable is being used, it too can be used to ground the tower, though a more resilient design is to separate the ground for the tower from the cable. To ground the cable, simply peel back a bit of cable at the point closest to the ground before it goes into the building, then attach a ground cable from that point, either by soldering or using a very conductive connector. This then needs to be waterproofed.

Power stabilizers & regulators

There are many brands of power stabilizers, but most are either digital or electromechanical. The latter are much cheaper and more common. Electromechanical stabilizers take power at 220V, 240V, or 110V and use that energy to turn a motor, which always produces the desired voltage (normally 220V). This is normally effective, but these units offer little protection from lightning or other heavy surges. They often burn out after just one strike. Once burnt, they can actually be fused at a certain (usually wrong) output voltage.

Digital regulators regulate the energy using resistors and other solid state components. They are more expensive, but are much less susceptible to being burnt.

Whenever possible, use a digital regulator. They are worth the added cost, and will offer better protection for the rest of your equipment. Be sure to inspect all components of your power system (including the stabilizer) after lightning activity.

9

Troubleshooting

How you establish the support infrastructure for your network is as important as what type of equipment you use. Unlike wired connections, problems with a wireless network are often invisible, and can require more skill and more time to diagnose and remedy. Interference, wind, and new physical obstructions can cause a long-running network to fail. This chapter details a series of strategies to help you build a team that can support your network effectively.

Building your team

Every village, company or family has individuals who are intrigued by technology. They are the ones found splicing the television cable, re-wiring a broken television or welding a new piece to a bicycle. These people will take interest in your network and want to learn as much about it as possible. Though these people are invaluable resources, you must avoid imparting all of the specialized knowledge of wireless networking to only one person. If your only specialist loses interest or finds better paying work somewhere else, they take the knowledge with them when they go.

There may also be many young and ambitious teenagers or young adults who will be interested and have the time to listen, help, and learn about the network. Again, they are very helpful and will learn quickly, but the project team must focus their attention on those who are best placed to support the network in the coming months and years. Young adults and teenagers will go off to university or find employment, especially the ambitious youth who tend to want to be involved. These youth also have little influence in the community, where an older individual is likely to be more capable of making decisions that positively affect the network as a whole. Even though these individuals might have less time to learn and might appear to be less interested, their involvement and proper education about the system can be critical.

Therefore, a key strategy in building a support team is to balance and to distribute the knowledge among those who are best placed to support the network for the long term.   You should involve the youth, but do not let them capitalize use or knowledge of these systems. Find people who are committed to the community, who have roots in the community, who can be motivated, and teach them. A complementary strategy is to compartmentalize functions and duties, and to document all methodology and procedures.   In this way, people can be trained easily, and substituted with little effort.

For example, in one project site the training team selected a bright young university graduate who had returned to his village. He was very motivated and learned quickly. Because he learned so quickly, he was taught more than had been foreseen, and he was able to deal with a variety of problems, from fixing a PC to rewiring Ethernet cable. Unfortunately, two months after the project launch he was offered a government job and left the community. Even a better salary could not keep him, since the prospect of a stable government job was too appealing. All of the knowledge about the network and how to support it left with him. The training team had to return and begin the training again. The next strategy was to divide functions, and to train people who were permanently rooted in the community: people who had houses and children, and were already employed. It took three times as long to teach three people as it took to train the young university grad, but the community will retain this knowledge for much longer.

Though this might seem to suggest that you should hand-pick who is to be involved, that is not often the best approach. It is often best to find a local partner organization or a local manager, and work with them to find the right technical team. Values, history, local politics, and many other factors will be important to them, while remaining completely unfathomable to people who are not from that community. The best approach is to coach your local partner, to provide them sound criteria, make sure that they understand that criteria, and to set firm boundaries. Such boundaries should include rules about nepotism and patronage, though these rules must consider the local situation. It may be impossible to say that you cannot hire kin, but it is best to provide a means of checks and balances.   Where a candidate is kin, there should be clear criteria and a second authority in deciding upon their candidacy.   It is also important that the local partner is given this authority and is not undermined by the project organizers, thus compromising their ability to manage. They will be best able to judge who will work best with them. If they are well educated in this process, then your requirements should be satisfied.

Troubleshooting and support of technology is an abstract art. The first time you look at an abstract painting, it may just look to you like a bunch of random paint splatters. After reflecting on the composition for a time, you may come to appreciate the work as a whole, and the "invisible" coherence becomes very real. The neophyte looking at a wireless network may see the antennas and wires and computers, but it can take a while for them to appreciate the point of the "invisible" network. In rural areas, it can often take a huge leap of understanding before locals will appreciate an invisible network that is simply dropped into their village. Therefore, a phased approach is needed to ease people into supporting technology systems. The best method is involvement. Once the participants are chosen and committed to the project, involve them as much as possible. Let them "drive". Give them the cable crimper or keyboard and show them how to do the work. Even if you do not have time to explain every detail and even if it will take longer, they need to be involved physically and see not only what has been done, but how much work was done.

The scientific method is taught in virtually all western schools. Many people learn about it by the time they reach high-school science class. Simply put, you take a set of variables, then slowly eliminate those variables through binary tests until you are left with one or only a few possibilities. With those possibilities in mind, you complete the experiment. You then test to see if the experiment yields something similar to the expected result. If it did not, you recalculate your expected result and try again. The typical agrarian villager may have been introduced to the concept, but likely will not have had the opportunity to troubleshoot complex problems. Even if they are familiar with the scientific method, they might not think to apply it to resolving real problems.

This method is very effective, although time consuming. It can be sped up by making logical assumptions. For example, if a long-running access point suddenly stops working after a storm, you might suspect a power supply related problem and thus skip most of the procedure. People charged with supporting technology should be taught how to troubleshoot using this method, as there will be times when the problem is neither known nor evident. Simple decision trees or flow charts can be made that test these variables, and try to eliminate the variables to isolate the problem. Of course, these charts should not be followed blindly.

It is often easier to teach this method using a non technological problem first. For example, have your student develop a problem resolution procedure on something simple and familiar, like a battery powered television. Start by sabotaging the television. Give them a battery that is not charged. Disconnect the aerial. Insert a broken fuse. Test the student, making it clear that each problem will show specific symptoms, and point the way as to how to proceed. Once they have fixed the television, have them apply this procedure to a more complicated problem. In a network, you can change an IP address, switch or damage cables, use the wrong SSID, or orient the antenna in the wrong direction. It is important that they develop a methodology and procedure to resolve these problems.

Proper troubleshooting technique

No troubleshooting methodology can completely cover all problems you will encounter when working with wireless networks.   But often, problems come down to one of a few common mistakes.   Here are a few simple points to keep in mind that can get your troubleshooting effort working in the right direction.

- **Don't panic.**   If you are troubleshooting a system, that means that it was working at one time, probably very recently.   Before jumping in and making changes, survey the scene and assess exactly what is broken.   If you have historical logs or statistics to work from, all the better.   Be sure to collect information first, so you can make an informed decision before making changes.

- **Is it plugged in?**   This step is often overlooked until many other avenues are explored.   Plugs can be accidentally (or intentionally) unplugged very easily.   Is the lead connected to a good power source?   Is the other end connected to your device?   Is the power light on?   It may sound silly, but you will feel even sillier if you spend a lot of time checking out an antenna feed line only to realize that the AP was unplugged the entire time.   Trust me, it happens more often than most of us would care to admit.

- **What was the last thing changed?**   If you are the only person with access to the system, what is the last change you made?   If others have access to it, what is the last change they made and when?   When was the last time the system worked?   Often, system changes have unintended consequences that may not be immediately noticed.   Roll back that change and see what effect it has on the problem.

- **Make a backup.**   This applies before you notice problems, as well as after.   If you make a complicated software change to a system, having a backup means that you can quickly restore it to the previous settings and start again.   When troubleshooting very complex problems, having a configuration that "sort-of" works can be much better than having a mess that doesn't work at all (and that you can't easily restore from memory).

- **The known good**.   This idea applies to hardware, as well as software.   A *known good* is any component that you can replace in a complex system to verify that its counterpart is in good, working condition.   For example, you may carry a tested Ethernet cable in a tool kit.   If you suspect problems with a cable in the field, you can easily swap out the suspect cable with the known good and see if things improve.   This is much faster and less error-prone than re-crimping a cable, and immediately tells you if the change fixes the problem. Likewise, you may also pack a backup battery, antenna cable, or a CD-ROM with a known good configuration for the system.   When fixing complicated problems, saving your work at a given point lets you return to it as a known good, even if the problem is not yet completely solved.

- **Change one variable at a time.** When under pressure to get a failed system back online, it is tempting to jump ahead and change many likely variables at once. If you do, and your changes seem to fix the problem, then you will not understand exactly what led to the problem in the first place. Worse, your changes may fix the original problem, but lead to more unintended consequences that break other parts of the system. By changing your variables one at a time, you can precisely understand what went wrong in the first place, and be able to see the direct effects of the changes you make.

- **Do no harm.** If you don't fully understand how a system works, don't be afraid to call in an expert. If you are not sure if a particular change will damage another part of the system, then either find someone with more experience or devise a way to test your change without doing damage. Putting a penny in place of a fuse may solve the immediate problem, but it may also burn down the building.

It is unlikely that the people who design your network will be on call twenty-four hours per day to fix problems when they arise. Your troubleshooting team will need to have good troubleshooting skills, but may not be competent enough to configure a router from scratch or crimp a piece of LMR-400. It is often much more efficient to have a number of backup components on-hand, and train your team to be able to swap out the entire broken part. This could mean having an access point or router pre-configured and sitting in a locked cabinet, plainly labeled and stored with backup cables and power supplies. Your team can swap out the failed component, and either send the broken part to an expert for repair, or arrange to have another backup sent in. Assuming that the backups are kept secure and are replaced when used, this can save a lot of time for everyone.

Common network problems

Often, connectivity problems come from failed components, adverse weather, or simple misconfiguration. Once your network is connected to the Internet or opened up to the general public, considerable threats will come from the network users themselves. These threats can range from the benign to the outright malevolent, but all will have impact on your network if it is not properly configured. This section looks at some common problems found once your network is used by actual human beings.

Locally hosted websites

If a university hosts its website locally, visitors to the website from outside the campus and the rest of the world will compete with the university's staff for Internet bandwidth. This includes automated access from search engines that periodically *spider* your entire site. One solution to this problem is to use split DNS and mirroring. The university mirrors a copy of its websites to a server at, say, a European hosting company, and uses split DNS to direct all users from outside the university network to the mirror site, while users on the university network access the same site locally. Details about how to set this up are provided in chapter three.

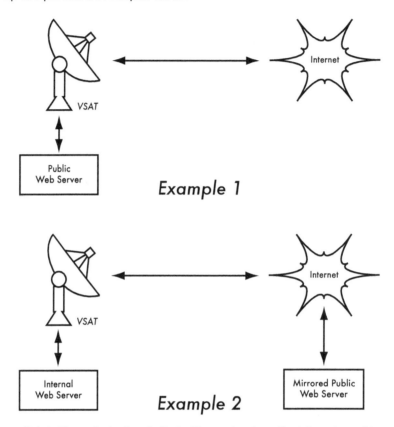

Figure 9.1: In Example 1, all website traffic coming from the Internet must traverse the VSAT. In Example 2, the public web site is hosted on a fast European service, while a copy is kept on an internal server for very fast local access. This improves the VSAT connection and reduces load times for web site users.

Open proxies

A proxy server should be configured to accept only connections from the university network, not from the rest of the Internet. This is because people elsewhere will connect and use open proxies for a variety of reasons, such as to avoid paying for international bandwidth. The way to configure this depends on the proxy server you are using. For example, you can specify the IP address range of the campus network in your **squid.conf** file as the only network that can use Squid. Alternatively, if your proxy server lies behind a border firewall, you can configure the firewall to only allow internal hosts to connect to the proxy port.

Open relay hosts

An incorrectly configured mail server will be found by unscrupulous people on the Internet, and be used as a relay host to send bulk email and spam. They do this to hide the true source of the spam, and avoid getting caught. To test for an open relay host, the following test should be carried out on your mail server (or on the SMTP server that acts as a relay host on the perimeter of the campus network). Use ***telnet*** to open a connection to port 25 of the server in question (with some Windows versions of telnet, it may be necessary to type 'set local_echo' before the text is visible):

```
telnet mail.uzz.ac.zz 25
```

Then, if an interactive command-line conversation can take place (for example, as follows), the server is an open relay host:

```
MAIL FROM: spammer@waste.com
250 OK - mail from <spammer@waste.com>
RCPT TO: innocent@university.ac.zz
250 OK - rcpt to spammer@waste.com
```

Instead, the reply after the first MAIL FROM should be something like:

```
550 Relaying is prohibited.
```

An online tester is available at sites such as *http://www.ordb.org/*. There is also information about the problem at this site. Since bulk emailers have automated methods to find such open relay hosts, an institution that does not protect its mail systems is almost guaranteed to be found and abused. Configuring the mail server not to be an open relay consists of specifying the networks and hosts that are allowed to relay mail through them in the MTA (eg., Sendmail, Postfix, Exim, or Exchange). This will likely be the IP address range of the campus network.

Peer-to-peer networking

Bandwidth abuse through peer-to-peer (P2P) file-sharing programs such as Kazaa, Morpheus, BitTorrent, WinMX and BearShare can be prevented in the following ways:

- **Make it impossible to install new programs on campus computers.** By not giving regular users administrative access to PC workstations, it is possible to prevent the installation of programs such as Kazaa. Many institutions also standardize on a desktop build, where they install the required operating system on one PC. They then install all the necessary applications on it, and configure these in an optimal way. The PC is also configured in a way that prevents users from installing new applications. A disk image of this PC is then cloned to all other PCs using software such as Partition Image (see *http://www.partimage.org/*) or Drive Image Pro (see *http://www.powerquest.com/*).

From time to time, users may succeed in installing new software or otherwise damaging the software on the computer (causing it to hang often, for example). When this happens, an administrator can simply put the disk image back, causing the operating system and all software on the computer to be exactly as specified.

- **Blocking these protocols is not a solution.** This is because Kazaa and other protocols are clever enough to bypass blocked ports. Kazaa defaults to port 1214 for the initial connection, but if that is not available it will attempt to use ports 1000 to 4000. If these are blocked, its uses port 80, making it look like web traffic. For this reason, ISPs don't block it but "throttle it", using bandwidth management tools.

- **If rate-limiting is not an option, change the network layout.** If the proxy server and mail servers are configured with two network cards (as described in chapter three) and these servers are not configured to forward any packets, this would block all P2P traffic. It would also block all other types of traffic, such as Microsoft NetMeeting, SSH, VPN software, and all other services not specifically permitted by the proxy server. In low bandwidth networks it may be decided that the simplicity of this design will outweigh the disadvantages.   Such a decision may be necessary, but shouldn't be taken lightly.   Network administrators simply cannot predict how users will make innovative use of a network. By preemptively blocking all access, you will prevent users from making use of any services (even low-bandwidth services) that your proxy does not support. While this may be desirable in extremely low bandwidth circumstances, it should never be considered as a good access policy in the general case.

Programs that install themselves (from the Internet)

There are programs that automatically install themselves and then keep on using bandwidth - for example, the so-called Bonzi-Buddy, the Microsoft Network, and some kinds of worms. Some programs are spyware, which keep sending information about a user's browsing habits to a company somewhere on the Internet. These programs are preventable to some extent by user education and locking down PCs to prevent administrative access for normal users. In other cases, there are software solutions to find and remove these problem programs, such as Spychecker (*http://www.spychecker.com/*) or Ad-Aware (*http://www.lavasoft.de/*).

Windows updates

The latest Microsoft Windows operating systems assume that a computer with a LAN connection has a good link to the Internet, and automatically downloads security patches, bug fixes and feature enhancements from the Microsoft Web site. This can consume massive amounts of bandwidth on an expensive Internet link. The two possible approaches to this problem are:

- **Disable Windows updates on all workstation PCs.** The security updates are very important for servers, but whether workstations in a protected private network such as a campus network need them is debatable.

- **Install a Software Update Server.** This is a free program from Microsoft that enables you to download all the updates from Microsoft overnight on to a local server and distribute the updates to client workstations from there. In this way, Windows updates need not use any bandwidth on the Internet link during the day. Unfortunately, all client PCs need to be configured to use the Software Update Server for this to have an effect. If you have a flexible DNS server, you can also configure it to answer requests for *windowsupdate.microsoft.com* and direct the updater to your update server. This is only a good option for large networks, but can save untold amounts of Internet bandwidth.

Blocking the Windows updates site on the proxy server is not a good solution because the Windows update service (Automatic Updates) keeps retrying more aggressively, and if all workstations do that, it places a heavy load on the proxy server. The extract below is from the proxy log (Squid access log) where this was done by blocking Microsoft's cabinet (.cab) files.

Much of the Squid log looks like this:

```
2003.4.2 13:24:17 192.168.1.21 http://windowsupdate.microsoft.com/ident.cab
  *DENIED* Banned extension .cab GET 0
2003.4.2 13:24:18 192.168.1.21 http://windowsupdate.microsoft.com/ident.cab
 *DENIED* Banned extension .cab GET 0
2003.4.2 13:24:18 192.168.1.21 http://windowsupdate.microsoft.com/ident.cab
 *DENIED* Banned extension .cab HEAD 0
2003.4.2 13:24:19 192.168.1.21 http://windowsupdate.microsoft.com/ident.cab
 *DENIED* Banned extension .cab GET 0
2003.4.2 13:24:19 192.168.1.21 http://windowsupdate.microsoft.com/ident.cab
 *DENIED* Banned extension .cab GET 0
2003.4.2 13:24:20 192.168.1.21 http://windowsupdate.microsoft.com/ident.cab
 *DENIED* Banned extension .cab GET 0
2003.4.2 13:24:21 192.168.1.21 http://windowsupdate.microsoft.com/ident.cab
 *DENIED* Banned extension .cab GET 0
2003.4.2 13:24:21 192.168.1.21 http://windowsupdate.microsoft.com/ident.cab
 *DENIED* Banned extension .cab GET 0
2003.4.2 13:24:21 192.168.1.21 http://windowsupdate.microsoft.com/ident.cab
 *DENIED* Banned extension .cab HEAD 0
```

While this may be tolerable for a few PC clients, the problem grows significantly as hosts are added to the network. Rather than forcing the proxy server to serve requests that will always fail, it makes more sense to redirect the Software Update clients to a local update server.

Programs that assume a high bandwidth link

In addition to Windows updates, many other programs and services assume that bandwidth is not a problem, and therefore consume bandwidth for reasons the user might not predict. For example, anti-virus packages (such as Norton AntiVirus) periodically update themselves automatically and directly from the Internet. It is better if these updates are distributed from a local server.

Other programs, such as the RealNetworks video player, automatically download updates and advertisements, as well as upload usage patterns back to a site on the Internet. Innocuous looking applets (like Konfabulator and Dashboard widgets) continually poll Internet hosts for updated information. These can be low bandwidth requests (like weather or news updates), or very high bandwidth requests (such as webcams). These applications may need to be throttled or blocked altogether.

The latest versions of Windows and Mac OS X also have a time synchronization service. This keeps the computer clock accurate by connecting to time servers on the Internet. It is more efficient to install a local time server and distribute accurate time from there, rather than to tie up the Internet link with these requests.

Windows traffic on the Internet link

Windows computers communicate with each other via **NetBIOS** and **Server Message Block** (**SMB**). These protocols work on top of TCP/IP or other transport protocols. It is a protocol that works by holding **elections** to determine which computer will be the **master browser**. The master browser is a computer that keeps a list of all the computers, shares and printers that you can see in **Network Neighborhood** or **My Network Places**. Information about available shares are also broadcast at regular intervals.

The SMB protocol is designed for LANs and causes problems when the Windows computer is connected to the Internet. Unless SMB traffic is filtered, it will also tend to spread to the Internet link, wasting the organization's bandwidth. The following steps might be taken to prevent this:

• **Block outgoing SMB/NetBIOS traffic on the perimeter router or firewall.** This traffic will eat up Internet bandwidth, and worse, poses a potential security risk. Many Internet worms and penetration tools actively scan for open SMB shares, and will exploit these connections to gain greater access to your network.

- **Install ZoneAlarm on all workstations (not the server)**. A free version can be found at *http://www.zonelabs.com/*. This program allows the user to determine which applications can make connections to the Internet and which ones cannot. For example, Internet Explorer needs to connect to the Internet, but Windows Explorer does not. ZoneAlarm can block Windows Explorer from doing so.

- **Reduce network shares.** Ideally, only the file server should have any shares. You can use a tool such as SoftPerfect Network Scanner (from *http://www.softperfect.com/*) to easily identify all the shares in your network.

Worms and viruses

Worms and viruses can generate enormous amounts 'of traffic. The W32/Opaserv worm, for example, is still prevalent, even though it is an old one. It spreads through Windows shares and is detected by other people on the Internet because it attempts to spread further. It is therefore essential that anti-virus protection is installed on all PCs. Furthermore, user education about executing attachments and responding to unsolicited email is essential. In fact, it should be a policy that no workstation or server should run unused services. A PC should not have shares unless it is a file server; and a server should not run unnecessary services either. For example, Windows and Unix servers typically run a web server service by default. This should be disabled if that server has a different function; the fewer services a computer runs, the less there is to exploit.

Email forwarding loops

Occasionally, a single user making a mistake can cause a problem. For example, a user whose university account is configured to forward all mail to her Yahoo account. The user goes on holiday. All emails sent to her in her absence are still forwarded to her Yahoo account, which can grow to only 2 MB. When the Yahoo account becomes full, it starts bouncing the emails back to the university account, which immediately forwards it back to the Yahoo account. An email loop is formed that might send hundreds of thousands of emails back and forth, generating massive traffic and crashing mail servers.

There are features of mail server programs that can recognize loops. These should be turned on by default. Administrators must also take care that they do not turn this feature off by mistake, or install an SMTP forwarder that modifies mail headers in such a way that the mail server does not recognize the mail loop.

Large downloads

A user may start several simultaneous downloads, or download large files such as 650MB ISO images. In this way, a single user can use up most of the bandwidth. The solutions to this kind of problem lie in training, offline downloading, and monitoring (including real-time monitoring, as outlined in chapter six). Offline downloading can be implemented in at least two ways:

- At the University of Moratuwa, a system was implemented using URL redirection. Users accessing **ftp://** URLs are served a directory listing in which each file has two links: one for normal downloading, and the other for offline downloading. If the offline link is selected, the specified file is queued for later download and the user notified by email when the download is complete. The system keeps a cache of recently downloaded files, and retrieves such files immediately when requested again. The download queue is sorted by file size. Therefore, small files are downloaded first. As some bandwidth is allocated to this system even during peak hours, users requesting small files may receive them within minutes, sometimes even faster than an online download.

- Another approach would be to create a web interface where users enter the URL of the file they want to download. This is then downloaded overnight using a ***cron job*** or scheduled task. This system would only work for users who are not impatient, and are familiar with what file sizes would be problematic for download during the working day.

Sending large files

When users need to transfer large files to collaborators elsewhere on the Internet, they should be shown how to schedule the upload. In Windows, an upload to a remote FTP server can be done using an FTP script file, which is a text file containing FTP commands, similar to the following (saved as **c:\ftpscript.txt**):

```
open ftp.ed.ac.uk
gventer
mysecretword
delete data.zip
binary
put data.zip
quit
```

To execute, type this from the command prompt:

```
ftp -s:c:\ftpscript.txt
```

On Windows NT, 2000 and XP computers, the command can be saved into a file such as **transfer.cmd**, and scheduled to run at night using the Scheduled Tasks (Start → Settings → Control Panel → Scheduled Tasks). In Unix, the same can be achieved by using *at* or **cron**.

Users sending each other files

Users often need to send each other large files. It is a waste of bandwidth to send these via the Internet if the recipient is local. A file share should be created on the local Windows / Samba /web Novell server, where a user can put the large file for others to access.

Alternatively, a web front-end can be written for a local web server to accept a large file and place it in a download area. After uploading it to the web server, the user receives a URL for the file. He can then give that URL to his local or international collaborators, and when they access that URL they can download it. This is what the University of Bristol has done with their FLUFF system. The University offers a facility for the upload of large files (FLUFF) available from *http://www.bristol.ac.uk/fluff/*. These files can then be accessed by anyone who has been given their location. The advantage of this approach is that users can give external users access to their files, whereas the file share method can work only for users within the campus network. A system like this can easily be implemented as a CGI script using Python and Apache.

10
Economic Sustainability

Achieving long-term sustainability is perhaps the most difficult goal when designing and operating wireless networks and telecenters in developing countries. The prohibitive cost of Internet connectivity in many developing countries imposes a substantial operating expense that makes these models sensitive to economic fluctuations and necessitates innovation to attain viability. Substantial progress in the use of wireless networks for rural communications has been accomplished over the past few years, due in large part to technological breakthroughs. Long-distance links have been constructed, high bandwidth designs are possible and secure means to access networks are available. In contrast, there have been fewer successes with the development of sustainable business models for wireless networks and telecenters, particularly for remote areas. Based on the authors' experiences and observations of existing networks, as well as knowledge from entrepreneurial development best practices, this chapter will focus on documenting methods for building sustainable wireless networks and telecenters.

In the past decade, there has been tremendous growth in Internet access across the developing world. Most developing world cities now have wireless or ADSL networks and fiber optic connections to the Internet, which is a substantial improvement. Nevertheless, outside urban areas, Internet access is still a formidable challenge. There is little wired infrastructure beyond the principal cities. Therefore, wireless remains one of the few choices for providing affordable Internet access. There are now proven models for rural access using wireless. In Macedonia, the Macedonia Connects project has now connected a majority of the country's schools to the Internet. This book was written for those wishing to connect their communities. The models described here are smaller in scale and use affordable designs. Our aim is to provide examples of how wireless networks can be designed to expand sustainable access where large telecommunications operators have not yet installed their networks into areas that would otherwise not be economically feasible by traditional models.

Two common misconceptions must be dispelled. First, many people assume that there is one preferred business model that will work in every community of the developing world, and the key to success is to find that one "eureka" solution. In practice, this is not the case. Each community, town or village is different. There is no prescribed model that meets the needs of all areas in the developing world. Despite the fact that some places may be similar in economic terms, the characteristics of a sustainable business model vary from community to community. Although one model may work in one village, another village nearby may not possess the same necessary qualities for this model to be sustainable. In this circumstance, other innovative models must be customized to fit the context of this particular community.

Another misconception is that sustainability has the same definition for all people. Although this term generally means that a system is built to persist indefinitely, this chapter focuses more on the discussion of the economic conditions (financial and managerial) than other aspects of sustainability. Also, instead of the horizon being indeterminate, it centers on a time period of five years – the period in which these ICT infrastructure and wireless technologies are expected to be useful. Thus, the term sustainability will be used to encapsulate a system designed to persist for approximately five or more years.

When determining and implementing the best model for a wireless network or telecenter, several key factors help to ensure its success. This chapter is not meant to be a guide for managing sustainable wireless networks. Rather, this "how-to" guide seeks to present an approach that will enable you to find the model that best fits your situation. The tools and information contained within this chapter will help people starting wireless networks in the developing world to ask the right questions and gather the necessary data to define the most appropriate components of their model. Keep in mind that determining the best model is not a sequential process where each step is followed until completion. In fact, the process is ongoing and iterative. All of the steps are integrally connected to each other, and often you will revisit steps several times as you progress.

Create a Mission Statement

What do you want to accomplish by setting up your network? It seems like a simple question. However, many wireless networks are installed without a clear vision of what they are doing and what they hope to accomplish in the future. The first step involves documenting this vision with the input of your entire team or staff. What is the purpose of the wireless network? Who does the network seek to serve? What does the network do to address the community's needs and to create value? What are the principles that guide the network? A good mission statement expresses the purpose of your network in a concise, meaningful way while articulating your values and services. Above all, your mission provides a vision of the aspirations for your wireless network.

It is important that every team member working to build the wireless network is included in the process of developing your mission, which helps create further buy-in. It will garner support and commitment not only from your staff, but also from customers, partners and donors, which will further your overall objectives. In the dynamic world of technology, the needs of customers and the best way to satisfy those needs change rapidly; therefore, the development of your mission is an ongoing process. After defining the initial mission with your team, you must conduct research to determine whether this first conception is aligned with the realities of your environment. Based on an analysis of the external environment and your internal competencies, you must constantly modify the mission throughout the life-cycle of the wireless network.

Evaluate the Demand for Potential Offerings

The next step in deriving your business model involves assessing the community's demand for the network's products and services. First, identify the individuals, groups and organizations in the community that have a need for information and would benefit from the wireless network's offerings. Potential users could consist of a wide variety of individuals and organizations that include, but are not limited to:

- Farmers' associations and cooperatives
- Women's groups
- Schools and universities
- Businesses and local entrepreneurs
- Health clinics and hospitals
- Religious groups
- International and local non-governmental organizations (NGOs)
- Local and national government agencies
- Radio stations
- Organizations in the tourist industry

Once you establish a list of all the potential user groups of the network, you must determine their needs for access to information and communication. Often, people confuse services with needs. A farmer may need to gather information on market prices and climatic conditions to improve his crop yield and sales. Perhaps the way in which he gets this information is through the Internet; however, the farmer could also receive this information through SMS over a mobile phone or through **Voice over Internet Protocol** (**VOIP**). It is important to differentiate between needs and services because there may be various ways to satisfy the farmer's needs. Your wireless network should look for the best way to fulfill the farmer's needs, thereby creating value at the lowest cost for the user.

When assessing the needs of the community, it is important to figure out where the network can bring the most value to its users. For instance, in the small town of Douentza, Mali, a telecenter manager evaluated the potential benefits of establishing a wireless network through discussions with several local organizations. He interviewed one local NGO that discussed its need to send monthly reports to its headquarters office in Bamako. At that time, there was no Internet access in Douentza. In order to email a copy of the report, the NGO sent one of its employees to Mopti once a month, resulting in transportation and lodging costs, as well as the opportunity cost of having the employee out of the office for several days each month. When the telecenter manager calculated the total monthly costs incurred by the NGO, he was able to demonstrate the value of an Internet connection through cost savings to the organization.

Assistance from key partners may also be necessary to secure sustainability for your wireless network. During this phase, you should connect with potential partners and explore mutually beneficial collaborations.

You can evaluate the demand in your community by contacting your potential customers and asking questions directly through surveys, focus groups, interviews or town hall meetings. Conducting research through a review of statistical documentation, industry reports, censuses, magazines, newspapers and other secondary data sources will also help to give you a better picture of your local environment. The goal of this data collection is to obtain a thorough understanding of the demand for information and communication in your community so that the network being created responds to those needs. Often, wireless networks that do not succeed in the developing world forget this key step. Your entire network should be based on the demand in the community. If you set up a wireless network in which the community does not find value or cannot afford its services, it will ultimately fail.

Establish Appropriate Incentives

Often, there is little economic incentive for such subsistence-based economic participants to access the Internet. In addition, the cost of acquiring a computer, learning to use it, and getting an Internet connection far outweighs the economic returns that it can provide. There has recently been some development of applications that address this lack of incentive, such as market information systems, quality standards imposed by importing countries, and commodities exchanges. Internet access becomes an obvious advantage in situations where knowing the day-to-day prices of products can make a significant difference in income.

Establishing appropriate economic incentives is paramount to the success of the network. The network must provide economic value to its users in a way that outweighs its costs, or it must be cheap enough that its costs are marginal and affordable to its users. It is crucial to design a network with viable economic uses and with costs that are less than the economic value provided by it. Additionally, to create a proper incentive structure, you must involve the community in the creation of the network from the beginning of the project, making sure that this initiative is organic and not imposed from the outside. To begin, you should try to answer the following questions:

1. What economic value can this network generate for the local economy and for whom?

2. How much perceivable economic value can be generated?

3. Can present impediments be overcome to allow the achievement of these economic returns?

By answering these questions, the network will be able to clearly articulate its value proposition for its users. For example, "By using this network you can improve your margins on commodity sales by 2%," or "Internet will allow you to save $X in phone charges and transportation costs per month." You must figure out how your network can improve efficiencies, reduce costs, or increase revenues for these customers.

For example, if providing market information for the local maize industry, the network should be located near to where farmers bring their crop for sale to merchants. Your network would then likely need to tie-into market information systems, providing daily price sheets ($1 each), or terminals to sellers and merchants ($2/hr). Your network might also provide the means for farmers to read about new techniques and to buy new products. You might also provide wireless connections to merchants and rent them thin-client terminals for Internet access. If the market was small, you might be able to reduce costs by limiting access to images and other bandwidth intensive services. Again, knowing how much value your network will create for these merchants will allow you to gauge how much they will be able to afford for your services.

Research the Regulatory Environment for Wireless

The regulatory environment for wireless networks also affects the type of business model that can be implemented. First, research whether any organization has the right to use 2.4 GHz frequencies without a license. In most situations, 2.4 GHz is free to use worldwide; however, some countries restrict who can operate a network or require expensive licenses to do so. Although wireless networks are legal in the Ukraine, the government requires an expensive license to use 2.4 GHz frequencies, which renders this shared usage prohibitive. Typically only well established Internet Service Providers in this country have sufficient cash flow to pay the license fees. This restriction makes it difficult for a small community to share a wireless network with other potentially interested parties or organizations. Other countries, such as the Republic of Mali, are more permissive. Because there are no such restrictions on wireless networks, the possibility to share Internet connectivity in small communities is a viable solution. The lesson is to do your research at the onset, ensuring your network will comply with the laws of the country and local community. Some project managers have been forced to shut down their wireless networks simply because they were unknowingly breaking the law.

You should also check into the legality of Voice over Internet Protocol (VoIP) services. Most countries in the developing world have not yet defined whether VoIP is permitted; in such countries, nothing would prevent you from offering the VoIP service. However, in some countries there are complicated rules surrounding VoIP. In Syria, VoIP is prohibited for all networks, not just wireless. In Ukraine, VoIP is legal for international calls only.

Analyze the Competition

The next phase in the evaluation of your community involves an analysis of the wireless network's competition. Competitors include organizations that provide similar products and services (e.g., another wireless Internet service provider or WISP), organizations viewed as substitutes or alternatives to the products and services your network provides (e.g., a cybercafé), and organizations defined as new entrants to the wireless market. Once you have identified your competitors, you should research them thoroughly. You can obtain information about your competitors through the Internet, telephone calls, their advertisements and marketing materials, surveys of their customers and visits to their site. Create a file for each competitor. The competitive information you gather can include a list of services (including price and quality information), their target clients, customer service techniques, reputation, marketing, etc. Be sure to collect anything that will help you determine how to position your network in the community.

It is important to evaluate your competition for many reasons. First, it helps you determine the level of market saturation. There have been several instances where a subsidized telecenter was established by a donor organization in a small village with limited demand, despite the fact that there was already a locally owned cybercafé there. In one circumstance, the subsidized center maintained low prices because it did not have to cover its costs. This scenario eventually caused the locally owned center to go out of business. After the funding stopped, the subsidized center went out of business as well, due to low revenues and high costs. Knowing what already exists will allow you to determine how your network can contribute value to the community. In addition, analyzing the competition can stimulate innovative ideas for your service offerings. Is there something that you can do better than the competitors to make your services more effectively fit the needs of the community? Finally, by analyzing your competitors from the customers' point of view and understanding their strengths and weaknesses, you can determine your competitive advantages in the community. Competitive advantages are those which cannot be easily replicated by the competition. For example, a wireless network that can exclusively offer a faster Internet connection than a competitor is a competitive advantage that facilitates client utilization.

Determine Initial and Recurring Costs and Pricing

When you are planning to set up and operate your wireless network, you must determine the resources needed to start your project and the recurring operating costs. Start-up costs include everything you must purchase to start your wireless network. These expenses can range from the initial investment you make in hardware, installations, and equipment for access points, hubs, switches, cables, UPS, etc. to the costs to register your organization as a legal entity. Recurring costs are what you must pay to continue to operate your wireless network, including the cost of Internet access, telephone, loans, electricity, salaries, office rental fees, equipment maintenance and repairs, and regular investments to replace malfunctioning or obsolete equipment.

Every piece of equipment will eventually break down or become outdated at some point, and you should set aside extra money for this purpose. An advisable and very common method to deal with this is to take the price of the device and divide it by the period of time you estimate that it will last. This process is called **depreciation**. Here is an example. An average computer is supposed to last for two to five years. If the initial cost to purchase the computer was $1,000 USD, and you will be able to use the computer for five years, your annual depreciation will be $200 USD. In other words, you will lose $16.67 USD every month so that you can eventually replace this computer. To make your project sustainable, it is of fundamental importance that you save the money to compensate for the depreciation of equipment each month. Keep these savings until you finally have to spend them for equipment replacement. Some countries have tax laws that determine the period of depreciation for different types of devices. In any case, you should try to be very realistic about the life-cycle of all the implemented gear and plan for their depreciation carefully.

Try to find out all your costs in advance and make realistic estimations on your expenses. The following grid (continued on the next page) shows you a way to classify and list all of your costs. It is a good tool to structure the different costs, and it will help you to distinguish between initial costs and recurring costs.

It is important to research all your start-up costs in advance, and make realistic estimations on your recurring expenses. It is always better to over-budget for expenses than to under-budget. With every wireless project, there are always unforeseen costs, especially during the first year of operations as you learn how to better manage your network.

Categories of Costs

	Initial / start-up costs	Recurring costs
Labor costs	• Check ups (analyses) and consultancies • Development costs for programming, testing, integration etc. • Installation costs • Recruiting costs • Training costs (introduction)	• Handling costs / salaries for employees or freelancer, including yourself • Equipment maintenance and support costs for software, hardware and ancillary equipment • Security personnel • Training costs (refreshers)

	Initial / start-up costs	Recurring costs
Material (non-labor) costs	• Acquisition and production costs (for hardware like PCs, VSAT, radio link equipment and software) • Ancillary equipment (e.g., switches, cables and cabling, generator, UPS, etc.) • Data protection and security • Start-up inventory (chairs, tables, lighting, curtains, tiles and carpeting) • Premises costs (new building, modification, air conditioning, electrical wiring and boxes, security grills) • Legal costs, such as business registration • Initial license costs (VSAT) • Initial marketing costs (flyers, stickers, posters, opening party)	• Operating costs for hardware and operating systems (Internet access, telephone, etc.) • Rent or leasing rates • Depreciation of hardware and equipment • License fees • Consumables and office supplies (e.g., data media, paper, binds, clips) • Operational costs to maintain data protection and security • Insurance premiums • Costs for energy and to ensure power supply • Loan payments, capital costs for paying back your setup costs • Costs for advertising • Local fees • Legal and accounting services

To improve your chances of sustainability, it is generally best to maintain the lowest cost structure for your network. In other words, keep your expenses as low as possible. Take time to thoroughly research all of your suppliers, particularly the ISPs, and shop around for the best deals on quality service. Once again, be certain that what you purchase from suppliers corresponds with the demand in the community. Before installing an expensive VSAT, ensure there is a sufficient number of individuals and organizations in your community willing and able to pay for using it. Depending upon demand for information access and ability to pay, an alternative method of connectivity may be more appropriate. Do not be afraid to think outside the box and be creative when determining the best solution.

Keeping your costs down should not be at the cost of quality. Because low-quality equipment is more likely to malfunction, you could be spending more on maintenance in the long run. The amount of money you will spend to maintain your ICT infrastructure is hard to guess. The larger and more complicated your infrastructure becomes, the more financial and labor resources you must allocate for its maintenance.

Many times this relation is not linear but exponential. If you have a quality problem with your equipment once it is rolled out, it can cost you an enormous amount of money to fix it. Concurrently, your sales will decrease because the equipment is not up and running. There is an interesting example of a major wireless internet service provider (WISP) who had more than 3,000 access points in operation for a while. However, the WISP never managed to break even because it had to spend too much money to maintain all the access points. In addition, the company underestimated the short life-cycle of such devices. ICT hardware tends to get cheaper and better as time goes on. As soon as the company had invested time and money to install the version of expensive first generation 802.11b access points, the new "g" standard was created. New competitors designed better and cheaper access points and offered faster Internet access for less money. Finally the first WISP was forced to close down the company, although it was initially the market leader. Look at the following table to get a better picture on the fast development of wireless standards and equipment:

Protocol	Release Date	Typical Data Rate
802.11	1997	< 1 Mbps
802.11b	1999	5 Mbps
802.11g	2003	20 Mbps
802.11a	1999, but rare until 2005	23 Mbps
802.11y	June 2008 (estimated)	23 Mbps
802.11n	June 2009 (estimated)	75 Mbps

Keep in mind the rapid advancement and changes in technology and think about how and when it may be time for you to reinvest in newer and cheaper (or better) devices to keep your infrastructure competitive and up-to-date. As mentioned before, it is highly important that you save enough to be able to do so, when necessary.

Once you have identified and mapped out your costs, you should also determine what and how to charge for your services. This is a complicated and time-consuming process to do correctly. These key tips will assist when making pricing decisions:

- Calculate the prices you charge so that you cover all costs to provide the service, including all recurring expenses

- Examine the prices of your competitors

- Evaluate what your customers are willing and able to pay for your services, and make sure your prices correspond with these

It is absolutely essential to make a financial plan before you start. You need to list all of your initial and recurring costs and make some calculations to find out if your project can be sustainable.

Secure the Financing

Once you have determined your initial and recurring costs and created your financial plan, you know how much financing you will need to run a successful wireless network. The next step is to research and secure the appropriate amount of money to start up and run your wireless network.

The most traditional method of receiving funding for wireless networks in the developing world is through grants given by donors. A donor is an organization that contributes funding and other types of donations to an organization or consortium of organizations to help them manage projects or support causes. Because this funding is provided in the form of grants or other donations, it is not expected to be repaid by the organizations implementing the wireless projects or by the project's beneficiaries. Such donors include large international organizations like the United Nations (UN) and various specialized UN agencies like the United Nations Development Program (UNDP) and United Nations Educational, Scientific and Cultural Organization (UNESCO). Government agencies that specialize in international development, such as the United States Agency for International Development (USAID), the United Kingdom's Department for International Development (DFID), and the Canadian International Development Agency (CIDA), are also considered donors. Large foundations like the Gates Foundation and the Soros Foundation Network and private companies are other types of donors.

Typically, receiving funding involves a competitive or a non-competitive process. The non-competitive process is more infrequent, so this chapter will focus on the competitive process at a very high level. Most donors have complicated procedures surrounding the distribution of funding. The authors in this book are by no means trying to oversimplify this in depth system of rules and regulations. The authors intend only to convey a general understanding of this process for communities attempting to establish wireless networks in the developing world. During the competitive bid process, the donor creates a **request for proposal** (**RFP**) or a **request for application** (**RFA**), which solicits various non-governmental organizations, private companies and their partners to submit proposals outlining their plans for projects within the constraints of the donors' objectives and guidelines. In response to this RFP or RFA, NGOs and other organizations compete through the submittal of their proposals, which are then evaluated by the donors based on specific established criteria. Finally, the donor organization selects the most appropriate and highest ranking proposal to fund the project. Sometimes donors also supply funding to support an organization's operations, but this type of funding is more unusual than the competitive bid process.

Another way of accessing the necessary funds to start and maintain a wireless network is through **microfinance**, or the provision of loans, savings and other basic financial services to the world's poorest people. Pioneered in the 1970's by organizations like ACCION International and Grameen Bank, microcredit, a type of microfinance, enables poor individuals and entrepreneurs to receive loans in small amounts of money to start up small enterprises. Despite the fact that these individuals lack many of the traditional qualifications needed to obtain loans like verifiable credit, collateral or steady employment, microcredit programs have been highly successful in many developing countries. Typically, the process involves an individual or a group completing and submitting a loan application in the hopes of receiving a loan, and the lender, the individual or organization that provides the loan, giving money on condition that it is returned with interest.

The use of microcredit to fund wireless networks does pose one constraint. Usually, microcredit involves very small sums of money. Unfortunately, because a large amount of capital is needed to purchase the initial equipment for wireless network set up, sometimes a microcredit loan is not sufficient. However, there have been many other successful applications of microcredit that have brought technology and its value to the developing world. An example includes the story of village phone operators. These entrepreneurs use their microcredit loans to purchase mobile phones and phone credits. They then rent the use of their mobile phones to community members on a per-call basis and earn enough money to repay their debt and make a profit for themselves and their families.

Another mechanism for getting funding to start a wireless network is angel funding. Angel investors are normally wealthy individuals that provide capital for business start-up in exchange for a high rate of return on their investment. Because the ventures in which they invest are start ups and, therefore, often high risk, angel investors tend to expect different things in addition to their return. Many expect a board position and maybe a role in the organization.

Some angels want to have a stake in the company, while others prefer shares in the company that can be easily redeemable at face value, thus providing a clear exit for the investor. To protect their investments, angels frequently ask the businesses not to make certain key decisions without their approval. Because of the high risk involved in developing markets, it is often challenging to find angel investors to help setup a wireless network, but not impossible. The best way to find potential investors is through your social network and through research online.

Evaluate the Strengths and Weaknesses of the Internal Situation

A network is only as good as the people who work and operate it. The team you put in place can mean the difference between success and failure. That is why it is important to reflect about your team's qualifications and skills, including those of staff and volunteers, in comparison to the competencies needed for a wireless project. First, make a list of all the competencies needed to run a wireless project successfully. Capacity areas should include technology, human resources, accounting, marketing, sales, negotiation, legal, and operations, among others. Afterwards, identify local resources to fulfill these skills. Map your team's skills sets to the competencies needed, and identify key gaps.

One tool often used to assist with this self-evaluation is an analysis of strengths, weaknesses, opportunities and threats, called SWOT. To conduct this analysis, specify your internal strengths and weaknesses, and elaborate upon the external opportunities and threats in your community. It is important to be realistic and honest about what you do well and what you are lacking. Be sure to distinguish between where your organization is at the beginning of this endeavor from where it could be in the future. Your strengths and weaknesses allow you to evaluate your capacities internally and better understand what your organization can do, as well as its limits. By understanding your strengths and weaknesses and comparing them to those of your competitors, you can determine your competitive advantages in the market. You can also note the areas where you can improve. Opportunities and threats are external, which enable you to analyze real world conditions and how these conditions influence your network.

The diagram below will help you in creating your own SWOT analysis for your organization. Be sure to respond to the questions asked and list your strengths, weaknesses, opportunities and threats in the spaces designated.

Strengths	Weaknesses
• What do you do well? • What unique resources can you draw on? • What do others see as your strengths? • • • •	• What could you improve? • Where do you have fewer resources than others? • What are others likely to see as weaknesses? • • • •
Opportunities	Threats
• What good opportunities are open to you? • What trends could you take advantage of? • How can you turn your strengths into opportunities? • • • •	• What trends could harm you? • What is your competition doing? • What threats do your weaknesses expose you to? • • • •

Putting it All Together

Once you have gathered all of the information, you are ready to put everything together and decide upon the best model for the wireless network in your community. Based on the results of your external and internal analyses, you must refine your mission and service offerings. All of the factors that you researched in the preceding steps come into play when determining your overall strategy. It is essential to employ a model that capitalizes on opportunities and works within the constraints of the local environment. To do this, you must often find innovative solutions to attain sustainability. By exploring several examples and discussing the components of the models implemented in those instances, you will better understand how to arrive at an appropriate model.

In the distant jungles of the Democratic Republic of Congo, there is a rural hospital in a village called Vanga in the province of Bandundu. It is so remote that patients travel for weeks to get there often through a combination of travel by foot and by river. This village, founded by Baptist missionaries in 1904, has served as a hospital for many years. Although it is extremely re-mote, it is renowned for being an excellent facility and has had the support of German and American missionaries who have kept this facility in operation. In 2004, a project sponsored by USAID established a telecenter in this village to help improve education in this isolated community; this Internet facility was also heavily used by the educated class in the community – the hospital's staff. The center had been a great boon to the community, offering access to the world's knowledge and even providing consultation with distant col-leagues in Switzerland, France and Canada. The center required near total subsidization to operate and cover its costs, and funding was to end by 2006. Although the center added great value to the community, it did have some shortcomings, primarily technical, economic, and political issues that limited its sustainability. A study was commissioned to consider options for its future. After reviewing the center's cost structure, it was determined that it needed to cut its costs and look for new ways to increase its revenues. The largest ex-penses were electricity and Internet access; therefore, creative models needed to be constructed to reduce the telecenter's costs and provide ac-cess in a way that was sustainable.

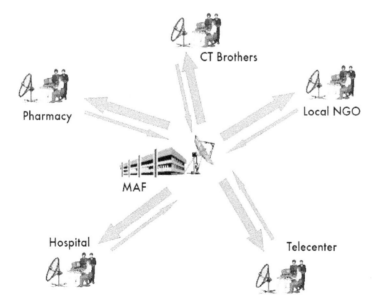

Figure 10.1: Shared Internet over wireless

In this instance, a traditional VSAT was used for connectivity. However, this model provided a unique way of accommodating local community groups' limited ability to pay for Internet services. Various organizations in the community share Internet access through a wireless network; they also share the costs associated with that connection. This model functions well due to specific conditions – namely an awareness and understanding of the value of the Internet among key community members, the necessary resources to support Internet access, and a regulatory system that permits wireless sharing. In Vanga, several organizations, including a hospital, a pharmacy, several missionary groups, a community resource center, and some non-profit organizations, have a need for Internet access and the means to pay for it. This arrangement enables the network of organizations to have a higher quality connection at a lower cost. Additionally, one organization in the village has the capacity and willingness to manage several aspects of the network's operations, including the billing and payment collection, technical maintenance and general business operations of the entire network. Therefore, this model works well in Vanga because it has been tailored to meet community demand and leverage local economic resources.

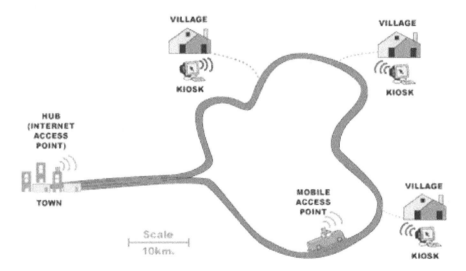

Figure 10.2: DakNet's roaming access point

Another example of a model adapted to fit the local context is that of First Mile Solutions' DakNet. This model has been deployed in villages in India, Cambodia, Rwanda, and Paraguay. By taking into account the limited buying power of villagers, this model addresses their communication needs in an innovative way. In the DakNet model, there is a franchise that exists in the country, and local entrepreneurs are recruited and trained to operate kiosks equipped with Wi-Fi antennas. Using pre-paid cards, villagers are able to asynchronously send and receive emails, texts, and voice mails, conduct web searches, and participate in e-commerce. Afterwards, these communications are stored in the local kiosk's server. When a bus or motorcycle with a mobile access point drives past a kiosk, the vehicle automatically receives the kiosk's stored data and delivers any incoming data. Once the vehicle reaches a hub with Internet connectivity, it processes all requests, relaying emails, messages, and shared files.

DakNet integrates both mobile access and franchise models to bring value to people in remote villages. For such a model to be sustainable, several key conditions need to be present. First, a franchise organization must exist to provide financial and institutional support, including an initial investment, working capital for certain recurring costs, advice on start-up practices, management training, standardized processes, reporting mechanisms, and marketing tools. Additionally, this model requires a highly motivated and dynamic individual in the village, with the appropriate skills to manage a business and willingness to accept certain requirements of the franchise organization. Because these entrepreneurs are often asked to commit their own resources to the start-up costs, they need to have sufficient access to financial resources. Finally, to ensure this model will sustain itself, there should be sufficient demand for information and communication and few competitors in the community.

Conclusion

No single business model will enable wireless networks to be sustainable in all environments of the developing world; different models must be used and adapted as the circumstances dictate. Every community has unique characteristics, and sufficient analysis must be conducted at the onset of a project to determine the most appropriate model. This analysis should consider several key factors in the local environment, including community demand, competition, costs, economic resources, etc. Although appropriate planning and execution will maximize the chances of making your network sustainable, there are no guarantees of success. However, by using the methods detailed in this chapter, you will help to ensure that your network brings value to the community in a way that corresponds with the users' needs.

11
Case Studies

No matter how much planning goes into building a link or node location, you will inevitably have to jump in and actually install something. This is the moment of truth that demonstrates just how accurate your estimates and predictions prove to be.

It is a rare day when everything goes precisely as planned. Even after you install your 1st, 10th, or 100th node, you will still find that things do not always work out as you might have intended. This chapter describes some of our more memorable network projects. Whether you are about to embark on your first wireless project or you are an old hand at this, it is reassuring to remember that there is always more to learn.

General advice

The economies of developing countries are very different from the developed world, and thus a process or solution designed for a more developed country may not be suitable in West Africa, or Southern Asia. Specifically, the cost of locally produced materials and the cost of labour will be negligible, whereas imported goods can be much more expensive when compared to its cost in the developed world. For example, one can manufacture and install a tower for a tenth of the cost of a tower in the United States, but the price of an antenna might be double. Solutions that capitalize on local competitive advantages, namely cheap labour and locally found materials, will be the easiest to replicate.

Finding the right equipment is one of the most difficult tasks in developing markets. Because transportation, communication and economic systems are not developed, the right materials or equipment can be difficult and often impossible to find. A fuse, for example, is difficult to find, thus finding wire that has a burn-up at a certain amperage and can substitute is a great advantage. Finding local substitutes for materials also encourages local entrepreneurship, ownership, and can save money.

Equipment enclosures

Cheap plastics are everywhere in the developing world, but they are made of poor materials and are thin, thus mostly unsuitable for enclosing equipment. PVC tubing is far more resilient and is made to be waterproof. In West Africa, the most common PVC is found in plumbing, sized from 90mm to 220mm. Access points such as the Routerboard 500 and 200 can fit into such tubing, and with end-caps that are torched-on, they can make very robust waterproof enclosures. They also have the added benefit of being aerodynamic and uninteresting to passers-by. The resulting space left around the equipment assures adequate air circulation. Also, it is often best to leave an exhaust hole at the bottom of the PVC enclosure. The author did find that leaving open holes can become a problem. In one instance ants decided to nest 25 meters above ground inside the PVC holding the access point. Using a wire mesh cover made from locally available screen material is advised to secure the exhaust hole from infestations.

Antenna masts

Recovering used materials has become an important industry for the poorest countries. From old cars to televisions, any material that has value will be stripped, sold, or re-used. For example, you will see vehicles torn apart piece by piece and day by day. The resulting metal is sorted and then tossed into a truck to be sold.   Local metal workers will already be familiar with how to make television masts from scrap metal. A few quick adaptations and these same masts can be re-purposed for wireless networks.

The typical mast is the 5 meter pole, comprised of a single 30mm diameter pipe which is then planted into cement. It's best to construct the mast in two parts, with a removable mast that fits into a base which is slightly larger in diameter. Alternately, the mast may be made with arms that can be securely cemented into a wall. This project is easy, but requires the use of a ladder to complete and therefore some caution is suggested.

This type of mast can be augmented by several meters with the use of guy lines. To sturdy the pole, plant three lines 120 degrees apart, forming an angle of at least 33 degrees with the tower.

Above all: involve the local community

Community involvement is imperative in assuring the success and sustainability of a project. Involving the community in a project can be the greatest challenge, but if the community is not involved the technology will not serve their needs, nor will it be accepted. Moreover, a community might be afraid and could subvert an initiative. Regardless of the complexity of the undertaking, a successful project needs support and buy-in from those it will serve.

An effective strategy in gaining support is to find a respected champion whose motives are palatable. Find the person, or persons whom are most likely to be interested in the project. Often, you will need to involve such champions as advisors, or as members of a steering committee. These people will already have the trust of the community, will know who to approach, and can speak the language of the community. Take your time and be selective in finding the right people for your project. No other decision will affect your project more than having effective, trusted local people on your team.

In addition, take note of key players in an institution, or community. Identify those people whom are likely to be opponents and proponents of your project. As early as possible, attempt to earn the support of the potential proponents and to diffuse the opponents. This is a difficult task and one that requires intimate knowledge of the institution or community. If the project does not have a local ally, the project must take time to acquire this knowledge and trust from the community.

Be careful in choosing your allies. A "town-hall" meeting is often useful to see local politics, alliances, and feuds in play. Thereafter, it is easier to decide on whom to ally, champion and whom to diffuse. Try to not build unwarranted enthusiasm. It is important to be honest, frank, and not to make promises that you cannot keep.

In largely illiterate communities, focus on digital to analog services such as Internet for radio stations, printing on-line articles and photos, and other non-textual applications. Do not try to introduce a technology to a community without understanding which applications will truly will serve the community. Often the community will have little idea how new technologies will help their problems. Simply providing new features is useless without an understanding of how the community will benefit.

When gathering information, verify the facts that you are given. If you want to know the financial status of a company/organization, ask to see an electricity bill, or phone bill. Have they been paying their bills? At times, potential beneficiaries will compromise their own values in hopes of winning funds or equipment. Most often, local partners who trust you will be very frank, honest, and helpful.

Another common pitfall is what I call "divorced parents" syndrome, where NGOs, donors, and partners are not told of each others involvement with the beneficiary. Savvy beneficiaries can earn handsome rewards by letting NGOs and donors lavish them with equipment, training and funds. It is important to know which other organizations are involved so you can understand how their activities might impact your own. For example, I once designed a project for a rural school in Mali. My team installed an open source system with used computers and spent several days training people how to use it. The project was deemed a success, but shortly after the installation, another donor arrived with brand-new Pentium 4 computers running Windows XP. The students quickly abandoned the older computers and lined-up to use the new computers. It would have been better to negotiate with the school in advance, to know their commitment to the project. If they had been frank, the computers that are now sitting unused could have been deployed to another school where they would be used.

In many rural communities in under-developed economies, law and policies are weak, and contracts can be effectively meaningless. Often, other assurances must be found. This is where pre-paid services are ideal, as they do not require a legal contract. Commitment is assured by the investment of funds before service is given.

Buy-in also requires that those involved invest in the project themselves. A project should ask for reciprocal involvement from the community.

Above all, the "no-go" option should always be evaluated. If a local ally and community buy-in cannot be had, the project should consider choosing a different community or beneficiary. There must be a negotiation; equipment, money, and training cannot be gifts. The community must be involved and they too must contribute.

—Ian Howard

Case study: Crossing the divide with a simple bridge in Timbuktu

Networks ultimately connect people together, and therefore always involve a political component. The cost of Internet in less developed economies is high and the ability to pay is low, which adds to the political challenges. Attempting to superimpose a network where human networks are not fully functioning is nearly impossible in the long term. Trying to do so can leave a project on unstable social ground, threatening its existence. This is where the low cost and mobility of a wireless network can be advantageous.

The author's team was asked by funders to determine how to connect a rural radio station with a very small (2 computer) telecentre to the Internet in Timbuktu, the desert capital of Mali. Timbuktu is widely known as an outpost in the most remote area of the world. At this site, the team decided to implement a model which has been called the **parasitic wireless model**. This model takes a wireless "feed" that is spliced from an existing network, and extends that network to a client site using a simple bridged network. This model was chosen because it requires no significant investment by the supporting organization. While it added a source of revenue for the telecentre, it did not add a significant operational cost. This solution meant that the client site could get cheap Internet, albeit not as fast or as reliable as a dedicated solution. Because of opposed usage patterns between an office and a telecentre there was no perceptible slowing of the network for either party. Though in an ideal situation it would be best to encourage more development of the small telecentre into an ISP, neither the telecentre nor the market were deemed ready. As is often the case, there were serious concerns about whether this telecentre could become self-sustaining once its funders departed. Thus, this solution minimized the initial investment while achieving two goals: first, it extended the Internet to the target beneficiary, a radio station, at an affordable cost. Second, it added a small additional revenue source for the telecentre while not increasing its operational costs, or adding complexity to the system.

The people

Timbuktu is remote, though having a world renowned name. Being a symbol of remoteness, many projects have wanted to "stake a flag" in the sands of this desert city. Thus, there are a number of information and communications technologies (ICT) activities in the area. At last count there were 8 satellite connections into Timbuktu, most of which service special interests except for the two carriers, SOTELMA and Ikatel. They currently use VSAT to link their telephone networks to the rest of the country. This telecentre used an X.25 connection to one of these telcos, which then relayed the connection back to Bamako. Relative to other remote cities in the country, Timbuktu has a fair number of trained IT staff, three existing telecentres, plus the newly installed telecentre at the radio station. The city is to some degree over saturated with Internet, precluding any private, commercial interests from being sustainable.

Design Choices

In this installation the client site is only 1 km away directly by line of sight. Two modified Linksys access points, flashed with OpenWRT and set to bridge mode, were installed. One was installed on the wall of the telecentre, and the other was installed 5 meters up the radio station's mast. The only configuration parameters required on both devices were the ssid and the channel. Simple 14 dBi panel antennas (from *http://hyperlinktech.com/*)

were used. At the Internet side, the access point and antenna were fastened using cement plugs and screws onto the side of the building, facing the client site. At the client site, an existing antenna mast was used. The access point and antenna were mounted using pipe rings.

To disconnect the client, the telecentre simply unplugs the bridge on their side. An additional site will eventually be installed, and it too will have its own bridge at the telecentre so that staff can physically disconnect the client if they have not paid. Though crude, this solution is effective and reduces risk that the staff would make a mistake while making changes to the configuration of the system. Having a bridge dedicated to one connection also simplified installation at the central site. as the installation team was able to choose the best spot for connecting the client sites.   Though it is not optimal to bridge a network (rather than route network traffic), when technology knowledge is low and one wants to install a very simple system this can be a reasonable solution for small networks. The bridge makes systems installed at the remote site (the radio station) appear as though they are simply connected to the local network.

Financial model

The financial model here is simple. The telecentre charges a monthly fee, about $30 per connected computer to the radio station. This was many times cheaper than the alternative. The telecentre is located in the court of the Mayor's office, so the principle client of the telecentre is the Mayor's staff. This was important because the radio station did not want to compete for clientele with the telecentre and the radio station's systems were primarily intended for the radio station staff. This quick bridge reduced costs, meaning that this selective client base could support the cost of the Internet without competing with the telecentre, its supplier. The telecentre also has the ability to easily disconnect the radio station should they not pay. This model also allowed sharing of network resources. For example, the radio station has a new laser printer, while the telecentre has a color printer. Because the client systems are on the same network, clients can print at either site.

Training

To support this network, very little training was required. The telecentre staff were shown how to install the equipment and basic trouble shooting, such as rebooting (power cycling) the access points, and how to replace the unit should one fail. This allows the author's team to simply ship a replacement and avoid the two day trek to Timbuktu.

Summary

The installation was considered an interim measure. It was meant to serve as a stop-gap measure while moving forward with a more complete solution. While it can be considered a success, it has not yet led to building more physical infrastructure. It has brought ICTs closer to a radio solution, and re-enforced local client/supplier relationships.

As it stands, Internet access is still an expensive undertaking in Timbuktu. Local politics and competing subsidized initiatives are underway, but this simple solution has proven to be an ideal use case. It took the team several months of analysis and critical thought to arrive here, but it seems the simplest solution provided the most benefit.

—*Ian Howard*

Case study: Finding solid ground in Gao

One day's drive east from Timbuktu, in Eastern Mali, is Gao. This rural city, which seems more more like a big village, sits up the the river Niger just before it dips South crossing into Niger and onto Nigeria. The city slopes into the river gently, and has few buildings taller than two stories. In 2004, a telecentre was installed in Gao. The project's goal was to provide information to the community in the hope that a better informed community would yield a healthier and more educated citizenry.

The centre provides information via CD-ROMs, films and radio, but the cornucopic source of information for the centre is the Internet. It is a standard telecentre, with 8 computers, an all-in-one printer, scanner, fax, a telephone and a digital camera. A small two room building was built to house the telecentre. It is located a bit outside of downtown, which is not an ideal location for attracting customers, but the site was chosen because of its sympathetic host. The site received funding for all construction needed, and equipment and initial training was supplied as well. The telecentre was expected to be self-sustaining after one year.

Several months after its opening, the telecentre was attracting few customers. It used a modem to dial-up to connect to an Internet provider in the capital. This connection was too slow and unreliable, and so the funder sponsored the installation of a VSAT system. There are a number of VSAT systems now available to the region; most of these services have just recently become available. Previously only C-band (which cover a larger area than Ku-band) systems were available. Recently, fiber has been laid in almost every subway tunnel and canal throughout Europe, and thus it has supplanted the more expensive satellite services. As a result, providers are now redirecting their VSAT systems to new markets, including middle and West-ern Africa, and South Asia. This has led to a number of projects which use satellite systems for an Internet connection.

After the VSAT was installed, the connection provided 128 kbps down and 64 kbps up, and cost about $400 per month. The site was having trouble earning enough revenue to pay for this high monthly cost, so the telecentre asked for help. A private contractor was hired, who had been trained by the author to install a wireless system. This system would split the connection between three clients: a second beneficiary, a radio station, and the telecen-tre, each paying $140. This collectively covered the costs of the VSAT, and the extra revenue from the telecentre and the radio station would cover sup-port and administration of the system.

The people

Though capable and willing, the author's team did not do the actual installa-tion. Instead, we encouraged the telecentre to hire the local contractor to do it. We were able to reassure the client by agreeing to train and support the contractor in the fulfillment of this installation. The premise of this decision was to discourage a reliance on a short-term NGO, and rather to build trust and relationships between domestic service providers and their clients. This design proved to be fruitful. This approach took much more time from the author's team, perhaps twice as much, but this investment has already be-gun to pay-off. Networks are still being installed and the author and his team are now home in Europe and North America.

Design choices

Initially, it was conceived that a backbone connection would be made to the radio station, which already had a 25 meter tower. That tower would be used to relay to the other clients, avoiding the need to install towers at the client sites, as this tower was well above any obstacles in the city. To do this, three approaches were discussed: installing an access point in repeater mode, using the WDS protocol, or using a mesh routing protocol. A repeater was not desirable as it would introduce latency (due to the one-armed repeater prob-lem) to an already slow connection. VSAT connections need to send packets up to the satellite and back down, often introducing up to 3000 ms in delay for a round trip. To avoid this problem, it was decided to use one radio to connect to clients, and a second radio for to the dedicated backbone connec-tion. For simplicity it was decided to make that link a simple bridge, so that the access point at the radio station would appear to be on the same physical LAN as the telecentre.

In testing this approach functioned, though in the real world, its performance was dismal. After many different changes, including replacing the access points, the technician decided that there must be a software or hardware bug affecting this design. The installer then decided to place the access point at the telecentre directly using a small 3 meter mast, and to not use a relay site at the radio station. The client sites also required small masts in this design. All sites were able to connect, though the connections were at times too feeble, and introduced massive packet loss.

Later, during the dust season, these connections became more erratic and even less stable. The client sites were 2 to 5 km away, using 802.11b. The team theorized that the towers on either side were too short, cutting off too much of the Fresnel zone. After discussing many theories, the team also realized the problem with the performance at the radio station: the radio frequency 90.0 MHz was about the same as the frequency of the high-speed (100BT) Ethernet connection. While transmitting, the FM signal (at 500 watts) was completely consuming the signal on the Ethernet cable. Thus, shielded cable would be required, or the frequency of the Ethernet link would need to be changed. The masts were then raised, and at the radio station the speed of the Ethernet was changed to 10 Mbps. This changed the frequency on the wire to 20 MHz, and so avoided interference from the FM transmission. These changes resolved both problems, increasing the strength and reliability of the network. The advantage of using mesh or WDS here would be that client sites could connect to either access point, either directly to the telecentre to the radio station. Eventually, removing the reliance on the radio station as a repeater likely made the installation more stable in the longer-term.

Financial model

The satellite system used at this site cost approximately $400 per month. For many IT for Development projects this expensive monthly cost is difficult to manage. Typically these projects can purchase equipment and pay for the establishment of a wireless network, but most are not able to pay for the cost of the network after a short period of time (including the recurring Internet costs and operational costs). It is necessary to find a model where the monthly costs for a network can be met by those who use. For most community telecenters or radio stations, this is simply too expensive. Often, the only feasible plan is to share the costs with other users. To make the Internet more affordable, this site used wireless to share the Internet to the community, allowing a greater number of organizations to access the Internet while reducing the cost per client.

Typically in Mali, a rural community has only a few organizations or companies that could afford an Internet connection. Where there are few clients, and the Internet connection cost is high, the model developed by his team included **anchor clients**: clients whom are solid and are low-risk. For this region, foreign NGOs (Non Governmental Organizations), the United Nations Agencies and large commercial enterprises are among the very few whom qualify.

Among the clients selected for this project were three anchor clients, who collectively paid the entire monthly cost of the satellite connection. A second beneficiary, a community radio station, was also connected. Any revenue earned from the beneficiaries contributed to a windfall, or deposit for future costs, but was not counted upon due to the small margins that both of these community services operated on. Those clients could be disconnected and could resume their service once they can afford it again.

Training needed: who, what, for how long

The contractor taught the telecentre technician the basics of supporting the network, which was fairly rudimentary. Any non-routine work, such as adding a new client, was contracted out. Therefore it was not imperative to teach the telecentre staff how to support the system in its entirety.

Lessons learned

By sharing the connection, the telecentre is now self-sustaining, and in addition, three other sites have Internet access. Though it takes more time and perhaps more money, it is valuable to find the right local talent and to encourage them to build relationships with clients. A local implementor will be able to provide the follow-up support needed to maintain and expand a network. This activity is building local expertise, and demand, which will allow subsequent ICT projects to build on this base.

—Ian Howard

Case Study: Fantsuam Foundation's Community Wireless Network

Kafanchan is a community of 83,000 people located 200 km northeast of Abuja, in central Nigeria. Kafanchan used to be known as a busy and thriving town as it was the host of one of the main junctions of the national railway. When the railway industry was booming, almost 80% of Kafanchan's populations relied on it in one way or another. Following the complete breakdown of the Nigerian railway system, the population of Kafanchan has been forced to go back to its original source of income, which is agriculture.

Kafanchan is a poorly connected area in terms of fixed telephony and Internet connectivity. Today, no fixed telephony (PSTN) is available in the area and GSM only just arrived in 2005. However, the GSM coverage is just as poor as the quality of the service. At the moment, SMS services are the most reliable communication service because voice conversations tend to cut off in the middle and suffer heavy noise.

Poor access to electricity brings further challenges to the people of Kafanchan. The national electric power company of Nigeria, generally known as NEPA (National Electric Power Authority), is more commonly known to Nigerians as "Never Expect Power Always". In 2005, NEPA changed its name to Power Holding Company of Nigeria (PHCN).

Kafanchan is receiving power from NEPA on an average of 3 hours per day. For the remaining 21 hours, the population relies on expensive diesel generators or kerosene for illumination and cooking. When NEPA is available on the grid, it provides an unregulated voltage in the range of 100-120 V in a system designed for 240 V. This voltage must be regulated to 240 V before most loads can be connected. Only light bulbs can be fed straight to the grid power since they can handle the low voltage without damage.

Project participants

Given the challenging background of Kafanchan, how could anyone come up with the idea of establishing the first rural Wireless ISP in Nigeria there? Fantsuam Foundation did and they made it happen.

Fantsuam Foundation is a local, non-governmental organization that has been working together with the community of Kafanchan since 1996 to fight poverty and disadvantage through integrated development programs. Fantsuam's focus lies on micro finance, ICT services and social development in rural communities of Nigeria. Becoming the first rural wireless ISP in Nigeria was part of their mission to be a recognized leader in the provision of rural development initiatives, as well as the foremost rural knowledge economy driver in Nigeria.

The Wireless ISP of Fantsuam Foundation, also know as *Zittnet*, is funded by IDRC, the International Development Research Centre of Canada. IT +46, a Swedish based consultancy company focusing on ICTs for development, has worked together with the Zittnet team to provide technical support for wireless communications, bandwidth management, solar energy, power backup systems and VoIP deployments.

Objectives

The main objective of Zittnet is to improve access to communications in the area of Kafanchan by implementing a community wireless network. The network provides intranet and Internet access to local partners in the community. The community network is formed by community-based organizations such as educational institutions, faith-based institutions, health services, small enterprises and individuals.

Power Backup System

In order to provide a reliable service to the community, Zittnet needed to be equipped with a stable power backup system that would make the network run independently of the NEPA.

A hybrid power system was designed for Fantsuam, consisting of a deep-cycle battery bank and 2 kW (peak) solar panels. The system can charge from three different sources: a diesel generator, a solar array, and from NEPA when electricity is available. The network operation center (NOC) of the organization runs completely from solar energy. The rest of the Fantsuam's premises runs from NEPA or the generator via the battery bank, which provides uninterrupted voltage stability. The NOC load has been separated from the rest of the load of Fantsuam to ensure a reliable power source to the critical infrastructure in the NOC, even when the battery bank is running low on power.

Figure 11.1: 24 solar panels with a nominal power of 80 W have been mounted to the roof of the NOC to provide power to the system 24/7.

Simulations with the best existing solar data reveal that Kaduna State, where Kafanchan is located, receives at least 4 sun peak hours during its worst months which stretch from June to August (the rainy season).

Each of the solar panels (Suntech 80 W peak) provides a maximum current of 5 A (when the solar radiation is highest during the day). In the worst months of the year, the system is expected to produce not less than 6 KWh/day.

The solar system has been designed to provide 12 and 24 V DC output in order to match the input voltage of all low power servers and workstations for NOC infrastructure and training classrooms.

The solar panels used are **Suntech STP080S-12/Bb-1** with the following specifications:

. Open-circuit Voltage (V_{OC}): **21.6 V**

. Optimum operating voltage (V_{MP}): **17.2 V**

. Short-circuit current (I_{SC}): **5 A**

. Optimum operating current (I_{MP}): **4.65 A**

. Maximum power at STC (P_{MAX}): **80 W (Peak)**

The minimum 6 KWh/day that feeds the NOC is used to power the following equipment:

Device	Hours/Day	Units	Power (W)	Wh
Access points	24	3	15	1080
Low power servers	24	4	10	960
LCD screens	2	4	20	160
Laptops	10	2	75	1500
Lamps	8	4	15	480
VSAT modem	24	1	60	1440
Total				**5620**

The power consumption for servers and LCD screens is based on Inveneo's Low Power Computing Station, *http://www.inveneo.org/?q=Computingstation*.

The total estimated power consumption of the NOC is 5.6 kWh/day which is less than the daily power generated from the solar panels in the worst month.

Figure 11.2: The NOC is built by locally made laterite brick stones, produced and laid by youths in Kafanchan.

Network Operating Center (NOC)

A new Network Operating Center was established to host the power backup system and server room facilities. The NOC was designed to provide a place safe from dust, with good cooling capabilities for the batteries and the inverters. The NOC uses natural methods and is made from locally available materials.

The building is comprised of four rooms: a battery storage room, a server room, a working space and a room for equipment storage.

The battery storage room hosts seventy 200 Ah deep cycle batteries, as well as five inverters (one of them pure sine wave), two solar regulators, power stabilizers and DC and AC disconnects. The batteries are stacked vertically on a metal shelf structure for better cooling.

The server space accommodates a rack unit for servers and a fan. The room has no regular windows, to avoid dust and overheating. The server room and battery room face south to improve natural cooling and to help keep the room at an appropriate temperature.

The server room and the battery space require effective low cost/low energy cooling as they need to operate 24x7. To achieve this goal, natural cooling techniques have been introduced in the NOC design: small fans and extractors and thick walls of bricks (double width) in the direction of the sunset.

The south side of the building hosts 24 solar panels in a shadow-free area on its metal roof. The roof was designed with an inclination of 20 degrees to host the panels and limit corrosion and dust. Extra efforts have been made to keep the panels easily reachable for cleaning and maintenance. The roof has also been strengthened in order to carry the extra load of 150-200 kg.

The NOC building is constructed of locally produced laterite mud bricks. The material is cheap since it is frequently used and comes from the top layer of soil. The bricks are produced locally by hand using a low-tech pressing technique. The NOC is unique for its kind in Kaduna State.

Figure 11.3: Omolayo Samuel, one of the staff of Zittnet, does not fear the height of the 45m tall tower as she is aligning the antennas hosted in the top of the tower.

Physical infrastructure: A communication mast

Most potential clients to Zittnet are located between 1 km and 10 km from the premises of Fantsuam. In order to reach these clients, Fantsuam established a communication mast on their premises. In October 2006, a 45m (150 foot) tall self-standing mast was installed at Fantsuam Foundation. The mast was equipped with grounding and lighting protection as well as a mandatory signal light.

A metal ring was buried at the base of the tower at a depth of 4 feet. All three legs of the mast were then connected to the grounding circuit. A lightning rod was mounted at the highest point of the mast to protect the equipment against lighting strikes. The rod is made of pure copper and is connected to the earth ring at the base of the mast using copper tape.

The signal light mounted at the top of the mast is a requirement from the Civil Aviation Authorities. The light is equipped with a photocell which enables automated switching based on the level of ambient light. In this way, the light comes on at night and goes off during the day.

Wireless backbone infrastructure

The wireless backbone infrastructure is built using SmartBridges multi-band access points and client units from the Nexus PRO™ TOTAL series. The units are designed for service providers and enterprises to establish high performance point-to-multipoint outdoor wireless links. They come with an integrated multi-band sectoral antenna that can operate both in 2.4 GHz and 5.1-5.8 GHz frequencies. The Nexus PRO™ TOTAL series offers QoS for traffic prioritization and bandwidth management per client using the IEEE 802.11e compliant WMM (WiFi Multimedia) extensions.

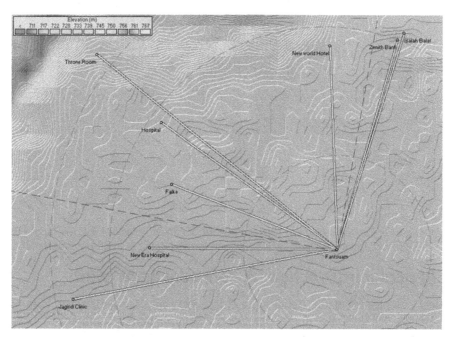

Figure 11.4: The network topology of Zittnet in October 2007.

Currently, the topology of the network is a star topology with two access points in the communication mast at Fantsuam's premises. One access point hosts a 90 degree sectoral antenna (blue dotted lines) and the other access point provides omnidirectional coverage to the surroundings (red dotted rings). Clients that are located within the area between the dotted lines are connected to the sectoral antenna, while the remaining clients are connected to the omnidirectional antenna.

Plans are underway to expand the wireless backbone by setting up two wireless repeaters. One repeater will be located in Kafanchan city using an existing NITEL tower to enhance the wireless coverage in the city center. The second repeater will be established in the Kagoro Hills, a small mountain group with a relative altitude to Kafanchan of about 500m, which is located about 7 km from Kafanchan. This repeater will provide coverage to many surrounding towns and may even enable a long-distance link to Abuja.

Zittnet connected its first client in early August 2007. Two months later, no less than eight clients are connected to Zittnet. These clients include:

- The general hospital
- New Era Hospital
- Jagindi Street Clinic (health clinic)
- Zenith Bank (for private use)
- Isaiah Balat (Internet café)
- New World Hotel
- Throne Room GuestHouse
- Fulke

Problems encountered

A few problem areas that have been constantly present throughout the project are as follows.

Low buildings

Most client premises are single-story buildings with a height of no more than 3 meters. Many houses have very weak roof structures which makes it impossible to mount equipment on the roof, as physical access is not possible. The low buildings force us to mount the equipment at a fairly low height, as clients can not afford to invest in small (10 m) masts to host the equipment. Most installations make use of water tanks or a simple 3 meter metal pole attached to the wall of the premise.

When the equipment is mounted low, the first Fresnel zone is not cleared and lower throughput is experienced. Although the landscape in Kafanchan is very flat, vegetation in the form of thick mango trees easily block the line-of-sight.

Lightning strikes

Heavy thunder storms are frequent during the rainy season in Kafanchan. In September 2007, a nearby lightning strike damaged equipment mounted on a mast, as well as its power supply. At the moment, the access point and its PoE injector are grounded to the tower itself. Further means need to be investigated to prevent damage to equipment caused by nearby lightning. The Zittnet team is currently working on improving the surge protection by adding extra coaxial surge arrestors. Furthermore, the shield of the UTP cable connecting the access point with the NOC will be grounded using grounding blocks and fasteners.

Low Quality Equipment

Unfortunately, a lack of quality products on the market is a widespread problem across the whole African continent. As most sub-Sahara countries lack policies for quality assurance of imported goods, the market is flooded by "cheap" and very low quality articles. Since quality products are hard to find, you often find yourself buying locally available merchandise that breaks even before it is put into operation. As no sort of warranty exists for these minor purchases, this ends up being very expensive. This problem is almost always present in common accessories such as power sockets, power bars, RJ45 connectors, CAT5 cabling, and other low-tech equipment.

Business Model

The only alternative for Internet access in Kafanchan is via satellite. During 2006, Fantsuam had a subscription of 128/64 kbps dedicated bandwidth at a cost of $1800 USD/month. This huge monthly cost of connectivity has been a big burden for Fantsuam and a constant stress of being unable to meet the monthly bill.

As an alternative to the high risk "flat fee" model, Fantsuam has implemented a system called **HookMeUP** provided by Koochi Communications. The system offers flexible Pay-As-You-Go charges over broadband VSAT Internet connections to countries across sub-Sahara Africa.

This kind of access model is typically found in airports, hotels or large shopping malls in western countries where end-users buy vouchers online and log in using an access code.

The HookMeUP system offers a 512/256 kbps dedicated VSAT connection to Fantsuam (from their ground station in the UK). Fantsuam buys vouchers from Koochi Communications and resells them to its local clients in Kafanchan. In this way, Fantsuam is no longer stuck with a fixed monthly cost but has only to pay Koochi for the bandwidth they actually have consumed. The risk of buying expensive international bandwidth has now been transferred to the Internet provider instead of the end user, at a cost of a higher price for the end user.

Fantsuam foundation now acts as a reseller of vouchers from Koochi and a supplier of wireless infrastructure to the end users. The Wireless Community Network now provides the Fantsuam Foundation with five sources of income:

1. Installation of client premises equipment (one occasion per client)

2. Leasing of wireless equipment (monthly cost per client)

3. Reselling wireless equipment (one occasion per client)

4. Installation of wireless hotspot at client's premise (one occasion per client)

5. Reselling of vouchers (continuously)

The voucher system is based on three parameters: **access time**, **data limit** and **validity time**. Whichever parameter runs out first will consume the voucher.

Access time	Data limit (MB)	Validity time	Price (USD)	USD / h	USD / 700 MB
30 min	5	1 day	0.80	1.60	112.00
60 min	10	5 days	1.28	1.28	89.60
12 hours	60	14 days	10.40	0.87	121.33
24 hours	150	30 days	26.00	1.08	121.33
1 month	500	1 month	71.50	0.10	100.10
3 months	1600	3 months	208.00	0.10	91.00
6 months	3500	6 months	416.00	0.10	83.20
12 months	7500	12 months	728.00	0.08	67.95

The greatest advantage of this system is that Fantsuam Foundation no longer has the burden of a huge monthly bill for international bandwidth. Having a flat-fee model means that you are forced to sell a certain amount of bandwidth every month. With the Pay-As-You-Go (PAYG) model, Fantsuam's income from reselling vouchers depends on how much bandwidth their clients consume. The client pays in advance (pre-paid model) with the result that Fantsuam will never end up in huge debt with the provider.

The pre-paid model works well in Africa since people are familiar with this model from mobile operators. It is even used by electricity companies in some counties. The pre-paid model is appreciated by many as it helps them to keep track of their expenditures. One of the main limitations of the PAYG model is the lack of flexibility and transparency. The current PAYG system provides very little feedback to the user about consumed time or volume. Only when the user logs off will he/she be informed about how many minutes are left to spend.

However, the business model seems to fit the local reality of Kafanchan and many other rural communities in Africa quite well. Although there is room for improvement, the advantage of avoiding debts is far greater than the disadvantages. With time, when the number of clients have increased and they can rely on a substantial monthly income from the wireless network, it might be beneficial to go back to the flat-fee model again.

Clients

The clients are free to use the Internet access for any purpose. For example, Isaiah Balat is reselling vouchers (that he bought from Fantsuam) to his clients. His Internet café hosts 10 computers that all are connected to Zittnet. The clients purchase vouchers from the owner with a margin of 25% over the price offered by Fantsuam. In return, clients that do not have access to a computer connected to Zittnet can access the network though the PC's at Isaiah Balat's café.

The New World Hotel is another client that aims to create a similar business model but on a larger scale. They will provide wireless Internet access to all of their rooms and offer access to Zittnet's uplink by reselling vouchers.

Other clients, like the General Hospital and the Jagindi Street Clinic, are using the Internet access for professional and private use without reselling access to its clients.

--Louise Berthilson

Case study: The quest for affordable Internet in rural Mali

For several years the international development community has promoted the idea of closing the digital divide. This invisible chasm that has formed separating access to the wealth of information and communications technologies (ICT) between the developed and the developing world. Access to information and communications tools has been shown to have a dramatic impact on quality of life. For many donors fatigued by decades of supporting traditional development activities, the installation of a telecentre in the developing world seems like a realizable and worthwhile effort. Because the infrastructure does not exist, this is much more expensive and difficult to do in the developing world than it is in the West. Moreover, few models have been shown to sustain these activities. To help mitigate some of the cost of bringing the Internet to rural areas of the developed world, the author's team has promoted the use of wireless systems to share the cost of an Internet connection. In November of 2004, an affiliated project asked the author's team to pilot such a wireless system at a recently installed telecentre in rural Mali, 8 hours South-West by four-by-four from Bamako, the capital.

This rural city, located on the margin of a man-made reservoir, holds water for the Manitali dam that powers a third of the country. This location is fortunate as hydroelectric power is much more stable and available than diesel generated power. While diesel generated power is far less stable, some rural communities are lucky to have any electricity at all.

The city is also endowed to be in one of the most fertile regions of the country, in its cotton belt, Mali's main cash crop. It was believed that this site would be the least difficult of the rural areas in Mali to make a self-sustaining telecentre. Like many experiments, this pilot was fraught with challenges.

Technologically it was a simple task. In 24 hours the team installed an 802.11b wireless network that shares the telecenter's VSAT Internet connection with 5 other local services: the Mayor, the Governor, the health service, the district's Mayor's council (CC) and the community advisory service (CCC).

These clients had been selected during a reconnaissance two months prior. During that visit the team had interviewed potential clients and determined which clients could be connected without complicated or expensive installations. The telecentre itself is housed at the community radio station. Radio stations tend to be great sites to host wireless networks in rural Mali as they are often well placed, have electricity, security and people who understand at least the basics of radio transmissions. They are also natural hubs for a village. Providing Internet to a radio station provides better information to its listeners. And for a culture which is principally oral, radio happens to be the most effect means to provide information.

From the list of clients above, you will note that the clients were all government or para-governmental. This proved to be a difficult mix, as there is considerable animosity and resentment between the various levels of government, and there were continuing disputes regarding taxes and other fiscal matters. Fortunately the director of the radio station, the network's champion, was very dynamic and was able to wade through most of these politics, though not all.

Design choices

The technical team determined that the access point would be installed at 20 meters up the radio station tower, just below the FM radio dipoles, and not so high as to interfere with coverage to client sites below in the bowl-like depression where most were found. The team then focused on how to connect each client site to this site. An 8 dBi omni (from Hyperlinktech, *http://hyperlinktech.com/*) would suffice, providing coverage to all client sites. The 8 dBi antenna that was chosen has a 15 degree vertical beamwidth, assuring that the two clients less than a kilometer away could still receive a strong signal. Some antennae have very narrow beam width and thus "overshoot" sites that are close. Panel antennae were considered, though at least two would be required and either a second radio or a channel splitter. It was deemed unnecessary for this installation. The following calculation shows how to calculate the angle between the client site's antenna and the base station's antenna, using standard trigonometry.

```
tan(x) = difference in elevation
       + height of base station antenna
       - height of CPE antenna
       / distance between the sites

tan(x) = 5m + 20m - 3m / 400m
     x = tan-1 (22m / 400m)
     x =~ 3 degrees
```

In addition to the equipment in the telecentre (4 computers, a laser printer, 16 port switch), the radio station itself has one Linux workstation installed by the author's project for audio editing. A small switch was installed in the radio station, an Ethernet cable was run through plastic tubing buried at 5 cm across to the telecentre, across the yard.

From the main switch, two cables run up to a Mikrotik RB220, access point. The RB220 has two Ethernet ports, one that connects to the VSAT through a cross-over cable, and the second that connects to the radio station's central switch. The RB 220 is housed in a D-I-Y PVC enclosure and an 8 dBi omni (Hyperlink Technologies) is mounted directly to the top of the PVC cap.

The RB220 runs a derivative of Linux, Mikrotik version 2.8.27. It controls the network, providing DHCP, firewall, and DNS-caching services, while routing traffic to the VSAT using NAT. The Mikrotik comes with a powerful command line and a relatively friendly and comprehensive graphical interface. It is a small x86 based computer, designed for use as an access point or embedded computer. These access points are POE capable, have two Ethernet ports, a mini-pci port, two PCMCIA slots, a CF reader (which is used for its NVRAM), are temperature tolerant and support a variety of x86 operating systems. Despite that the Mikrotik software requires licensing, there was already a substantial user base in Mali. The system has a powerful and friendly graphical interface that was superior to other products. Due to the above factors the team agreed to use these systems, including the Mikrotik software to control these networks. The total cost of the RB220, with License Level 5, Atheros mini-pci a/b/g and POE was $461. You can find these parts at Mikrotik online at *http://www.mikrotik.com/routers.php#linx1part0*.

The network was designed to accommodate expansion by segregating the various sub-networks of each client; 24 bit private subnets were alloted. The AP has a virtual interface on each subnet and does all routing between, also allowing fire-walling at the IP layer. Note: this does not provide a firewall at the network layer, thus, using a network sniffer like tcpdump one can see all traffic on the wireless link.

To limit access to subscribers, the network uses MAC level access control. There was little perceived security risk to the network. For this first phase, a more thorough security system was left to be implemented in the future, when time could be found to find an easier interface for controlling access. Users were encouraged to use secure protocols, such as https, pops, imaps etc.

The affiliate project had installed a C-band VSAT (DVB-S) system. These satellite systems are normally very reliable and are often used by ISPs. It is a large unit, in this case the dish was 2.2 meters in diameter and expensive, costing approximately $12,000 including installation. It is also expensive to operate. A 128 kbps down and 64 kbps up Internet connection costs approximately $700 per month. This system has several advantages compared to a Ku system though, including: greater resilience to bad weather, lower contention rates (number of competing users on the same service) and it is more efficient at transferring data.

The installation of this VSAT was not ideal. Since the system ran Windows, users were able to quickly change a few settings, including adding a password to the default account. The system had no UPS or battery back up, so once a power outage occurred the system would reboot and sit waiting for a password, which had since been forgotten. To make this situation worse, because the VSAT software was not configured as an automatic background service it did not automatically launch and establish the link. Though the C-band systems are typically reliable, this installation caused needless outages which could have been resolved with the use of a UPS, proper configuration of the VSAT software as a service, and by limiting physical access to the modem. Like all owners of new equipment, the radio station wanted to display it, hence it was not hidden from view. Preferably a space with glass doors would have kept the unit secure while keeping it visible.

The wireless system was fairly simple. All of the client sites selected were within 2 km of the radio station. Each site had a part of the building that could physically see the radio station. At the client site, the team chose to use commercial, client grade CPEs: Based on price, the Powernoc 802.11b CPE bridge, small SuperPass 7 dBi patch antennas and home-made Power Over Ethernet (POE) adaptors. To facilitate installation, the CPE and the patch antenna were mounted on a small piece of wood that could be installed on the outside wall of the building facing the radio station.

In some cases the piece of wood was an angled block to optimize the position of the antenna. Inside, a POE made from a repurposed television signal amplifier (12V) was used to power the units. At the client sites there were not local networks, so the team also had to install cable and hubs to provide Internet for each computer. In some cases it was necessary to install Ethernet adapters and their drivers (this was not determined during the assessment). It was decided that because the client's networks were simple, that it would be easiest to bridge their networks. Should it be required, the IP architecture could allow future partitioning and the CPE equipment supported STA mode. We used a PowerNOC CPE bridge that cost $249.

Local staff were involved during the installation of the wireless network. They learned everything from wiring to antenna placement. An intensive training program followed the installation. It lasted several weeks, and was meant to teach the staff the day to day tasks, as well as basic network troubleshooting.

A young university graduate who had returned to the community was chosen to support the system, except for the cable installation, which the radio station technician quickly learned. Wiring Ethernet networks is very similar to coaxial cable repairs and installations which the radio technician already performed regularly. The young graduate also required little training. The team spent most of its time helping him learn how to support the basics of the system and the telecentre. Soon after the telecentre opened, students were lined up for the computer training, which offered 20 hours of training and Internet use per month for only $40, a bargain compared to the $2 an hour for Internet access. Providing this training was a significant revenue and was a task that the young computer savvy graduate was well suited for.

Unfortunately, and somewhat unsurprisingly, the young graduate left for the capital, Bamako, after receiving an offer for a government job. This left the telecentre effectively marooned. Their most technically savvy member, and the only one who was trained in how to support the system, had left. Most of the knowledge needed to operate the telecentre and network left with him. After much deliberation, the team determined that it was best not to train another tech savvy youth, but rather to focus on the permanent local staff, despite their limited technical experience. This took much more time. Our trainers have had to return for a total of 150 hours of training. Several people were taught each function, and the telecentre support tasks were divided among the staff.

Training did not stop there. Once the community services were connected, they too needed access. It seemed that although they were participating, the principals, including the mayor, were not using the systems themselves. The team realized the importance of assuring that the decision makers used the system, and provided training for them and their staff. This did remove some of the mystique of the network and got the city's decision makers involved.

Following training, the program monitored the site and began to provide input, evaluating ways that this model could be improved. Lessons learned here were applied to other sites.

Financial Model

The community telecentre was already established as a non-profit, and was mandated to be self-sustaining through the sale of its services. The wireless system was included as a supplementary source of revenue because early financial projections for the telecentre indicated that they would fall short of paying for the VSAT connection.

Based on the survey, and in consultation with the radio station that manages the telecentre, several clients were selected. The radio station negotiated contracts with some support from its funding partner. For this first phase, clients were selected based on ease of installation and expressed ability to pay. Clients were asked to pay a subscription fee, as described later.

Deciding how much to charge was a major activity which required consultation and expertise that the community did not have in financial projections. The equipment was paid for by the grant, to help offset the costs to the community, but clients were still required to pay a subscription fee, which served to assure their commitment. This was equivalent to one month of the service fee.

To determine the monthly cost for an equal slice of bandwidth we started with the following formula:

```
VSAT + salaries + expenses (electricity, supplies) =
telecentre revenue + wireless client revenue
```

We had estimated that the telecentre should earn about $200 to $300 per month in revenue. Total expenses were estimated to be $1050 per month, and were broken down as: $700 for the VSAT, $100 for salaries, $150 for electricity, and about $100 for supplies. About $750 in revenue from the wireless clients was required to balance this equation. This amounted to roughly $150 from each client. This was just tolerable by the clients, and looked feasible, but required fair weather, and had no room for complications.

Because this was becoming complicated, we brought in business geeks, who modified the formula as such:

```
Monthly expenses + amortization + safety funds = total
revenue
```

The business experts were quick to point out the need of amortization of the equipment, or one could say "re-investment funds" as well as safety funds, to assure that the network can continue if a client defaults, or if some equipment breaks. This added about $150 per month for amortization (equipment valued at about $3,000, amortized over 24 months) and the value of one client for default payments, at $100. Add another 10% to account for currency devaluation ($80), and that equals an expense of $1380 per month. In trying to implement this model, it was finally determined that amortization is a concept that was too difficult to convey to the community, and that they would not consider that clients might default on payment. Thus, both formulae were used, the first by the telecentre and the second for our internal analysis.

As was soon discovered, regular payments are not part of the culture in rural Mali. In an agrarian society everything is seasonal, and so too is income. This means that the community's income fluctuates wildly. Moreover, as many public institutions were involved, they had long budget cycles with little flexibility. Although they theoretically had the budget to pay for their service, it would take many months for the payments to be made. Other fiscal complications arose as well. For example, the mayor signed on and used the back-taxes owed by the radio to pay for its subscription. This of course did not contribute to cash flow. Unfortunately, the VSAT providers have little flexibility or patience, as they have limited bandwidth and only have room for those that can pay.

Cash flow management became a primary concern. First, the revenue foreseen in financial projections showed that even with an optimistic outlook, they would not only have trouble earning enough revenue on time to pay the fee, but getting the money to the Bamako-based bank also presented a problem. Roads near the village can be dangerous, due to the number of smugglers from Guinea and wayward rebels from the Ivory Coast. As projected, the telecentre was not able to pay for its service and its service was suspended, thereby suspending payment from their clients as well.

Before the project was able to find solutions to these problems, the cost of the VSAT already began to dig the telecentre into debt. After several months, due to technical problems, as well as concerns raised in this analysis, the large C-band VSAT was replaced with a cheaper Ku band system. Although cheaper, it still sufficed for the size of the network. This system was only $450, which by ignoring amortization and safety margins is affordable by the network. Unfortunately, due to default payments, the network was not able to pay for the VSAT connection after the initial subsidized period.

Conclusions

Building a wireless network is relatively easy, but making it work is much more of a business problem than a technical problem. A payment model that considers re-investment and risk is a necessity, or eventually the network will fail. In this case, the payment model was not appropriate as it did not conform to fiscal cycles of the clients, nor did it conform to social expectations. A proper risk analysis would have concluded that a $700 (or even a $450) monthly payment left too narrow a margin between revenue and expenses to compensate for fiscal shortcomings. High demand and education needs limited the expansion of the network.

Following training the network operated for 8 months without significant technical problems. Then, a major power surge caused by a lightning strike destroyed much of the equipment at the station, including the access point and VSAT. As a result, the telecentre was still off-line at the time that this book was written. By that time this formula was finally deemed an unsuitable solution.

—Ian Howard

Case study: Commercial deployments in East Africa

Describing commercial wireless deployments in Tanzania and Kenya, this chapter highlights technical solutions providing solid, 99.5% availability Internet and data connectivity in developing countries. In contrast to projects devoted to ubiquitous access, we focused on delivering services to organizations, typically those with critical international communications needs. I will describe two radically different commercial approaches to wireless data connectivity, summarizing key lessons learned over ten years in East Africa.

Tanzania

In 1995, with Bill Sangiwa, I founded CyberTwiga, one of the first ISPs in Africa. Commercial services, limited to dialup email traffic carried over a 9.6 kbps SITA link (costing over $4000/month!), began in mid-1996. Frustrated by erratic PSTN services, and buoyed by a successful deployment of a 3-node point-multipoint (PMP) network for the Tanzania Harbours authority, we negotiated with a local cellular company to place a PMP base station on their central mast. Connecting a handful of corporations to this WiLan proprietary 2.4 GHz system in late 1998, we validated the market and our technical capacity to provide wireless services.

As competitors haphazardly deployed 2.4 GHz networks, two facts emerged: a healthy market for wireless services existed, but a rising RF noise floor in 2.4 GHz would diminish network quality. Our merger with the cellular carrier, in mid-2000, included plans for a nationwide wireless network built on the existing cellular infrastructure (towers and transmission links) and proprietary RF spectrum allocations.

Infrastructure was in place (cellular towers, transmission links, etc.) so wireless data network design and deployment were straightforward. Dar es Salaam is very flat, and because the cellular partner operated an analog network, towers were very tall. A sister company in the UK, Tele2, had commenced operations with Breezecom (now Alvarion) equipment in 3.8/3.9 GHz, so we followed their lead.

By late 2000, we had established coverage in several cities, using fractional E1 transmission circuits for backhaul. In most cases the small size of the cities connected justified the use of a single omnidirectional PMP base station; only in the commercial capital, Dar es Salaam, were 3-sector base stations installed. Bandwidth limits were configured directly on the customer radio; clients were normally issued a single public IP address. Leaf routers at each base station sent traffic to static IP addresses at client locations, and prevented broadcast traffic from suffocating the network. Market pressures kept prices down to about $100/month for 64 kbps, but at that time (mid/late 2000) ISPs could operate with impressive, very profitable, contention ratios. Hungry applications such as peer-peer file sharing, voice, and ERPs simply did not exist in East Africa. With grossly high PSTN international charges, organizations rapidly shifted from fax to email traffic, even though their wireless equipment purchase costs ranged from $2000-3000.

Technical capabilities were developed in-house, requiring staff training overseas in subjects such as SNMP and UNIX. Beyond enhancing the company skills set, these training opportunities generated staff loyalty. We had to compete in a very limited IT labor market with international gold mining companies, the UN, and other international agencies.

To insure quality at customer sites, a top local radio and telecoms contractor executed installations, tightly tracking progress with job cards. High temperatures, harsh equatorial sunlight, drenching rain, and lightning were among the environmental insults tossed at outside plant components; RF cabling integrity was vital.

Customers often lacked competent IT staff, burdening our employees with the task of configuring many species of network hardware and topology.

Infrastructure and regulatory obstacles often impeded operations. The cellular company tightly controlled towers, so that if there was a technical issue at a base station hours or days could pass before we gained access. Despite backup generators and UPS systems at every site, electrical power was always problematic. For the cellular company, electrical mains supplies at base stations were less critical. Cellular subscribers simply associated with a different base station; our fixed wireless data subscribers went offline.

On the regulatory side, a major disruption occurred when the telecoms authority decided that our operation was responsible for disrupting C-band satellite operations for the entire country and ordered us to shut down our network.

Despite hard data demonstrating that we were not at fault, the regulator conducted a highly publicized seizure of our equipment. Of course the interference persisted, and later was determined to emanate from a Russian radar ship, involved in tracking space activities. We quietly negotiated with the regulator, and ultimately were rewarded with 2 x 42 MHz of proprietary spectrum in the 3.4/3.5 GHz bands. Customers were switched over to dialup in the month or so it took to reconfigure base stations and install new CPE.

Ultimately the network grew to about 100 nodes providing good, although not great, connectivity to 7 cities over 3000+km of transmission links. Only the merger with the cellular operator made this network feasible—the scale of the Internet/data business alone would not have justified building a data network of these dimensions and making the investments needed for proprietary frequencies. Unfortunately, the cellular operator took the decision to close the Internet business in mid-2002.

Nairobi

In early 2003 I was approached by a Kenyan company, AccessKenya, with strong UK business and technical backup to design and deploy a wireless network in Nairobi and environs.   Benefiting from superb networking and business professionals, improved wireless hardware, progress in internet-working, and bigger market we designed a high availability network in line with regulatory constraints.

Two regulatory factors drove our network design. At the time in Kenya, Internet services were licensed separately from public data network operators, and a single company could not hold both licenses. Carrying traffic of multiple, competing ISPs or corporate users, the network had to operate with total neutrality. Also, "proprietary" frequencies, namely 3.4/3.5 GHz, were not exclusively licensed to a single provider, and we were concerned about interference and the technical ability/political will of the regulator to enforce. Also, spectrum in 3.4/3.5 GHz was expensive, costing about USD1000 per MHz per year per base station.   Restated, a base station using 2 x 12 MHz attracted license fees of over $10,000 year. Since Nairobi is a hilly place with lots of tall trees and valleys, wireless broadband networks demanded many base stations.   The licensing overheads simply were not sensible. In contrast, 5.7/5.8 GHz frequencies were subject only to an annual fee, about USD 120, per deployed radio.

To meet the first regulatory requirement we chose to provide services using point-point VPN tunnels, not via a network of static IP routes. An ISP would deliver a public IP address to our network at their NOC. Our network conducted a public-private IP conversion, and traffic transited our network in private IP space. At the customer site, a private-public IP conversion delivered the globally routable address (or range) to the customer network.

Security and encryption added to network neutrality, and flexibility, as unique sales properties of our network.   Bandwidth was limited at the VPN tunnel level. Based on the operating experience of our sister UK company, VirtuallT, we selected Netscreen (now subsumed under Juniper Networks) as the vendor for VPN firewall routers.

Our criteria for wireless broadband equipment eliminated big pipes and feature-rich, high performance gear. Form factor, reliability, and ease of installation and management were more important than throughput. All international Internet connections to Kenya in 2003, and at this writing, are carried by satellite. With costs 100X greater than global fiber, satellite connectivity put a financial ceiling on the amount of bandwidth purchased by end-users. We judged that the bulk of our user population required capacity on the order of 128 to 256 kbps.   We selected Motorola's recently introduced Canopy platform in line with our business and network model.

Broadband Access, Ltd., went live in July 2003, launching the "Blue" network. We started small, with a single base station. We wanted demand to drive our network expansion, rather than relying on a strategy of building big pipes and hoping we could fill them.

Canopy, and third-party enhancements such as omnidirectional base stations, permitted us to grow our network as traffic grew, softening initial capital expenditures. We knew the tradeoff was that as the network expanded, we would have to sectorize traffic and realign client radios. The gentle learning curve of a small network paid big dividends later. Technical staff became comfortable with customer support issues in a simple network environment, rather than have to deal with them on top of a complex RF and logical framework. Technical staff attended two-day Motorola training sessions.

A typical PMP design, with base stations linked to a central facility via a Canopy high-speed microwave backbone, the network was deployed on building rooftops, not antenna towers. All leases stipulated 24x7 access for staff, mains power and, critically, protected the exclusivity of our radio frequencies. We did not want to restrict landlords from offering roof space to competitors, rather to simply guarantee that our own services would not be interrupted.

Rooftop deployments provided many advantages. Unlimited physical access, unconstrained by night or rain, helped meet the goal of 99.5% network availability. Big buildings also housed many big clients, and it was possible to connect them directly into our core microwave network. Rooftop sites did have the downside of more human traffic—workers maintaining equipment (a/c) or patching leaks would occasionally damage cabling. As a result all base stations were set up with two sets of cabling for all network elements, a primary and a spare.

Site surveys confirmed radio path availability and client requirements. Survey staff logged GPS positions for each client, and carried a laser rangefinder to determine height of obstacles. Following receipt of payment for hardware, contractors under the supervision of a technical staffer performed installations. Canopy has the advantage that the CPE and base station elements are light, so that most installations do not need extensive civil works or guying. Cabling Canopy units was also simple, with outdoor UTP connecting radios directly to customer networks. Proper planning enabled completion of many installations in less than an hour, and contractor crews did not need any advanced training or tools.

As we compiled hundreds of customer GPS positions we began to work closely with a local survey company to overlay these sites on topographical maps. These became a key planning tool for base station placement.

Note that the point-point VPN tunnel architecture, with its separate physical and logical layers, required clients to purchase both wireless broadband and VPN hardware. In order to tightly control quality, we categorically refused to permit clients to supply their own hardware—they had to buy from us in order to have service and hardware guarantees. Every client had the same hardware package. Typical installations cost on the order of USD 2500, but that compares to the $500-600 monthly charges for 64 to 128 kbps of bandwidth. A benefit of the VPN tunnel approach was that we could prevent a client's traffic from passing over the logical network (i.e. if their network was hit by a worm or if they didn't pay a bill) while the radio layer remained intact and manageable.

As it grew from one base station to ten, and service was expanded to Mombasa, the network RF design evolved and wherever possible network elements (routers) were configured with fallover or hot swap redundancy. Major investments in inverters and dual conversion UPS equipment at each base station were required to keep the network stable in the face of an erratic power grid. After a number of customer issues (dropped VPN connections) were ascribed to power blackouts, we simply included a small UPS as part of the equipment package.

Adding a portable spectrum analyzer to our initial capital investment was costly, but hugely justified as we operated the network. Tracing rogue operators, confirming the operating characteristics of equipment, and verifying RF coverage enhanced our performance.

Fanatical attention to monitoring permitted us to uptweak network performance, and gather valuable historical data. Graphed via MRTG or Cacti (as described in chapter six), parameters such as jitter, RSSI, and traffic warned of rogue operators, potential deterioration of cable/connectors, and presence of worms in client networks. It was not uncommon for clients to claim that service to their site had been interrupted for hours/days and demand a credit. Historical monitoring verified or invalidated these claims.

The Blue network combined a number of lessons from Tanzania with improved RF and networking technologies.

Lessons learned

For the next few years satellite circuits will provide all international Internet connectivity in East Africa. Several groups have floated proposals for submarine fiber connectivity, which will energize telecommunications when it happens. Compared to regions with fiber connectivity, bandwidth costs in East Africa will remain very high.

Wireless broadband networks for delivery of Internet services therefore do not need to focus on throughput. Instead, emphasis should be placed on reliability, redundancy, and flexibility.

Reliability for our wireless networks was our key selling point. On the network side this translated into sizable investments in infrastructure substitution, such as backup power, and attention to details such as crimping and cabling. The most ordinary reasons for a single customer to lose connectivity were cabling or crimping issues. Radio failures were essentially unheard of. A key competitive advantage of our customer installation process is that we pushed contractors to adhere to tight specifications. It was common for well-managed customer sites to remain connected for hundreds of days with zero unscheduled downtime. We controlled as much of our infrastructure as possible (i.e building rooftops).

As attractive as potential alliances with cellular providers seem, in our experience they raise more problems than they solve. In East Africa, Internet businesses generate a fraction of the revenue of mobile telephony, and so are marginal to the cellular companies. Trying to run a network on top of infrastructure that doesn't belong to you and is, from the point of view of the cellular provider, a goodwill gesture, will make it impossible to meet service commitments.

Implementing fully redundant networks, with fail-over or hotswap capability is an expensive proposition in Africa. Nonetheless the core routers and VPN hardware at our central point of presence were fully redundant, configured for seamless fail-over, and routinely tested. For base stations we took the decision not to install dual routers, but kept spare routers in stock. We judged that the 2-3 hours of downtime in the worst case (failure at 1AM Sunday morning in the rain) would be acceptable to clients. Similarly weekend staff members had access to an emergency cupboard containing spare customer premises equipment, such as radios and power supplies.

Flexibility was engineered into both the logical and RF designs of the network. The point-to-point VPN tunnel architecture rolled out in Nairobi was extraordinarily flexible in service of client or network needs. Client connections could be set to burst during off-peak hours to enable offsite backup, as a single example. We could also sell multiple links to separate destinations, increasing the return on our network investments while opening up new services (such remote monitoring of CCTV cameras) to clients.

On the RF side we had enough spectrum to plan for expansion, as well as cook up an alternative radio network design in case of interference. With the growing number of base stations, probably 80% of our customer sites had two possible base station radios in sight so that if a base station were destroyed we could restore service rapidly.

Separating the logical and RF layers of the Blue network introduced an additional level of complexity and cost. Consider the long-term reality that radio technologies will advance more rapidly than internetworking techniques. Separating the networks, in theory, gives us the flexibility to replace the existing RF network without upsetting the logical network. Or we may install a different radio network in line with evolving technologies (Wimax) or client needs, while maintaining the logical network.

Finally, one must surrender to the obvious point that the exquisite networks we deployed would be utterly useless without unrelenting commitment to customer service. That is, after all, what we got paid for.

More information

- Broadband Access, Ltd.: *http://www.blue.co.ke/*
- AccessKenya, Ltd.: *http://www.accesskenya.com/*
- VirtualIT: *http://www.virtualit.biz/*

--Adam Messer, Ph.D

Case study: Dharamsala Community Wireless Mesh Network

The Dharamsala Wireless-Mesh Community Network came to life in February 2005, following the deregulation of WiFi for outdoor use in India. By the end of February 2005, the mesh had already connected 8 campuses.

Extensive testing during February of 2005 showed that the hard mountainous terrain is most suitable for mesh networking, as conventional point-to-multipoint networks, cannot overcome the line-of-sight limitations presented by the mountains. mesh topology also offered much larger area coverage, while the "self healing" nature of mesh routing, proved to be essential in places where electricity supply is very erratic at best.

The mesh backbone includes over 30 nodes, all sharing a single radio channel. Broadband Internet services are provided to all mesh members. The total upstream Internet bandwidth available is 6 Mbps. There are over 2,000 computers connected to the mesh, The broadband internet connection is putting the mesh under great load. At present, the system seems to handle the load without any increase in latency or packet-loss. It is clear that scalability will become an issue if we continue to use a single radio channel. To solve this problem, new mesh routers with multiple radio channel support are being developed and tested in Dharamsala, with an emphasis on products that meet our technical requirements and our economically viable. The initial results are very promising.

The mesh network is based on recurring deployments of a hardware device, which is designed and built locally – known as the ***Himalayan-Mesh-Router*** (*http://drupal.airjaldi.com/node/9*). The same mesh-routers are installed at every location, with only different antennas, depending on the geographical locations and needs. We use a wide range of antennas, from 8 - 11 dBi omnidirectional, to 12 - 24 dBi directional antennas and occasionally some high-gain (and cost) sector antennas.

The mesh is primarily used for:

• Internet access

• File-sharing applications

• Off-site backups

• Playback of high quality video from remote archives.

A central VoIP, software-based PBX is installed (Asterisk) and it provides advanced telephony services to members. The Asterisk PBX is also interfacing the PSTN telephone network. However, due to legal issues it is presently used only for incoming calls into the mesh. Subscribers use a large variety of software-phones, as well as numerous ATAs (Analog Telephone Adaptors) and full-featured IP phones.

Figure 11.5: Dharamsala installer working on a tower

The encrypted mesh back-bone does not allow access to roaming mobile devices (notebooks and PDAs), so we have placed multiple 802.11b access-points at many of the same locations where mesh-routers are installed. The mesh provides the backbone infrastructure while these APs provide access to mobile roaming devices, where needed.

Access to the mesh back-bone is only possible by mesh-routers. Simple wireless clients lack the intelligence needed to "speak" the mesh routing protocols and strict access policies. The mesh channel is therefore encrypted (WPA), and also "hidden" to prevent mobile devices from finding it or attempting to access it. Allowing access to the mesh only by mesh-routers allows for strict access control policies and limitations to be enforced at the CPE (Client Premises Equipment) which is a crucial element needed to achieve end-to-end security, traffic-shaping, and quality-of-service.

Power consumption of the mesh-Router is less than 4 Watts. This makes them ideal for using with solar panels. Many of the Dharamsala Mesh routers are powered solely by small solar panels. The use of solar power in combination with small antennas and low power routers is ideally suitable for disaster areas, as it very likely to survive when all other communication infrastructure is damaged.

--AirJaldi, http://airjaldi.com/

Case study: Networking Mérida State

The city of Mérida lies at the foot of the highest mountain in Venezuela, on a plateau at about 1600 m. It is the capital of the state of Mérida, and home to a two- centuries-old university, with some 35,000 students. The University of Los Andes (ULA) deployed the first academic computer network in 1989 which, despite economic limitations, has grown to encompass 26 km of fiber optic cable over which both a TDM and an ATM (asynchronous transfer mode) network are overlaid.   In 2006, over the same fiber optic cable, a 50 km Gigabit Ethernet network has been deployed.

Figure 11.6: Mérida is one of the three mountainous states of Venezuela, where the Andes reach 5000 m.

Nevertheless, many places in the city and the surrounding villages are out of reach of the fiber optic ring. The university operates a communication server with telephone lines to provide remote access to its network, but local calls are charged by the minute and many villages lack phone lines altogether.

For these reasons, efforts to develop wireless access to the university's network, called RedULA, were undertaken from the very beginning. The first attempts took advantage of the existing packet network operated by radio amateurs. As early as 1987, amateurs had a gateway with an **HF** (**High Frequency**) station working at 300 bps for contacts overseas, as well as several **VHF** (**Very High Frequency**) stations linked at 1200 bps that crisscrossed the country.

While the rugged mountains of the region are a big obstacle for laying cables and building roads, they can be helpful in deploying a radio network. This task is aided by the existence of a cable car system, reputedly the highest in the world, which links the city to a 4765 m peak.

Figure 11.7: On its way to the peak, the cable car passes by an intermediate station called La Aguada, which is 3450 m high and has an astounding view of the city of Mérida and other villages at distances up to 50 km.

Packet radio

Local amateurs operate a packet radio network. Initially it worked at 1200 bps, using VHF amateur FM voice radios connected to a personal computer by means of a **terminal node controller** (**TNC**). The TNC is the interface between the analog radio and the digital signals handled by the PC.

The TNC keys the Push To Talk circuits in the radio to change from transmit to receive, performs modulation/demodulation and the assembly/disassembly of packets using a variation of the X.25 protocol known as **AX.25**. Gateways between VHF and HF radios were built by attaching two modems to the same TNC and computer. Typically, a gateway would connect the local VHF packet network to stations overseas by means of HF stations that could span thousands of kilometers, albeit at a speed of only 300 bps. A national packet radio network was also built, which relayed on **digipeaters** (digital repeaters, essentially a TNC connected to two radios with antennas pointing in different directions), to extend the network from Mérida to Caracas by means of just two such repeater stations. The digipeaters operated at 1200 bps and allowed for the sharing of programs and some text files among amateurs.

Phil Karn, a radio amateur with a strong background in computer networks, wrote the KA9Q program that implements TCP/IP over AX.25. Using this program, named after the call sign of its developer, amateurs all over the world were soon able to connect to the Internet using different kinds of radios. KA9Q keeps the functions of the TNC to a bare minimum, harnessing the power of the attached PC for most processing functions. This approach allows for much greater flexibility and easy upgrades. In Mérida, we were soon able to upgrade our network to 9600 bps by use of more advanced modems, and several radio amateurs were now able to access the Internet through the RedULA wired network. The limit on the radio bandwidth available on the VHF band puts a cap on the highest attainable speed. To increase that speed, one must move to higher frequency carriers.

Amateurs are allowed to use 100 kHz wide channels using **UHF** (**Ultra-High Frequency**) signals. Digital radios coupled with 19.2 kbps modems doubled the transmission bandwidth. A project was developed using this technology to link the House of Science in the city of El Vigia, to Mérida and the Internet. UHF antennas were built at LabCom, the communications laboratory of ULA.

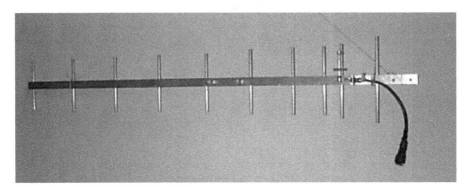

Figure 11.8: A UHF antenna for packet radio developed at ULA, LabCom.

Although El Vigia is only 100 km from Mérida by road, the mountainous terrain called for the use of two repeaters. One is located at La Aguada, at 3600 m altitude, and the other at Tusta, at 2000 m. The project was financed by FUNDACITE MERIDA, a government institution that promotes science and technology in the state. FUNDACITE also operates a pool of 56 kbps telephone modems to provide Internet access for institutions and individuals. The need for two repeater stations underscores the limitations imposed by using higher frequency carriers, which require line of sight to establish a reliable transmission. In the much lower VHF band, signals are easily reflected and can reach beyond hills.

Sometimes it is possible to reflect signals using a ***passive repeater,*** which is made by connecting two directional antennas back to back with a coaxial cable, without any radio. This scheme was tested to connect my residence to LabCom. The distance is only 11 km, but there is a hill in between that blocks radio signals. A connection was made by using a passive repeater to reflect off La Aguada, with the two antennas of the repeater pointing 40 degrees apart. While this was very exciting and certainly much cheaper than access through the telephone modems, a faster medium would obviously be needed for a wireless backbone to connect remote villages.

We therefore explored the use of 56 kbps modems developed by Dale Heatherington. These modems are housed in a PI2 card built by Ottawa amateurs, and connected directly to a PC using Linux as the network operating system. While this system functions very well, the emergence of the World Wide Web with its plethora of images and other bandwidth-hogging files made it clear that if we were to satisfy the needs of schools and hospitals we had to deploy a higher bandwidth solution, at least on the backbone. This meant the use of even higher carrier frequencies in the microwave range, which entailed high costs.

Fortunately, an alternative technology widely used in military applications was becoming available for civilian uses at affordable prices. Called ***spread spectrum***, it first found a use in civilian applications as a short-reach wireless local area network, but soon proved to be very useful in places where the electromagnetic spectrum is not overcrowded, allowing the bridging of distances of several kilometers.

Spread spectrum

Spread spectrum uses low power signals with its spectrum expanded on purpose to span all the allocated bandwidth, while at the same time allowing a number of users to share the medium by using different codes for each subscriber.

There are two ways to accomplish this: ***Direct Sequence Spread Spectrum*** (***DSSS***) and ***Frequency Hopping Spread Spectrum*** (***FHSS***).

- In DSSS the information to be transmitted is digitally multiplied by a higher frequency sequence, thereby augmenting the transmission bandwidth. Although this might seem to be a waste of bandwidth, the recovery system is so efficient that it can decode very weak signals, allowing for the simultaneous use of the same spectrum by several stations.

- In FHSS, the transmitter is constantly changing its carrier frequency inside the allotted bandwidth according to a specified code. The receiver must know this code in order to track the carrier frequency.

Both techniques exchange transmission power for bandwidth, allowing many stations to share a certain portion of the spectrum. During the First Latin American Networking School (EsLaRed '92), held in Mérida in 1992, we were able to demonstrate this technique. We established some trial networks making use of external antennas built at the LabCom, allowing transmission at several kilometers. In 1993, the Venezuelan Ministry of Telecommunications opened up four bands for use with DSSS:

- 400 - 512 MHz

- 806 - 960 MHz

- 2.4 - 2.4835 GHz

- 5.725 - 5.850 GHz

In any of the above bands, maximum transmitter power was restricted to 1 Watt and the maximum antenna gain to 6 dBi, for a total EIRP (effective isotropic radiated power) of 36 dBm. This ruling paved the way for the deployment of a DSSS network with a nominal bandwidth of 2 Mbps in the 900 MHz band. This technology satisfied the needs caused by the surge in World Wide Web activity.

The network started at LabCom, where the connection to RedULA was available. LabCom housed an inhouse-built Yagi antenna pointed towards a corner reflector at Aguada. This provided a 90 degree beamwidth, illuminating most of the city of Mérida. Several subscriber sites, all sharing the nominal 2 Mbps bandwidth, were soon exchanging files, including images and video clips. Some subscriber sites that required longer cables between the antenna and the spread spectrum radio were accommodated by the use of bidirectional amplifiers.

These encouraging results were reported to a group set up at the International Centre for Theoretical Physics (ICTP) in Trieste, Italy, in 1995. This group was aimed at providing connectivity between the Computer Center, Physical Sciences Building, and the Technology Building at the University of Ile-Ife in Nigeria. Later that year, the network was set up by ICTP staff with funding from the United Nations University and has been running satisfactorily ever since, proving to be a much more cost-effective solution than the fiber optic network originally planned would have been.

Back in Mérida, as the number of sites increased, the observed throughput per user declined. We started looking at the 2.4 GHz band to provide additional capacity. This band can carry three simultaneously independent 2 Mbps streams, but the effective range is lower than what can be achieved in the 900 MHz band. We were very busy planning the extension of the backbone using

2.4 GHz when we found out about a start-up company that was offering a new solution that promised longer distances, dramatically higher throughput, and the possibility of frequency reuse with narrowband microwaves.

Broadband delivery system

After visiting the Nashua, New Hampshire, facilities of Spike Technologies, we were convinced that their proprietary antenna and radio system was the best solution for the requirements of our state network, for the following reasons:

Their broadband delivery system employs a special sectored antenna (**Figure 11.9**), with 20 dBi gain on each of up to 22 independent sectors. Each sector transmits and receives on independent channels at 10 Mbps full duplex, for an aggregate throughput of 440 Mbps. Frequency reuse on interleaved sectors makes for a spectrally efficient system.

THE SECTORED APPROACH

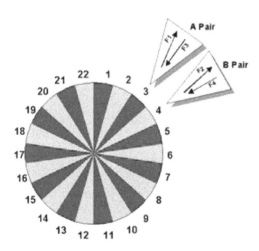

- PRIZM BDS utilizes a patented, sectored single aperture that allows spectral reuse of two channel pairs

- Spectral efficiency of this model results in a ratio of 11:1

Figure 11.9: Spike Technologies' full duplex, high density sectoral system.

The narrowband digital radios can operate anywhere from 1 to 10 GHz, with a coverage of up to 50 km. The radios work with a variety of cable TV modems, delivering a standard 10Base-T LAN connection to the subscriber. At the base station, the sectors are interconnected with a high-speed switch that has a very small latency (see **Figure 11.10**), allowing applications such as streaming video at up to 30 frames per second. Each sector acts as an independent Ethernet LAN.

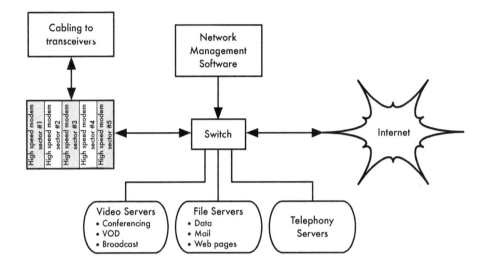

Figure 11.10: Spike Technologies' system interconnections.

At the subscriber site, a similar radio and modem provide a 10BaseT connection to the local Ethernet.

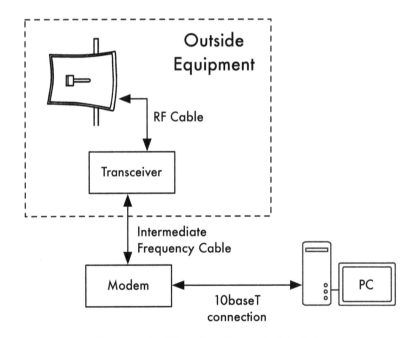

Figure 11.11: The subscriber end of the link.

With funding from Fundacite, a trial system was soon installed in Mérida, with the base station located just above the cable car station of La Aguada at an altitude of 3600 m.

Figure 11.12: Installation above Mérida at La Aguada, at 3600 meters.

Initially only 5 sectors were installed, with a beamwidth of 16 degrees each. The first subscriber site was at Fundacite´s premises, where a satellite system provides Internet access. Sector two served the Governor's Palace. Sector three served FUNDEM, a relief organization of the local government. Sector four served a penitentiary near the town of Lagunillas, about 35 km from Mérida. The fifth sector transmitted to a mountaintop repeater close to the village of La Trampa, 40 km from La Aguada. From La Trampa, another 41 km link extended the network to the House of Science in the town of Tovar.

On January 31, 1998, a videoconference between the penitentiary and the Justice Palace in Mérida proved that, aside from Internet access, the system could also support streaming video. In this case it was used for the arraignment of prisoners, thus avoiding the inconveniences and risks of their transportation.

The success of the trial prompted the state government to allocate the funding for a complete system to give high-speed Internet access to the state health system, educational system, libraries, community centers, and several governmental agencies. In January 1999 we had 3 hospitals, 6 educational institutions, 4 research institutions, 2 newspapers, 1 TV station, 1 public library, and 20 social and governmental institutions sharing information and accessing the Internet. Plans call for 400 sites to be connected within this year at full duplex 10 Mbps speed, and funding has already been allocated for this purpose.

Figure 11.13 shows a map of the state of Mérida. The dark lines show the initial backbone, while the light lines show the extension.

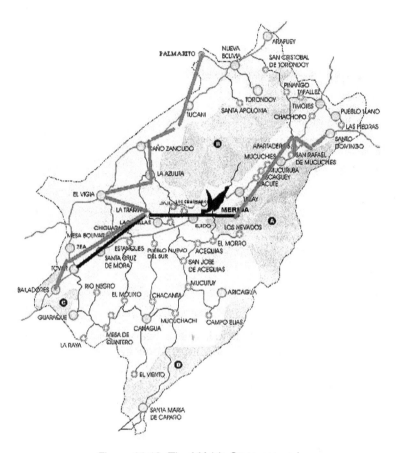

Figure 11.13: The Mérida State network

Among the many activities supported by the network, it is worthwhile to mention the following:

- **Educational**: Schools have found an endless supply of material of the highest quality for pupils and teachers, especially in the areas of geography, languages, and sciences, and as a tool to communicate with other groups that share common interests. Libraries have rooms with computers accessible to the general public with full Internet capabilities. Newspaper and TV stations have an amazing source of information to make available to their audience.

- **Health**: The university hospital has a direct link to the intensive care unit, where a staff of specialist physicians is always on duty. These doctors are available to be queried by their colleagues in remote villages to discuss specific cases. A group of researchers at the university is developing several telemedicine applications based on the network.

- **Research**: The astronomic observatory of Llano del Hato, located on a mountain at 3600 m and 8 degrees off the equator will soon be linked, allowing astronomers from all over the world access to the images collected there. Field researchers in many villages will enjoy Internet access.

- **Government**: Most government agencies are already connected and starting to put information online for the citizens. We expect this to have a profound impact on the relationship of citizens with the government. Relief agencies and law enforcement agencies make heavy use of the network.

- **Entertainment and Productivity**: For people living outside the city, the opportunities offered by the Net have a significant impact on the quality of their lives. We hope that this will help to reverse the trend of migrating out of the countryside, alleviating the overcrowding of the urban areas. Farmers have access to information about the commanding prices of their crops and supplies, as well as improved agricultural practices.

SUPERCOMM '98, held in Atlanta in June, cited the Mérida broadband delivery network as winner of the SUPERQuest award in category 8-Remote Access as the best in that particular field of nominees.

Training

Since our earliest efforts to establish a computer network, we realized that training was of paramount importance for the people involved in the network construction, management, and maintenance. Given our very limited budget, we decided that we had to pool our resources with those of other people who also required training. In 1990 the ICTP organized the First International School on computer network analysis and management, which was attended by Professor Jose Silva and Professor Luis Nunez from our university. Upon returning to Mérida, they proposed that we should somehow emulate this activity in our university. To this end, taking advantage of my sabbatical, I spent three months at Bellcore in Morristown, New Jersey, and three more months at the ICTP helping in the preparation of the Second Networking School in 1992, where I was joined by my colleague Professor Edmundo Vitale. I spent the rest of my sabbatical at SURANET in College Park, Maryland, under the guidance of Dr. Glenn Ricart, who introduced me to Dr. Saul Hahn of the Organization of American States, who offered financial support for a training activity in Latin America. These experiences allowed us to launch the First Latin American Networking School (EsLaRed'92) in Mérida, attended by 45 participants from 8 countries in the region, with instructors from Europe, the United States, and Latin America. This hands-on training lasted three weeks, and wireless technologies were emphasized.

EsLaRed'95 gathered again in Mérida with 110 participants and 20 instructors. EsLaRed'97 had 120 participants, and it was endorsed by the Internet Society, which also sponsored a Spanish and Portuguese first Networking

Workshop for Latin America and the Caribbean, held in Rio de Janeiro in 1998 with EsLaRed responsible for the training content. Now ten years later, Es-LaRed continues to expand its training efforts throughout South America.

Concluding remarks

The Internet has an even more profound impact in developing countries than elsewhere, owing to the high cost of international phone calls, faxes, magazines, and books. This is obviously exacerbated by the lower average income of people. Some dwellers in remote villages that do not have telephones are experiencing a transition from the 19th to the 21st century thanks to wireless networking. It is hoped that this will contribute to the improvement of lifestyles in the fields of health, education, entertainment, and productivity, as well as create a more equitable relationship between citizens and government.

References

- Karn, Phil, "The KA9Q Internet (TCP/IP) Package: A Progress Report," Sixth ARRL Computer Networking Conference, Redondo Beach, CA, 29 August 1987.

- Heatherington, D., "A 56 kilobaud RF modem," Sixth ARRL Computer Networking Conference, Redondo Beach, CA, 29 August 1987.

- Conatel, Comision Nacional de Comunicaciones, Ministerio de Transporte y Comunicaciones, "NORMAS PARA LA OPERACION DE SISTEMAS DE TELECOMUNICACIONES CON TECNOLOGIA DE BANDA ESPARCIDA (SPREAD SPECTRUM)," Caracas, 17 November 1993.

- International Centre For Theoretical Physics, "Programme of Training and System Development on Networking and Radiocommunications," Trieste, Italy, 1996, *http://www.ictp.trieste.it/*

- Escuela Latinoamericana de Redes, *http://www.eslared.org.ve/*

--Ermanno Pietrosemoli

Case study: Chilesincables.org

Recent wireless data transmission technologies allow the creation of high speed, geographically separated networks at a relatively low cost. If these networks are built around the idea of removing restrictions to data access, we call them *free networks.* Such networks can bring great benefits to every user, independent of the their political, economic, or social conditions. This kind of network is a direct response to the often restrictive commercial model ruling over much of our modern western society.

In order for free networks to flourish, wireless technologies must be adapted and put to the best possible use. This is carried out by groups of hackers who do the research, investigation, development and implementation of projects, as well as permit free access to the knowledge gained.

Chilesincables.org endeavors to promote and organize wireless free networks in Chile in a professional way. We do this by providing education about the related legal and technical aspects of wireless networking; encouraging the adaptation of new technologies through adequate research; and stimulating the adaptation of these technologies to meet the specific needs of Chilean communities and society.

Description of technology

We employ a variety of wireless technologies, including IEEE 802.11a/b/g. We are also investigating recent innovations in the field, such as WiMAX. In most cases, the equipment has been modified in order to be accept external locally built antennas which meet local telecommunications regulations.

Even though a majority of wireless hardware available on the market will suit our goals, we encourage utilization and exploration of a few vendors that allow for better control and adaptation to our needs (without necessarily increasing the prices). These include Wi-Fi cards with chipsets offered by Atheros, Prism, Orinoco, and Ralink, as well as some models of access points manufactured by Linksys, Netgear, and Motorola. The hacker community has developed firmware that provides new functionality on this equipment.

For the network backbone itself, we employ Open Source operating systems, including GNU/Linux, FreeBSD, OpenBSD, and Minix. This fits our needs in the areas of routing as well as implementation of services such as proxies, web and FTP servers, etc. In addition, they share our project's philosophy of being free technology with open source code.

Uses and applications

The networks implemented so far allow the following tasks:

- Transfer of data via FTP or web servers
- VoIP services
- Audio and video streaming
- Instant messaging
- Exploration and implementation of new services such as LDAP, name resolution, new security methods, etc.
- Services provided by the clients. The users are free to use the net's infrastructure in order to create their own services.

Administration and maintenance

The operational unit of the network is the **node**. Each node allows clients to associate to the network and obtain basic network services. In addition, each node must be associated to at least another node, by convention. This allows the network to grow and to make more services available to every client.

A node is maintained by an administrator who is a member of the community committed to the following tasks:

- Maintenance of an adequate uptime (over 90%).
- Providing basic services (typically web access).
- Keeping the clients updated about the node's services (for example, how to get access to the network). This is generally provided by a captive portal.

The general administration of the network (specifically, tasks related to deployment of new nodes, selection of sites, network's topology, etc.) is carried out by the board of the community, or by technicians trained for this purpose.

Chilesincables.org is currently in the process of acquiring legal organization status, a step that will allow the regulation of its internal administrative procedures and the formalization of the community in our society.

Training and capacity building

Chilesincables.org considers training of its members and clients to be of vital importance for the following reasons:

- The radio spectrum must be kept as clear as possible in order to guarantee adequate quality of wireless connections. Therefore, training in radio communications techniques is essential.

- The employment of materials and methods approved by the current regulations is a requirement for the normal development of the activities.

- In order to comply with Internet standards, all of our network administrators are trained in TCP/IP networking.

- To ensure continuity in network operations, knowledge of networking technology must be transferred to the users.

To support these principles, Chilesincables.org undertakes the following activities:

- **Antenna Workshop.** Attendees are trained in the construction of antennas, and introduced to basic concepts of radio communication.

- **Operating Systems Workshop.** Training on the implementation of routers and other devices based on GNU/Linux or other software such as m0n0wall or pfsense. Basic networking concepts are also taught.

- **Promotion and Advertising.** Events for different communities that pursue our same goals are promoted. These include college workshops, lectures, free software gatherings, etc.

- **Updating of Materials.** Chilesincables.org maintains a number of free-access documents and materials made available to people interested in a specific activity.

The pictures on the following pages present a brief account of the activities in our community.

Figure 11.14: Omnidirectional slotted antenna workshop. In this session, attendants learned about building antennas and related theory.

Figure 11.15: One of our staff members lecturing on the implementation of a m0nowall-based router in the administration of a node.

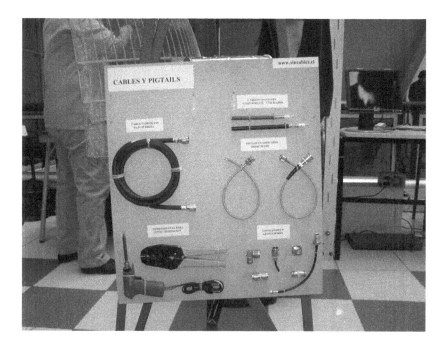

Figure 11.16: Detail of mini tower with samples of antennas, cables and pigtails.

Figure 11.17: Wireless station and parabolic antenna used for the transmission of
Santiago-2006 FLISOL via streaming video.

Figure 11.18: Location of the other end of the link.

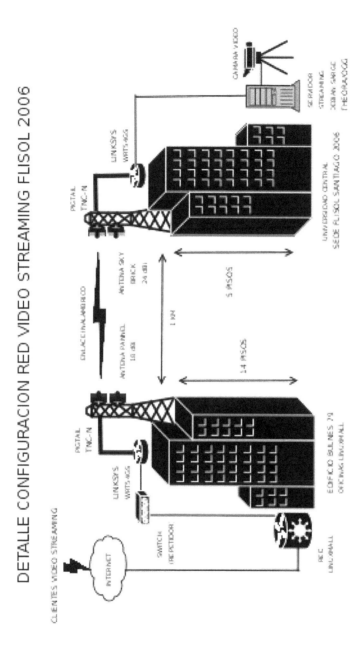

Figure 11.19: Schematic representing Santiago-2006 FLISOL video streaming transmission, using free software. The wireless transmission speed achieved was 36 Mbps at 1 km.

Figure 11.20: Quiani node. This is one of the world's highest nodes. Its located at an elevation of 4000 m, about 2000 km north of the country's capital.

Figure 11.21: Node in southern Santiago, consisting of a 15 m tower, a Trevor Marshall 16+16 antenna, and 30 clients. The node is connected to a downtown node more than 12 km away.

Figure 11.22: Panoramic view of a node from the top of the tower.

Figure 11.23: Downtown node connected to the Santiago southern node. Note the parabolic antenna for backhaul and the slotted antenna to connect the clients.

Figure 11.24: Implementation of node over a water tower in Batuco, Metropolitan Region, providing backhaul to Cabrati telecenter.

Figure 11.25: Workshop on Yagi antennas organized by our community. Participants are building their own antennas.

Credits

Our community is made up of a group of committed volunteer associates among which are worthy of notice:

Felipe Cortez (Pulpo), Felipe Benavides (Colcad), Mario Wagenknecht (Kaneda), Daniel Ortiz (Zaterio), Cesar Urquejo (Xeuron), Oscar Vasquez (Machine), Jose San Martin (Packet), Carlos Campano (Campano), Christian Vasquez (Crossfading), Andres Peralta (Cantenario), Ariel Orellana (Ariel), Miguel Bizama (Picunche), Eric Azua (Mr. Floppy), David Paco (Dpaco), Marcelo Jara (Alaska).

--Chilesincables.org

Case study: Long Distance 802.11

Thanks to a favorable topography, Venezuela already has some long range WLAN links, like the 70 km long operated by Fundacite Mérida between Pico Espejo and Canagua.

To test the limits of this technology, it is necessary to find a path with an unobstructed line of sight and a clearance of at least 60% of the first Fresnel zone.

While looking at the terrain in Venezuela, in search of a stretch with high elevation at the ends and low ground in between, I first focused in the Guayana region. Although plenty of high grounds are to be found, in particular the famous "tepuys" (tall mesas with steep walls), there were always obstacles in the middle ground.

My attention shifted to the Andes, whose steep slopes (rising abruptly from the plains) proved adequate to the task. For several years, I have been traveling through sparsely populated areas due to my passion for mountain biking. In the back of my head, I kept a record of the suitability of different spots for long distance communications.

Pico del Aguila is a very favorable place. It has an altitude of 4200 m and is about a two hour drive from my home town of Mérida. For the other end, I finally located the town of El Baúl, in Cojedes State. Using the free software Radio Mobile (available at *http://www.cplus.org/rmw/english1.html*), I found that there was no obstruction of the first Fresnel zone (spanning 280 km) between Pico del Aguila and El Baúl.

Action Plan

Once satisfied with the existence of a suitable trajectory, we looked at the equipment needed to achieve the goal. We have been using Orinoco cards for a number of years. Sporting an output power of 15 dBm and receive threshold of -84 dBm, they are robust and trustworthy. The free space loss at 282 km is 149 dB. So, we would need 30 dBi antennas at both ends and even that would leave very little margin for other losses.

On the other hand, the popular Linksys WRT54G wireless router runs Linux. The Open Source community has written several firmware versions for it that allow for a complete customization of every transmission parameter. In particular, OpenWRT firmware allows for the adjustment of the acknowledgment time of the MAC layer, as well as the output power. Another firmware, DD-WRT, has a GUI interface and a very convenient site survey utility. Furthermore, the Linksys can be located closer to the antenna than a laptop. So, we decided to go with a pair of these boxes. One was configured as an AP (access point) and the other as a client. The WRT54G can operate at 100 mW output power with good linearity, and can even be pushed up to 200 mW. But at this value, non linearity is very severe and spurious signals are generated, which should be avoided. Although this is consumer grade equipment and quite inexpensive, after years of using it, we felt confident that it could serve our purpose. Of course, we kept a spare set handy just in case.

By setting the output power to 100 mW (20 dBm), we could obtain a 5dB advantage compared with the Orinoco card. Therefore, we settled for a pair of WRT54Gs.

Pico del Águila site survey

On January 15, 2006, I went to Pico Águila to check out the site that Radio Mobile had reported as suitable. The azimuth towards El Baúl is 86°, but since the magnetic declination is 8° 16', our antenna should be pointed to a magnetic bearing of 94°.

Unfortunately, when I looked towards 94°, I found the line of sight obstructed by an obstacle that had not been shown by the software, due to the limited resolution of the digital elevation maps that are freely available.

I rode my mountain bike for several hours examining the surrounding area looking for a clear path towards the East. Several promising spots were identified, and for each of them I took photos and recorded the coordinates with a GPS for later processing with the Radio Mobile software. This led me to refine my path selection, resulting in the one depicted in **Figure 11.26** using Google Earth:

Figure 11.26: View of the 280 km link. Maracaibo's Lake is to the West, and the Peninsula of Paraguaná is to the North.

The radio profile obtained with Radio Mobile is shown in **Figure 11.27**:

Figure 11.27: Map and profile of the proposed path between Pico Aguila, and Morrocoy hill, near the town of El Baúl.

The details of the wireless link are displayed in **Figure 11.28**:

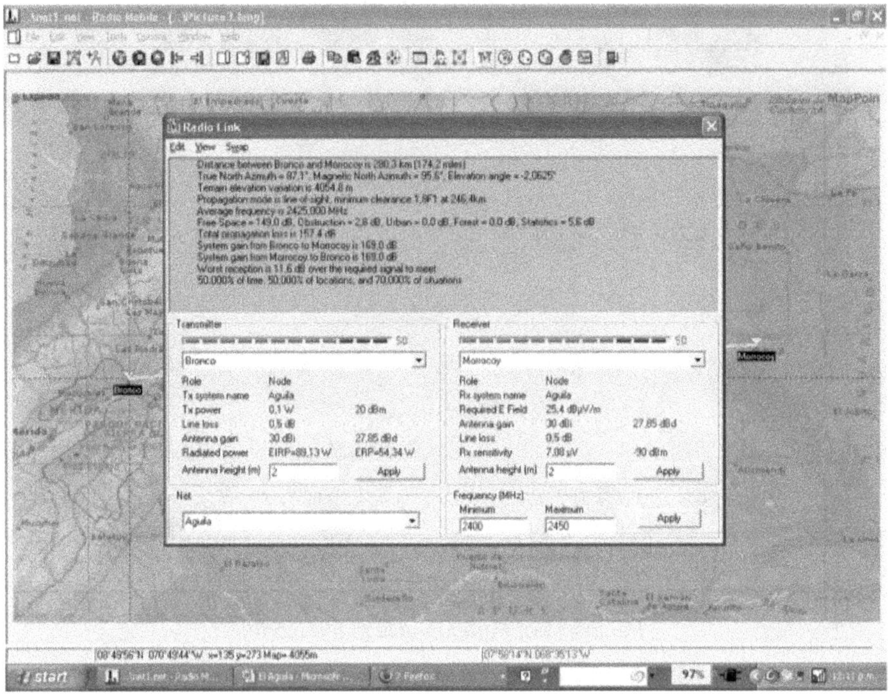

Figure 11.28: Propagation details of the 280 km link.

In order to achieve a reasonable margin of some 12 dB for the link, we needed antennas with at least 30 dBi gain at each end.

Antennas

High gain antennas for the 2.4 GHz band are not available in Venezuela. The importation costs are considerable, so we decided instead to recycle parabolic reflectors (formerly used for satellite service) and replaced the feed with one designed for 2.4 GHz. We proved the concept with an 80 cm dish. The gain was way too low, so we tried an offset fed 2.4 m reflector. This offered ample gain, albeit with some difficulties in the aiming of the 3.5° beam. The 22.5° offset meant that the dish appeared to be pointing downwards when it was horizontally aligned.

Several tests were performed using various cantennas and a 12 dBi Yagi as a feed. We pointed the antenna at a base station of the university wireless network that was located 11 km away on a 3500 m mountain. The test site sits at 2000 m and therefore the elevation angle is 8°. Because of the offset feed, we pointed the dish 14° downward, as can be seen in the following picture:

Figure 11.29: 2.4 m offset fed reflector with a 12 dBi antenna at its focus, looking 14° down. The actual elevation is 8° up.

We were able to establish a link with the base station at Aguada, but our efforts to measure the gain of the setup using Netstumbler were not successful. There was too much fluctuation on the received power values of live traffic.

For a meaningful measurement of the gain, we needed a signal generator and spectrum analyzer. These instruments were also required for the field trip in order to align the antennas properly.

While waiting for the required equipment, we looked for an antenna to be used at the other end, and also a pointing system better suited to the narrow radio beam.

In February 2006, I traveled to Trieste to partake in the annual wireless training event that I have been attending since 1996. While there, I mentioned the project to my colleague Carlo Fonda, who was immediately thrilled and eager to participate.

The collaboration between the **Latin American Networking School** (**Es-LaRed**) and the **Abdus Salam International Centre for Theoretical Physics** (**ICTP**) goes back to 1992, when the first Networking School was held in Mérida with ICTP support. Since then, members of both institutions have collaborated in several activities. Some of these include an annual training school on wireless networking (organized by ICTP) and another on computer networks (organized by EsLaRed) that are hosted in several countries throughout Latin America. Accordingly, it was not difficult to persuade Dr. Sandro Radicella, the head of the Aeronomy and Radio Propagation Laboratory at ICTP, to support Carlo Fonda's trip in early April to Venezuela in order to participate in the experiment.

Back at home, I found a 2.75 m parabolic central fed mesh antenna at a neighbors house. Mr. Ismael Santos graciously lent his antenna for the experiment.

Figure 11.30 shows the disassembly of the mesh reflector.

Figure 11.30: Carlo and Ermanno disassembling the satellite dish supplied by Mr. Ismael Santos.

We exchanged the feed for a 2.4 GHz one, and aimed the antenna at a signal generator that was located on top of a ladder some 30 m away. With a spectrum analyzer, we measured the maximum of the signal and located the focus. We also pinpointed the boresight for both the central fed and the offset antennas. This is shown in **Figure 11.31**:

Figure 11.31: Finding the focus of the antennas with the 2.4 GHz feed

We also compared the power of the received signal with the output of a commercial 24 dBi antenna. This showed a difference of 8 dB, which led us to believe that the overall gain of our antenna was about 32 dBi. Of course, there is some uncertainty about this value. We were receiving reflected signals, but the value agreed with the calculation from the antenna dimension.

El Baúl Site Survey

Once we were satisfied with the proper functioning and aim of both antennas, we decided to do a site survey at the other end of the El Baúl link. Carlo Fonda, Gaya Fior and Ermanno Pietrosemoli reached the site on April 8th. The following day, we found a hill (south of the town) with two telecom towers from two cell phone operators and one belonging to the mayor of El Baúl. The hill of Morrocoy is some 75 m above the surrounding area, about 125 m above sea level. It provides an unobstructed view towards El Aguila. There is a dirt road to the top, a must for our purpose, given the weight of the antenna.

Performing the experiment

On Wednesday April 12th, Javier Triviño and Ermanno Pietrosemoli traveled towards Baúl with the offset antenna loaded on top of a four-wheel drive truck. Early the morning of April 13th, we installed the antenna and pointed it at a compass bearing of 276°, given that the declination is 8° and therefore the true Azimuth is 268°.

At the same time, the other team (composed by Carlo Fonda and Gaya Fior from ICTP, with assistance of Franco Bellarosa, Lourdes Pietrosemoli and José Triviño) rode to the previously surveyed area at Pico del Aguila in a Bronco truck that carried the 2.7 m mesh antenna.

Figure 11.32: Pico del Águila and surrounds map with Bronco truck.

Poor weather is common at altitudes of 4100 m above sea level. The Aguila team was able to install and point the mesh antenna before the fog and sleet began. **Figure 11.33** shows the antenna and the rope used for aiming the 3° radio beam.

Power for the signal generator was supplied from the truck by means of a 12 VDC to 120 VAC inverter. At 11 A.M in El Baúl, we were able to observe a -82 dBm signal at the agreed upon 2450 MHz frequency using the spectrum analyzer. To be sure we had found the proper source, we asked Carlo to switch off the signal. Indeed, the trace on the spectrum analyzer showed only noise. This confirmed that we were really seeing the signal that originated some 280 km away.

After turning the signal generator on again, we performed a fine tuning in elevation and azimuth at both ends. Once we were satisfied that we had attained the maximum received signal, Carlo removed the signal generator and replaced it with a Linksys WRT54G wireless router configured as an access point. Javier substituted the spectrum analyzer on our end for another WRT54G configured as a client.

Figure 11.33: Aiming the antenna at el Águila.

At once, we started receiving "beacons" but ping packets did not get through.

This was expected, since the propagation time of the radio wave over a 300 km link is 1 ms. It takes at least 2 ms for an acknowledgment to reach the transmitter.

Fortunately, the OpenWRT firmware allows for adjusting the ACK timing. After Carlo adjusted for the 3 orders of magnitude increase in delay above what the standard Wi-Fi link expects, we began receiving packets with a delay of about 5 ms.

Figure 11.34: El Baúl antenna installation. Actual elevation was 1° upward, since the antenna has an offset of 22.5°.

We proceeded to transfer several PDF files between Carlo's and Javier's laptops. The results are shown in **Figure 11.35**.

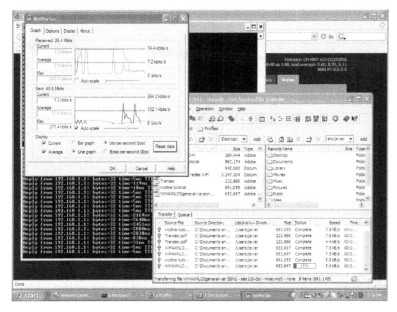

Figure 11.35: Screenshot of Javier's laptop showing details of PDF file transfer from Carlo's laptop 280 km away, using two WRT54G wireless routers, no amplifiers.

Note the ping time of a few milliseconds.

Figure 11.36: Javier Triviño (right) and Ermanno Pietrosemoli beaming from the El Baúl antenna

Figure 11.37: Carlo Fonda at the Aguila Site

Mérida, Venezuela, 17 April 2006.

One year after performing this experiment, we found the time and resources to repeat it. We used commercial 30 dBi antennas, and also a couple of wireless routers which had been modified by the TIER group led by Dr. Eric Brewer of Berkeley University.

The purpose of the modification of the standard WiFi MAC is to make it suitable for long distance applications by replacing the CSMA Media Access Control with TDMA. The latter is better suited for long distance point-to-point links since it does not require the reception of ACKs. This eliminates the need to wait for the 2 ms round trip propagation time on a 300 km path.

On April 28th, 2007, a team formed by Javier Triviño, José Torres and Francisco Torres installed one of the antennas at El Aguila site. The other team, formed by Leonardo González V., Leonardo González G., Alejandro González and Ermanno Pietrosemoli, installed the other antenna at El Baúl.

A solid link was quickly established using the Linksys WRT54G routers. This allowed for video transmission at a measured throughput of 65 kbps. With the TDMA routers, the measured throughput was 3 Mbps in each direction. This produced the total of 6 Mbps as predicted by the simulations done at Berkeley.

Can we do better?

Thrilled by these results, which pave the way for really inexpensive long distance broadband links, the second team moved to another location previously identified at 382 km from El Aguila, in a place called Platillón. Platillón is 1500 m above sea level and there is an unobstructed first Fresnel zone towards El Aguila (located at 4200 m above sea level). The proposed path is shown in **Figure 11.38**:

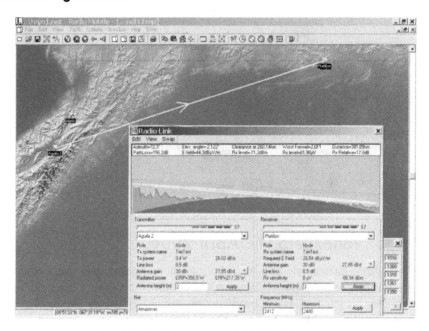

Figure 11.38: Map and profile of the 380 km path.

Again, the link was quickly established with the Linksys and the TIER supplied routers. The Linksys link showed approximately 1% packet loss, with an average round trip time of 12 ms. The TIER equipment showed no packet loss, with propagation times below 1 ms. This allowed for video transmission, but the link was not stable. We noticed considerable signal fluctuations that often interrupted the communication.

However, when the received signal was about -78 dBm, the measured throughput was a total of 6 Mbps bidirectional with the TIER routers implementing TDMA.

Figure 11.39: The team at el Aguila, José Torres (left), Javier Triviño (center) and Francisco Torres (right)

Although further tests must be conducted to ascertain the limits for stable throughput, we are confident that Wi-Fi has a great potential for long distance broadband communication. It is particularly well suited for rural areas were the spectrum is still not crowded and interference is not a problem, provided there is good radio line of sight.

Acknowledgments

We wish to express our gratitude to Mr. Ismael Santos for lending the mesh antenna to be installed at El Aguila and to Eng. Andrés Pietrosemoli for supplying the special scaffolding joints used for the installation and transportation of the antennas.

We'd also like to thank the Abdus Salam International Centre of Theoretical Physics for supporting Carlo Fonda's trip from Italy to Venezuela.

*Figure 11.40: The team at Platillon. From left to right: Leonardo González V.,
Leonardo González G., Ermanno Pietrosemoli and Alejandro González .*

The 2006 experiment was performed by Ermanno Pietrosemoli, Javier
Triviño from EsLaRed, Carlo Fonda, and Gaya Fior from ICTP. With the help
of Franco Bellarosa, Lourdes Pietrosemoli, and José Triviño.

For the 2007 experiments, Dr. Eric Brewer from Berkeley University provided
the wireless routers with the modified MAC for long distance, as well as en-
thusiastic support through his collaborator, Sonesh Surana. RedULA, CPTM,
Dirección de Servicios ULA Universidad de los Andes and Fundacite Mérida
contributed to this trial.

This work was funded by ICA-IDRC.

References

- Fundación Escuela Latinoamericana de Redes, Latin American Networking School, *http://www.eslared.org.ve/*

- Abdus Salam International Centre for Theoretical Physics, *http://wireless.ictp.it/*

- OpenWRT Open Source firmware for Linksys, *http://openwrt.org/*

- Fundacite Mérida, *http://www.funmrd.gov.ve/*

--Ermanno Pietrosemoli

Appendix A: Resources

We recommend these resources for learning more about the various aspects of wireless networking. For more links and resources, see our website at *http://wndw.net/*.

Antennas and antenna design

- Cushcraft technical papers on antenna design and radio propagation, *http://www.cushcraft.com/comm/support/technical-papers.htm*

- Free antenna designs, *http://www.freeantennas.com/*

- Hyperlink Tech, *http://hyperlinktech.com/*

- Pasadena Networks LLC, *http://www.wlanparts.com/*

- SuperPass, *http://www.superpass.com/*

- Unofficial NEC2 code archives, *http://www.nec2.org/*

- Unofficial NEC2 radio modeling tool home page, *http://www.nittany-scientific.com/nec/*

- USB WiFi dish designs, *http://www.usbwifi.orcon.net.nz/*

Network troubleshooting tools

- Bing throughput measurement tool, *http://fgouget.free.fr/bing/index-en.shtml*

- Cacti network monitoring package, *http://www.cacti.net/*

- DSL Reports bandwidth speed tests, *http://www.dslreports.com/stest*

- EaKiu spectrum analysis tool, *http://www.cookwareinc.com/EaKiu/*

- EtherApe network traffic monitor, *http://etherape.sourceforge.net/*

- Flowc open source NetFlow collector, *http://netacad.kiev.ua/flowc/.*

- Iperf network performance testing tool, *http://dast.nlanr.net/Projects/Iperf/*

- iptraf network diagnostic tool, *http://iptraf.seul.org/*

- MRTG network monitoring and graphing tool,
  http://people.ee.ethz.ch/~oetiker/webtools/mrtg/

- My TraceRoute network diagnostic tool, *http://www.bitwizard.nl/mtr/*

- Nagios network monitoring and event notification tool,
  http://www.nagios.org/

- NetFlow, the Cisco protocol for collecting IP traffic information,
  http://en.wikipedia.org/wiki/Netflow

- ngrep network security utility for finding patterns in data flows,
  http://ngrep.sourceforge.net/

- Network monitoring implementation guides and tutorials,
  http://wiki.debian.org/Network_Monitoring

- Ntop network monitoring tool, *http://www.ntop.org/*

- RRDtool round robin database graphing utility,
  http://people.ee.ethz.ch/~oetiker/webtools/rrdtool/

- SmokePing network latency and packet loss monitor,
  http://people.ee.ethz.ch/~oetiker/webtools/smokeping/

- SoftPerfect network analysis tools, *http://www.softperfect.com/*

- Squid transparent http proxy HOWTO,
  http://tldp.org/HOWTO/TransparentProxy.html

- ttcp network performance testing tool, *http://ftp.arl.mil/ftp/pub/ttcp/*

- Wireshark network protocol analyzer, *http://www.wireshark.org/*

Security

- AntiProxy http proxy circumvention tools and information,
  http://www.antiproxy.com/

- Anti-spyware tools, *http://www.spychecker.com/*

- Driftnet network monitoring utility, *http://www.ex-parrot.com/~chris/driftnet/*

- Etherpeg network monitoring utility, *http://www.etherpeg.org/*

- Introduction to OpenVPN, *http://www.linuxjournal.com/article/7949*

- Lavasoft Ad-Aware spyware removal tool, *http://www.lavasoft.de/*

- Linux security and admin software,
  http://www.linux.org/apps/all/Networking/Security_/_Admin.html

- OpenSSH secure shell and tunneling tool, *http://openssh.org/*

- OpenVPN encrypted tunnel setup guide, *http://openvpn.net/howto.html*

- Privoxy filtering web proxy, *http://www.privoxy.org/*
- PuTTY SSH client for Windows, *http://www.putty.nl/*
- Sawmill log analyzer, *http://www.sawmill.net/*
- Security of the WEP algorithm,
  http://www.isaac.cs.berkeley.edu/isaac/wep-faq.html
- Stunnel Universal SSL Wrapper, *http://www.stunnel.org/*
- TOR onion router, *http://www.torproject.org/*
- Weaknesses in the Key Scheduling Algorithm of RC4,
  http://www.crypto.com/papers/others/rc4_ksaproc.ps
- Windows SCP client, *http://winscp.net/*
- Your 802.11 Wireless Network has No Clothes,
  http://www.cs.umd.edu/~waa/wireless.pdf
- ZoneAlarm personal firewall for Windows, *http://www.zonelabs.com/*

Bandwidth optimization

- Cache heirarchies with Squid,
  http://squid-docs.sourceforge.net/latest/html/c2075.html
- dnsmasq caching DNS and DHCP server,
  http://www.thekelleys.org.uk/dnsmasq/doc.html
- Enhancing International World Wide Web Access in Mozambique Through the Use of Mirroring and Caching Proxies,
  http://www.isoc.org/inet97/ans97/cloet.htm
- Fluff file distribution utility, *http://www.bristol.ac.uk/fluff/*
- Linux Advanced Routing and Traffic Control HOWTO, *http://lartc.org/*
- Microsoft Internet Security and Acceleration Server,
  http://www.microsoft.com/isaserver/
- Microsoft ISA Server Firewall and Cache resource site,
  http://www.isaserver.org/
- Optimising Internet Bandwidth in Developing Country Higher Education,
  http://www.inasp.info/pubs/bandwidth/index.html
- Pittsburgh Supercomputing Center's guide to Enabling High Performance Data Transfers, *http://www.psc.edu/networking/perf_tune.html*
- Planet Malaysia blog on bandwidth management,
  http://planetmy.com/blog/?p=148

- RFC 3135: Performance Enhancing Proxies Intended to Mitigate Link-Related Degradations, *http://www.ietf.org/rfc/rfc3135*
- Squid web proxy cache, *http://squid-cache.org/*

Mesh networking

- Champaign-Urbana Community Wireless Network software, *http://cuwireless.net/download*
- Freifunk OLSR mesh firmware for the Linksys WRT54G, *http://www.freifunk.net/wiki/FreifunkFirmware*
- MIT Roofnet Project, *http://pdos.csail.mit.edu/roofnet/doku.php*
- OLSR mesh networking daemon, *http://www.olsr.org/*
- Real-time OLSR topology viewer, *http://meshcube.org/nylon/utils/olsr-topology-view.pl*
- AirJialdi Mesh Router, *http://drupal.airjaldi.com/node/9*

Wireless operating systems and drivers

- DD-WRT wireless router OS, *http://www.dd-wrt.com/*
- HostAP wireless driver for the Prism 2.5 chipset, *http://hostap.epitest.fi/*
- m0n0wall wireless router OS, *http://m0n0.ch/wall/*
- MadWiFi wireless driver for the Atheros chipset, *http://madwifi.org/*
- Metrix Pyramid wireless router OS, *http://pyramid.metrix.net/*
- OpenWRT wireless router OS for Linksys access points, *http://openwrt.org/*
- Tomato wireless router OS for Linksys access points, *http://www.polarcloud.com/tomato*

Wireless tools

- Chillispot captive portal, *http://www.chillispot.info/*
- Interactive Wireless Network Design Analysis Utilities, *http://www.qsl.net/n9zia/wireless/page09.html*
- KisMAC wireless monitor for Mac OS X, *http://kismac.macpirate.ch/*
- Kismet wireless network monitoring tool, *http://www.kismetwireless.net/*
- MacStumbler wireless network detection tool for Mac OS X, *http://www.macstumbler.com/*

- NetStumbler wireless network detection tool for Windows and Pocket PC, *http://www.netstumbler.com/*

- NoCatSplash captive portal, *http://nocat.net/download/NoCatSplash/*

- PHPMyPrePaid prepaid ticketing system, *http://sourceforge.net/projects/phpmyprepaid/*

- RadioMobile radio performance modeling tool, *http://www.cplus.org/rmw/*

- Terabeam wireless link calculation tools, *http://www.terabeam.com/support/calculations/index.php*

- Wellenreiter wireless network detection tool for Linux, *http://www.wellenreiter.net/*

- WiFiDog captive portal, *http://www.wifidog.org/*

- Wireless Network Link Analysis tool by GBPRR, *http://my.athenet.net/~multiplx/cgi-bin/wireless.main.cgi*

General wireless related information

- DefCon long distance WiFi shootout, *http://www.wifi-shootout.com/*

- Homebrew wireless hardware designs, *http://www.w1ghz.org/*

- Linksys wireless access point information*, http://linksysinfo.org/*

- Linksys WRT54G resource guide, http://seattlewireless.net/index.cgi/LinksysWrt54g

- NoCat community wireless group, *http://nocat.net/*

- Ronja optical data link hardware, *http://ronja.twibright.com/*

- SeattleWireless community wireless group, *http://seattlewireless.net/*

- SeattleWireless Hardware comparison page, *http://www.seattlewireless.net/HardwareComparison*

- Stephen Foskett's Power Over Ethernet (PoE) Calculator, *http://www.gweep.net/~sfoskett/tech/poecalc.html*

Networking services

- Access Kenya ISP, *http://www.accesskenya.com/*

- Broadband Access Ltd. wireless broadband carrier, *http://www.blue.co.ke/*

- Virtual IT outsourcing, http://www.virtualit.biz/

- wire.less.dk consultancy and services, *http://wire.less.dk/*

Training and education

- Association for Progressive Communications wireless connectivity projects, *http://www.apc.org/wireless/*
- International Network for the Availability of Scientific Publications, *http://www.inasp.info/*
- Makere University, Uganda, *http://www.makerere.ac.ug/*
- Radio Communications Unit of the Abdus Salam International Center for Theoretical Physics, *http://wireless.ictp.trieste.it/*
- World Summits on Free Information Infrastructures, *http://www.wsfii.org/*

Miscellaneous links

- Cygwin Linux-like environment for Windows, *http://www.cygwin.com/*
- Graphvis graph visualization tool, *http://www.graphviz.org/*
- ICTP bandwidth simulator, *http://wireless.ictp.trieste.it/simulator/*
- ImageMagick image manipulation tools and libraries, *http://www.imagemagick.org/*
- NodeDB war driving map database, *http://www.nodedb.com/*
- Open Relay DataBase, *http://www.ordb.org/*
- Partition Image disk utility for Linux, *http://www.partimage.org/*
- RFC 1918: Address Allocation for Private Internets, *http://www.ietf.org/rfc/rfc1918*
- Rusty Russell's Linux Networking Concepts, *http://www.netfilter.org/documentation/HOWTO/ networking-concepts-HOWTO.html*
- Ubuntu Linux, *http://www.ubuntu.com/*
- VoIP-4D Primer, *http://www.it46.se/voip4d/voip4d.php*
- wget web utility for Windows, *http://xoomer.virgilio.it/hherold/*
- WiFiMaps war driving map database, *http://www.wifimaps.com/*
- WiSpy spectrum analysis tool, *http://www.metageek.net/*

Books

- *802.11 Networks: The Definitive Guide, 2nd Edition*. Matthew Gast, O'Reilly Media. ISBN #0-596-10052-3

- *802.11 Wireless Network Site Surveying and Installation.* Bruce Alexander, Cisco Press. ISBN #1-587-05164-8

- The *ARRL Antenna Book, 20th Edition.* R. Dean Straw (Editor), American Radio Relay League. ISBN #0-87259-904-3

- The *ARRL UHF/Microwave Experimenter's Manual*. American Radio Relay League. ISBN #0-87259-312-6

- *Building Wireless Community Networks, 2nd Edition*. Rob Flickenger, O'Reilly Media. ISBN #0-596-00502-4

- *How To Accelerate Your Internet,* A free book about bandwidth optimization. *http://bwmo.net/.* ISBN #978-0-9778093-1-8

- *Deploying License-Free Wireless Wide-Area Networks.* Jack Unger, Cisco Press. ISBN #1-587-05069-2

- TCP/IP Illustrated, Volume 1. W. Richard Stevens, Addison-Wesley. ISBN #0-201-63346-9

- *Wireless Hacks, 2nd Edition*. Rob Flickenger and Roger Weeks, O'Reilly Media. ISBN #0-596-10144-9

Appendix B: Channel Allocations

The following tables list the channel numbers and center frequencies used for 802.11a and 802.11b/g. Note that while all of these frequencies are in the unlicensed ISM and U-NII bands, not all channels are available in all countries. Many regions impose restrictions on output power and indoor / outdoor use on some channels. These regulations are rapidly changing, so always check your local regulations before transmitting.

Note that these tables show the center frequency for each channel. Channels are 22MHz wide in 802.11b/g, and 20MHz wide in 802.11a.

802.11b / g			
Channel #	Center Frequency (GHz)	Channel #	Center Frequency (GHz)
1	2.412	8	2.447
2	2.417	9	2.452
3	2.422	10	2.457
4	2.427	11	2.462
5	2.432	12	2.467
6	2.437	13	2.472
7	2.442	14	2.484

802.11a	
Channel #	Center Frequency (GHz)
34	5.170
36	5.180
38	5.190
40	5.200
42	5.210
44	5.220
46	5.230
48	5.240
52	5.260
56	5.280
60	5.300
64	5.320
149	5.745
153	5.765
157	5.785
161	5.805

Appendix C: Path Loss

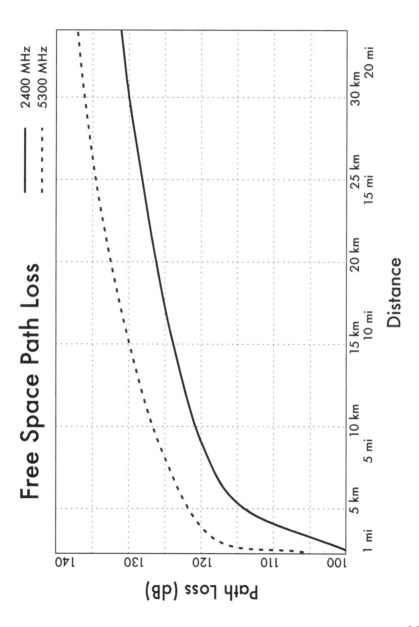

Appendix D: Cable Sizes

Wire gauge, diameter, current capacity, and resistance at 20°C. These values can vary from cable to cable. When in doubt, consult the manufacturer's specifications.

AWG Gauge	Diameter (mm)	Ohms / Meter	Max Amperes
0000	11.68	0.000161	302
000	10.40	0.000203	239
00	9.27	0.000256	190
0	8.25	0.000322	150
1	7.35	0.000406	119
2	6.54	0.000513	94
3	5.83	0.000646	75
4	5.19	0.000815	60
5	4.62	0.001028	47
6	4.11	0.001296	37
7	3.67	0.001634	30
8	3.26	0.002060	24
9	2.91	0.002598	19
10	2.59	0.003276	15

Appendix E: Solar Dimensioning

Use these tables to collect the necessary data to estimate the required size of your solar energy system.

General Data

Site Name	
Site Latitude (°)	

Irradiation Data

$G_{dm}(0)$, in kWh / m² per day)

Jan	Feb	Mar	Apr	May	Jun	Jul	Aug	Sep	Oct	Nov	Dec
Worst Irradiation Month											

Reliability and System Operational Voltage

Days of Autonomy (N)	
Nominal Voltage (V_{NEquip})	

Component Characteristics

Solar Panels	
Voltage @ Maximum Power (V_{pmax})	
Current @ Maximum Power (I_{pmax})	
Panel Type/Model and Power (W_p)	

Batteries	
Nominal Capacity @ 100 H (C_{NBat})	
Nominal Voltage (V_{NBat})	
Maximum Depth of Discharge (DoD_{MAX}) or Usable Capacity (C_{UBat})	

Regulator	
Nominal Voltage (V_{NReg})	
Maximum Current (I_{maxReg})	

DC/AC Inverter (if needed)	
Nominal Voltage (V_{NConv})	
Instantaneous Power (P_{IConv})	
Performance @ 70% Load	

Loads

Estimated Energy Consumed by the Loads (DC)				
Month of Greatest Consumption				
Description	# of Units	x Nominal Power	x Usage Hours / Day	= Energy (Wh/day)
E_{TOTAL} DC				

Estimated Energy Consumed by the Loads (AC)				
Month of Greatest Consumption				
Description	# of Units	x Nominal Power	x Usage Hours / Day	= Energy (Wh/day)
E_{TOTAL} AC (before converter)				
E_{TOTAL} AC (after converter) = E_{TOTAL} AC / 70%				

Finding the Worst Month

		J	F	M	A	M	J	J	A	S	O	N	D
Site Name													
Site Latitude (°)													
Nominal Voltage of the Installation V_N													
(Month)		J	F	M	A	M	J	J	A	S	O	N	D
Inclination ß													
G_{dm} (ß) (kWh/m^2 × day)													
E_{TOTAL} (DC) (Wh/day)													
E_{TOTAL} (AC) (Wh/day)													
E_{TOTAL} (AC + DC)=													
I_m (A) = E_{TOTAL} (Wh/day) × 1kW/m^2/ (G_{dm}(ß) × V_N)													

Worst Month Summary	
Worst Month	
I_m (A)	
I_{mMAX} (A) = 1.21 × I_m	
E_{TOTAL} (AC + DC)	

Final Calculations

Panels		
Panels in Series (N_{PS})	$N_{PS} = V_N / V_{Pmax} =$	
Panels in Parallel (N_{PP})	$N_{PP} = I_{mMAX} / I_{Pmax} =$	
Total Number of Panels	$N_{TOT} = N_{PS} \times N_{PP} =$	

Batteries		
Necessary Capacity (C_{NEC})	E_{TOTAL}(WORST MONTH) / $V_N \times N$	
Nominal Capacity (C_{NOM})	C_{NEC} / DoD_{MAX}	
Number of Batteries in Series (N_{BS})	V_N / V_{NBAT}	

Cables			
	Panels > Batteries	Batteries > Converter	Main Line
Voltage Drop ($V_a - V_b$)			
Thickness (Section) $r \times L \times I_{mMAX} / (V_a - V_b)$			

For cable thickness computation, $r = 0.01286\ \Omega$ mm^2/m (for copper) and L is the length in meters.

Glossary

0 - 9

802.11. While 802.11 is a wireless protocol in its own right, 802.11 is often used to refer to a family of wireless networking protocols used mainly for local area networking. Three popular variants include 802.11b, 802.11g, and 802.11a. See also: ***Wi-Fi.***

A

AC see ***Alternating Current***

access point (AP). A device that creates a wireless network that is usually connected to a wired Ethernet network. See also: ***CPE, master mode***

accumulator. Another name for a ***battery***.

ad-hoc mode. A radio mode used by 802.11 devices that allows the creation of a network without an access point. Mesh networks often use radios in ad-hoc mode. See also: ***managed mode, master mode, monitor mode***

Address Resolution Protocol (ARP). A protocol widely used on Ethernet networks to translate IP addresses into MAC addresses.

address space. A group of IP addresses that all reside within the same logical subnet.

advertised window. The portion of a TCP header that specifies how many additional bytes of data the receiver is prepared to accept.

Alternating Current (AC). An electrical current which varies over time in a cyclic manner. AC current is typically used for lighting and appliances. See also: ***Direct Current***

amortization. An accounting technique used to manage the expected cost of replacement and obsolescence of equipment over time.

amplifier. A device used to increase the transmitted power of a wireless device.

amplitude. The distance from the center of a wave to the extreme of one of its peaks.

anchor clients. Business clients of a subscription system who are reliable and can be considered low-risk.

AND logic. A logical operation that only evaluates as true if all of the items being compared also evaluate as true. See also: **OR logic**.

anonymizing proxy. A network service that hides the source or destination of communications. Anonymizing proxies can be used to protect people's privacy and to reduce an organization's exposure to legal liability for the actions of its users.

anonymity. In computer networks, communications that cannot be linked to a unique individual are said to be anonymous. The trade-off of anonymity versus accountability in communications is an ongoing debate online, and rules about anonymous communications vary widely around the world. See also: **authenticated**

antenna diversity. A technique used to overcome multipath interference by using two or more physically separated receiving antennas.

antenna gain. The amount of power concentrated in the direction of strongest radiation of an antenna, usually expressed in dBi. Antenna gain is reciprocal, which means that the effect of gain is present when transmitting as well as receiving.

antenna pattern. A graph that describes the relative strength of a radiated field in various directions from an antenna. See also: **rectangular plot, polar plot, linear polar**

coordinates, logarithmic polar coordinates

AP see **Access Point**

application layer. The topmost layer in the OSI and TCP/IP network models.

Argus see **Audit Record Generation and Utilization System**

ARP see **Address Resolution Protocol**

associated. An 802.11 radio is associated to an access point when it is ready to communicate with the network. This means that it is tuned to the proper channel, in range of the AP, using the correct SSID and other authentication parameters, etc.

at. A Unix facility that allows timed, one-shot execution of programs. See also: **cron**

attenuation. The reduction of available radio power as it is absorbed along a path, such as through trees, walls, buildings, or other objects. See also: **free space loss, scattering**

Audit Record Generation and Utilization System (Argus). An open source network monitoring tool used for tracking flows between hosts. Argus is available from *http://www.qosient.com/argus* .

authenticated. A network user that has proven their identity to a service or device (such as an access point) beyond a shadow of a doubt, usually by some means of cryptography. See also: **anonymity**

azimuth. The angle that measures deviation with respect to the south in the northern hemisphere, and with respect to the north in the southern hemisphere. See also: *inclination*

B

bandwidth. A measure of frequency ranges, typically used for digital communications. The word bandwidth is also commonly used interchangeably with *capacity* to refer to the theoretical maximum data rate of a digital communications line. See also: *capacity, channel, throughput*

battery. A device used to store energy in a photovoltaic system. See also: *solar panel, regulator, load, converter, inverter*

beamwidth. The angular distance between the points on either side of the main lobe of an antenna, where the received power is half that of the main lobe. The beamwidth of an antenna is usually stated for both the horizontal and vertical planes.

benchmarking. Testing the maximum performance of a service or device. Benchmarking a network connection typically involves flooding the link with traffic and measuring the actual observed throughput, both on transmit and receive.

BGAN see *Broadband Global Access Network*

BNC connector. A coaxial cable connector that uses a "quick-connect" style bayonet lug. BNC connectors are typically found on 10base2 coaxial Ethernet.

bridge. A network device that connects two networks together at the *data link layer*. Bridges do not route packets at the *network layer*. They simply repeat packets between two *link-local* networks. See also: *router* and *transparent bridging firewall*.

bridge-utils. A Linux software package that is required for creating 802.1d Ethernet bridges. *http://bridge.sourceforge.net/*

Broadband Global Access Network (BGAN). One of several standards used for satellite Internet access. See also: *Digital Video Broadcast (DVB-S)* and *Very Small Aperture Terminal (VSAT)*.

broadcast address. On IP networks, the broadcast IP address is used to send data to all hosts in the local subnet. On Ethernet networks, the broadcast MAC address is used to send data to all machines in the same collision domain.

bypass diodes. A feature found on some solar panels that prevents the formation of *hot-spots* on shaded cells, but reduces the maximum voltage of the panel.

C

CA see *Certificate Authority*

Cacti (*http://www.cacti.net/*). A popular web-based monitoring tool written in PHP.

capacity. The theoretical maximum amount of traffic provided by a digital communications line. Often used interchangeably with *bandwidth*.

captive portal. A mechanism used to transparently redirect web browsers to a new location. Captive portals are often used for authentication or for interrupting a user's online session (for example, to display an Acceptable Use Policy).

cell. Solar panels are made up of several individual cells, which are electrically connected to provide a particular value of current and voltage. Batteries are also made up of individual cells connected in series, each of which contributes about 2 volts to the battery.

Certificate Authority. A trusted entity that issues signed cryptographic keys. See also: *Public Key Infrastructure, SSL*

channel capacity. The maximum amount of information that can be sent using a given bandwidth. See also: *bandwidth, throughput, data rate*

channel. A well defined range of frequencies used for communications. 802.11 channels use 22 MHz of bandwidth, but are only separated by 5 MHz. See also: *Appendix B.*

CIDR see *Classless Inter-Domain Routing*

CIDR notation. A method used to define a network mask by specifying the number of bits present. For example, the netmask 255.255.255.0 can be specified as /24 in CIDR notation.

circular polarization. An electromagnetic field where the electric field vector appears to be rotating with circular motion about the direction of propagation, making one full turn for each RF cycle. See also: *horizontal polarization, vertical polarization*

Class A, B, and C networks. For some time, IP address space was allocated in blocks of three different sizes. These were Class A (about 16 million addresses), Class B (about 65 thousand addresses), and Class C (255 addresses). While CIDR has replaced class-based allocation, these classes are often still referred to and used internally in organizations using private address space. See also: *CIDR notation*.

Classless Inter-Domain Routing. CIDR was developed to improve routing efficiency on the Internet backbone by enabling route aggregation and network masks of arbitrary size. CIDR replaces the old class-based addressing scheme. See also: *Class A, B, and C networks*.

client. An 802.11 radio card in *managed mode*. Wireless clients will join a network created by an access point, and automatically change the channel to match it. See also: *access point, mesh*

closed network. An access point that does not broadcast its SSID, often used as a security measure.

coax. A round (coaxial) cable with a center wire surrounded by a dielectric, outer conductor, and tough insulating jacket. Antenna cables are usually made of coax. Coax is short for "of common axis".

collision. On an Ethernet network, a collision occurs when two devices connected to the same physical segment attempt to transmit at the same time. When collisions are detected, devices delay retransmission for a brief, randomly selected period.

conductor. A material that easily allows electric or thermal energy to flow through without much resistance. See also: *dielectric, insulator*

connectionless protocol. A network protocol (such as UDP) that requires no session initiation or maintenance. Connectionless protocols typically require less overhead than session oriented protocols, but do not usually offer data protection or packet reassembly. See also: *session oriented protocol*.

consistent platform. Maintenance costs can be reduced by using a consistent platform, with the same hardware, software, and firmware for many components in a network.

constructive interference. When two identical waves merge and are in phase, the amplitude of the resulting wave is twice that of either of the components. This is called constructive interference. See also: *destructive interference*

controls. In *NEC2*, controls define the RF source in an antenna model. See also: *structure*

converter. A device used to convert DC signals into a different DC or AC voltage. See also: *inverter*

CPE see *Customer Premises Equipment*

cron. A Unix facility that allows timed and repeated execution of programs. See also: *at*

Customer Premises Equipment. Network equipment (such as a *router* or *bridge*) that is installed at a customer's location.

D

data link layer. The second layer in both the OSI and TCP/IP network models. Communications at this layer happen directly between nodes. On Ethernet networks, this is also sometimes called the MAC layer.

data rate. The speed at which 802.11 radios exchange symbols, which is always higher than the available throughput. For example, the nominal data rate of 802.11g is 54 Mbps, while the maximum throughput is about 20 Mbps). See also: *throughput*

dB see *decibel*

DC see *Direct Current*

DC/AC Converter. A device that converts DC power into AC power, suitable for use with many appliances. Also known as an *inverter*.

DC/DC Converter. A device that changes the voltage of a DC power source. See also: ***linear conversion, switching conversion***

decibel (dB). A logarithmic unit of measurement that expresses the magnitude of power relative to a reference level. Commonly used units are dBi (decibels relative to an isotropic radiator) and dBm (decibels relative to a milliwatt).

default gateway. When a router receives a packet destined for a network for which it has no explicit route, the packet is forwarded to the default gateway. The default gateway then repeats the process, possibly sending the packet to its own default gateway, until the packet reaches its ultimate destination.

default route. A network route that points to the default gateway.

Denial of Service (DoS). An attack on network resources, usually achieved by flooding a network with traffic or exploiting a bug in an application or network protocol.

depreciation. An accounting method used to save money to cover the eventual break down of equipment.

destructive interference. When two identical waves merge and are exactly out of phase, the amplitude of the resulting wave is zero. This is called destructive interference. See also: ***constructive interference***

DHCP see ***Dynamic Host Configuration Protocol***

dielectric. A non-conductive material that separates conducting wires inside a cable.

Digital Elevation Map (DEM). Data that represents the height of terrain for a given geographic area. These maps are used by programs such as ***Radio Mobile*** to model electromagnetic propagation.

Digital Video Broadcast (DVB-S). One of several standards used for satellite Internet access. See also: ***Broadband Global Access Network (BGAN)*** and ***Very Small Aperture Terminal (VSAT)***.

dipole antenna. The simplest form of ***omnidirectional antenna***.

Direct Current (DC). An electrical current which remains constant over time. DC current is typically used for network equipment, such as access points and routers. See also: ***Alternating Current***

Direct Sequence Spread Spectrum (DSSS). The radio modulation scheme used by 802.11b.

directional antenna. An antenna that radiates very strongly in a particular direction. Examples of directional antennas include the yagi, dish, and waveguide antennas. See also: ***omnidirectional antenna, sectorial antenna***

directivity. The ability of an antenna to focus energy in a particular direction when transmitting, or to receive energy from a particular direction when receiving.

diversity see **antenna diversity**

DNS see **Domain Name Service**

DNS caching. By installing a DNS server on your local LAN, DNS requests for an entire network may be cached locally, improving response times. This technique is called DNS caching.

dnsmasq. An open source caching DNS and DHCP server, available from *http://thekelleys.org.uk/*

Domain Name Service (DNS). The widely used network protocol that maps IP addresses to names.

dominant mode. The lowest frequency that can be transmitted by a waveguide of a given size.

DoS see **Denial of Service**

DSSS see **Direct Sequence Spread Spectrum**

DVB-S see **Digital Video Broadcast.**

Dynamic Host Configuration Protocol (DHCP). A protocol used by hosts to automatically determine their IP address.

E

eavesdropper. Someone who intercepts network data such as passwords, email, voice data, or online chat.

edge. The place where one organization's network meets another. Edges are defined by the location of the external **router**, which often acts as a **firewall**.

electromagnetic spectrum. The very wide range of possible frequencies of electromagnetic energy. Parts of the electromagnetic spectrum include radio, microwave, visible light, and X rays.

electromagnetic wave. A wave that propagates through space without the need for a propagating medium. It contains an electric and a magnetic component. See also: **mechanical wave**

elevation see **inclination**

end span injectors. An 802.3af **Power over Ethernet** device that provides power via the Ethernet cable. An Ethernet switch that provides power on each port is an example of an end span injector. See also: **mid span injectors**

end-to-end encryption. An encrypted connection negotiated by both ends of a communications session. End-to-end encryption can provide stronger protection than **link layer encryption** when used on untrusted networks (such as the Internet).

EtherApe. An open source network visualization tool. Available at *http://etherape.sourceforge.net/*

Ethereal see **Wireshark**.

Extended Service Set Identifier (ESSID). The name used to identify an 802.11 network. See also: **closed network**

external traffic. Network traffic that originates from, or is destined for, an IP address outside your internal network, such as Internet traffic.

F

firestarter. A graphical front-end for configuring Linux firewalls available from *http://www.fs-security.com/*.

filter. The default table used in the Linux netfilter firewall system is the filter table. This table is used for determining traffic that should be accepted or denied.

firewall. A router that accepts or denies traffic based on some criteria. Firewalls are one basic tool used to protect entire networks from undesirable traffic.

flush. To remove all entries in a routing table or netfilter chain.

forwarding. When routers receive packets that are destined for a different host or network, they send the packet to the next router closest to its ultimate destination. This process is called forwarding.

forwarding loops. A routing misconfiguration where packets are forwarded cyclically between two or more routers. Catastrophic network failure is prevented by using the TTL value on every packet, but forward-

ing loops need to be resolved for proper network operations.

free space loss. Power diminished by geometric spreading of the wavefront, as the wave propagates through space. See also: **attenuation, free space loss, Appendix C**

frequency. The number of whole waves that pass a fixed point in a period of time. See also: **wavelength, Hertz**

front-to-back ratio. The ratio of the maximum **directivity** of an antenna to its directivity in the opposite direction.

full duplex. Communications equipment that can send and receive at the same time (such as a telephone). See also: **half duplex**

fwbuilder. A graphical tool that lets you create **iptables** scripts on a machine separate from your server, and then transfer them to the server later. *http://www.fwbuilder.org/*

G

gain. The ability of a radio component (such as an antenna or amplifier) to increase the power of a signal. See also: **decibel**

gain transfer. Comparing an antenna under test against a known standard antenna, which has a calibrated gain.

gasification. The production bubbles of oxygen and hydrogen that occurs when a battery is **overcharged**.

globally routable. An address issued by an ISP or RIR that is reachable from any point on the Internet. In IPv4, there are approximately four billion possible IP addresses, although not all of these are globally routable.

H

half duplex. Communications equipment that can send or receive, but never both at once (such as a handheld radio). See also: **full duplex**.

Heliax. High quality coaxial cable that has a solid or tubular center conductor with a corrugated solid outer conductor which enables it to flex. See also: **coax**

Hertz (Hz). A measure of **frequency**, denoting some number of cycles per second.

HF (**High-Frequency**). Radio waves from 3 to 30 MHz are referred to as HF. Data networks can be built on HF that operate at very long range, but with very low data capacity.

hop. Data that crosses one network connection. A web server may be several hops away from your local computer, as packets are forwarded from router to router, eventually reaching their ultimate destination.

horizontal polarization. An electromagnetic field with the electric component moving in a linear horizontal direction. See also: **circular polarization, vertical polarization**

hot-spot. In wireless networks, a hot-spot is a location that provides Internet access via **Wi-Fi**, typically by use of a **captive portal**. In **photovoltaic systems**, a hot-spot occurs when a single **cell** in a **solar panel** is shaded, causing it to act as a resistive load rather than to generate power.

hub. An Ethernet networking device that repeats received data on all connected ports. See also: **switch**.

Huygens principle. A wave model that proposes an infinite number of potential wavefronts along every point of an advancing wavefront.

Hz see **Hertz**

I

IANA see **Internet Assigned Numbers Authority**

ICMP see **Internet Control Message Protocol**

ICP see **Inter-Cache Protocol**

impedance. The quotient of voltage over current of a transmission line, consisting of a resistance and a reactance. The load impedance must match the source impedance for maximum power transfer (50Ω for most communications equipment).

inbound traffic. Network packets that originate from outside the local network (typically the Internet) and are bound for a destination inside the local network. See also: *outbound traffic*.

inclination. The angle that marks deviation from a horizontal plane. See also: *azimuth*

infrastructure mode see *master mode*

insulator see *dielectric*

Inter-Cache Protocol (ICP). A high performance protocol used to communicate between web caches.

Internet Assigned Numbers Authority (IANA). The organization that administers various critical parts of Internet infrastructure, including IP address allocation, DNS root name servers, and protocol service numbers.

Internet Control Message Protocol (ICMP). A Network Layer protocol used to inform nodes about the state of the network. ICMP is part of the Internet protocol suite. See also: *Internet protocol suite*.

Internet layer see *network layer*

Internet Protocol (IP). The most common network layer protocol in use. IP defines the hosts and networks that make up the global Internet.

Internet protocol suite (TCP/IP). The family of communication protocols that make up the Internet. Some of these protocols include TCP, IP, ICMP, and UDP. Also called the *TCP/IP protocol suite*, or simply *TCP/IP*.

Intrusion Detection System (IDS). A program that watches network traffic, looking for suspicious data or behavior patterns. An IDS may make a log entry, notify a network administrator, or take direct action in response to undesirable traffic.

inverter see *DC/AC Converter*

IP see *Internet Protocol*

iproute2. The advanced routing tools package for Linux, used for traffic shaping and other advanced techniques. Available from *http://linux-net.osdl.org/*

iptables. The primary command used to manipulate netfilter firewall rules.

irradiance. The total amount of solar energy that lights a given area, in W/m^2

ISM band. ISM is short for Industrial, Scientific, and Medical. The ISM band is a set of radio frequencies set aside by the ITU for unlicensed use.

isotropic antenna. A hypothetical antenna that evenly distributes power in all directions, approximated by a dipole.

IV characteristic curve. A graph that represents the current that is provided based on the voltage generated for a certain solar radiation.

K

knetfilter. A graphical front-end for configuring Linux firewalls. Available from *http://venom.oltrelinux.com/*

known good. In troubleshooting, a known good is any component that can be substituted to verify that its counterpart is in good, working condition.

L

lag. Common term used to describe a network with high ***latency***.

lambda (λ) see ***wavelength***

LAN see ***Local Area Network***

latency. The amount of time it takes for a packet to cross a network connection. It is often (incorrectly) used interchangeably with Round Trip Time (RTT), since measuring the RTT of a wide-area connection is trivial compared to measuring the actual latency. See also: ***Round Trip Time***.

lead-acid batteries. Batteries consisting of two submerged lead electrodes in an electrolytic solution of water and sulfuric acid. See also: ***stationary batteries***

lease time. In DHCP, IP addresses are assigned for a limited period of time, known as the lease time. After this time period expires, clients must request a new IP address from the DHCP server.

Line of Sight (LOS). If a person standing at point A has an unobstructed view of point B, then point A is said to have a clear Line of Sight to point B.

linear polar coordinates. A graph system with equally spaced, graduated concentric circles representing an absolute value on a polar projection. Such graphs are typically used to represent antenna radiation patterns. See also: ***logarithmic polar coordinates***

linear conversion. A DC voltage conversion method that lowers the voltage by converting excess energy to heat. See also: ***switching conversion***

linear polarization. An ***electromagnetic wave*** where the electric field vector stays in the same plane all the time. The electric field may leave the antenna in a vertical orientation, a horizontal orientation, or at some angle between the two. See also: ***vertical polarization, horizontal polarization***

link budget. The amount of radio energy available to overcome path losses. If the available link budget exceeds the path loss, minimum receive sensitivity of the receiving radio, and any obstacles, then communications should be possible.

link layer encryption. An encrypted connection between ***link-local*** devices, typically a wireless ***client*** and an ***access point***. See also: ***end-to-end encryption***

link-local. Network devices that are connected to the same physical segment communicate with each other directly are said to be link-local. A link-local connection cannot cross a router boundary without using some kind of encapsulation, such as a *tunnel* or a *VPN*.

listen. Programs that accept connections on a TCP port are said to listen on that port.

load. Equipment in a photovoltaic system that consumes energy. See also: *battery, solar panel, regulator, converter, inverter*

Local Area Network (LAN). A network (typically Ethernet) used within an organization. The part of a network that exists just behind an ISP's router is generally considered to be part of the LAN. See also: *WAN*.

logarithmic polar coordinates. A graph system with logarithmically spaced, graduated concentric circles representing an absolute value on a polar projection. Such graphs are typically used to represent antenna radiation patterns. See also: *linear polar coordinates*

long fat pipe network. A network connection (such as VSAT) that has high capacity and high latency. In order to achieve the best possible performance, TCP/IP must be tuned to match the traffic on such links.

LOS see *Line of Sight*

M

MAC layer see *data link layer*

MAC address. A unique 48 bit number assigned to every networking device when it is manufactured. The MAC address is used for link-local communications.

MAC filtering. An access control method based on the MAC address of communicating devices.

MAC table. A network switch must keep track of the MAC addresses used on each physical port, in order to efficiently distribute packets. This information is kept in a table called the MAC table.

maintenance-free lead-acid batteries see *lead-acid batteries*

Man-In-The-Middle (MITM). A network attack where a malicious user intercepts all communications between a client and a server, allowing information to be copied or manipulated.

managed hardware. Networking hardware that provides an administrative interface, port counters, SNMP, or other interactive features is said to be managed.

managed mode. A radio mode used by 802.11 devices that allows the radio to join a network created by an access point. See also: *master mode, ad-hoc mode, monitor mode*

master browser. On Windows networks, the master browser is the computer that keeps a list of all the computers, shares and printers that are available in **Network Neighborhood** or **My Network Places**.

master mode. A radio mode used by 802.11 devices that allows the radio to create networks just as an access point does. See also: *managed mode, ad-hoc mode, monitor mode*

match condition. In netfilter, a match condition specifies the criteria that determine the ultimate target for a given packet. Packets may be matched on MAC address, source or destination IP address, port number, data contents, or just about any other property.

Maximum Depth of Discharge (DoD$_{max}$). The amount of energy extracted from a battery in a single discharge cycle, expressed as a percentage.

Maximum Power Point (P$_{max}$). The point where the power supplied by a solar panel is at maximum.

MC-Card. A very small microwave connector found on Lucent / Orinoco / Avaya equipment.

mechanical wave. A wave caused when some medium or object is swinging in a periodic manner. See also: *electromagnetic wave*

Media Access Control layer see *data link layer*

mesh. A network with no hierarchical organization, where every node on the network carries the traffic of every other as needed. Good mesh network implementations are self-healing, which means that they automatically detect routing problems and fix them as needed.

message types. Rather that port numbers, ICMP traffic uses message types to define the type of information being sent. See also: *ICMP*.

method of the worst month. A method for calculating the dimensions of a standalone photovoltaic system so it will work in the month in which the demand for energy is greatest with respect to the available solar energy. It is the worst month of the year, as this month with have the largest ratio of demanded energy to available energy.

MHF see *U.FL*

microfinance. The provision of small loans, savings and other basic financial services to the world's poorest people.

mid span injectors. A *Power over Ethernet* device inserted between an Ethernet switch and the device to be powered. See also: *end span injectors*

milliwatts (mW). A unit of power representing one thousandth of a Watt.

MITM see *Man-In-The-Middle*

MMCX. A very small microwave connector commonly found on equipment manufactured by Senao and Cisco.

monitor mode. A radio mode used by 802.11 devices not normally used for communications that allows the radio passively monitor radio traffic. See also: **master mode, managed mode, ad-hoc mode**

monitor port. On a managed switch, one or more monitor ports may be defined that receive traffic sent to all of the other ports. This allows you to connect a traffic monitor server to the port to observe and analyze traffic patterns.

Multi Router Traffic Grapher (MRTG). An open source tool used for graphing traffic statistics. Available from *http://oss.oetiker.ch/mrtg/*

multipath. The phenomenon of reflections of a signal reaching their target along different paths, and therefore at different times.

multipoint-to-multipoint see **mesh**

mW see **milliwatt**

My TraceRoute (mtr). A network diagnostic tool used as an alternative to the traditional traceroute program. *http://www.bitwizard.nl/mtr/*. See also: **traceroute / tracert**.

N

N connector. A sturdy microwave connector commonly found on out-door networking components, such as antennas and outdoor access points.

Nagios (*http://nagios.org/*) A real-time monitoring tool that logs and notifies a system administrator about service and network outages.

NAT see **Network Address Translation**

nat. The table used in the Linux netfilter firewall system to configure Network Address Translation.

NEC2 see **Numerical Electromagnetics Code**

NetBIOS. A session layer protocol used by Windows networking for file and printer sharing. See also: **SMB**.

netfilter. The packet filtering framework in modern Linux kernels is known as netfilter. It uses the iptables command to manipulate filter rules. *http://netfilter.org/*

netmask (**network mask**). A netmask is a 32-bit number that divides the 16 million available IP addresses into smaller chunks, called subnets. All IP networks use IP addresses in combination with netmasks to logically group hosts and networks.

NeTraMet. An open source network flow analysis tool available from *freshmeat.net/projects/netramet/*

network address. The lowest IP number in a subnet. The network address is used in routing tables to specify the destination to be used when sending packets to a logical group of IP addresses.

Network Address Translation (NAT). NAT is a networking technology that allows many computers to share a single, globally routable IP address. While NAT can help to solve the problem of limited IP address space, it creates a technical challenge for two-way services, such as Voice over IP.

network detection. Network diagnostic tools that display information about wireless networks, such as the network name, channel, and encryption method used.

network layer. Also called the Internet layer. This is the third layer of the OSI and TCP/IP network models, where IP operates and Internet routing takes place.

network mask see **netmask**

ngrep. An open source network security utility used to find patterns in data flows. Available for free from *http://ngrep.sourceforge.net/*

node. Any device capable of sending and receiving data on a network. Access points, routers, computers, and laptops are all examples of nodes.

Nominal Capacity (C_N). The maximum amount of energy that can be extracted from a fully charged battery. It is expressed in Ampere-hours (Ah) or Watt-hours (Wh).

Nominal Voltage (V_N). The operating voltage of a photovoltaic system, typically 12 or 24 volts.

ntop. A network monitoring tool that provides extensive detail about connections and protocol use on a local area network. *http://www.ntop.org/*

null. In an antenna radiation pattern, a null is a zone in which the effective radiated power is at a minimum.

nulling. A specific case of **multipath** interference where the signal at the receiving antenna is zeroed by the **destructive interference** of reflected signals.

number of days of autonomy (N). The maximum number of days that a photovoltaic system can operate without significant energy received from the sun.

Numerical Electromagnetics Code (NEC2). A free antenna modeling package that lets you build an antenna model in 3D, and then analyze the antenna's electromagnetic response. *http://www.nec2.org/*

OFDM see **Orthogonal Frequency Division Multiplexing**

omnidirectional antenna. An antenna that radiates almost equally in every direction in the horizontal plane. See also: **directional antenna, sectorial antenna**

one-arm repeater. A wireless repeater that only uses a single radio, at significantly reduced throughput. See also: **repeater**

onion routing. A privacy tool (such as **Tor**) that repeatedly bounces your TCP connections across a number of servers spread throughout the Internet, wrapping routing information in a number of encrypted layers.

OR logic. A logical operation that evaluates as true if any of the items being compared also evaluate as true. See also: **AND logic**.

Orthogonal Frequency Division Multiplexing (OFDM)

OSI network model. A popular model of network communications defined by the ISO/IEC 7498-1 standard. The OSI model consists of seven interdependent layers, from the physical through the application. See also: **TCP/IP network model**.

outbound traffic. Network packets that originate from the local network and are bound for a destination outside the local network (typically somewhere on the Internet). See also: **inbound traffic**.

overcharge. The state of a battery when charge is applied beyond the limit of the battery's capacity. If energy is applied to a battery beyond its point of maximum charge, the electrolyte begins to break down. **Regulators** will allow a small amount of overcharge time to a battery to avoid **gasification**, but will remove power before the battery is damaged.

overdischarge. Discharging a battery beyond its **Maximum Depth of Discharge**, which results in deterioration of the battery.

oversubscribe. To allow more users than the maximum available bandwidth can support.

P

packet. On IP networks, messages sent between computers are broken into small pieces called packets. Each packet includes a source, destination, and other routing information that is used to route it to its ultimate destination. Packets are reassembled again at the remote end by TCP (or another protocol) before being passed to the application.

packet filter. A firewall that operates at the Internet layer by inspecting source and destination IP addresses, port numbers, and protocols. Packets are either permitted or discarded depending on the packet filter rules.

partition. A technique used by network hubs to limit the impact of computers that transmit excessively. Hubs will temporarily remove the abusive computer (partition it) from the rest of the network, and reconnect it again after some time. Excessive partitioning indicates the presence of an excessive bandwidth consumer, such as a peer-to-peer client or network virus.

passive POE injector see **Power over Ethernet**

path loss. Loss of radio signal due to the distance between communicating stations.

Peak Sun Hours (PSH). Average value of daily irradiation for a given area.

photovoltaic generator see *solar panel*

photovoltaic solar energy. The use of solar panels to collect solar energy to produce electricity. See also: *thermal solar energy*

photovoltaic system. An energy system that generates electrical energy from solar radiation and stores it for later use. A standalone photovoltaic system does this without any connection to an established power grid. See also: *battery, solar panel, regulator, load, converter, inverter*

physical layer. The lowest layer in both the OSI and TCP/IP network models. The physical layer is the actual medium used for communications, such as copper cable, optic fiber, or radio waves.

pigtail. A short microwave cable that converts a non-standard connector into something more robust and commonly available.

ping. A ubiquitous network diagnostic utility that uses ICMP echo request and reply messages to determine the round trip time to a network host. Ping can be used to determine the location of network problems by "pinging" computers in the path between the local machine and the ultimate destination.

PKI see *Public Key Infrastructure*

plomb. A heavy piece of metal buried in the earth to improve a ground connection.

PoE see *Power over Ethernet*

point-to-multipoint. A wireless network where several nodes connect back to a central location. The classic example of a point-to-multipoint network is an access point at an office with several laptops using it for Internet access. See also: *point-to-point, multipoint-to-multipoint*

point-to-point. A wireless network consisting of only two stations, usually separated by a great distance. See also: *point-to-multipoint, multipoint-to-multipoint*

Point-to-Point Protocol (PPP). A network protocol typically used on serial lines (such as a dial-up connection) to provide IP connectivity.

polar plot. A graph where points are located by projection along a rotating axis (radius) to an intersection with one of several concentric circles. See also: *rectangular plot*

polarization. The direction of the electric component of an electromagnetic wave as it leaves the transmitting antenna. See also: *horizontal polarization, vertical polarization, circular polarization*

polarization mismatch. A state where a transmitting and receiving antenna do not use the same polarization, resulting in signal loss.

policy. In netfilter, the policy is the default action to be taken when no other filtering rules apply. For example, the default policy for any chain may be set to ACCEPT or DROP.

port counters. Managed switches and routers provide statistics for each network port called port counters. These statistics may include inbound and outbound packet and byte counts, as well as errors and retransmissions.

power. The amount of energy in a certain amount of time.

Power over Ethernet (PoE). A technique used to supply DC power to devices using the Ethernet data cable. See also: *end span injectors, mid span injectors*

PPP see *Point to Point Protocol*

presentation layer. The sixth layer of the OSI networking model. This layer deals with data representation, such as MIME encoding or data compression.

private address space. A set of reserved IP addresses outlined in RFC1918. Private address space is frequently used within an organization, in conjunction with Network Address Translation (NAT). The reserved private address space ranges include 10.0.0.0/8, 172.16.0.0/12, and 192.168.0.0/16. See also: *NAT*.

Privoxy (*http://www.privoxy.org/*). A web proxy that provides anonymity through the use of filters. Privoxy is often used in conjunction with *Tor*.

proactive routing. A *mesh* implementation where every node knows about the existence of every other node in the mesh cloud as well as which nodes may be used to route traffic to them. Each node maintains a routing table covering the whole mesh cloud. See also: *reactive routing*

protocol analyzer. A diagnostic program used to observe and disassemble network packets. Protocol analyzers provide the greatest possible detail about individual packets.

protocol stack. A set of network protocols that provide interdependent layers of functionality. See also: *OSI network model* and *TCP/IP network model*.

PSH see *Peak Sun Hours*

Public key cryptography. A form of encryption used by SSL, SSH, and other popular security programs. Public key cryptography allows encrypted information to be exchanged over an untrusted network without the need to distribute a secret key.

Public Key Infrastructure (PKI). A security mechanism used in conjunction with *public key cryptography* to prevent the possibility of *Man-In-The-Middle* attacks. See also: *certificate authority*

Q

quick blow. A type of fuse that immediately blows if the current flowing through it is higher than their rating. See also: **slow blow**

R

radiation pattern see **antenna pattern.**

radio. The portion of the electromagnetic spectrum in which waves can be generated by applying alternating current to an antenna.

reactive routing. A **mesh** implementation where routes are computed only when it is necessary to send data to a specific node. See also: **proactive routing**

realtime monitoring. A network monitoring tool that performs unattended monitoring over long periods, and notifies administrators immediately when problems arise.

reciprocity. An antenna's ability to maintain the same characteristics regardless if whether it is transmitting or receiving.

recombinant batteries see **lead-acid batteries**

rectangular plot. A graph where points are located on a simple grid. See also: **polar plot**

Regional Internet Registrars (RIR). The 4 billion available IP addresses are administered by the IANA. The space has been divided into large subnets, which are delegated to one of the five regional Internet registries, each with authority over a large geographic area.

regulator. The component of a **photovoltaic system** that assures that the **battery** is working in appropriate conditions. It avoids **overcharging** or **undercharging** the battery, both of which are very detrimental to the life of the battery. See also: **solar panel, battery, load, converter, inverter**

repeater. A node that is configured to rebroadcast traffic that is not destined for the node itself, often used to extend the useful range of a network.

Request for Comments (RFC). RFCs are a numbered series of documents published by the Internet Society that document ideas and concepts related to Internet technologies. Not all RFCs are actual standards, but many are either approved explicitly by the IETF, or eventually become de facto standards. RFCs can be viewed online at *http://rfc.net/.*

return loss. A logarithmic ratio measured in dB that compares the power reflected by the antenna to the power that is fed into the antenna from the transmission line. See also: **impedance**

reverse polarity (RP). Proprietary microwave connectors, based on a standard connector but with the genders reversed. The **RP-TNC** is probably the most common reverse polarity connector, but others (such as RP-SMA and RP-N) are also commonplace.

RF transmission line. The connection (typically ***coax***, ***Heliax***, or a ***waveguide***) between a radio and an antenna.

RIR see ***Regional Internet Registrars***

Round Trip Time (RTT). The amount of time it takes for a packet to be acknowledged from the remote end of a connection. Frequently confused with ***latency***.

rogue access points. An unauthorized access point incorrectly installed by legitimate users, or by a malicious person who intends to collect data or do harm to the network.

Round Robin Database (RRD). A database that stores information in a very compact way that does not expand over time. This is the data format used by RRDtool and other network monitoring tools.

router. A device that forwards packets between different networks. The process of forwarding packets to the next hop is called ***routing.***

routing. The process of forwarding packets between different networks. A device that does this is called a ***router***.

routing table. A list of networks and IP addresses kept by a router to determine how packets should be forwarded. If a router receives a packet for a network that is not in the routing table, the router uses its default gateway. Routers operate at the Network Layer. See also: ***bridge*** and ***default gateway***.

RP see ***Reverse Polarity***

RP-TNC. A common proprietary version of the TNC microwave connector, with the genders reversed. The RP-TNC is often found on equipment manufactured by Linksys.

RRD see ***Round Robin Database***

RRDtool. A suite of tools that allow you to create and modify RRD databases, as well as generate useful graphs to present the data. RRDtool is used to keep track of time-series data (such as network bandwidth, machine room temperature, or server load average) and can display that data as an average over time. RRDtool is available from *http://oss.oetiker.ch/rrdtool/*

rsync (*http://rsync.samba.org/*). An open source incremental file transfer utility used for maintaining mirrors.

RTT see ***Round Trip Time***

S

SACK see ***Selective Acknowledgment***

scattering. Signal loss due to objects in the path between two nodes. See also: ***free space loss, attenuation***

sectorial antenna. An antenna that radiates primarily in a specific area. The beam can be as wide as 180 degrees, or as narrow as 60 degrees. See also: *directional antenna, omnidirectional antenna*

Secure Sockets Layer (SSL). An end-to-end encryption technology built into virtually all web browsers. SSL uses *public key cryptography* and a trusted *public key infrastructure* to secure data communications on the web. Whenever you visit a web URL that starts with https, you are using SSL.

Selective Acknowledgment (SACK). A mechanism used to overcome TCP inefficiencies on high latency networks, such as VSAT.

Server Message Block (SMB). A network protocol used in Windows networks to provide file sharing services. See also: *NetBIOS*.

Service Set ID (SSID) see *Extended Service Set Identifier*

session layer. Layer five of the OSI model, the Session Layer manages logical connections between applications.

session oriented protocol. A network protocol (such as TCP) that requires initialization before data can be exchanged, as well as some clean-up after data exchange has completed. Session oriented protocols typically offer error correction and packet reassembly, while connectionless protocols do not. See also: *connectionless protocol*.

shared medium. A *link-local* network where every node can observe the traffic of every other node.

Shorewall (*http://shorewall.net/*). A configuration tool used for setting up netfilter firewalls without the need to learn iptables syntax.

sidelobes. No antenna is able to radiate all the energy in one preferred direction. Some is inevitably radiated in other directions. These smaller peaks are referred to as sidelobes.

signal generator. A transmitter that emits continuously at a specific frequency.

Simple Network Management Protocol (SNMP). A protocol designed to facilitate the exchange of management information between network devices. SNMP is typically used to poll network switches and routers to gather operating statistics.

site-wide web cache. While all modern web browsers provide a local data cache, large organizations can improve efficiency by installing a site-wide web cache, such as Squid. A site-wide web cache keeps a copy of all requests made from within an organization, and serves the local copy on subsequent requests. See also: *Squid*.

slow blow. A fuse that allows a current higher than its rating to pass for a short time. See also: *quick blow*

SMA. A small threaded microwave connector.

SMB see **Server Message Block**

SmokePing. A latency measurement tool that measures, stores and displays latency, latency distribution and packet loss all on a single graph. SmokePing is available from *http://oss.oetiker.ch/smokeping/*

SNMP see **Simple Network Management Protocol**

Snort (*http://www.snort.org/*). A very popular open source intrusion detection system. See also: **Intrusion Detection System**.

SoC see **State of Charge**

solar module see **solar panel**

solar panel. The component of a **photovoltaic system** used to convert solar radiation into electricity. See also: **battery, regulator, load, converter, inverter**

solar panel array. A set of **solar panels** wired in series and/or parallel in order to provide the necessary energy for a given **load**.

solar power charge regulator see **regulator**

spectrum see **electromagnetic spectrum**

spectrum analyzer. A device that provides a visual representation of the electromagnetic spectrum. See also: **Wi-Spy**

Speed. A generic term used to refer to the responsiveness of a network connection. A "high-speed" network

should have low latency and more than enough capacity to carry the traffic of its users. See also: **bandwidth**, **capacity**, and **latency**.

split horizon DNS. A technique used to serve different answers to DNS requests based on the source of the request. Split horizon is used to direct internal users to a different set of servers than Internet users.

spoof. To impersonate a network device, user, or service.

spot check tools. Network monitoring tools that are run only when needed to diagnose a problem. Ping and traceroute are examples of spot check tools.

Squid. A very popular open source web proxy cache. It is flexible, robust, full-featured, and scales to support networks of nearly any size. *http://www.squid-cache.org/*

SSID see **Extended Service Set Identifier**

SSL see **Secure Sockets Layer**

standalone photovoltaic system see **photovoltaic system**

State of Charge (SoC). The amount of charge present in a battery, determined by the current voltage and type of battery.

stateful inspection. Firewall rules that are aware of the the state associated with a given packet. The state is not part of the packet as transmitted over the Internet, but is determined by the firewall itself. New, established, and related connections may all be taken into consideration when filtering packets. Stateful inspection is sometimes called connection tracking.

stationary batteries. Batteries designed to have a fixed location and in scenarios where the power consumption is more or less irregular. Stationary batteries can accommodate deep discharge cycles, but they are not designed to produce high currents in brief periods of time. See also: ***lead-acid batteries***

structure. In ***NEC2***, a numerical description of where the different parts of the antenna are located, and how the wires are connected up. See also: ***controls***

subnet mask see ***netmask***

subnets. A subset of a range of IP networks, defined by ***netmasks***.

switch. A network device that provides a temporary, dedicated connection between communicating devices. See also: ***hub***.

switching conversion. A DC voltage conversion method that uses a magnetic component to temporarily store the energy and transform it to another voltage. Switching conversion is much more efficient than ***linear conversion***.

T

target. In netfilter, the action to be taken once a packet matches a rule. Some possible netfilter targets in-clude ***ACCEPT***, ***DROP***, ***LOG***, and ***REJECT***.

TCP see ***Transmission Control Protocol***

TCP acknowledgment spoofing

TCP window size. The TCP parameter that defines how much data that may be sent before an ACK packet is returned from the receiving side. For instance, a window size of 3000 would mean that two packets of 1500 bytes each will be sent, after which the receiving end will either ACK the chunk or request retransmission.

TCP/IP see ***Internet protocol suite***

TCP/IP network model. A popular simplification of the OSI network model that is used with Internet networks. The TCP/IP model consists of five interdependent layers, from the physical through the application. See also: ***OSI network model***.

tcpdump. A popular open source packet capture and analysis tool available at *http://www.tcpdump.org/*. See also: ***WinDump*** and ***Wireshark***.

Temporal Key Integrity Protocol (TKIP). An encryption protocol used in conjunction with ***WPA*** to improve the security of a communications session.

thermal solar energy. Energy collected from the sun in the form of heat. See also: ***photovoltaic solar energy***

thrashing. The state when a computer has exhausted the available RAM and must use the hard disk for temporary storage, greatly reducing system performance.

throughput. The actual amount of information per second flowing through a network connection, disregarding protocol overhead.

throughput testing tools. Tools that measure the actual bandwidth available between two points on a network.

Time To Live (TTL). A TTL value acts as a deadline or emergency brake to signal a time when the data should be discarded. In TCP/IP networks, the TTL is a counter that starts at some value (such as 64) and is decremented at each router hop. If the TTL reaches zero, the packet is discarded. This mechanism helps reduce damage caused by routing loops. In DNS, the TTL defines the amount of time that a particular zone record should be kept before it must be refreshed. In Squid, the TTL defines how long a cached object may be kept before it must be again retrieved from the original website.

TKIP see **Temporal Key Integrity Protocol**

TNC connector. A common, sturdy threaded microwave connector.

Tor (*http://www.torproject.org/*). An **onion routing** tool that provides good protection against traffic analysis.

traceroute / tracert. A ubiquitous network diagnostic utility often used in conjunction with ping to determine the location of network problems. The Unix version is called traceroute, while the Windows version is tracert. Both use ICMP echo requests with increasing TTL values to determine which routers are used to connect to a remote host, and also display latency statistics. Another variant is tracepath, which uses a similar technique with UDP packets. See also: **mtr**.

traction batteries see **lead-acid batteries**

Transmission Control Protocol (TCP). A session oriented protocol that operates at the Transport Layer, providing packet reassembly, congestion avoidance, and reliable delivery. TCP is an integral protocol used by many Internet applications, including HTTP and SMTP. See also: **UDP**.

transmission power. The amount of power provided by the radio transmitter, before any antenna gain or line losses.

transparent bridging firewall. A firewall technique that introduces a bridge that selectively forwards packets based on firewall rules. One benefit of a transparent bridging firewall is that it does not require an IP address. See also: **bridge**.

transparent cache. A method of implementing a site-wide web cache that requires no configuration on the web clients. Web requests are silently redirected to the cache, which makes the request on behalf of the client. Transparent caches cannot use authentication, which makes it impossible to implement traffic accounting at the user level. See also: *site-wide web cache*, *Squid*.

transparent proxy. A caching proxy installed so that users' web requests are automatically forwarded to the proxy server, without any need to manually configure web browsers to use it.

transport layer. The third layer of the OSI and TCP/IP network models, which provides a method of reaching a particular service on a given network node. Examples of protocols that operate at this layer are *TCP* and *UDP*.

trending. A type of network monitoring tool that performs unattended monitoring over long periods, and plots the results on a graph. Trending tools allow you to predict future behavior of your network, which helps you plan for upgrades and changes.

TTL see *Time To Live*

tunnel. A form of data encapsulation that wraps one protocol stack within another. This is often used in conjunction with encryption to protect communications from potential eavesdroppers, while eliminating the need to support encryption within the application itself. Tunnels are often used conjunction with *VPN*s.

U

U.FL. A very tiny microwave connector commonly used on mini-PCI radio cards.

UDP see *User Datagram Protocol*

unintentional users. Laptop users who accidentally associate to the wrong wireless network.

Unshielded Twisted Pair (UTP). Cable used for 10baseT and 100baseT Ethernet, consisting of four pairs of twisted wires.

Useful Capacity (C_u). The usable capacity of a battery, equal to the product of the *Nominal Capacity* and the *Maximum Depth of Discharge*.

User Datagram Protocol (UDP). A *connectionless protocol* (at the *transport layer*) commonly used for video and audio streaming.

UTP see *Unshielded Twisted Pair*

V

valve regulated lead acid battery (VRLA) see *lead-acid batteries*

vertical polarization. An electromagnetic field with the electric component moving in a linear vertical direction. Most wireless consumer electronic devices use vertical polarization. See also: *circular polarization, vertical polarization*

Very Small Aperture Terminal (VSAT). One of several standards used for satellite Internet access. VSAT is the most widely deployed satellite technology used in Africa. See also: **Broadband Global Access Network (BGAN)** and **Digital Video Broadcast (DVB-S)**.

video sender. A 2.4 GHz video transmitter that can be used as an inexpensive **signal generator**.

Virtual Private Network (VPN). A tool used to join two networks together over an untrusted network (such as the Internet). VPNs are often used to connect remote users to an organization's network when traveling or working from home. VPNs use a combination of encryption and tunneling to secure all network traffic, regardless of the application being used. See also: **tunnel**.

VoIP (**Voice over IP**). A technology that provides telephone-like features over an Internet connection. Examples of popular VoIP clients include Skype, Gizmo Project, MSN Messenger, and iChat.

VPN see **Virtual Private Network**.

VRLA see **valve regulated lead acid battery**

VSAT see **Very Small Aperture Terminal**

Very Small Aperture Terminal (VSAT). One of several standards used for satellite Internet access. VSAT is the most widely deployed satellite technology used in Africa.

See also: **Broadband Global Access Network (BGN)** and **Digital Video Broadcast (DVB-S)**.

W

WAN see **Wide Area Network**

War drivers. Wireless enthusiasts who are interested in finding the physical location of wireless networks.

wavelength. The distance measured from a point on one wave to the equivalent part of the next, for example from the top of one peak to the next. Also known as **lambda (λ)**.

WEP see **Wired Equivalent Privacy**

wget. An open source command line tool for downloading web pages. http://www.gnu.org/software/wget/

Wi-Fi. A marketing brand owned by the Wi-Fi Alliance that is used to refer to various wireless networking technologies (including 802.11a, 802.11b, and 802.11g). Wi-Fi is short for **Wireless Fidelity**.

Wi-Fi Protected Access (WPA). A fairly strong **link layer encryption** protocol supported by most modern **Wi-Fi** equipment.

Wi-Spy. An inexpensive 2.4 GHz spectrum analysis tool available from http://www.metageek.net/.

Wide Area Network (WAN). Any long distance networking technology. Leased lines, frame relay, DSL, fixed wireless, and satellite all typically implement wide area networks. See also: **LAN**.

wiki. A web site that allows any user to edit the contents of any page. One of the most popular public wikis is *http://www.wikipedia.org/*

window scale. A TCP enhancement defined by RFC1323 that allows TCP window sizes larger than 64KB.

WinDump. The Windows version of tcpdump. It is available from *http://www.winpcap.org/windump/*

Wired Equivalent Privacy (WEP). A somewhat secure **link layer encryption** protocol supported by virtually all 802.11a/b/g equipment.

Wireless Fidelity see **Wi-Fi**.

wireshark. A free network protocol analyzer for Unix and Windows. *http://www.wireshark.org/*

WPA see **Wi-Fi Protected Access**

Z

Zabbix (*http://www.zabbix.org/*) A realtime monitoring tool that logs and notifies a system administrator about service and network outages.

www.ingramcontent.com/pod-product-compliance
Lightning Source LLC
Chambersburg PA
CBHW080144060326
40689CB00018B/3847